Education and
Gender Equality

Education and Gender Equality

Edited by

Julia Wrigley

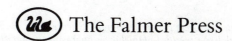 **The Falmer Press**

(A member of the Taylor & Francis Group)

London • Washington, D.C.

UK The Falmer Press, 4 John Street, London, WC1N 2ET
USA The Falmer Press, Taylor & Francis Inc., 1900 Frost Road, Suite 101, Bristol, PA 19007

First published 1992

The editor is grateful to the American Sociological Association for granting permission to reproduce the following material from *Sociology of Education* 62, pp. 1–74 (1989): Aaron Benavot, 'Education, Gender, and Economic Development: A Cross-National Study'; Nancy E. Durbin and Lori Kent, 'Postsecondary Education of White Women in 1990'; Saundra Gardner, Cynthia Dean and Deo McKaig, 'Responding to Differences in the Classroom: The Politics of Knowledge, Class and Sexuality'; Roslyn Arlin Mickelson, 'Why Does Jane Read and Write So Well? The Anomaly of Women's Achievement'; and Wendy Luttrell, 'Working-Class Women's Ways of Knowing: Effects of Gender, Race, and Class'.

A catalogue record for this book is available from the British Library

ISBN 1 85000 945 7
ISBN 1 85000 946 5 (pbk)

Library of Congress Cataloging-in-Publication Data are available on request

Jacket design by Caroline Archer

Typeset in 9.5/11pt Bembo
by Graphicraft Typesetters Ltd., Hong Kong

Printed in Great Britain by Burgess Science Press, Basingstoke, on paper which has a specified pH value on final paper manufacture of not less than 7.5 and is therefore 'acid free'.

Contents

Contents

Preface

This book grew out of a special issue of *Sociology of Education*. Philip Wexler, the journal's editor, asked Rachel Rosenfeld and me to coedit a special issue on gender and education. This request marked the journal's acknowledgment of the rapidly expanding world of feminist scholarship on education. The special issue contained five articles, and an additional seven articles, all but one newly written, were solicited for this book.

There is no simple relation between education and gender equality. As with social class relations, schools both reinforce subordination and create new possibilities for liberation, and these contradictions occur at every level and in every aspect of education. Schools are sites of pervasive gender socialization, but they offer girls a chance to use their brains and develop their skills. Education does far more than reproduce inequalities, sometimes spurring students to think beyond the ideological limits laid out for them. Countless girls have endured schooling designed to fit them for domestic roles, but countless others have demanded more. The feminist movement made visible both the entrenched gender discrimination of schools and the rebellion of women against what they experienced.

To explore education and gender is to examine the bridge between the public world of occupations and the private world of families. Schools link the families from which young children come and the sex- and race-segregated occupational worlds to which they are sent. Educational systems represent state penetration into family life and state interest in children's training for the work force. Official ideologies of equality reach their greatest intensity in the educational sphere. Occupying an extraordinarily important and sensitive juncture, the educational system reflects the pervasive social inequalities of gender, class, and race, and it also absorbs the political shocks of protest movements against these inequalities.

Because schools link public and private worlds, help to form consciousness, and structure inequalities, there are many ways to look at gender and education. In this book, the chapters break into four major topic areas. The first section, with four chapters, analyzes gender and education from a comparative and historical perspective, with particular attention to the role of the state. In the first chapter, I consider feminist rethinking of the welfare state and how it might apply to gender and education. Aaron Benavot offers a cross-national study of the contribution of women's education to national economic development. Ingrid

Jönsson analyzes the interesting case of Sweden, a country where the government has tried to reduce gender inequality, but where women remain occupationally subordinate and men continue to have an educational advantage. Nancy Durbin and Lori Kent argue that we can only understand women's move into higher education if we consider the specific types of schooling women sought and how these fit with their social circumstances and occupational goals.

The book's second section, on 'Diversity, Social Control, and Resistance in Classrooms', contains three chapters on gender and social relations within schools and universities. While very different in their specifics, each chapter is based on classroom observation and involves careful analysis of interactions between people and how they reflect power relations. Linda Grant explores the interaction of race and gender in the schooling of African-American and white girls. Barrie Thorne argues that gender segregation in elementary school is widespread but more fluid and socially conditioned than is usually acknowledged by those stressing sex roles. Saundra Gardner, Cynthia Dean and Deo McKaig discuss feminist pedagogy in the face of student differences along lines of social class, feminist knowledge and sexual orientation.

The third section, on 'Gender and Knowledge', considers the social context of learning and, more basically, of defining intelligence and knowledge. Those immersed in mainstream sociology of education customarily operate with a restricted view of knowledge and achievement. People who succeed at school-defined academic tasks are considered intelligent, and much sociological energy has gone into figuring out what makes some people more 'intelligent' and successful than others. The authors in this section take a broader view of their subject. Rather than asking which women succeed in school and why, Roslyn Mickelson asks a question that is too seldom addressed: Given their limited rewards for school success, why do women in general do as well in school as they do? She provides an analytical review of competing theoretical perspectives which yield different answers to this question. Taking a step further, Wendy Luttrell analyzes working-class white and African-American women's definitions of intelligence, suggesting that they do not accept notions of intelligence measured in terms of academic achievement and book knowledge. On a more macro level, Deborah Perkins Jones and David P. Baker look at the social context of girls' mathematics achievement. Biological determinists have made their last stand on the issue of girls' math underachievement compared with that of boys but, using cross-national data, Jones and Baker show that girls' mathematics scores are socially influenced. In countries where women have a shot at good jobs, including technical jobs, girls are likely to do better at math than in countries where women have little chance to use their education.

Two chapters on families and schools comprise the book's last section. The authors seek to understand the many ways in which the private worlds of families and the public worlds of schools intersect. They see the link as conditioned by social class and gender. Both chapters are based mainly on interviews with women from working-class and middle-class backgrounds. Annette Lareau examines the broadening of mothers' roles to include the management of their children's educational careers. Middle-class mothers, in particular, take on this management as a result of the confluence of their socially defined class and gender roles, as they seek to invest their 'cultural capital' in their children. Merrilee Finley followed a group of working-class and middle-class young women over five years as they made the transition from high school to work or higher education. Her detailed interviews enabled her to develop a very specific under-standing of how the middle-class women were aided by the class resources of their families, while nearly all the working-class women suffered disappointment in their educational hopes.

I should like to thank the many women and girls (and some men) who indirectly made this book possible by challenging sexism in education. Their activism and raised consciousness has had reverberations on classrooms and academicians alike. I should also like to thank Rachel Rosenfeld for her very great contribution in coediting the special journal of *Sociology of Education* on gender and education. Philip Wexler made the special issue possible and provided much encouragement and practical support in turning the issue into a book. The American Sociological Association gave permission for the reprinting of the five articles drawn from the special issue and facilitated the publication process. Hartry Field gave moral support. Elizabeth Wrigley-Field made it clear she thought sexism has no place in education.

Section 1

Gender, the State, and Education

1 Gender and Education in the Welfare State

Julia Wrigley

In varying degrees, Western industrial societies have developed social welfare programs which protect citizens over the life course. All provide pensions for the aged, income protection for the unemployed, and some form of assistance for impoverished families with children. With the exception of the United States, they also provide national health care systems or insurance. This vast expansion of the state role means that gender relations no longer play themselves out mainly within family and market contexts. State social policy is shaped by gender assumptions and in turn affects women's degree of social and economic independence from men. Feminists have argued that programs have often been designed which reinforce women's subordination and, while feminist writers differ greatly among themselves, they have developed a critique both of social welfare policy and of scholarship about it (Nelson 1990; Linda Gordon 1990). It is my purpose in this chapter to extend the analysis to gender and social policy in the educational sphere.

Feminist writers on both sides of the Atlantic have criticized the vast literature on the welfare state for ignoring gender in the shaping of social provision (Linda Gordon 1990; Sapiro 1990). Theorists have long debated the role of social class in accounting for the different trajectories of welfare state development, but most paid no attention to gender. They did not focus on the frequent division of social welfare payments into what has been called a 'male channel' and a 'female channel', with men receiving more generous benefits than women (Nelson 1990). To the feminist writers, this is not a small or accidental feature of social welfare programs, but goes to their heart. The 'family wage' ideology, the notion that a male worker should receive enough to support a dependent wife and children, not only governed trade union strategy but also helped account for the scope and form of government benefit programs. Women have received benefits based on family status rather than based on a concept of earned right, such as applied to male workers (Quadagno 1990). Virginia Sapiro puts the point succinctly: 'Most social policy aimed at women has been designed explicitly to benefit them in their capacity as wives and mothers and more particularly, to benefit those who depend upon them for nurturance and domestic service: husbands, children, and elderly relatives' (1990, p. 45). When women and their dependents lacked the support of a male breadwinner, they could turn to aid from the state. While countries differ in their social provision, most have not allowed women sufficient income or freedom to become independent of paternalistic authority, whether that authority has been exercised by individual men or by state agencies.

Those stressing gender have made many astute observations about government social policy. They have pointed out that men have not only received more generous benefits than women, but have generally experienced less bureaucratic harassment in the social welfare system. Men seldom face moral tests of their character, as women receiving public assistance often do. Women on welfare have had to endure government surveillance and intrusion, while men receiving unemployment insurance have not expected administrators to pry into their personal lives. Critics have pointed out that it is not 'gender neutral' to tie benefit programs to jobs, as men have had privileged access to the most secure and best-paying jobs. They have also noted that programs primarily serving women and children have more often been means-tested than those programs more geared to men. Further, in the United States, Social Security, the premier social welfare program, operates on a national basis and with national standards, while programs with a more heavily female constituency tend to be operated on state and local bases. Local administration allows for pronounced expression of racial and gender biases and for widely varying levels of provision (Abramovitz 1988).

The differences between male and female benefits can in part be quantified: on average, for example, women receive only two-thirds the old age insurance received by men (Quadagno 1990, p. 14). Beyond this, there are qualitative differences in the treatment experienced by men and women. It adds up to a pattern of profound gender bias in state social provision. It should be noted that the feminist analysis is itself not fully developed. Some feminists and social theorists have a straightforward social control theory, seeing expanded welfare services as coopting recipients and fragmenting the working class along lines of race, class, and gender. Others contend that public programs have operated overall to expand women's opportunities and to reduce their dependence on individual men. Women have also gained from their extensive employment in the public sphere (Piven 1990). These authors challenge the notion that expanded social provision has reduced women's power (Pascall 1986).

Many questions need to be answered about how social class and race fit in with a gender-based analysis. With stable jobs being the key to receiving good benefits, men as well as women have suffered from benefit limitations and exclusions. The racial biases in the US social welfare system have been glaringly evident, with a conservative Southern white elite historically keeping a stranglehold over benefits for black men and women in order to preserve a low-wage labor force (Amott 1990). Some analysts try to integrate race and gender in their discussions of social welfare programs (e.g., Quadagno 1990; Mink 1990; Piven 1990) and many also recognize the social class aspects of benefit differences. On the whole, though, the interplay of race, class, and gender factors has undoubtedly been more complex than has been captured by either traditional writers on the welfare state or by feminist critics.

In the large literature on the welfare state, most authors discuss pensions, family assistance programs, unemployment insurance, and other types of income transfer mechanisms. As one notes, 'By convention, in the United States welfare policy consists of those public programs providing money, goods in kind, or services that are made available to offset regularly occurring events outside the control of individuals' (Nelson 1990, p. 126). Education does not fit within this definition, yet in a larger sense education can be considered a social welfare program. It is, at least, as Barbara Nelson puts it, one of the 'flanking subsystems' of welfare policies (1990, p. 127). Government entry into the educational sphere and the establishment of income transfer programs both represent major expansions of state roles in ways that profoundly affect the welfare of individual citizens. In the one case, income transfer programs help safeguard living standards over the life cycle; in the other, education helps govern individuals' chances for jobs, their places in the marriage market (Mare 1991), and their economic rewards. The transition of states from 'night watchman' roles to broad social ones has involved proactive policies in the educational sector as well as in narrower kinds of social welfare provision.

In the United States, the major social policy initiatives of state and local governments prior to the 1930s involved commitment to mass public education (Weir, Orloff and Skocpol 1988a, p. 6). These initiatives gave a distinctive cast to American policy development; in Germany, government commitment to social security programs predated expansion of the educational system by several decades, while in the United States the reverse held true (Heidenheimer 1981, p. 295). Analysts have suggested that governments in effect made choices between fostering educational entitlement and social security entitlement (Kaelbe 1981; Heidenheimer 1981). By the 1960s, the United States and Western European countries had developed rather more similar policy profiles, as education expanded in Europe and social welfare programs became more extensive and inclusive in the United States. Debates over why governments began investing heavily in education parallel debates over why they established old age pensions and unemployment insurance. In each case, some argue that these programs have primarily served the purposes of state-building elites, while others have contended that they arose in response to working-class pressure.

In this chapter, I will suggest that there are analytic parallels to be drawn between gender biases in the educational and social welfare systems. While feminists have written a great deal on gender discrimination in schools, they have focused on classroom practices, textbook biases, and the gender values of teachers; M. Sadker, D. Sadker and Klein (1991) provide an excellent review of this literature. This research has sensitized us to the many subtle and not-so-subtle ways girls get messages of subordination, and to issues of feminist pedagogy (see Gardner, Dean and McKaig, this volume), but it has paid less attention to larger structural inequalities and how they affect women's education. While theorists have developed broad arguments about how race and class interact to affect children's educational prospects (Ogbu 1978), feminist work has been narrower. In connecting gender inequality in education to the new and rapidly expanding literature on gender inequality in state programs, we can go further in developing a structural view of how inequalities between men and women arise and are maintained.

In this chapter, I shall outline main elements in the feminist analysis of gender-based social welfare provision, and shall assess the extent to which these apply in the educational sector. While those who study gender and the welfare state vary in their emphases, there are some common points in their work. Typically, they stress disparities in state resources received by men and women, with women receiving fewer resources and more moral scrutiny than men. They argue that tying benefits to work history privileges men and assumes women's dependence. They also analyze how women's caregiving work has restricted their labor market opportunity and attendant social welfare benefits. Several such writers have stressed how women have played central roles in staffing and reforming social welfare programs (Piven 1990; Sapiro 1990). I shall take up each of these points in regard to gender and the educational system. The chapter will conclude with a discussion of possible changes in the importance of gender as an axis of educational inequality. Throughout, I shall draw upon the work of contributors to this volume, showing how their work, diverse as it is in method and theme, clarifies many different aspects of the relation between gender, education, and state policy.

State Provision and Gender Bias in Education

The US social welfare system rests on a mixture of public and private resources. The Scandinavian social democracies have created social welfare systems designed to protect people from the vagaries of the market, but the United States has followed a quite different path. Social welfare programs are designed to strengthen, not undermine or replace, the market (Esping-Andersen 1990). Those with good jobs rely on private pensions and private health insurance to augment limited government benefits. For the average wage earner, Social Security payments replace only about two-fifths of preretirement income, necessitating private supplement for those wanting to preserve their living standards (Rosenbaum 1991, p. A10).[1] The social welfare system's orientation toward the market has been particularly damaging to women and to minorities; their labor market disadvantages are compounded because benefits are tied to jobs. They receive lower government benefits than those with steady, high-paying work; they also generate fewer private resources with which to supplement their public benefits.

In addition to their liabilities in the social welfare system, women have suffered disadvantages in state educational provision. These disadvantages arise at every level of schooling, although they are most pronounced at the point where education becomes relevant for occupational preparation (Pascall 1986, p. 115). The different likely occupational destinies of males and females have historically served as warrants for their different treatment (and unequal receipt of state resources) in the educational system, whether in high school up through the mid-twentieth century or in college during the postwar era. The sex-segregated labor market helps produce gender-defined schooling.

There are many ways in which state resources can be distributed unequally in the educational system. Inequalities accepted as politically legitimate in one era can become suspect in another, generally through political mobilization of those being shortchanged. The maintenance of racially segregated school systems in the South facilitated unequal spending on black and white students; in the North, as ghettoization intensified in big cities, resource disparities between black and white schools increased (Homel 1984). In the United States, schools have been segregated much more frequently by race than by gender, which made it hard to provide grossly unequal resources for the sexes as was done for the races. In a comprehensive study of coeducation in American schools, Tyack and Hansot argue that, throughout its educational history, the United States has been conspicuous for the widespread gender equality to be found in its public schools

(1990). Boys and girls usually attended the same schools, worked from the same books, and had the same teachers. Children's shared educational experiences limited sex-based spending disparities.

Coeducation undoubtedly constrained public authorities, but expenditure disparities did exist and they were important. They were most pronounced in school vocational and sports programs. In the early 1900s, high school vocational education programs were almost entirely sex segregated. Training for skilled trades was reserved for boys, while girls took courses in home economics or garment work (Tyack and Hansot 1990, p. 210). African-American girls fared even worse than white girls; schools often trained them to be servants or laundry workers. Such courses were cheap for school districts to run, no expensive equipment was required, and schools made only minimal investment in instruction.

Girls gained no occupational advantage from home economics courses, but business courses prepared them for jobs in the expanding white-collar sector. High school education mattered more for girls than it did for boys (Carter and Prus 1982). Employers invested in boys' on-the-job training, while girls applying for clerical jobs were expected to arrive with skills. This explains why many more girls than boys stayed in high school, even at the cost of foregone wages. They (and their families) had to bear the cost of their skill development. Girls got an economic payoff from commercial courses, but school districts did not have to spend heavily on girls' training. Tyack and Hansot note that 'The most popular subjects — bookkeeping, shorthand, and typing — were relatively cheap and easy to start up' (1990, p. 214). Many girls and their families also invested in private commercial courses, paying from their own resources for occupational training that boys could expect to receive on the job.

Schools spent more on boys outside as well as inside the classroom, most particularly on sports programs. Competitive school sports teams took root in America's schools in the first several decades of the 1900s. They bound local communities to the schools and created a male sports culture. Girls remained on the sidelines, cheering on male athletes. The passage of Title IX of the 1972 Education Amendments, which required schools to equalize funds and programs for girls and boys, marked a challenge to one of the most entrenched of school expenditure inequalities. At the time the law was passed, 'The ratio of expenditures for girls' sports in comparison to boys' ranged from 1:8 to 1:450 in eight communities. In two states, public schools spent no funds on girls' sports, while in Minneapolis the school district spent more on one football team than on all girls' sports in the eleven city high schools' (Tyack and Hansot 1990, p. 263). Even after Title IX was passed, equalization occurred only where women's activists organized themselves.

The decentralized American educational system, with uncertain quality control, vast inter-ethnic competition, and local political pressure for expanded opportunity, fueled credentialism and early expansion of post-secondary education (Heidenheimer 1981; Collins 1979). College involves heavy public and private expense, and families must bear the burden of tuition and of students' forgone wages and living expenses. Many families can meet these expenses only with state aid (Hearn, Fenske and Curry 1985). Since the Second World War the federal government has not only contributed heavily to universities and colleges, but it has also underwritten college expenses through loans and grants to individual students.

The federal government first began funding scholarships after the Second World War, initially choosing a funding method that ensured gender bias. Revenue growth generated by extended federal income tax provisions led to several national social policy initiatives in the postwar period, most notably in the fields of housing and education (Weir, Orloff and Skocpol 1988a, p. 8). In a break from previous policy, the federal government underwrote the college educations of millions of returning veterans through the GI bill. Veterans of previous wars had not received educational benefits (except for disabled veterans of the First World War); rather they were given bonuses or health care (Mosch 1975, p. 11; Levitan and Zickler 1973). The passage of the GI bill reflected the increasing popularity and importance of college attendance. Experts rank the GI bill with the 1862 Morrill Act (which established land grant colleges) as the two most important pieces of educational legislation in American history (Mosch 1975, p. 3). More than fourteen million people received some form of assistance through the GI bill (Mosch 1975, p. 2), the overwhelming majority of them men.

The Social Security Act benefited men more than women, although no explicit gender bias permeated the act. Similarly, the first federal provision of college scholarships benefited men far more than women, although women were not barred from participation. In each case, the basis of benefit allocation — jobs or military service — served men better than women. At the time the GI bill was passed, some legislators called for a national scholarship program that was not tied to previous military service, but the idea was rejected (Mosch 1975).

The GI bill proved so popular that the government extended the program into the cold war era. Veterans of the Korean and Vietnam wars have also received government aid to attend college or receive other post-secondary training. Less than 2 percent of the veterans of the Second World War, the Korean war, or the Vietnam war have been women (Levitan and Zickler 1973, p. 11; Veterans Administration 1981, p. 1). Women veterans have had higher average educational levels than their male counterparts, but have used their educational benefits under the GI bill at a lower rate, despite a typical pattern of more-educated veterans relying more heavily on the GI bill.[2]

Women's disadvantages in securing higher education go far beyond their limited participation in different versions of the GI bill. They typically command fewer public and private resources of all sorts than men. As women have increasingly entered the labor market, they have sought more education. Between 1970 and 1980, women's enrollment in college increased by 77.4 percent while that of men increased by 22.6 percent (Moran 1986, p. 1). Due to limited resources, women tend to enroll at cheaper institutions than do men.

> Trends in college enrollment since 1960 show that the participation of females is directly related to costs: the higher the tuition and living costs, the less likely women are to enroll. Women consequently depend on low-cost institutions, outnumbering males in undergraduate public four-year and two-year colleges, while males outnumber females in high-cost private institutions (Moran 1986, p. 2).

Women outnumber men in community colleges nearly two to one (Moran 1986, p. 5). Of these, substantial numbers are women with dependent children, a group with high levels of unmet need for financial assistance (Hearn, Fenske and

Curry 1985). Community colleges spend much less per student than do four-year colleges; in 1985, expenditures were $8297 a year less for full-time equivalent students at community colleges than for students at four-year colleges (Monk-Turner 1990). The limited expenditure on students helps lead to a generally lower quality of education and to low prestige for graduates. Women who attend community colleges suffer a depreciated occupational return for each year of education compared with those who attend four-year colleges. The small number of women in elite private colleges, in contrast, earn a high return on their education. It is even more beneficial for women than for men to attend highly selective institutions, perhaps because their high-status degrees reassure male gatekeepers that they are worthy of employment (Kingston and Smart 1990, p. 156). For the great bulk of women this is not an issue, however, as they disproportionately enroll in low-cost colleges.

The GI bill paved the way for government entry into other forms of scholarship provision for students, including many programs that are not tied to military status. More than 80 percent of student financial aid comes from the federal government; this includes aid in the form of loans, grants, and work study programs (Moran 1986, p. 9). In 1986, the federal government spent more than $10 billion on student aid. Given how large this sum is, gender differences in its receipt can be of great importance. Women receive less such aid than do men and they are particularly disadvantaged in terms of the most prestigious and valuable forms of aid. Women receive 84 percent as much in government loans as do men, and 73 percent as much in grants (Moran 1986, p. 10). Grants help students advance through their programs without acquiring a large burden of debt. Women are particularly likely to find a debt burden discouraging, as they typically earn much less than men once they get their degrees and often major in subjects which lead them into relatively low-wage, sex-segregated occupations, such as teaching and nursing. Male and female college seniors report quite different income expectations, in part at least reflecting the economic reality awaiting them (Smith and Powell 1990). The sex segregation of jobs has repercussions back down the ladder into the educational system, as, looking ahead at their future work, women become reluctant to persevere in educational expenditures. Helen Astin reports that women who rely largely on loans are more likely to quit school than those who receive grants (cited in Moran 1986, p. 14).[3]

Women often do not fare well on loans, but they have less chance than men of receiving merit-based scholarships. They receive substantially fewer National Merit Scholarships than do men, perhaps because the selection committees for these and other scholarships tend to be male-dominated (Moran 1986, pp. 16–17). The well-known gender gap in scores on the math SATs and GREs is a major liability for women, as many scholarships are tied to performance on these exams. The gender gap in performance on the math SATs can be attributed to the particular test make-up, as well as to girls' lesser exposure to high school math courses (Linn and Hyde 1989), but scholarship committees tend to treat these tests as indicators of basic quantitative ability. Merit tends to be defined in ways that benefit males; Moran points out that 'the award of merit-based scholarships is highly discretionary and thus more subject to biases based on gender' than are awards based on need (1986, p. 16).

Feminist critics have pointed to the decentralized nature of many US social welfare programs as adding to the liabilities of the powerless. Local elites have

7

been able to control the administration of programs and have frequently set arbitrary and discriminatory rules which have had negative consequences for women and minorities. In a similar way, women have been disadvantaged by the decentralized nature of much decision-making about who will receive fellowships and student research and teaching jobs. Academic departments (or even subsections of departments) typically make these decisions, and in fields where women are few and far between, they are subject to decisions made very largely by male faculty members (Moran 1986, pp. 26–8). Women graduate students receive fewer posts as research assistants than do men; this can limit their professional socialization and ability to publish while still in school.

In addition to direct biases in government funding of students, gender biases in social welfare programs have contributed to women's difficulties in attending college. Because men typically have longer work histories, they are more likely than women to receive unemployment insurance, workmen's compensation, and disability payments. These types of social provision fall into the 'male channel' and involve less stigma and restriction than do the 'welfare' payments more often received by women. Those receiving transfer payments through the 'male channel' can generally use these payments to help them attend college. Women, the main recipients of Aid to Families with Dependent Children, are vulnerable to state-by-state variations in program rules, and in many states recipients lose their benefits, or have them reduced, if they enroll in college (Moran 1986, pp. 24–5). The complexity and variability of program rules often discourage welfare recipients from trying to enroll in higher education, even when it might technically be possible. Not only do rules vary from place to place, but individual caseworkers can make arbitrary decisions on eligibility.

In 1981, a Social Security rules change limited the ability of widows to send their children to college. Until that year, full-time students between 18 and 21 had been eligible for monthly payments if they had a deceased parent who was covered by Social Security. Congress deleted this provision, negatively affecting women, as they often outlive their husbands. Widows no longer receive state support for children in college (Moran 1986, p. 25).

The pattern of state aid for education disadvantages women in that historically (and to some extent today) they have received fewer resources in high school, have received less government aid in attending college, and have faced social service rules which have restricted their ability to go to college themselves or, if they are widows, to send their children. The educational system mirrors the inequalities in social provision which occur elsewhere. The limitations of social provision in the United States thrust women back on private resources and here too they suffer in comparison with men.

Gender and Private Resources for Education

Inequalities in private resources are most evident across social class lines, but they also occur within families. Theoretically, family resources could be distributed in gender-neutral ways, but in practice, as men do better in the labor market, this increases their power within families (Hochschild 1989). The intra-family division of labor and resources tends to follow market lines, with the weaker parties (women) doing more work and having fewer family resources invested in them, while the main earners (men) have their time, skills, and energies protected.

There is evidence that parents attach greater value to their sons' college attendance than that of their daughters. In the early 1900s, 'daughters sometimes worked to help finance their brothers' schooling' (Durbin and Kent, this volume, p. 71), and they still take second place to sons. Women's chances of attending college are reduced if they have brothers (Powell and Steelman 1989), as families funnel their resources toward the sons, leaving less for the daughters. As Powell and Steelman note, 'Gender is one of the most powerful bases for the allocation of privileges and penalties' (p. 145), and it operates within families as well as outside them. Unlike some other resources, such as certain types of 'cultural capital' which are jointly shared by all within the home, parental investment in children's college costs can and often does involve substantial inequities between siblings. Students with brothers are far more likely to get college loans and to graduate with higher levels of indebtedness than are students without brothers; they are also more likely to seek, and obtain, outside funding through grants and to hold part-time jobs. The presence of sisters in the family does not produce these effects. In the competition between siblings, sisters emerge as less favored claimants on family resources, at least when there is not enough to go around.

It is working-class daughters who suffer the most from gender inequities in the distribution of family resources. Middle-class families can often muster the money to send all their children, regardless of sex, to college. In working-class families, parents must sometimes make a choice, and they typically support a son rather than a daughter. Merrilee Finley's chapter in this volume explores this process. Finley interviewed young working-class and middle-class women in Southern California over five years as they made the transition from high school to college, work, or motherhood. She found that for both the middle-class and working-class women, 'There was often a special advantage in not having a brother ... This common situation made a greater difference to the working-class women, because there were fewer family resources to begin with' (p. 225). Finley found that the working-class families in her sample who sent daughters to college disproportionately had no sons.

The picture is, however, more complicated than this. Just as lack of alternatives meant that in the early 1900s young women were more likely to stay in high school than were young men, even though they and their families had to bear the burden of their forgone earnings, so families sometimes have no choice but to spend more on their daughters' college than on their sons'. Men have more chance of getting external funding than do women. They get more public and private scholarship money and, due to their better labor market position, they also have higher earnings during summer employment and greater savings. This means that in families where college-going is the norm, parents sometimes have to provide more for their daughters' college expenses because the daughters have fewer other ways of getting funds. As Moran comments, the parents 'contribute more because they have to' (1986, p. 36). Thus, within a given family, parents may bear a higher proportion of the children's college costs for daughters than for sons (Steelman and Powell 1989), but in families too poor to make a disproportionate contribution, daughters may miss the chance to go to college at all. Parents can help redress the balance between the opportunities of their sons and daughters by providing more private resources for daughters but, depending on their own gender ideologies, some go in the opposite direction and spend more on sons. In this common situation, inequalities in the public and private spheres do not counteract, but intensify, each other.

Women as Caregivers and Restricted Opportunity

Women cannot expend all their energy in paid employment because most also look after their families in a highly unequal intra-family division of labor (Abel and Nelson 1990; Fuchs 1988). Even girls have heavier caregiving duties than their brothers, providing more care for younger siblings, sometimes at the cost of their school grades (Smith 1984). Women pay an immediate labor market price if they work part time so they can look after children or frail parents; they pay a later price when they receive only limited Social Security payments or private pensions. Women's caregiving role conflicts with their realization of economic reward for their educational investment. Women have reduced prospects for economic independence because others depend on them for care, limiting their ability to operate freely in the labor market (Sapiro 1990, p. 48).

Traditionally, women have met the needs of the old, the young, and the sick within their families, but these needs are socially defined. Standards of mothering, for example, vary from era to era and from social class to social class. The increasing importance of education has led mothers to add a new element to their caregiving roles. Many now serve as the managers of their children's educational careers. As education has become critical in obtaining good jobs, children's school success has mattered more within families. Parents increasingly worry about their children's performance and cognitive capacities. A content analysis of popular literature directed toward parents from 1900 to 1985 showed a great increase in the percentage of articles which discussed the need for young children's intellectual stimulation (Wrigley 1988). Mothers gauge their success as parents not only by how likable their children are, but by how well their children do in school. This is particularly the case for middle-class parents, many of whom got their own jobs through their educational credentials and who hope to transmit their class advantages to their children.

The American educational system, like most other aspects of its social welfare services, is decentralized rather than nationally controlled. This allows for variable standards of social provision and for the expression of local biases in the provision of benefits or services (Weir, Orloff and Skocpol 1988a, p. 7). The differences in social provision can be very substantial. Heidenheimer notes that, 'Although those American programs that are totally administered by federal agencies, such as social security pensions, usually have nationally uniform benefit rates, benefit levels in education and social assistance have varied by factors of 4:1 among American states and localities' (1981, p. 286).

Decentralization has led to great variation in the nature and quality of schools from one area or even neighborhood to another. Countries with standardized national curricula and with high-quality standards for teachers minimize local variations in what is taught (Stevenson and Baker 1991; Hage, Garnier and Fuller 1988). In the United States, however, curricular and quality variability can be substantial, as teachers have considerable autonomy and respond in part to local standards and pressures. The social class implications of this are clear, but there is an indirect, but important, gender effect as well. The gender effect arises because the US system rewards educational intervention by parents, and it is typically mothers who accomplish this intervention. Decentralization rewards parental activity in two ways: schools vary in their quality and they are also permeable to parental influence.

American schooling arrangements put a premium on active parental efforts to secure 'good' schooling for their children. Those parents who want their children to succeed in school typically do not rest once they have supplied a home environment conducive to learning. They also investigate schooling options and, if need be, move to new neighborhoods, pay for private schools, or work through the educational bureaucracy to get their children into desirable public schools. Once they have their children in what they consider acceptable schools, many try to get their children good teachers and get them into high-track courses. As Baker and Stevenson put it, 'Parents must do a long series of small things to assist their child toward maximum educational attainment. This may range from monitoring performance to managing a specific school problem' (1986, p. 165). This kind of bureaucratic intervention takes time, information, and vigilance. Annette Lareau's chapter in this volume shows it to be gender-specific work. Overwhelmingly, mothers maintain contact with the schools, pick up information from networks of other mothers, and monitor their children's educational progress. Educated mothers do not invest their cultural capital only in their own careers; they also invest in their children's careers. For young children, they provide intellectually stimulating environments; for older children, they invest time and bureaucratic know-how as educational managers.

Looking ahead, young women in school and college recognize that caregiving roles will fall largely to them. Data from the 1977 Quality of Employment Survey showed that married working women gave priority to their families in balancing their work and family identities, while married men did not feel they had to stress one identity over the other (Bielby and Bielby 1989, p. 786). Women perceive that spending time on their families will detract from their economic success. 'Marriage', Smith and Powell comment, 'tends to increase the wages of men while parenthood lessens the labor force attachment and earnings of women' (1990, p. 205). This is one factor that helps keep women out of careers in science. In a national survey, high school girls reported that they see scientific careers as incompatible with family life (Ware and Lee 1988). College women in the 1980s reported the same, while family-oriented college men were more inclined to go into science than those not geared toward families. Caregiving demands, both actual and anticipated, help shape women's educational choices and funnel them into low-paying, sex-segregated occupations; once employed, mothers expend energy on their children's educational careers and other caregiving tasks. Many aspects of the American social welfare system rest partly on the unpaid labor of family members. When public hospitals are distant and overcrowded, someone has to drive children or aged parents to appointments and then wait; when the elderly have insufficient money to live by themselves, it is their children, and particularly their daughters, who take on their care. So too in the educational system, there is a vast world of private support and caregiving that bolsters the public world of the school, and this is largely provided by women. This care, the actual personal mixing of public and private resources, damages women's ability to extract their own resources from the private labor market and, ultimately, the public benefits system.

Moral Critique of those Receiving Benefits

Feminist writers have pointed out that social policy has been based on the assumption that women can and will depend on men for economic support. Policy-makers accepted patriarchal norms without question and built programs around the idea of men earning a 'family wage' and supporting women and children. In their narrow calculus, male-headed households constituted the norm, both practically and ideologically. They ignored the many households where men earned less than a family wage or where they failed to give their wives and children an adequate share of the family income. They also ignored those women who lived without men. Men's economic security depended on their ability to hold a job; for most women, such security depended on their ability (and willingness) to maintain a relationship with a wage-earning man. Both strategies for finding economic security involved risk, but without question the risk to women was much greater. The state provided only the most meager and paltry of alternatives to women who lacked men's economic support.

Some authors have emphasized the social control aspect of welfare policy, as well as its economic effects. They believe capitalists and state officials wanted to penalize women who violated gender norms and to reinforce women's dependence on individual men or on the patriarchal state. Linda Gordon depicts welfare programs as driven by an 'autonomous agenda of regulating family structure, domestic labor, and the reproductive and sexual behavior of single women' (1988, p. 617). Other writers, including Piven and Cloward, have critiqued this notion, arguing that, while there has been much rhetoric about supporting families, policy-makers have mainly sought welfare programs that guaranteed a cheap labor supply (1988). In their view, moral criticisms of 'welfare mothers' and punitive behavior toward them reflect a desire to keep welfare rolls low and to maintain labor discipline.

Feminist authors may differ on the centrality of social control goals to welfare bureaucrats, but the programs clearly were not designed to foster women's independence. Similarly, girls' education was usually designed to reinforce their domestic roles rather than to prepare them for social or economic independence. Until after the Second World War, white girls attending school were assumed to be preparing for domestic lives; the schools did not hold out motherhood as salvation for African-American girls, as their lives were expected to involve paid labor (Pascall 1986). Except among a minority of highly educated women, gender inequalities in schooling caused little concern, even among those dedicated to rooting out class or race inequalities.

The taken-for-granted nature of sexist assumptions in the social policy arena rendered them nearly invisible. They became evident mainly in the attacks leveled against those women who violated gender norms. Feminist writers have called attention to the sustained and sometimes savage moral criticism that has been directed toward single women on welfare. This moral condemnation has proven a durable means of attacking welfare. Sexist and racist prejudices have been activated as a way of reducing public support for welfare and creating what could be termed a 'righteousness gulf' between those on Social Security and those on AFDC, a gulf that has shaped the politics of US social provision (Weir, Orloff and Skocpol 1988b). Conventional images of gender have been used to call aspects of the social welfare system into question. This moral critique has become a potent political factor in its own right.

While women on welfare have been particularly vulnerable, as they have committed the crime of market vulnerability, women in the educational sphere have also faced moral attack if they have ventured past accepted gender boundaries. Restrictions on women's learning have complex roots, but criticism of high-achieving women has helped keep women in their place. The social costs of deviating from the gender norm have been high, even when the women were deviating in the direction of achievement. Here, as elsewhere in the social welfare system, women have been accorded a narrow role, and to burst its boundaries has been to bring obloquy and sometimes social isolation.

There is an analytical link between moral attacks on single women on welfare and on women who achieved unusual degrees of educational success. In both cases, the women have displayed personal independence rather than dependence on individual men. Women on welfare have paid the price of subjection to repressive rules; women in the educational system have had their behavior controlled. Women who pioneered in college attendance in the late 1800s found that even institutions dedicated to educating women imposed moral constraints. When Wellesley College opened in 1875, for example, its founders promulgated regulations designed to make the college function very much like a seminary (Lynn Gordon 1990, p. 29), but the women rebelled and eventually a more secular leadership emerged. A similar conflict took place at Mount Holyoke. The University of Chicago was founded as a coeducational institution in 1892, but President William Rainey Harper tried to segregate the sexes in the early 1900s. He argued that coeducation had brought about 'too many cases of young women who have lost some of the fine attractiveness which somewhat closer reserve would have attained' (quoted in Lynn Gordon 1990, p. 113). Well-known male faculty members endorsed the move toward segregation, contending that coeducation had led away from 'gracious womanhood' (p. 114), but women professors and students successfully fought back.

Women on welfare have suffered both harsh institutional rules and social stigma; university women have been among the highly privileged, but, along with their class privilege, they have suffered institutional constraints (compared with male college students) and have also borne a measure of social disapproval. In the late nineteenth century, women training to be doctors had to endure abuse and taunts from male students (Pascall 1986). While college-educated men fared well in the marriage market, Claudia Goldin summed up the women's situation:

> The powerful norms that defined appropriate work for women succeeded, in part, because inappropriate behavior entailed severe social costs. The most extreme cost for many women was to forgo marriage entirely.... Occupations with the greatest barriers to women were generally those for which women who gained entry never married. The young women who entered college or library school in the late nineteenth and early twentieth centuries, for example, might well have entered a convent, so few eventually married (1990, pp. 204–5).

Education increased the respect accorded to men, but women were often socially devalued if they pursued higher education. This began to change after the first decades of the twentieth century, as college-educated women became more common. These women had more chance to marry than had their pioneering sisters, but if they married and continued working they found that their education brought them less economic reward than it did their single classmates. Married women got lower returns on their education than did single women (Goldin 1990, pp. 178–9). In a labor market already segregated by sex, married women occupied a still more confined corner, and throughout the 1940s married women faced legal and institutional bars to employment. Marriage bars never took hold in industrial employment, but were strongly enforced in many white-collar settings. Highly educated women could remain single, enhancing their opportunity to earn, or they could get married, reducing the rate of return on their education. They had little way around this dilemma. Highly educated women had become socially acceptable, but essentially they still faced a choice between marriage and (relative) occupational success. If they tried for both, they were commonly criticized for stealing jobs from men and venturing beyond their sphere (Oppenheimer 1970). Educated women had to make painful choices about their gender roles and faced condemnation if they pressed the boundaries of those roles.

Mass education for girls and boys has become a global phenomenon, with schooling standing at the intersection of the public worlds of jobs and the private worlds of families (Pascall 1986). Benavot, in this volume, assesses the economic impact of women's education on economic development in ninety-six countries; he finds expanded education among primary school girls has stronger effects on economic productivity than does education for boys. He speculates that this could be due to education's ability to redefine previously marginal groups as valuable and to restructure traditional roles. It is this very restructuring that helps create moral controversy around those women and girls who establish new educational paths.

Marriage bars are now illegal in the United States, and women make up an ever-larger proportion of college students, but both women and girls still risk criticism if they violate gender roles within the educational system. Girls, historically and today, are subject to social demands that they demonstrate feminine behavior within schools. If they are too ambitious or assertive, they can pay a social price among their peers and teachers. In this volume, Linda Grant explores the complexity of the social roles of African-American and white girls in elementary school classrooms. The white girls tend to be teacher-oriented, seeking adult approval. Those who reject typical feminine styles of speech or behavior face harsh criticism, including moral condemnation by teachers as 'bad girls'. Teachers describe misbehaving boys as breaking rules, but do not globally condemn them, while girls who misbehave are seen as morally deficient. No matter how young the girls, some teachers see resistant behavior as indicating a future life of sexual promiscuity. African-American girls had more complex roles in the classroom. They served as social go-betweens, able to mediate between adult authorities (the teachers) and other students, partly because they were less teacher-identified than the white girls. Many of the African-American girls observed by Grant were socially skillful, but they paid a price for their go-between roles. Teachers tended to downgrade or not notice their academic skills.

Not only are girls more readily evaluated in moral terms than are boys, but, on a more subtle level, there are gendered expectations about which courses and subject matters are suitable for girls. After years of feminist activism around schools, there are still distinct patterns of male and female student coursetaking, patterns based on traditional notions of femininity and on coercive forms of social control (Jacobs 1989). The feminist movement has challenged informal social controls and accompanying institutional barriers, with some degree of success; there has been a larger decline in sex segregation (defined in terms of the likelihood of men and women sharing the same majors) in college than in the work world (Jacobs 1989, p. 118). On the basis of extensive analysis of data, Jacobs reports:

> While occupational segregation by sex has declined slowly since the 1960s, higher education has experienced substantial change. Higher education appears far more susceptible than private employers to the influence of government decree and organized pressure groups. Yet the formal equality of education continues to coexist with substantial segregation in the studies men and women pursue (1989, p. 118).

Math and science courses remain an area of considerable segregation. Girls (and African-American and Hispanic students of both sexes) take fewer math and science courses than do Caucasian boys (US Congress 1988). Gender differences in mathematics experiences start early. Using a large sample of fourth through sixth grade classes, Hallinan and Sorensen studied ability grouping in math. They found that girls with high levels of tested mathematics achievement were less likely to be in high-ability groups than were boys with similar levels of achievement (1987), although these grouping practices did not seem to undermine girls' achievement. At the high school level, a gender gap in mathematics learning emerges, although it is diminishing (Sadker, Sadker and Klein 1991; Linn and Hyde 1989). Differences in mathematics learning have long-term consequences. Even as women have increasingly entered fields such as law and business, once nearly all male, they have made few inroads into fields highly dependent on mathematics (Wilson and Boldizar 1990). High school women's aspirations for college majors predict their eventual selection of curricula which require little math and which have low income potential.

Girls' lack of encouragement to pursue mathematics and science courses has deleterious effects on their self-esteem as well as on their future earnings. In 1990 the American Association of University Women commissioned a national survey of girls and boys aged nine to fifteen. Both male and female teenagers suffered drops in self-esteem, but this was particularly true for teenage girls. Many boys, even if not good at school work, declared that they were 'good at doing things'. Luttrell's chapter in this volume shows that this belief in male ability to 'do things' carries over into adulthood, with working-class women esteeming men's practical knowledge and implicitly devaluing their own skills. In the AAUW study, most girls had a less global sense of competence than boys, but fared well if they had good school performance. Their sense of academic competence was impaired, however, by a feeling on the part of many that they were not good at science and math. Only one in seven high school girls said she was good at math (compared with one in four boys). Male and female students attribute lack of success at math to different causes. The report's authors conclude that 'Girls interpret their problems with math as personal failures. Boys project it more as a problem with the subject matter itself' (American Association of University Women 1990, p. 13). These differences contribute to an expectation gap, with girls much more likely than boys to say they are 'not smart enough' for their preferred careers. Gender expectations lead to differences in coursetaking, and these help lead to differences in (self) perceived competence; for girls these differences contribute to a general decline in self-esteem and a sense that they will not be able to reach their goals.

It is not surprising that it is at the secondary level that girls begin to lose their self-confidence and academic ambition. Pascall points out that in Britain, as well as in the United States, for girls

> the period of looking forward to adulthood is one of contracting horizons, of negotiating with the realities of a segregated labour market, of intensified 'femininity' and preoccupation with a romantic and domestic future. It is when girls look beyond school that their commitment to academic achievement may decline (1986, p. 120).

This view is supported by data on girls' and boys' relative levels of mathematics achievement in sixteen countries (Jones and Baker, this volume). In countries where secondary school girls have a reasonable expectation that desirable occupations will be open to them, they perform better at math than do girls in countries with rigid sex-typing of jobs. The relative openness of the social structure filters down into the schools and inclines girls to learn typical 'male' subjects.

Gender expectations are not unvarying. In some countries at some periods, girls have more ability to break through into new roles than in others. Similarly, even within the confines of one school, there are settings where gender roles are tightly enforced and others where boys and girls mingle more freely and counteract gender stereotypes. The fluidity of social roles is emphasized by Barrie Thorne in her chapter in this volume. When gender expectations are fluid, the cost of violating them is likely to be smaller than when girls are subjected to across-the-board restrictions on their behavior. Female students at every level of schooling have increasing personal freedom, but there can still be a price to pay, and a moral critique to endure, if they stray far from conventional notions of how they should look, behave, and learn.

Women and Employment in the Social Welfare System

Theorists disagree over the extent to which gender issues have shaped the social welfare system, but there is no disagreement over the importance of expanded social provision for women's employment. Women disproportionately staff the social welfare sector, serving as caseworkers, clerks, aides, nurses, and teachers, while men continue to hold the top jobs in a state-created gender hierarchy (Pascall 1986, p. 31). Frances Fox Piven writes that 'By 1980, fully 70 percent of the 17.3 million social service jobs on all levels of government, including education, were held by women, accounting for about one-third of all female nonagricultural employment and for the larger part of female job gains since

1960' (1990, p. 255). Women are intricately involved with the welfare state, both as clients and staff, and nowhere is this more evident than in the educational sector.

Teaching has historically been the occupation *par excellence* for middle-class women seeking employment. The vast expansion of the educational system through the late nineteenth and the twentieth centuries brought with it increased demand for women as teachers. They received much lower wages than male teachers, but teaching paid well compared with other women's jobs (Carter and Prus 1982). Men had little incentive to enter teaching, as they could earn better wages elsewhere,[4] but this was not true for women, millions of whom entered upon a direct employment relation with the state. By 1900, nearly three-quarters of all teachers in the United States were women (Durbin and Kent, this volume). As late as the 1960s, teaching remained one of a handful of professional occupations open to college-educated women (nursing, social work, and library work being the others). A national survey covering the years from 1957 to 1964 showed that 54 percent of employed women college graduates were teachers (Goldin 1990, p. 206). The funneling of women into teaching ultimately helped fuel the women's liberation movement, as college-educated women became increasingly frustrated with their narrow occupational choices (Goldin 1990). Heavily female teaching forces helped give women a vehicle for political expression even in the early 1900s. Treated with condescension by male-dominated professional associations, paid much less than their male colleagues, and kept out of administrative jobs, women teachers found ample reason to organize. In Chicago, San Antonio, Atlanta, New York, and other cities, women elementary school teachers took the lead in unionizing (Herbst 1989, p. 190). Occupying a strategic position as government-employed, white-collar workers, in some cities organized women teachers served as links between middle-class reform women and unionized blue-collar workers (Wrigley 1982). This gave women entree into political worlds typically closed to them. Linda Gordon has stressed that the activism of women clients in demanding services from the social welfare bureaucracy must be understood as political behavior (1988). Her point is well taken, but it is worth noting that, as public employees, women teachers had much more chance of engaging in conscious, collective political action than did individual clients, whatever the clients' level of personal militancy and resistance. Women teachers, in some cities at some times, had the means to formulate explicit political agendas. Holding jobs and able to form unions or federations, they could also carve distinctive paths separate from those of middle-class club women, while sometimes engaging them as allies.

Organized women teachers protested against rules barring married women from teaching and fought to throw off moral scrutiny and regulation. As with women who worked elsewhere in the social welfare system, sometimes they themselves oppressed those they served: female teachers could enforce traditional notions of feminine behavior on their female students. Other teachers, however, served as strong role models for the girls they taught, presenting images of caring along with economic independence. Teachers continue strongly to influence their students, with a special impact on female students. A national survey of students found that almost 75 percent of the elementary school girls sampled and more than half of high school girls wanted to be teachers (far higher proportions than among the boys) (AAUW 1990, p. 11). With their sustained, year-long involvement with students, teachers, more than any others who staff social welfare programs, are likely to have an impact on those they serve and, knowingly or unknowingly, to help shape their own gender identities and expectations.

Women's disproportionate employment in state social services and schools may give them a political stake in the expansion of social welfare. In Sweden, with a highly developed public sector, gender bifurcation between the public and private realms is far advanced. Women are heavily concentrated in public employment; they accounted for 87 percent of employment growth in the health, education, and welfare sectors in Sweden from 1965 to 1985, resulting in a 'unique feminization of the welfare state' (Esping-Andersen 1990, p. 202). Gender segregation in the Swedish economy has profound implications for efforts to reduce sexist practices in the country's educational system, as explored by Ingrid Jönsson in her chapter in this volume. The extreme gender split between public and private employment may be unique to Sweden, but a broadly similar pattern is emerging in the United States. Women's economic fortunes as clients and workers are increasingly tied up with the state; their political empowerment depends on their ability to generate and command state resources (Piven 1990). Women teachers proved to be the forerunners of a much larger female-dominated social welfare work force, and this, along with a female predominance in welfare state services, may lead to an increasing gender gap in political reactions to the welfare state.

Conclusion

The social welfare state has had profound importance for women and vice versa (Sapiro 1990, p. 48). Conventionally defined, most social welfare programs involve income transfers, whether through social security, welfare or other means. Education does not involve such transfers, except indirectly. From an analytic point of view, however, debates over the origin and development of the welfare state, and specifically over the role gender played in shaping it, apply with equal force to education. Schooling stands at the intersection of the public and private realms, embodying the gender contradictions found in each. Education acts both to limit women's aspirations and to expand their opportunities.

The educational system prepares students for labor market entry, but women and people of color do not receive the same rewards in the labor market as do white men. This affects women at many points in their educational lives, as Mickelson explores in her chapter in this book. Even in an officially gender-neutral educational system, a sex-segregated occupational structure limits women's ability to secure resources for their schooling, and these limitations occur at numerous points. Parents choose to invest more heavily in sons when resources are scarce; they do this perhaps because of traditional preferences regarding sons and their importance, but also because investing in sons is likely to lead to a larger economic payoff. Because women earn less than men, they accumulate smaller savings and have more trouble paying their own way through college. Once in college, women have lower income expectations than men, which makes them reluctant to take on heavy loans to pay college expenses. They frequently end up in gender-segregated majors. When women emerge from the educational system, they must seek jobs in a world with pervasive sexual segregation and wage discrimination (England et al. 1988).

Women's experiences in the educational system have paralleled those of women in the social welfare system at large. In both spheres, they have received fewer public resources than have men, their caregiving roles have lessened their ability to operate autonomously, their use of educational or social services has subjected them to a kind of moral criticism seldom leveled against men, and they have had special employment relations with the state. In education, as in other areas of the social welfare system, poor and working-class women have had the worst treatment and the most limited access to benefits (Pascall 1986).

The welfare rights movement of the 1960s brought changes in long-standing sexist practices within the social welfare bureaucracy. The United States edged toward the type of non-capricious social entitlement found in more developed welfare states in Western Europe (Heidenheimer 1981). Similarly, women made strides in the educational sector. In both spheres, the conservative political climate of the 1970s and 1980s helped stall or in some cases even reverse previous gains (Hearn, Fenske and Curry 1985). Over the longer term, highly educated women appear increasingly to be entering privileged male jobs (Esping-Andersen 1990, p. 209). They have penetrated a number of occupations once solidly dominated by men and have more chances for professional jobs than did women a generation before them (Goldin 1990). In 1960, only 3 percent of all first professional degrees went to women, compared with 35 percent in 1987 (p. 215). Only 15 percent of those graduating from law school were women in 1975, while ten years later women made up 38 percent of law school graduates. They have also flocked to business schools, partly because business careers hold out the promise of high incomes and partly because they do not require extensive technical and mathematical skills (Wilson and Boldizar 1990). Changes are most visible among young women who are recent college graduates (Goldin 1990).

Data on declining sex segregation of occupations must be interpreted with a large grain of salt, as a great deal of segregation occurs within job categories (Bielby and Baron 1986). Discrimination and segregation remain powerfully entrenched in the occupational structure. It is possible, however, that we are seeing the beginning of a long-term process whereby highly educated women make strides toward greater parity with men, while less-educated women remain trapped in female job ghettoes. Based on extensive study of occupational data for three models of welfare states, Esping-Andersen (1990) suggests that an increasingly dualistic job structure has emerged in the United States. The American occupational structure combines a large group of precarious and ill-paid jobs at the bottom and a substantial group of good jobs at the top. Women, African-Americans, and Hispanics remain heavily overrepresented in poor jobs, but the more privileged in each of these categories have increasingly entered 'good' jobs once reserved for white men.

If current trends continue we may see increasing inequality within race and gender categories, as Wilson (1991) has long argued has occurred within the African-American population. Even as some women and some people of color break down occupational barriers, racism and sexism imprison many others in low-wage jobs. African-Americans of all social degrees experience high levels of day-to-day racism and abuse (Feagin 1991). Similarly, no women escape sexist assumptions and practices. While the exclusion of women and minorities from good jobs used to be almost total, however, some now reap economic rewards even while experiencing other aspects of the negative treatment accorded those of their race or gender. Their economic success can bring them into favored positions in the social welfare system, where benefits are strongly tied to stable, good jobs.

If polarization within categories does increase, awareness of inequality could be high while political mobilization remains low. Those entering jobs previously reserved for white males might detach themselves from larger social struggles, and there is some evidence to suggest that this may be occurring. Davis and Robinson (1991) found, based on survey data, that well-educated American women have a high awareness of gender inequality but do not favor government action to improve women's position. Social transformation is not likely to come from these women but from those who remain more on the margins of the social welfare system and the occupational structure, those who have experienced few of the benefits of the welfare state.

Notes

1   The percentage of preretirement income replaced varies with the wage earner's salary level. While Social Security tax deductions are regressive, payout policies are progressive (Rosenbaum 1991).
2   Although women use educational benefits at a lower rate than men, they are more likely to use their benefits for college training (as compared with on-the-job training or training at a proprietary school) and to train full time. Because of these patterns, they are likely to use as much of their benefit entitlement as do male veterans (Veterans Administration 1981). In addition to overwhelmingly serving males, the GI bill has disproportionately aided white veterans; more than one-third of white veterans have received educational benefits, compared with only one-fourth of African-American veterans. This has occurred partly because the program favors those attending college, as compared with those receiving more vocational training (Levitan and Zickler 1973, p. 58).
3   Loans can create an additional problem for women, as pregnancy is not considered sufficient reason for delaying loan payback.
4   Jurgen Herbst writes that 'Men teachers were expected either to be incapable of other work or to be students earning their way through college' (1989, p. 186).

References

ABEL, E. and NELSON, M. (Eds) (1990) *Circles of Care: Work and Identity in Women's Lives*, Albany, State University of New York Press.

ABRAMOVITZ, M. (1988) *Regulating the Lives of Women: Social Welfare Policy from Colonial Times to the Present*, Boston, South End Press.

AMERICAN ASSOCIATION OF UNIVERSITY WOMEN (1990) *Shortchanging Girls, Shortchanging America*, Washington, DC, Greenberg-Lake Analysis Group.

AMOTT, T. (1990) 'Black Women and AFDC: Making Entitlement out of Necessity', in GORDON, L. (Ed.) *Women, the State, and Welfare*, Madison, University of Wisconsin Press, pp. 280–98.

BAKER, D. and STEVENSON, D. (1986) 'Mothers' Strategies for Children's School Achievement: Managing the Transition to High School', *Sociology of Education* 59, July, pp. 156–66.

BIELBY, W. and BARON, J. (1986) 'Men and Women at Work: Sex Segregation and Statistical Discrimination', *American Journal of Sociology* 91, 759–99.

BIELBY, W. and BIELBY, D. (1989) 'Family Ties: Balancing Commitments to Work and Family in Dual Earner Households', *American Sociological Review* 54, October, pp. 776–89.

CARTER, S. and PRUS, M. (1982) 'The Labor Market and the American High School Girl 1890–1928', *Journal of Economic History* 42, March, pp. 163–71.

COLLINS, R. (1979) *The Credential Society: An Historical Sociology of Education and Stratification*, New York, Academic Press.

DAVIS, N. and ROBINSON, R. (1991) 'Men's and Women's Consciousness of Gender Inequality: Austria, West Germany, Great Britain, and the United States', *American Sociological Review* 56, February, pp. 72–84.

ENGLAND, P., FARKAS, G., KILBOURNE, B. and DOU, T. (1988) 'Explaining Occupational Sex Segregation and Wages: Findings from a Model with Fixed Effects', *American Sociological Review* 53, August, pp. 544–58.

ESPING-ANDERSEN, G. (1990) *The Three Worlds of Welfare Capitalism*, Princeton, Princeton University Press.

FEAGIN, J. (1991) 'The Continuing Significance of Race: Antiblack Discrimination in Public Places', *American Sociological Review* 56, February, pp. 101–16.

FUCHS, V. (1988) *Women's Quest for Economic Equality,* Cambridge, Harvard University Press.

GOLDIN, C. (1990) *Understanding the Gender Gap: An Economic History of American Women*, New York, Oxford University Press.

GORDON, LINDA (1988) 'What does Welfare Regulate?', *Social Research* 55, Winter, pp. 609–30.

GORDON, LINDA (1990) 'The New Feminist Scholarship on the Welfare State', in GORDON, LINDA (Ed.) *Women, The State, and Welfare*, Madison, University of Wisconsin Press, pp. 9–35.

GORDON, LYNN, D. (1990) *Gender and Higher Education in the Progressive Era*, New Haven, Yale University Press.

HAGE, J., GARNIER, M. and FULLER, B. (1988) 'The Active State, Investment in Human Capital, and Economic Growth: France 1825–1975', *American Sociological Review* 53, December, pp. 824–37.

HALLINAN, M. and SORENSEN, A. (1987) 'Ability Grouping and Sex Differences in Mathematics Achievement', *Sociology of Education* 60, April, pp. 63–72.

HEARN, J., FENSKE, R. and CURRY, D. (1985) 'Unmet Financial Need Among Postsecondary Students: A Statewide Study', *Journal of Student Financial Aid* 15, Fall, pp. 31–44.

HEIDENHEIMER, A. (1981) 'Education and Social Security Entitlements in Europe and America', in FLORA, P. and HEIDENHEIMER, A. (Eds) *The Development of Welfare States in Europe and America*, New Brunswick, Transaction Books, pp. 269–304.

HERBST, J. (1989) *And Sadly Teach: Teacher Education and Professionalization in American Culture*, Madison, University of Wisconsin Press.

HOCHSCHILD, A., with MACHUNG, A. (1989) *The Second Shift: Working Parents and the Revolution at Home*, New York, Viking.

HOMEL, M. (1984) *Down from Equality: Black Chicagoans and the Public Schools 1920–41*, Urbana, University of Illinois Press.

JACOBS, J. (1989) *Revolving Doors: Sex Segregation and Women's Careers*, Stanford, Stanford University Press.

KAELBE, H. (1981) 'Educational Opportunities and Government Policies in Europe in the Period of Industrialization', in FLORA, P. and HEIDENHEIMER, A. (Eds) *The Development of Welfare States in Europe and America*, New Brunswick, Transaction Books, pp. 239–68.

KINGSTON, P. and SMART, J. (1990) 'The Economic Pay-Off to Prestigious Colleges', in KINGSTON, P. and LEWIS, L. (Eds) *The High-Status Track: Studies of Elite Schools and Stratification*, Albany, State University of New York Press, pp. 147–74.

LEVITAN, S. and ZICKLER, J. (1973) *Swords into Plowshares: Our GI Bill*, Salt Lake City, Olympus Publishing Company.

LINN, M. and HYDE, J. (1989) 'Gender, Mathematics, and Science', *Educational Researcher* 18, pp. 17–19, 22–7.

MARE, R. (1991) 'Five Decades of Educational Assortative Mating', *American Sociological Review* 56, February, pp. 15–32.

MINK, G. (1990) 'The Lady and the Tramp: Gender, Race, and the Origins of the American Welfare State', in GORDON, LINDA (Ed.) *Women, the State, and Welfare*, Madison, University of Wisconsin Press, pp. 92–122.

MONK-TURNER, E. (1990) 'The Occupational Achievements of Community and Four-Year College Entrants', *American Sociological Review* 55, October, pp. 719–25.

MORAN, M. (1986) *Student Financial Aid and Women: Equity Dilemma?*, ASHE-ERIC Higher Education Report No. 5, Washington, DC, Association for the Study of Higher Education.

MOSCH, T. (1975) *The GI Bill: A Breakthrough in Educational and Social Policy in the United States*, Hicksville, New York, Exposition Press.

NELSON, B. (1990) 'The Origins of the Two-Channel Welfare State: Workmen's Compensation and Mothers' Aid', in GORDON, LINDA (Ed.) *Women, the State, and Welfare*, Madison, University of Wisconsin Press, pp. 123–51.

OGBU, J. (1978) *Minority Education and Caste: The American System in Cross-Cultural Perspective*, New York, Academic Press.

OPPENHEIMER, V. (1970) *The Female Labor Force in the United States: Demographic and Economic Factors Governing its Growth and Changing Composition*, Berkeley, Institute of International Studies, University of California.

PASCALL, G. (1986) *Social Policy: A Feminist Analysis*, London, Tavistock.

PIVEN, F. (1990) 'Ideology and the State: Women, Power, and the Welfare State', in GORDON, LINDA (Ed.) *Women, the State, and Welfare*, Madison, University of Wisconsin Press, pp. 250–64.

PIVEN, F. and CLOWARD, R. (1988) 'Welfare Doesn't Shore Up Traditional Family Roles: A Reply to Linda Gordon', *Social Research* 55, Winter, pp. 631–47.

POWELL, B. and STEELMAN, L. (1989) 'The Liability of Having Brothers: Paying For College and the Sex Composition of the Family', *Sociology of Education* 62, April, pp. 134–47.

QUADAGNO, J. (1990) 'Race, Class, and Gender in the US Welfare State: Nixon's Failed Family Assistance Plan', *American Sociological Review* 55, February, pp. 11–28.

ROSENBAUM, D. (1991) 'Washington Talk: A Question of Fairness in Social Security', *New York Times*, March 22, p. A10.

SADKER, M., SADKER, D. and KLEIN, S. (1991) 'The Issue of Gender in Elementary and Secondary Education', in GRANT, G. (Ed.) *Review of Research in Education* 17, pp. 269–334.

SAPIRO, V. (1990) 'The Gender Basis of American Social Policy', in GORDON, LINDA (Ed.) *Women, the State, and Welfare*, Madison, University of Wisconsin Press, pp. 36–54.

SMITH, H. and POWELL, B. (1990) 'Great Expectations: Variations in Income Expectations among College Seniors', *Sociology of Education* 63, July, pp. 194–207.

SMITH, T. (1984) 'School Grades and Responsibility for Younger Siblings: An Empirical Study of the "Teaching Function"', *American Sociological Review* 49, April, pp. 248–60.

STEELMAN, L. and POWELL, B. (1989) 'Acquiring Capital for College: The Constraints of Family Configuration', *American Sociological Review* 54, October, pp. 844–55.

STEVENSON, D. and BAKER, D. (1991) 'State Control of the Curriculum and Classroom Instruction', *Sociology of Education* 64, January, pp. 1–10.

TYACK, D. and HANSOT, E. (1990) *Learning Together: A History of Coeducation in American Public Schools*, New Haven, Yale University Press.

US CONGRESS, OFFICE OF TECHNOLOGY ASSESSMENT (1988) *Elementary and Secondary Education for Science and Engineering — A Technical Memorandum*, Washington, DC, US Government Printing Office, OTA-TM-SET-41, December.

VETERAN'S ADMINISTRATION (1981) *Women Veterans' Use of Educational Benefits Under the GI Bill*, Washington, DC, Office of Reports and Statistics US Government Printing Office, Series W-81-1, September.

WARE, N. and LEE, V. (1988) 'Sex Differences in Choice of College Science Majors', *American Educational Research Journal* 25, Winter, pp. 593–614.

WEIR, M., ORLOFF, A. and SKOCPOL, T. (1988a) 'Understanding American Social Politics', in WEIR, M., ORLOFF, A. and SKOCPOL, T. (Eds) *The Politics of Social Policy in the United States*, Princeton, Princeton University Press, pp. 3–27.

WEIR, M., ORLOFF, A. and SKOCPOL, T. (1988b) "Epilogue: The Future of Social Policy in the United States: Political Constraints and Possibilities', in WEIR, M., ORLOFF, A. and SKOCPOL, T. (Eds) *The Politics of Social Policy in the United States*, Princeton, Princeton University Press, pp. 421–45.

WILSON, K. and BOLDIZAR, J. (1990) 'Gender Segregation in Higher Education: Effects of Aspirations, Mathematics Achievement, and Income', *Sociology of Education* 63, January, pp. 62–74.

WILSON, W. (1991) 'Studying Inner-City Social Dislocations: The Challenge of Public Agenda Research', *American Sociological Review* 56, February, pp. 1–14.

WRIGLEY, J. (1982) *Class Politics and Public Schools: Chicago, 1900–1950*, New Brunswick, Rutgers University Press.

WRIGLEY, J. (1988) 'Do Young Children Need Intellectual Stimulation? Experts' Advice to Parents, 1900–1985', *History of Education Quarterly* 29, Spring, pp. 41–75.

2 Education, Gender and Economic Development: A Cross-National Analysis

Aaron Benavot

Introduction

This chapter addresses two issues: Do gender differences in educational expansion have different effects on national economic growth? If so, what are the main mechanisms through which these differential effects occur? In past comparative research, these issues were either ignored or explained in relation to education's impact on women's participation in the labor force and reproductive behavior. The study presented here analyzed cross-national data on ninety-six countries from 1960 to 1985 and found clear evidence that in less-developed countries, especially some of the poorest, educational expansion among school-age girls at the primary level has a stronger effect on long-term economic prosperity than does educational expansion among school-age boys. This effect is not mediated by women's rates of participation in the wage labor force or by fertility rates. These findings provide qualified support for institutional theories of education's impact on society.

Models of the impact of education on economic development largely ignore the issue of gender. Whether rooted in concepts of human capital, modernization or economic dependence, few consider how the long-term effects of increased education may differ for school-age girls and boys. In retrospect, the neglect of this issue seems unjustified and short-sighted, especially in the context of Third World development. Evidence, mainly from individual-level research in developing countries, is accumulating regarding the particularly dynamic effects of educational expansion among school-age girls — on labor force participation, migration into the cities, changing family arrangements, the age at first marriage, and reproductive behavior (Caldwell 1982; Cochrane 1979; Smock 1981; Standing 1981). Although this emerging line of research has underlined the importance of analyzing the issue of development through the prism of gender, few studies have directly examined the interaction of schooling and gender for *long-term* economic growth.

Consider some of the key questions involved: Does education make women workers more or less productive than men workers in land cultivation or wage labor? Does educational expansion alter the proportion of cash to non-cash economic transactions that men and women conduct? Does education do more than differentially allocate men and women to various positions in the labor market? Does it have direct 'institutional' effects on the economy: creating new sources of economic value, delegitimating traditional economic roles isolated from the wage market, redefining the societal value attached to different privatized and communal pursuits? If so, are all levels of educational expansion of equal importance in these matters? Finally, what, if any, differences result from educational expansion among girls and boys?

The cross-national study reported in this chapter sought to explore these issues by analyzing the impact of gender differences in education on economic growth from 1960 to 1985. It compared the long-term effects of female versus male educational expansion at the mass (primary) and elite (secondary) levels after controlling for a number of important intervening variables. The chapter begins by surveying current models of the role of education in economic development and then examines recent lines of critique and argumentation. After testing the main predictions of three distinct theoretical perspectives in a cross-national research design, it concludes by discussing several explanations for the consistently strong effect of mass female education on economic growth in many of the poorest developing countries in the world.

Education and Economic Growth

The theoretical debate over the conditions and causes of economic growth has shifted dramatically in recent years. Arguments rooted in the modernization and human capital perspectives, which dominated social science discourse in the 1960s and early 1970s, have been sharply attacked and partially supplanted by neo-Marxist conceptualizations rooted in the dependency and world system perspectives. Proponents of the earlier models argued that the transformation of certain key social-structural arrangements — the mechanization of agriculture, rural-urban migration, the expansion and integration of a national market, a mass communications network, a decline in mortality and fertility rates, and an increase in political participation — were necessary conditions for sustained economic growth (see, for example, Apter 1965; Lerner 1958; Levy 1966; Rostow 1960).

Recent theoretical work, however, has focused on the dynamics of the world system that structures and conditions economic transformations in both the core and periphery of the world economy. One line of thought argues that the prevalence of foreign investment capital, the presence of multinational corporations, the concentration on exporting primary products and the dependence on imported technologies and manufactured goods constrains long-term economic development (Bornschier and Chase-Dunn 1985; Delacroix and Ragin 1978; Meyer-Fehr 1979; Nemeth and Smith 1985). A second line of thought discusses how certain features of the world polity — state fiscal strength, degree of regime centralization, and external political integration — may contribute to economic growth in the Third World (Meyer 1980; Ramirez and Thomas 1981; Rubinson 1979).

Another notable theoretical shift, though perhaps less dramatic, revolves around education's purported role in the process of economic development. Education enjoyed a prominent place in the arguments of early theorists on human capital and modernization (Denison 1964; Inkeles and Smith 1974; McClelland 1961; Schultz 1961). Human capital theorists, for example, viewed workers as 'holders of capital' (by virtue of the skills they acquire through education) who have the 'capacity to invest' in themselves (Karabel and Halsey 1977, p. 13). To them, the provision of education was not a form of consumption but a productive investment in society's 'stock' of human capital. Educational expansion (society's investment in the population) was a social investment at least as profitable, if not more so, than investment in physical capital. One source of evidence of the importance of human capital was social rates of return on educational investment that were greater than the traditional 'yardstick' of 10 percent (for a review, see Psacharopoulos and Woodhall 1985).

The main contribution of education to economic growth was to increase the level of cognitive skills possessed by the work force and consequently to improve their marginal productivity. Basic literacy and numeracy augment the productivity of workers in low-skill occupations; instruction that demands logical or analytical reasoning or provides technical and specialized knowledge increases the marginal productivity of workers in high-skill or professional positions. Education even enhances the productivity of farmers (Lockheed, Jamison and Lau 1980). Thus, in the aggregate, the greater the provision of schooling, the greater the stock of human capital in society and the greater the increases in national productivity and economic growth.[1]

Whereas human capital theorists emphasize how education increases the productivity and efficiency of workers, modernization theorists focus on how education transforms individual values, beliefs, and behavior (see, for example, Lerner 1958; McClelland 1961). Inkeles and Smith's (1974) statement of the modernization perspective on this issue is probably the clearest. These authors argue that exposure to 'modernizing' institutions (schools, factories and the mass media) inculcates 'modern' values and attitudes, such as the openness to new ideas, independence from traditional authority, a willingness to plan and calculate future exigencies, and a growing sense of personal and social efficacy. These normative and attitudinal changes continue throughout the life cycle, permanently altering an individual's relationship to the social structure. The compounding effects of this process are crucial: the greater the number of people exposed to modernizing institutions such as schools, the greater the level of 'individual modernity' attained by the population (Inkeles 1978, p. 471). Once a critical segment of the population changes in this way, the pace of societal modernization and economic development quickens. Thus, educational expansion, through its effects on individual values and beliefs, sets into motion the necessary building blocks for a more productive work force and for sustained economic growth (see also Halsey, Floud and Anderson 1961; McClelland 1966; Peaslee 1965).

During the 1970s, models rooted in the human capital and modernization perspectives were the focus of much criticism and debate, especially in the context of Third World development (Frank 1972; Portes 1973). For example, critics pointed to the contradictions resulting from rapid educational expansion and slow-growing wage employment. Evidence of widespread unemployment among school graduates — because of their inability to find employment at an appropriate level or their unwillingness to work in lower-status jobs — and the deleterious impact it was thought to have on economic growth were widely discussed (Colclough 1982, pp. 168–70; Irizarry 1980; Turnhan 1970). It was also pointed out that educated individuals with 'modern' attitudes and values, including many highly skilled professionals, were emigrating to industrialized nations to seek more suitable work positions or greater monetary rewards. Although rational from the individual perspective, the out-migration of educated labor (the notorious 'brain drain') was of questionable value from the perspective of the sender nations (Palmer 1982; Watanabe 1969). The drain of educated people created shortages in trained personnel, deprived developing countries of potential entrepreneurs, and increased the likelihood of slow and uneven economic development.

Clearly, earlier theories had failed to recognize several unintended consequences of rapid educational expansion: escalating public expenditures for education, increasing rates of dropout and grade repetition, and longer periods of unemployment for graduates. The logic of educational expansion placed new pressures on all students to seek higher credentials so they could compete for the few prestigious and well-paid positions in each country. As a result, learning relevant skills and specialized knowledge became secondary to acquiring the necessary credentials (Collins 1979). The unsatiated demand for education increased the preponderance of credentialism, educational inflation, and vocationalism, thereby placing severe constraints on the limited resources of developing economies (Berg 1971; Dore 1976; Grubb 1985). These trends reinforced the proposition that the effects of education on economic development were far more problematic and contradictory than earlier theories had assumed. The widespread circulation of neo-Marxist theories of underdevelopment (Amin 1973; Frank 1978) and of education's role in the reproduction of social and economic inequalities (Carnoy 1974) further undermined the assertion that education was a necessary condition for economic growth. It is not surprising, then, that many commentators during this period became more cautious and skeptical about the presumed positive economic impact of education (Weiler 1978).

Education, Women and Development

One thing should be clear from this brief review of the literature on education and development: the issue of gender has, for the most part, been ignored. The various strands of modernization theory, for example, had little to say about differences (attitudinal or behavioral) that may result from the schooling of men in contrast to the schooling of women. Educating women may transform them into modern actors, but this change was not considered to be qualitatively different from the impact of educating men. The basic assumption was that, as the process of modernization proceeded, educational and occupational opportunities would expand, women's traditional roles in the family would weaken, and women's overall status would inevitably improve (see Jaquette 1982). However, even if the erosion of traditional social structures in Third World societies presented women with greater opportunities to enter the wage labor force, this was not seen as a central component of the modernization model. Furthermore, few of the neo-Marxist or critical theorists just mentioned discussed the possibility of a differential impact from educating men and women.

Beginning in the 1970s, important feminist critiques of the models of development emerged. In her classic work *Woman's Role in Economic Development*, Boserup (1970) showed that in many African nations improvements in agricultural techniques and practices actually lowered the status of women by reducing their access to productive work roles. Later studies provided additional support for Boserup's insight that women's traditional work in agriculture — work of relatively high status, though unaccounted for in official statistics (Beneria 1982; Dixon-Mueller 1985) — could be marginalized though agricultural mechanization and industrialization and that their access to economic and political resources could decline in relation to men (see, for example, Dauber and Cain 1981; Tinker and Bramsen 1976).

Although it lacked an overarching theoretical paradigm, this growing body of feminist inquiry (usually referred to as the 'women and development' literature) sparked several lines of research into the relationship between socioeconomic development, the sexual division of labor, and the changing status of women. One line of research focused on the causes of women's overall and sector-specific participation in the labor force (Boulding 1977; Pampel and Tanaka 1986; Semyonov 1980; Youssef 1974); another explored the role of economic development and the accumulation of capital in the maintenance of patriarchal relations (Beneria and Sen 1981; see the review by Schuster 1982). The traditional interest of demographers in the causes of fertility (Cain 1984; Cochrane 1979; Curtin 1982) was reevaluated and later incorporated into comparative studies of the impact of the world economy and the international division of labor on the productive and reproductive statuses of women (see, for example, London 1988; Marshall 1985; Nash and Fernandez-Kelly 1983; Ward 1984).

The role of education was evident, though rarely central, in these feminist studies. Boserup (1970), for example, argued that women's education lessens the negative impact of economic development on women's status by increasing their access to urban labor markets and to improved agricultural techniques. But research on the issue of women's education generally focused on sex inequalities in the access to national educational systems (Acker, Megarry and Nisbet 1984; Deble 1980; Kelly and Elliot, 1982; Smock, 1981) or on sex differences in educational attainment (Finn, Dulberg and Reis 1979). Of the limited research on the long-term impact of women's participation in the educational enterprise, two issues have predominated: labor force participation and fertility.

Labor Force Participation

Many economic and sociological theories predict that education increases women's participation in the labor force. This prediction is premised on the notion that education favorably affects women's willingness and ability to enter the wage labor market. Specifically, it is asserted that the increased schooling of females (1) raises their potential earning power and thus provides them with a strong inducement to seek employment, (2) raises their occupational aspirations, (3) changes their attitudes toward women's traditional roles in the household and in the workplace, and (4) provides them with the necessary credentials for employment in many jobs (see Ram 1982; Standing 1981). Demographic theories also provide a rationale for the applicability of this prediction to less-developed countries. The propensity for rural-urban migration in these countries is especially high among the more educated, among the young, and among women. If women constitute a majority of these migrants, the result, because of changing opportunity costs, is higher rates of labor market participation among both urban and rural women (see Standing, 1981).

Nevertheless, empirical evidence supporting the hypothesized positive link between education and women's participation in the labor market has been mixed (Ram 1982; Smock 1981; Standing and Sheehan 1978). In some countries, market participation rates among women increase with greater educational attainment, but in others they are curvilinear. In the latter case, those with little or no schooling have high rates of participation, those with more schooling have lower rates, and those with the highest levels of schooling also have high participation rates. The rate among women in the middle category is thought to result from segmentation of the labor force (Standing 1981) or the fact that education, rather than a means of increasing income, is simply being used to increase the marital status of daughters from middle-class families (Goode 1963; Papanek 1985).

Do increases in women's labor force participation lead to increases in national productivity and economic production? Within more-developed countries, this proposition receives strong empirical validation (Mincer 1985), but within less-developed countries the evidence is sparse. Few studies have directly addressed the question. In an unusual study of the productivity of men and women farmers, the gain in productivity from education was higher for women than for men (Moock 1976). As women increase their educational attainments, many transfer from traditional agricultural positions to employment in the modern service sector and a wider range of occupations (Smock 1981). But does this redistribution of women workers produce a larger economic pie? We simply do not know.

Women workers as a group invariably earn less than do men as a group. The average ratio of women's to men's wages in more-developed countries was 63.6 percent in 1960 and 73.5 percent in 1980; in less-developed countries, the ratio is even lower (Mincer 1985). Human capital theorists argue that women's increased educational attainments will reduce the wage differentials between men and women because women will increase their commitment to wage employment, work in fewer part-time jobs, and have more continuous employment histories. Women's increased educational attainments should also cause sex differentials in the rate of return on education to decrease. However, in the few countries for which sex-specific rates of return on educational investment have been calculated, the rate of return for men is usually higher than that for women, although for secondary and tertiary education the average difference between male and female rates of return is less than 2.5 percent (Psacharopoulos 1973; 1985). In several countries, the rates of return to investment in education are actually higher for women. Yet all this means is that more-educated women are somewhat better off than less-educated women. It does not mean that educated women receive better paying positions in the occupational structure than do educated men.

The specific links between women's participation in the labor force and economic growth are unclear. However, as educational opportunities for men and women become equalized, women's rates of participation in the industrial and service sectors are likely to increase. Greater educational attainments among women will also lower the relative value of educational credentials attained by older men. Manufacturing firms and transnational corporations, in their constant search for cheaper, more 'stable' sources of labor, will have new justifications to replace men, especially older men, with younger women (UNESCO 1981). How these patterns augur for economic growth is not readily apparent, but a strong case (at least in terms of increased labor force participation) can be made for the dynamic effects of the expansion of the education of females.

Fertility

Let us examine the second issue — women's education and fertility — and consider the impact that this relationship may have on economic growth. Most scholars believe that rapid population growth has negative consequences for economic development (Coale and Hoover 1958; National Academy of Sciences 1971), although this conventional wisdom is being challenged and debated (National Research Council 1986; Simon 1981). The rapid increase in the population of less-developed countries occurs because they are experiencing lower mortality rates (especially infant and child mortality) concurrent with high birth rates (World Bank 1984). Educational expansion, it is argued, reduces population growth in the Third World by raising the age at first marriage, reducing the demand for children, and increasing the knowledge and use of birth control methods (Cochrane 1979). Thus, education primarily affects population growth by lowering fertility rates. An examination (United Nations 1983, pp. 84–6) of findings from the World Fertility Study generally supported this conclusion:

> Education has a negative effect on fertility, but not universally so; often the relationship, instead of being monotonic, is hump-shaped and contains an educational 'threshold' [on the average, three to four years of education] prior to which fertility either remains stationary or increases as the level of education rises.... Curvilinear patterns ... are common among countries just beginning to develop; the pattern becomes monotonically negative and thresholds disappear in middle-income, high-literacy countries.... Contraceptive use, moreover, was found to be positively linked to education monotonically (that is, without thresholds).

Also significant is the finding that the education of women has a stronger negative effect on fertility (by almost three times) than does the education of men (Cochrane 1983). It appears, therefore, that the education of women is especially critical in lowering the rates of population growth in middle-income and, to a lesser extent, in low-income countries. Thus education, by its impact on demographic processes such as fertility, becomes an important condition for sustained economic growth.

Note, however, that the two intervening mechanisms examined thus far, labor force participation and fertility, are conceptualized in terms of the *individual-level* effects of education on women. The underlying logic involves either the acquisition of skills or socialization: education affects the skills, behavior, and attitudes of individual women, making them more likely to enter wage employment rather than non-remunerative labor and to favor practices that limit the number of children they bear. This traditional conceptualization of educational effects may tell only part of the story.

Institutional Perspective

Several scholars have recently advanced *institutional-level* explanations of the impact of mass and elite education on society (see Boli, Ramirez, and Meyer 1985; Caldwell 1980; 1982; Meyer 1977; Thomas et al. 1987). Proponents of this perspective maintain that the expansion of formal schooling directly alters important institutional arrangements in society. For example, new and more expanded definitions of the individual and the self are created, new categories of professional personnel and specialized elites are constructed, the use of education-related rules for the allocation of jobs and promotions is intensified, the corporate identity and authority relations of the family are restructured, and the flow of net wealth in the family economy (from wife to husband and from child to parent) changes direction.

For developing nations in the Third World, the advent and expansion of primary education is particularly crucial in this regard. Mass education extends citizenship rights and duties to traditionally marginal segments of society (such as women, children, and the non-propertied classes), thereby increasing their integration into the economy and polity (Ramirez and Rubinson 1979; Ramirez and Weiss 1979). It also creates a new array of familial and societal dependencies, since the costs of raising children increases, children's potential for work (both inside and outside the home) is reduced, and children come to be seen as future rather than present producers (Caldwell 1980). These institutional changes, it is argued, have impacts on the non-schooled as well as the schooled, on the parental generation as well as the school-age generation, and on the status of social classes who are not exposed to schooling as well as the status of those who are.

In economic terms, institutional explanations contend that education constructs new categories of economic value, undercuts the legitimacy of 'traditional' economic pursuits (usually isolated from the wage economy), and redefines many formerly private or communal pursuits as deserving remuneration. In this way, education contributes directly to economic growth, independent of individual-level effects, by redefining the economic value attached to a wide range of economic and social activities that, ultimately, become incorporated in aggregate measures of national wealth such as the gross national product (GNP).

These arguments have important implications for the changing status of women and economic growth. They predict that the underlying ideology of modern school expansion, with its emphasis on citizenship, middle-class values and national progress, will construct new rights and duties for women as potentially productive citizens in the national economy and will begin to erode the role of women in the traditional family economy. In contrast to the theoretical arguments outlined earlier, which, if they focus on women's education at all, view its impact primarily as mediated by participation in the paid labor force or by lower overall fertility, this perspective predicts institutional effects of the education of women on economic growth which are independent of these mechanisms. Whether these institutional effects are more pronounced for mass education or elite education is not specifically discussed, though this issue will be addressed in the analyses that follow.

In sum, there are three general sets of predictions. First is the modernization perspective, which does not predict significant differences in the effects of the education of men versus that of women; when they are strong or weak, they should be strong or weak for both sexes. In addition, the impact of education should decline slightly when measures of women's participation in the labor force and reproductive behavior are introduced. Second, the human capital and demographic perspectives generally predict that women's education will have stronger long-term effects than will men's education but that these effects will decline significantly (or even disappear) once appropriate controls for labor force participation and fertility rates are included. Third, the institutional perspective generally predicts that the education of women and, to lesser extent, that of men, will have strong, direct effects on economic growth, effects that are not mediated by labor force participation or fertility rates.

Research Design and Methodology

The research reported here followed a comparative, cross-national research design. Alternative hypotheses were tested using different samples of developed and less-developed countries. A panel regression methodology was used to investigate the long-term economic impact of the enrollment expansion of males and females at the primary and secondary levels over a 25-year period, from 1960 to 1985.

Multiple regression analysis using panel data, usually called panel regression analysis, is a widely used technique for delineating the causes of societal change over time (Hannan 1979; Hannan and Young 1977). In panel regression models the dependent variable at some time point (in this case, 1985) is regressed on a lagged value of the dependent variable at some previous time point (in this case, 1960) and a set of independent variables also measured at previous time points.[2] In this way, panel models directly estimate the effects of the independent variables on change in the dependent variable, thereby reducing the problem of reverse causation and simultaneity that is common to cross-sectional research designs.

This study used per capita GNP to measure changes in levels of economic development over time. Data on GNP for 1960 and 1985 came from the fourth edition of the *World Tables* and are reported in constant 1985 US dollars (World Bank 1988). Population figures came from a recent series of estimates by the United Nations (United Nations 1986b). Since measures of economic development, such as the per capita GNP, have extremely skewed distributions (which violates an important assumption of ordinary least-squares regression techniques), all analyses used the log transformation of per capita GNP.

It is important to note that the quality, accuracy and comparability of GNP data have been questioned on several grounds. The biggest problem revolves around goods produced and services performed that do not pass (or have not passed) through markets, since the value of such goods and services is excluded from GNP estimates. In less-developed countries, where such transactions are particularly important, many workers make their livelihood in the 'informal' sector of the economy as small-scale vendors, porters, scribes, hawkers, and transporters (Portes and Sassen-Koob 1987). Since a good portion of the goods and services that are exchanged in the informal sector are not recorded in official accounts, their value must be estimated indirectly from other measures of income.

An additional problem is how the commercialization of trade and the transformation of subsistence activities affects estimates of GNP over time. As the economies of less-developed countries grow in size and scale, many formerly unaccounted and nonpecuniary productive activities (performed informally in households or in various communal arrangements) enter commercial markets and become incorporated in measures of the national product. Especially important in this respect are the economic activities of women, from childrearing and house-hold maintenance to agricultural production traded and exchanged locally, which often go unmeasured or underrated in official accounts of national output (ICRW 1980; Beneria 1982). If nonmarket subsistence activities and 'nonmarketable goods' take on cash values over time and, as a consequence, become incorporated in international accounts of national product, then the comparability of measures such as GNP is considerably weakened.

It is possible partially to circumvent these and other problems related to official GNP data by utilizing more refined measures of national income and product (e.g., Kravis, Heston and Summers 1982; Summers and Heston 1984; United Nations 1986a) or alternative measures of socio-economic development such as per capita energy consumption. For the purposes of the present study, suffice it to say that analyses using measures other than per capita GNP were performed and that no significant differences in the overall pattern of educational effects (from those reported in the next section) were found.

Data for the main independent variables came from several sources. Information on national enrollment rates was taken from UNESCO (1970) and the World Bank (1982, pp. 154–5). In addition, four other variables were employed in the analyses: (1) a dummy variable for countries that are major exporters of minerals or oil, (2) the concentration of export commodities, which measures one aspect of economic dependence known to have a negative effect on economic growth (World Bank 1983), (3) the total fertility rate, which refers to the average number of children that would be borne by a group of women in the childbearing ages (15–44) if they experienced no mortality (United Nations 1986b), and (4) the rates of women's participation in the industrial and service sectors of the labor force (International Labour Office 1986). The latter variables are included as intervening measures to test arguments advanced by theorists of the demographic and human capital perspectives. Since both theoretical perspectives assume that the impact of education will occur *after* women complete their studies and enter the wage labor force and/or begin a family, then a valid test of these arguments should incorporate a lag structure of five to ten years for each intervening variable to reflect the lagged effects of education. Therefore, in all the analyses reported below, I measured fertility rates at 1970 and women's rates of labor force partici-pation in the industrial and service sectors at 1965.

Finally, the category 'less-developed countries' consists of all countries in Latin America, the Caribbean, Africa, Asia (except Japan), the Middle East (except Kuwait) and Oceania (except Australia and New Zealand). A complete list of the countries included in the analyses is presented in the Appendix (p. 42).

Analyses and Findings

This section reports results from the main series of empirical analyses. Table 2.1 presents means and standard deviations for each variable used in the analyses for

Table 2.1   Means and Standard Deviations for All Variables in Panel Analyses, by Level of Development

Variables	All Countries (n=96)		More-developed Countries (n=20)		Less-developed Countries (n=76)	
	Mean	S.D.	Mean	S.D.	Mean	S.D.
Logged per capita GNP 1985	3.05	0.58	3.84	0.29	2.88	0.48
Logged per capita GNP 1960	2.84	0.49	3.49	0.35	2.70	0.40
Primary Enrollment Ratio 1960	69.50	28.50	93.90	5.70	63.50	28.60
Secondary Enrollment Ratio 1960	19.20	19.60	49.70	18.20	11.60	11.50
Tertiary Enrollment Ratio 1960	3.00	3.60	8.60	6.10	1.80	2.60
Female Primary Enrollment Ratio 1960	61.00	32.10	92.10	2.40	54.20	31.60
Male Primary Enrollment Ratio 1960	76.20	26.60	96.60	2.10	71.80	27.40
Female Secondary Enrollment Ratio 1960	16.60	19.00	45.80	16.10	10.20	12.40
Male Secondary Enrollment Ratio 1960	23.00	21.40	56.10	14.80	15.80	14.90
Total Fertility Rate 1970	5.00	1.90	2.20	0.40	5.60	1.50
Women's Rate of Participation in the Industrial Labor Force 1965	3.00	3.00	7.20	2.90	2.10	2.10
Women's Rate of Participation in the Service Sector Labor Force 1965	7.20	5.70	14.30	4.90	5.60	4.50
Dummy Variable for Mining/Oil Exporters	0.18	0.38	0.06	0.24	0.20	0.40
Export Commodity Concentration	54.40	29.50	15.50	16.40	62.80	24.60
Ratio of Female Primary Rate to Male Primary Rate, 1960	0.80		0.95		0.75	
Ratio of Female Secondary Rate to Male Secondary Rate, 1960	0.72		0.82		0.65	

the entire sample of countries and for subsets of twenty more-developed and seventy-six less-developed countries. Sex-specific enrollment rates refer to the number of male or female pupils enrolled at each educational level, standardized by the appropriate school-age population for each sex. These ratios range in value from 0 to 100 percent.[3] As others have documented (Deble 1980; Kelly and Elliot 1982), the average enrollment rates for males are higher than those for females at both the primary and secondary levels, especially in the Third World. In 1960, for example, 70 percent of all primary-age boys but only 54 percent of all primary-age girls in less-developed countries were enrolled in school. In the same year, about 16 percent of the male secondary-age group and 10 percent of the female secondary-age group were enrolled in secondary schools. Thus, the enrollment rates for females were, on the average, about 75 percent of the primary and 65 percent of the secondary enrollment rates for males. This disparity in mean enrollment rates was less marked among the twenty more-developed countries in the sample.

Table 2.2 reports intercorrelations among the main variables used in the panel regression analyses. The relatively high correlations between the two sex-specific enrollment ratios at the primary and secondary levels make it difficult to estimate the unique effects of each educational variable (see Hannan 1979). To ensure that the results are not adversely affected by high collinearity, I analyzed the impact of the enrollment rates of males and females in separate equations.

Table 2.2   Correlation Matrix of Variables Used in Panel Regression Analyses

	(1)	(2)	(3)	(4)	(5)	(6)	(7)	(8)	(9)	(10)	(11)	(12)	(13)	(14)
1. GNP per capita 1985	*													
2. GNP per capita 1960	.94	*												
3. Primary Education 1960	.72	.63	*											
4. Secondary Education 1960	.80	.77	.66	*										
5. Tertiary Education 1960	.65	.66	.51	.81	*									
6. Female Primary 1960	.72	.62	n/a	.67	.60	*								
7. Male Primary 1960	.68	.58	n/a	.55	.53	.83	*							
8. Female Secondary 1960	.78	.77	.67	n/a	.80	.70	.54	*						
9. Male Secondary 1960	.77	.71	.67	n/a	.78	.67	.56	.94	*					
10. Total Fertility Rate 1970	−.80	−.72	−.71	−.85	−.64	−.74	−.60	−.83	−.85	*				
11. Women's Rate of Participation in Industrial LF 1965	.67	.61	.56	.69	.53	.59	.49	.72	.73	−.76	*			
12. Women's Rate of Participation in Service LF 1965	.73	.77	.62	.78	.65	.66	.50	.85	.74	−.74	.75	*		
13. Dummy for Mining/ Oil Countries	−.01	.04	.07	−.13	−.16	−.01	−.05	−.07	−.09	.09	−1.5	−0.7	*	
14. Export Commodity Concentration	−.69	−.60	−.49	−.64	−.52	−.48	−.46	−.59	−.64	.66	−.65	−.52	.06	*

n/a = not applicable
LF = Labor Force

Certain correlations between sex-specific enrollment rates and the intervening variables are also relatively high. As a consequence, I tested for the impact of multicollinearity using various collinearity diagnostics (see Belsley, Kuh and Welsch 1980) and closely checked the consistency of the effects across different model specifications. These tests and checks indicated that multicollinearity was not a problem in the analyses reported below.

Table 2.3 examines the overall effects of primary, secondary, and tertiary education on economic growth in the 1960–85 period in three different model specifications. In the first model, the effects of the educational variables were estimated without controlling for the two main intervening mechanisms (fertility rates and women's labor force participation in the industrial and service sectors). In the next model the total fertility rate in 1970 was introduced, and in the last model both types of intervening variables were included together with the educational variables. The latter two models are direct tests of human capital and demographic arguments, which contend, respectively, that education increases employment in the wage labor market or alters the reproductive behavior of educated individuals. In all three model specifications, the lagged dependent

Table 2.3   Panel Analyses of the Effects of Education on Economic Growth, 1960–1985[†]

Equation Number: Number of Cases	1 96	2 96	3 96
Educational Enrollment Rates in 1960			
Primary Education	0.0036**	0.0030**	0.0032**
Secondary Education	0.0033*	0.0010	0.0021
Tertiary Education	–0.0142*	–0.0133*	–0.0120
Control Variables			
Lagged Dependent Variable	0.84**	0.84**	0.90**
Mining/Oil Exporters	–0.07*	–0.07*	–0.07*
Export Commodity Concentration	–0.003**	–0.003**	–0.002**
Intervening Variables			
Total Fertility Rate in 1970		–0.04**	–0.04**
Women's Participation Rate in Industrial Labor Force, 1965			0.008
Women's Participation Rate in Service Labor Force, 1965			–0.015**
Adjusted R^2	0.916	0.919	0.923
Constant	0.57	0.84	0.71

[†] Unstandardized regression coefficients are reported; dependent variable is logged GNP per capita, 1985.
* Unstandardized regression coefficient is at least 1.5 times its standard error.
** Unstandardized regression coefficient is at least 2.0 times its standard error.

variable as well as variables for major oil exporters and for trade dependence are included.

Table 2.3 shows that when the intervening variables are omitted, both primary and secondary education have significant positive effects on economic growth while tertiary education has a significant negative effect. When the intervening variables are included, the direction of the educational effects remains the same, but only primary education attains significance. This pattern of educational effects (positive effects of mass education and weak, negative effects of higher education) is basically similar to that reported in earlier studies (see, for example, Meyer et al. 1979; Benavot 1986). The finding that the economic impact of secondary education is weaker than previously reported is in all probability due to differences in the size of the sample, specification of the model, and the historical period examined.

In the next series of analyses, tertiary education was dropped and the models were reestimated using separate measures of educational expansion for females and males at the primary and secondary levels.[4] Table 2.4 shows that the primary enrollment rates of both females and males have strong positive effects on economic growth which weaken only slightly when fertility and labor force measures are included. On the whole, the parameter estimates associated with the primary education of females are not substantially different from those associated with the primary education of males. At the secondary level, the effects of the education of females are negative but generally weak and nonsignificant. The impact of the education of males is positive and significant but weakens considerably with the inclusion of fertility and labor force measures. In each model, the strength of

Table 2.4   Effects of Gender Differences in Education on Economic Growth, 1960–1985[†]

Equation Number:	1	2	3	4	5	6
Number of Cases	96	96	96	96	96	96
Sex-Specific Educational Enrollment Rates in 1960:						
Female Primary	0.0073**	0.0058**	0.0063**			
Male Primary				0.0071**	0.0063**	0.0061**
Female Secondary	−0.0016	−0.0062*	−0.0004			
Male Secondary				0.0054**	0.0010	0.0025
Control Variables:						
Lagged Dependent Variable	0.86**	0.86**	0.91**	0.81**	0.80**	0.86**
Mining/Oil Exporters	−0.06	−0.05	−0.05	−0.05	−0.05	−0.05
Export Commodity Concentration	−0.003**	−0.003**	−0.002**	−0.003*	−0.002**	−0.002**
Intervening Variables:						
Total Fertility Rate in 1970		−0.05**	−0.04**		−0.04**	−0.05**
Women's Participation Rate in Industrial Labor Force, 1965			0.009			0.006
Women's Participation Rate in Service Labor Force, 1965			−0.017**			−0.013**
Adjusted R^2	0.915	0.920	0.924	0.917	0.921	0.924
Constant	0.58	0.89	0.73	0.56	0.88	0.77

[†] Unstandardized regression coefficients are reported; dependent variable is logged GNP per capita, 1985.
* Unstandardized regression coefficient is at least 1.5 times its standard error.
** Unstandardized regression coefficient is at least 2.0 times its standard error.

the effect of the secondary education of males is greater than that of the secondary education of females.

In terms of the control and intervening variables that were entered, export commodity concentration and fertility had strong negative effects on economic growth during this period. Countries with economies based primarily on mining and mineral extraction did not experience greater rates of economic growth. What is perhaps surprising is that the rate of women's labor force participation in the industrial sector had a weak but positive impact on economic growth, whereas their rate of participation in the service sector had a significant negative impact.[5]

It should be borne in mind that the findings discussed thus far report the impact of education on economic growth for the entire sample of ninety-six countries. Since most of the arguments and predictions outlined earlier refer specifically to less-developed nations in the Third World, this subsample of countries will be isolated in the remaining analyses (see Table 2.5). After first reporting results for all seventy-six less-developed countries, this group of countries is divided along three criteria: by region (Africa, Central and South America, and Asia); by wealth (those less-developed countries with a per capita GNP of more than or less than $475); and by nonachievement of 'universal' primary education (in other words, those countries with a gross primary enrollment rate of less than 95 percent). In each case a fully specified model is estimated in which all control and intervening variables were entered. As before,

Table 2.5 The Effects of Female and Male Educational Expansion on Economic Growth, 1960–85, in Select Subsamples of Less-developed Countries [†]

Equation[‡]		Female Primary	Male Primary	Female Secondary	Male Secondary	Constant	Adjusted R^2
1. World sample	a.	0.0063**		−0.0004		0.73	0.924
(n=96)	b.		0.0061**		0.0025	0.77	0.924
2. All less-developed	a.	0.0064**		0.0033		0.65	0.859
countries (n=76)	b.		0.0056**		0.0078*	0.60	0.858
3. Less-developed	a.	0.0081**		0.0376		−0.06	0.751
countries in Africa	b.		0.0046*		0.0306	0.36	0.726
(n=34)							
4. Less-developed	a.	0.0061*		−0.0029		0.28	0.845
countries in the	b.		0.0055*		0.0010	0.25	0.835
Americas (n=23)							
5. Less-developed	a.	0.0024		0.0159		0.57	0.930
countries in Asia	b.		0.0027		0.0123*	0.32	0.935
(n=19)							
6. Poor less-developed	a.	0.0053**		0.0202		1.28	0.643
countries (below	b.		0.0041		0.0060	1.39	0.569
$475) (n=39)							
7. Richer less-developed	a.	0.0060**		0.0052		0.14	0.794
countries (above	b.		0.0076**		0.0110*	−0.10	0.855
$475) (n=37)							
8. Less-developed	a.	0.0060**		0.0101		0.55	0.833
countries without	b.		0.0038*		0.0104	0.59	0.819
universal primary							
education (n=56)							

[†] The dependent variable is the logged per capita GNP, 1985; unstandardized regression coefficients are reported.
[‡] Each equation in this table was estimated with the same control and intervening variables as those reported in Table 2.4 (Equations 3 and 6). To simplify the presentation of results, the parameters associated with these variables are not shown.
* Unstandardized regression coefficient is at least 1.5 times the standard error.
** Unstandardized regression coefficient is at least 2.0 times the standard error.

the effects of the educational expansion of females and of males are analysed separately. To simplify the presentation of results, Table 2.5 does not include regression coefficients associated with each control and intervening variable.

The main findings presented in Table 2.5 are as follows:

1 In a subsample of all less-developed countries (Equation 2), the primary education of both males and females has strong positive effects on economic growth. The parameter associated with the primary education of females (0.0064) is slightly higher than that associated with the primary education of males (0.0056). At the secondary level, the effect of the education of females changes direction but is still nonsignificant; the effect of the secondary education of males is positive and now significant.

2 In regional subsamples of less-developed countries (Equations 3, 4 and 5), the impact of the primary education of females is stronger than is the primary education of males in African nations and, to a lesser extent, in Central and South American nations. In Asian countries, the effects of the primary education of both females and males are positive but

considerably weaker because of the limited sample and the fact that most less-developed countries in this region have attained 'universal' primary education. The effects of secondary education vary somewhat by region and sex, but, for the most part, these generally positive effects are weak and nonsignificant.

3 When less-developed countries are divided into two groups by level of development (Equations 6 and 7), an interesting pattern emerges: in the poorer countries, the effects of the primary and secondary education of females are stronger than those of males while the opposite pattern occurs in the richer countries.

4 Finally, if only those less-developed countries that do not have 'universal' primary education are isolated (Equation 8), primary education, especially that of females, has a strong positive effect on economic growth, and the impact of secondary education, while positive, is weak and nonsignificant.

What picture emerges from this detailed analysis of less-developed countries? On the one hand, it is clear that the expansion of primary education, for both girls and boys, has a strong, positive and statistically significant effect on economic growth in the Third World, an effect that is not mediated by fertility rates or by women's rates of participation in the wage labor force. The effect of the expansion of secondary education, on the other hand, is more conditional. Although the secondary education of males has positive effects on economic growth in some parts of the Third World (for example, in Asia and in the richer, less-developed countries), the effect of the secondary education of females is generally weak and nonsignificant. The inconsistency of secondary education effects (in terms of both gender and world region) leads one to conclude that the economic impact of this type of schooling (which is far more elitist, selective, and vocationally oriented than is primary schooling) is mediated, to a much greater degree, by demographic and labor force processes.

Overall, one of the most interesting findings these analyses report concerns the relationship of primary education, gender, and economic growth in the Third World. In the poorest nations of the world (especially in Africa) and in countries in which primary schooling is not universally available, educational expansion among school-age girls at the primary level has a considerably stronger effect on long-term economic prosperity than does educational expansion among school-age boys. There is no evidence that the strong effect of the primary education of females on economic growth is mediated by variations in fertility rates or in women's participation in the wage labor force.

Conclusion

How much of the relationship between education and economic development is altered by integrating the issue of gender into existing theoretical models? Let us first consider the demographic perspective. A wealth of individual-level evidence demonstrates that increased educational attainments among women have pronounced (though not always linear) effects on the use of contraceptives, knowledge of birth control methods, and fertility rates. The standard of living and economic health of many countries are related to the rate of population growth, if only by the latter's impact on the denominator of all measures of economic development. By definition, slower population growth in a stagnant economy increases economic growth, since the total economic pie is divided among fewer mouths.

The consistently strong effect of the primary education of females is indicative of, but only partially explained by, this process. Important pieces of contradictory evidence cannot be accounted for by the demographic perspective. First, educational expansion for women at the secondary level does not have the predicted effect; on the contrary, the evidence suggests that its impact is weak and inconsistent. If education affects women mainly by altering their reproductive behavior, then all levels of educational expansion among females should have positive effects (albeit to different degrees) on economic growth. Second, in equations in which measures of fertility rates are controlled, the primary education of females continues to have a strong positive effect, which suggests that other mechanisms are at work. Thus, demographic explanations of the dynamics of women's education present, at best, a partial picture of its long-term impact.

On the one hand, proponents of modernization theory do not explicitly argue that 'modern' women will be more productive than will 'modern' men. Human capital theorists, by contrast, expect that rising levels of educational attainment among women increase the incentives for women to enter the labor market and induce them to take part-time or full-time jobs for wages. As more women move into the paid labor force, their productivity (as measured by official statistics) increases and their contribution to the national product grows. Yet the findings reported here suggest that the expansion of the primary education of females has a direct effect on economic growth over and above any indirect effects through women's participation in the paid labor force, whether in industry or services. Furthermore, not all forms of women's participation in the wage labor force increase national income levels as measured by GNP (women's employment in the service sector has a negative effect on economic growth). In sum, evidence corroborating the general predictions of the human capital perspective is weak.

The institutional perspective argues that education will construct new categories of economic value, integrate formerly marginal groups into the economic and political mainstream of society, and restructure authority relations and patterns of the flow of wealth in the traditional family economy. The main findings of this study are not inconsistent with this line of thinking, especially when one considers the strong effect of the primary education of females on economic growth, even after the rates of fertility and participation in the labor force are controlled. Primary education definitely affects two important groups of persons who are traditionally unincorporated in society and are thought to have minimal competencies in public life: women and children. The provision of mass education for girls and the ideology undergirding its expansion can, as they evidently do, expand the citizenship rights and duties of all women by redefining women as potentially productive wage earners in the national economy. On a global level, there are signs that the 'invisible' work traditionally done by women is slowly being incorporated into national and international accounts of economic output (see Joekes 1987). Expanding school places for girls, even in extremely patriarchal societies, comes to be seen as rational because school-age girls are increasingly viewed as a potentially valuable asset of the nation-state. Although gender inequalities and inequities in education and wages persist, the primary education of females appears to have important institutional effects on the economies of Third World nations.

Even so, this perspective overstates the positive benefits of secondary and tertiary education for economic development. The expansion of these levels of schooling may, indeed, construct and validate new elite and professional roles in society. But under conditions of highly dependent export production and a weak economic infrastructure, conditions that are characteristic of many less-developed countries today, such processes result in a disproportionate amount of scarce resources being directed to certain specialized positions (for example, positions in the public sector and management positions in foreign enterprises) whose long-term productivity is dubious at best. In addition, this perspective ignores the tendency of the higher levels of the educational system to orient their graduates to the centers of world culture and, by doing so, to contribute to the emigration of highly educated labor. This tendency accounts for the negative effects of tertiary education and the relatively weak impact of secondary education on economic growth in less developed countries. Furthermore, this perspective minimizes the importance of 'non-rational' reasons for women (or their families) to decide to attend secondary schools — for example, to confer status on parents or to increase the chances of finding a suitable (high-status) mate — which may account for the weak impact of the secondary education of females on economic growth.

In sum, there is clear evidence that primary education substantially contributed to the expansion of national economies in the post-Second World War period, but there are important gender differences which are highlighted in this study. A clearer picture of the education-gender-economic development nexus, as well as a more concise formulation of the mediating mechanisms involved in this process, is long overdue.

Appendix Countries Included in the Analyses (N=96)

North America	Spain	*South America*
Canada	Sweden	Argentina
USA	United Kingdom	Bolivia
	Yugoslavia	Brazil
Europe		Chile
Austria	*Cent. America/Caribbean*	Colombia
Finland	Barbados	Ecuador
France	Costa Rica	Guyana
West Germany	Dominican Rep.	Paraguay
Greece	El Salvador	Peru
Hungary	Guatemala	Uruguay
Iceland	Haiti	Venezuela
Italy	Honduras	
Malta	Jamaica	*Asia*
Netherlands	Mexico	Bangladesh
Norway	Nicaragua	Burma
Portugal	Trinidad & Tobago	Cyprus

Hong Kong	Fiji	Lesotho
India	Papua/New Guinea	Liberia
Indonesia		Libya
Israel	*Africa*	Madagascar
Japan	Algeria	Malawi
Malaysia	Angola	Mali
Nepal	Benin	Morocco
Pakistan	Botswana	Niger
Philippines	Burundi	Nigeria
Singapore	Cameroon	Rwanda
South Korea	Central African Rep.	Senegal
Sri Lanka	Chad	Somalia
Syria	Congo	Sudan
Thailand	Egypt	Swaziland
Turkey	Ethiopia	Tanzania
	Gabon	Togo
Oceania	Ghana	Zaire
Australia	Ivory Coast	Zambia
New Zealand	Kenya	Zimbabwe

Notes

1   Some researchers who are sympathetic to the human capital perspective have expressed more cautious opinions about the impact of educational expansion on economic growth. They discuss the 'inefficiencies' associated with educational expansion in less-developed countries (such as poor-quality schools, high drop-out rates, much grade repetition) which consequently lower the real 'stock' of human capital in the labor force. According to this reasoning, it is not the level of educational provision (measured by educational enrollment rates) that is critical to economic growth, but the actual amount of educational attainment embodied in the paid labor force (Psacharopoulos and Arriagada 1986). Since data on this latter measure, broken down by sex, are not available, it was not possible to examine this argument directly.

2   The inclusion of a lagged dependent variable guarantees a large R^2 that, although a positive result in cross-sectional analyses, is of little consequence in panel models. Instead of evaluating the results of panel regression models on the basis of the R^2 value obtained, emphasis is placed here on the size, direction, and significance of the partial regression coefficients. Furthermore, it is also known that lagged dependent variables, by explaining a large portion of the variation in the dependent variable, work against the explanatory power of the other independent variables in the equation (Hannan 1979; Heise 1970). As such, they provide a fairly conservative test of the effects of the main educational variables in each equation.

3   In some countries, numerous underage and overage pupils are enrolled in primary level programs, which may produce a primary enrollment ratio exceeding the hypothetical ceiling of 100 percent. In the analysis reported here, the primary enrollment rate in such instances has been set at 95 percent.

4   The impacts of primary and secondary education are the main focus because tertiary education has a weak effect on economic growth, and sex-specific enrollment rates at the tertiary level generally mirror those at the secondary level. Since both secondary and tertiary education are highly selective and elitist in most

developing countries, no pertinent information is lost by dropping tertiary education from the main analyses.

5 One problem in interpreting the negative effect of women's rate of participation in the service sector concerns the broad range of jobs that are included in this category in official statistics, from low-skilled service jobs, such as private housemaids, cooks, launderers and the like, to high-skilled professional jobs in law, medicine, teaching, and public administration. Thus, the exact relationship between the service sector and economic growth is not readily apparent. A 1983 cross-national study, however, found that the prevalence of low-skilled personal services has a significant negative effect on economic growth while the prevalence of high-status professional services has little impact on economic development (Fiala and Ramirez 1983). Thus, the negative effect documented in the present study tends to support the argument advanced by these and other authors (see, for example, Evans and Timberlake 1980) that the service sector is one factor mediating the negative impact of dependence on economic growth.

References

ACKER, S., MEGARRY, J. and NISBET, S. (1984) *World Yearbook of Education: Women and Education*, London, Kogan Page.

AMIN, S. (1973) *Neocolonialism in West Africa*, London, Penguin Books.

APTER, D. (1965) *The Politics of Modernization*, Chicago, University of Chicago Press.

BELSLEY, D., KUH, E. and WELSCH, R. (1980) *Regression Diagnostics*, New York, John Wiley.

BENAVOT, A. (1986) 'Education and Economic Growth in the Modern World System, 1913–1985'. Unpublished Ph.D. Dissertation, Department of Sociology, Stanford University.

BENERIA, L. (1982) 'Accounting for Women's Work', in BENERIA, L. (Ed.) *Women and Development: The Sexual Division of Labor in Rural Societies*, New York, Praeger, pp. 119–47.

BENERIA, L. and SEN, G. (1981) 'Accumulation, Reproduction and Women's Role in Economic Development: Boserup Revisited', *Signs* 7, 2, pp. 279–98.

BERG, I. (1971) *Education and Jobs: The Great Training Robbery*, Boston, Beacon Press.

BOLI, J., RAMIREZ, F. and MEYER, J. (1985) 'Explaining the Origins and Expansion of Mass Education', *Comparative Education Review* 29, May, pp. 145–70.

BORNSCHIER, V. and CHASE-DUNN, C. (1985) *Transnational Corporations and Underdevelopment*, New York, Praeger.

BOSERUP, E. (1970) *Woman's Role in Economic Development*, New York, St Martin's Press.

BOULDING, E. (1977) *Women in the Twentieth Century World*, New York, Halsted Press.

CAIN, M. (1984) *Women's Status and Fertility in Developing Countries*, World Bank Staff Working Paper 682, Washington, DC, World Bank.

CALDWELL, J. (1980) 'Mass Education as a Determinant in the Timing of Fertility Decline', *Population and Development Review* 6, June, pp. 225–55.

CALDWELL, J. (1982) *Theory of Fertility Decline*, London, Academic Press.

CARNOY, M. (1974) *Education as Cultural Imperialism*, New York, David McKay.

COALE, A.J. and HOOVER, E.M. (1958) *Population Growth and Economic Development in Low-Income Countries*, Princeton, Princeton University Press.

COCHRANE, S. (1979) *Fertility and Education*, Baltimore, Johns Hopkins University Press.

COCHRANE, S. (1983) 'Effects of Education and Urbanization on Fertility', in BULATAO, R. and LEE, R. (Eds) *Determinants of Fertility in Developing Countries*, Vol. 2, New York, Academic Press, pp. 587–626.

COLCLOUGH, C. (1982) 'The Impact of Primary Schooling on Economic Development', *World Development* 10, March, pp. 166–85.

COLLINS, R. (1979) *The Credential Society*, New York, Academic Press.

CURTIN, L. (1982) *Status of Women: A Comparative Analysis of Twenty Developing Countries*, Washington, DC, Population Reference Bureau.

DAUBER, R. and CAIN, M. (Eds) (1981) *Women and Technological Change in Developing Countries*, Boulder, Westview Press.

DEBLE, I. (1980) *The School Education of Girls*, Paris, France, UNESCO.

DELACROIX, J. and RAGIN, C. (1978) 'Modernizing Institutions, Mobilization and Third World Development', *American Journal of Sociology* 84, July, pp. 123–49.

DENISON, E.F. (1964) *Measuring the Contribution of Education and the Residual to Economic Growth*, Paris, France, Organization for Economic Cooperation and Development.

DIXON-MUELLER, R. (1985) *Women's Work in Third World Agriculture*, Geneva, Switzerland, International Labour Office.

DORE, R. (1976) *The Diploma Disease*, Berkeley, University of California Press.

EVANS, P. and TIMBERLAKE, M. (1980) 'Dependence, Inequality and the Growth of the Service Sector', *American Sociological Review* 45, August, pp. 531–52.

FIALA, R. and RAMIREZ, F. (1983) 'Dependence, Service Sector Growth and Economic Development in Lesser Developed Countries', Paper presented at the annual meeting of the American Sociological Association, Detroit.

FINN, J., DULBERG, L. and REIS, J. (1979) 'Sex Differences in Educational Attainment', *Harvard Educational Review* 49, November, pp. 477–503.

FRANK, A.G. (1972) *Lumpenbourgeosie, Lumpendevelopment: Dependence, Class and Politics in Latin America*, New York, Monthly Review Press.

FRANK, A.G. (1978) *Dependent Accumulation and Underdevelopment*, New York, Monthly Review Press.

GOODE, W.J. (1963) *World Revolution and Family Patterns*, New York, Free Press.

GRUBB, W.N. (1985) 'The Convergence of Educational Systems and the Role of Vocationalism', *Comparative Education Review* 29, November, pp. 526–48.

HALSEY, A., FLOUD, J. and ANDERSON, C. (Eds) (1961) *Education, Economy and Society*, New York, Free Press.

HANNAN, M. (1979) 'Issues in Panel Analysis of National Development', in MEYER, J. and HANNAN, M. (Eds) *National Development and the World System*, Chicago, University of Chicago Press, pp. 17–36.

HANNAN, M. and YOUNG, A. (1977) 'Estimation in Panel Models: Results in Pooling Cross-sections and Time Series', in HEISE, D. (Ed.) *Sociological Methodology*, San Francisco, Jossey-Bass, pp. 52–83.

HEISE, D. (1970) 'Causal Inference from Panel Data', in BORGATTA, E.R. and BOHRNSTEDT, G.W. (Eds) *Sociological Methodology 1970*, San Francisco, Jossey Bass.

INTERNATIONAL CENTER FOR RESEARCH ON WOMEN (ICRW) (1980) *Keeping Women Out*, Washington, DC, Agency for International Development.

INTERNATIONAL LABOUR OFFICE (1986) *Economically Active Population, 1950–2025*, 3rd ed. (5 volumes), Geneva, ILO.

INKELES, A. (1978) 'The Future of Individual Modernity', in YINGER, J.M. and CUTLER, S.J. (Eds) *Major Social Issues: A Multidisciplinary View*, New York, Free Press, pp. 459–75.

INKELES, A. and SMITH, D. (1974) *Becoming Modern*, London, Heinemann Educational.

IRIZARRY, R. (1980) 'Overeducation and Unemployment in the Third World', *Comparative Education Review* 24, October, pp. 338–52.

JACQUETTE, J. (1982) 'Women and Modernization Theory', *World Politics* 34, January, pp. 267–84.

JOEKES, S. (1987) *Women in the World Economy: An INSTRAW Study*, New York, Oxford University Press.

KARABEL, J. and HALSEY, A.H. (1977) 'Educational Research: A Review and an Interpretation', in KARABEL, J. and HALSEY, A.H. (Eds) *Power and Ideology in Education*, New York, Oxford University Press, pp. 1–87.

KELLY, G. and ELLIOT, C. (Eds) (1982) *Women's Education in the Third World*, Albany, State University of New York Press.

KRAVIS, I., HESTON, A. and SUMMERS, R. (1982) *World Product and Income*, Baltimore, Johns Hopkins University Press.

LERNER, D. (1958) *The Passing of Traditional Society*, Glencoe, Free Press.

LEVY, M. (1966) *Modernization and the Structure of Societies*, Princeton, Princeton University Press.

LOCKHEED, M., JAMISON, D. and LAU, L. (1980) 'Farmer Education and Farmer Efficiency', in KING, T. (Ed.) *Education and Income*, Washington, DC, World Bank, pp. 111–52.

LONDON, B. (1988) 'Dependence, Distorted Development and Fertility Trends in Noncore Nations', *American Sociological Review* 53, August, pp. 606–18.

MARSHALL, S. (1985) 'Development, Dependence and Gender Inequality in the Third World', *International Studies Quarterly* 29, June, pp. 217–40.

McCLELLAND, D. (1961) *The Achieving Society*, New York, Free Press.

McCLELLAND, D. (1966) 'Does Education Accelerate Economic Growth?', *Economic Development and Cultural Change* 14, April, pp. 257–78.

MEYER, J.W. (1977) 'The Effects of Education as an Institution', *American Journal of Sociology* 83, July, pp. 55–77.

MEYER, J.W. (1980) 'The World Polity and the Authority of the Nation-state', in BERGESON, A. (Ed.) *Studies of the Modern World-System*, New York, Academic Press, pp. 109–37.

MEYER, J.W., HANNAN, M., RUBINSON, R. and THOMAS, G. (1979) 'National Economic Development 1950–1970: Social and Political Factors', in MEYER, J.W. and HANNAN, M. (Eds) *National Development and the World System*, Chicago, University of Chicago Press, pp. 85–116.

MEYER-FEHR, P. (1979) 'Technologieabhangigkeit und Wirtschaftswachstum', *Schweizerische Zeitschrift für Soziologie* 5, pp. 79–96.

MINCER, J. (1985) 'Intercountry Comparisons of Labor Force Trends and of Related Developments', *Journal of Labor Economics* 3, January, pp. S1–S32.

MOOCK, P. (1976) 'The Efficiency of Women as Farm Managers', *American Journal of Agricultural Economics* 58, December, pp. 831–5.

NASH, J. and FERNANDEZ-KELLY, M. (Eds) (1983) *Women, Men and the International Division of Labor*, Albany, State University of New York Press.

NATIONAL ACADEMY OF SCIENCES (1971) *Rapid Population Growth*, Baltimore, Johns Hopkins University Press.

NATIONAL RESEARCH COUNCIL (Working Group on Population Growth and Economic Development) (1986) *Population Growth and Economic Development*, Washington, DC, National Academy Press.

NEMETH, R. and SMITH, D. (1985) 'International Trade and World-system Structure: A Multiple Network Analysis', *Review* 8, 4, pp. 517–60.

PALMER, R. (1982) 'Education and Emigration from Developing Countries', in ANDERSON, L. and WINDHAM, D. (Eds) *Education and Development*, Lexington, Lexington Books, pp. 113–28.

PAMPEL, F. and TANAKA, K. (1986) 'Economic Development and Female Labor Force Participation', *Social Forces* 64, March, pp. 599–619.

PAPANEK, H. (1985) 'Class and Gender in Education-Employment Linkages', *Comparative Education Review* 29, August, pp. 317–46.

PEASLEE, A. (1965) 'Elementary Education as a Prerequisite for Economic Growth', *International Development Review* 7, September, pp. 19–24.

PORTES, A. (1973) 'Modernity and Development: A Critique', *Studies in Comparative International Development* 8, 3, pp. 251–75.

PORTES, A. and S. SASSEN-KOOB (1987) 'Making it Underground', *American Journal of Sociology* 93, 1, pp. 30–61.

PSACHAROPOULOS, G. (1973) *Returns to Education: An International Comparison*, San Francisco, Jossey-Bass.

PSACHAROPOULOS, G. (1985) 'Returns to Education: A Further International Update and Implications', *Journal of Economic Resources* 20, 4, pp. 583–97.

PSACHAROPOLOUS, G. and ARRIAGADA, A. (1986) 'The Educational Composition of the Labour Force', *International Labor Review* 125, 5, pp. 561–74.

PSACHAROPOULOS, G. and WOODHALL, M. (1985) *Education for Development*, New York, Oxford University Press.

RAM, R. (1982) 'Sex Differences in the Labor Market Outcomes of Education', in KELLY, G. and ELLIOT, C. (Eds) *Women's Education in the Third World*, Albany, State University of New York Press, pp. 203–27.

RAMIREZ, F. and RUBINSON, R. (1979) 'Creating Members: The Political Incorporation and Expansion of Public Education', in MEYER, J.W. and HANNAN, M. (Eds) *National Development and the World System*, Chicago, University of Chicago Press, pp. 72–84.

RAMIREZ, F. and THOMAS, G. (1981) 'Structural Antecedents and Consequences of Statism', in RUBINSON, R. (Ed.) *Dynamics of World Development*, Beverly Hills, Sage Publications, pp. 139–66.

RAMIREZ, F. and WEISS, J. (1979) 'The Political Incorporation of Women', in MEYER, J.W. and HANNAN, M. (Eds) *National Development and the World System*, Chicago, University of Chicago Press, pp. 238–49.

ROSTOW, W.W (1960) *The Stages of Economic Growth*, Cambridge, England, Cambridge University Press.

RUBINSON, R. (1979) 'Dependence, Government Revenue and Economic Growth, 1955–70', in MEYER, J.W. and HANNAN, M. (Eds) *National Development and the World System*, Chicago, University of Chicago Press, pp. 207–22.

SCHULTZ, T.W. (1961) 'Investment in Human Capital', *American Economic Review* 51, March, pp. 1–17.

SCHUSTER, I. (1982) 'Review Article: Recent Research on Women and Development', *Journal of Development Studies* 18, July, pp. 511–35.

SEMYONOV, M. (1980) 'The Social Context of Women's Labor Force Participation', *American Journal of Sociology* 86, November, pp. 534–50.

SIMON, J. (1981) *The Ultimate Resource*, Princeton, Princeton University Press.

SMOCK, A.C. (1981) *Women's Education in Developing Countries*, New York, Praeger.

STANDING, G. (1981) *Labor Force Participation and Development*, 2nd ed., Geneva, International Labour Office.

STANDING, G. and SHEEHAN, G. (Eds) (1978) *Labour Force Participation in Low-Income Countries*, Geneva, International Labour Office.

SUMMERS, R. and HESTON, A. (1984) 'Improved International Comparisons of Real Product and its Composition: 1950–1980', *The Review of Income and Wealth* 30, June, pp. 207–62.

THOMAS, G., MEYER, J.W., RAMIREZ, F. and BOLI, J. (1987) *Institutional Structure*, Beverly Hills, Sage Publications.

TINKER, I. and BRAMSEN, M.B. (Eds) (1976) *Women and World Development*, Washington, DC, Overseas Development Council.

TURNHAM, D. (1970) *The Employment Problem in Less Developed Countries*, Paris, France, Organization for Economic Cooperation and Development.

UNITED NATIONS (1983) *Relationships Between Fertility and Education*, New York, UN.

UNITED NATIONS (1986a) *World Population Trends, Estimates and Projections as Assessed in 1984*, New York, Department of International Economic and Social Affairs, UN.

UNITED NATIONS (1986b) *World Comparisons of Purchasing Power and Real Product for 1980*, New York, UN.

UNESCO (United Nations Educational, Scientific and Cultural Organization) (1970) *Statistical Yearbook*, Paris, UNESCO.

UNESCO (1981) *Women and Development: Indicators of their changing role*, New York, UNESCO.

WATANABE, S. (1969) 'The Brain Drain from Developing Countries to Developed Countries', *International Labour Review* 4, pp. 400–35.

WARD, K. (1984) *Women in the World System*, New York, Praeger.

WEILER, H. (1978) 'Education and Development', *Comparative Education* 14, pp. 179–98.

WORLD BANK (1982) *World Development Report*, New York, Oxford University Press.

WORLD BANK (1983) *World Tables*, 3rd ed., New York, Oxford University Press.

WORLD BANK (1984) *World Development Report*, New York, Oxford University Press.

WORLD BANK (1988) *World Tables, 1987*, 4th ed., New York, Oxford University Press.

YOUSSEF, N. (1974) *Women and Work in Developing Societies*, Berkeley, University of California Press.

3　Women in Education from a Swedish Perspective

Ingrid Jönsson

During the postwar period the Swedish government has made deliberate efforts to decrease socio-economic differences in terms of income and wealth distribution, income growth and economic security. In the late 1960s another important dimension was added to the political agenda, namely the achievement of equality between the sexes (Persson-Tanimura 1988). The 'equality' platform drawn up by the Social Democratic Party in 1968 placed women among other disadvantaged groups, such as the young, the old, the handicapped, the unemployed, low-income groups and rural dwellers. The aims of the Swedish equal opportunities policy were also laid down in the document *The Status of Women in Sweden* (Sandlund 1971) which was submitted to the United Nations in the same year.

> The aim of a *long-term* program for women must be that every individual, irrespective of sex, shall have the same *practical* opportunities, not only for education and employment, but also, in principle, the same responsibilities for his and her maintenance as well as shared responsibility for the upbringing of the children and the upkeep of the home (p. 5).

The aims agreed in 1968 are still supported by the government.

In the 1950s women were encouraged to get an education in order to prepare for work after raising their children. Depending on where they were in the life cycle, women were either supposed to work or to take care of their family and children (Myrdahl and Klein 1956/1970). Women still carried the main responsibility for children and family, though they could work before having children or after the children had grown up. Feminists criticized this 'conditioned liberation' of women, and since the 1960s more attention has been given to the possibility of men participating in the care of their children.

At a time when it was mainly unmarried women who entered the labour market, the changes that were fought for included equal rights to education, equal access to all kinds of jobs, and equal pay for the same job. In Sweden, as in many other western countries, women's participation in the labor force rapidly increased during the postwar period, especially in the 1970s and onwards. The increased participation of married women with children led to other political demands, such as reforms in economic, social, and family policy. The introduction of separate taxation for husbands and wives and the expansion of public child-care facilities and parental insurance contributed to this increase in women's participation in the labour market. In 1988 about 85 percent of all adult women (20–64 years old) worked outside the home compared with 90 percent of men. Among women aged 25–44 with small children (younger than 7 years) an even higher percentage (86 percent) were in the labor force (AKU, 1988).[1]

Education has been given an important role in the struggle for equality between women and men as well as between different social groups. In the first nationwide Curriculum for the Comprehensive School (1962) it was assumed that boys and girls would show traditional differences with respect to behavior, interest and abilities, while in the 1969 revised version equality between the sexes was emphasized. Equality retains a very prominent position in the latest version of the curriculum (1980).[2] In 1988 the official long-term goal of equal opportunity in education was defined as achieving a situation where each specific study program in upper secondary school was attended by at least 40 percent boys or girls (Regeringens proposition 1987/88:105).

In the 1970s and 1980s the measures taken in education to promote equality between women and men have primarily been intended to broaden female pupils' choices of education and careers. Except for some small progress in recruiting more girls to longer technical education in secondary schools and at university level the results have been discouraging, and differentiation by sex at all levels of the educational system and in the labor market is still very marked. During the late 1980s there was even a regression. The experiment of giving priority to pupils who make a non-traditional choice of education in upper secondary school has not influenced the number of girls who choose male-dominated education. Boys have instead benefited when applying for female-dominated subjects (Civildepartmentet 1990). The drop-out rate among girls in male-dominated educational programs is much higher than the drop-out rate among boys in female-dominated study programs (Liljegren 1984; Bjarka 1984).

In understanding why these explicit aims have not been successfully achieved, we have to consider the historical male dominance of both education and the labor market and how this dominance has changed over time. There is a movement in society away from gender segregation to an ideal of integration though, even as many formal restrictions and obstacles have disappeared, male dominance has appeared in new and informal ways:

> There is a movement away from a society based on gender segregation
> to one in which more integration has become the ideal. There is further-
> more a movement from a society where gender differences are seen as an
> expression of a social order, to one where attempts are made to lessen
> such differences. Gender differences, then, are seen more and more as
> illegitimate (Haavind 1985, p. 18).

Our understanding of the present situation must therefore encompass women's strategies and responses to new forms of male dominance as well as to the constraints and opportunities created by social and economic structures. Social class exerts an important influence on individuals' choices of education and careers; this requires that the experiences of boys and girls from different social backgrounds must be considered. We need to include both the influence of the social structure on the individual's social background and the ways in which individuals act and reflect about their situation; or, as formulated by Kessler and his associates, 'First, we must find ways of talking about large-scale structures without reifying them and about practical practices without losing their larger-scale context' (Kessler et al. 1985, p. 35).

A historical perspective must be preserved, as domination changes over time and appears in new forms. Economic and social structures make up the framework of human action, but the reproduction of both class and gender relations is not mechanical and unchangeable. Consequently, an understanding of the present situation of women in education and working life must include women's own reflections about choices of education and careers in the context of relevant social changes. To get the full story we must try to include biography and history and their intersections within social structure (Mills 1959).

Both the knowledge taught and the ways it is taught are dominated by the values of privileged groups in society, but education is generally assumed to function in a class-neutral way (Bourdieu 1976). The school system is also assumed to function in a gender-neutral way but both in the past and now the educational system was and is controlled by men.[3] It is important to bear this in mind as equal opportunity strategies used in institutions such as schools are mostly class-blind in a way that makes them liable to be class-biased (Kessler et al. 1985, pp. 45–6). The different content of sex roles and the importance given to competition and participation in working life in different social milieus influence how equal opportunity measures appeal to girls from working-class and middle-class backgrounds (Anyon 1983; Berner 1984). Consequently, this can lead to different types of accommodation or resistance by working-class and middle-class girls:

> It should come as no surprise that it has been girls from the upper classes, where an ideology of individual mobility through education is strong, who so far have been the most prepared to break the occupational stereotypes and study subjects such as technology. They are also the ones most likely to benefit from the various measures taken to get more women into technical work (Berner 1984, p. 11).

Most measures taken to rectify gender inequalities are directed towards girls, but in Sweden some measures have been directed towards men. 'Positive discrimination' was used to get more men into pre-school teaching. The experiment was not very successful, however, as many male pre-school teachers did not stay in their jobs with the children but were promoted to administrative posts (Wernersson and Lander 1979).

Boys' and Girls' Education in a Historical Perspective

What used to be separate schools for boys and girls have gradually been integrated into one school system throughout the course of the twentieth century. Educational goals have explicitly differed according to gender as well as class and historical period. The introduction of compulsory schooling in 1842 meant that boys and girls from less privileged classes attended the same school. Most upperclass parents continued to send their children to private, single-sex schools. It was also clearly understood that boys and girls from different social classes were to fill different positions in society.

The classical academic education of upper-class boys was gradually supplemented and replaced by education which included the more practical knowledge needed by expanding commerce and industry (Williams, 1961/1975). Upper-class girls were educated at home or in private schools, and were primarily taught the skills required for their roles as wives and mothers. In the nineteenth century middle-level education was opened to unmarried middle-class girls as a way to support themselves, for expanding trade and commerce required clerks, secretaries, telephone operators, and the like.

During the late nineteenth and the early twentieth century both Liberals and Social Democrats tried to establish a six-year universal elementary school. However, a political compromise in the late 1920s resulted in a four-year universal elementary school followed by a choice between another two years in elementary school or grammar school. This formal division of the pupils constituted two different educational routes, with different knowledge taught and different social composition among the pupils. The two school routes led either to vocational training and manual work or to upper secondary schools, sometimes university studies, and intellectual work.

At the end of the nineteenth century most boys and girls from the lower classes were poorly educated. Compulsory schools were unevenly spread over the country and the length of schooling varied a great deal for the first fifty years after the establishment of compulsory education. After leaving elementary school, some male working-class youths acquired vocational training in the form of apprenticeship, but this option was formally closed to women. Expanding industry gradually demanded better qualified employees, which led to the opening of schools operating in the young workers' spare time, such as in the evenings and on Sundays. Young men attended technical courses, while women's courses were oriented towards household and office work. Educational options offered to upper- and middle- as well as working-class girls were inferior to boys' schooling both in quantity and quality (Kyle 1979). The reform of girls' education came second to boys', and still does (Lundahl 1986; Fürst 1990).[4] When vocational education developed in the public sector in 1918 it was also theoretically open to both sexes, though in practice girls could only attend up to a certain level. Technical education at higher levels remained a male domain.

The growth of the public sector was accompanied by the need for a greater number of well-educated women, and this strengthened their educational possibilities. Formally, all barriers to women's education and training were removed, but women still had the responsibility for the care of home and children. To work outside the home was not attractive, and the motive for vocational education was more or less to protect oneself for the future. The depression period of the 1930s, accompanied by a high rate of unemployment and a falling birthrate, perpetuated the idea of staying at home.

Upper-class and middle-class girls and women were primarily educated in private girls' schools. Some public schools opened to girls in the 1910s, but even as late as the 1920s about 75 percent of girls attended private girls' schools. In the early 1920s girls were admitted to public upper secondary schools provided that there were enough places for boys as well. In the late 1920s this provision was removed and in many towns separate upper secondary schools for girls were established. Girls' schools offering middle-level education were also set up by the state, and in the 1930s and 1940s elementary school was gradually extended. The number of girls acquiring middle-level education increased more than five times between 1910 and 1960, and the number of girls attending upper secondary schools was ten times higher in 1960 than at the beginning of the century. Separate girls' schools continued to exist as late as the 1960s (Lundahl 1986). In the 1870s women were admitted to higher medical and scientific training, yet higher technical schooling was closed until the early 1920s (Berner 1982).

The Contemporary School System

Political agreement on the importance of education in the upbringing of citizens in a democracy, together with economic growth in the Swedish economy after the Second World War, made the expansion of the school system possible. In the 1950s and 1960s the nine-year comprehensive school was gradually introduced, while the dual school system, designed for middle- and working-class children respectively, was eliminated. The school reforms aimed at creating equal educational opportunities for all children irrespective of class, gender or geographical residence within one common school, and disadvantaged families received economic support. The change from a selective school system to one based on election was a cornerstone in the democratization of education constituted by the School Act of 1962. Henceforth, each child was free to choose any study program according to his or her own interest and without the direction of teachers and head teachers.

From the 1950s onward the goal has been to keep pupils in the same classes throughout their nine years in comprehensive school, in order to avoid streaming. However, for about one-third of the lessons at senior level (grades 7–9) students are divided into a more and a less advanced course in mathematics and English and into optional subjects. The combinations of courses and subjects imply a formal distribution of various educational routes, which lead to different future positions. Boys and girls choose the two alternatives in mathematics and English to about the same extent. Optional subjects, however, are chosen in a very traditional way. Girls prefer to study a second foreign language while boys prefer an extra course in technology or natural sciences. Even so, class differences are much more articulated than gender differences, and upper-class pupils of both sexes choose, to a much larger extent than boys and girls from working-class homes, a combination involving the best preparation for theoretical studies in upper secondary school. All other subjects are common, irrespective of sex and ability. Sex education, domestic science and child care have been taught to both girls and boys since the 1950s, and technology was made a compulsory subject for both girls and boys in the 1980s. Furthermore, the experiences gained from a special project on sex roles in Swedish schools in the 1970s led to recommendations in 1977 for actions to promote educational equality between girls and boys. The recommendations focused on curriculum choices, vocational guidance, teachers' education and in-service training, cooperation with other authorities, and research and development of teaching material.

Since 1971 all education at the upper secondary level has been integrated in one school, which contains all longer and shorter academic courses as well as

Table 3.1 Upper Secondary School Lines Completed By Boys and Girls from Social Classes I and III, 1984.[6]

	Social Class I		Social Class III	
	Boys (%)	Girls (%)	Boys (%)	Girls (%)
Theoretical three- and four-year lines	59	48	18	17
Theoretical two-year lines	11	15	11	16
Vocational two-year lines	13	12	42	33
In upper secondary school in 1985*	10	13	3	2
Drop-outs	3	9	10	12
Did not apply or application not accepted	3	1	14	18
Unknown	1	2	2	2
Total	100	100	100	100
Number of cases	269	258	716	798

* The majority of the pupils left upper secondary school in 1983 and 1984. Some of the pupils leaving upper secondary school in 1985 completed the fourth year of the engineering course program, but most of them were pupils who had taken a year out of school to be exchange students in American high schools.

vocational training. However, research that my colleagues and I have conducted (Arnman and Jönsson 1983, 1986; Jönsson and Arnman 1989a, 1989b) shows very clearly that integration has succeeded only superficially. The integrated upper secondary school still contains different educational routes taken by pupils from different social backgrounds, and these routes lead to different positions in the labor market. Pupils attending both shorter and longer theoretical course programs ('lines') in upper secondary school have quite different social backgrounds from pupils taking vocational education. This is clearly illustrated in Table 3.1, which shows the different ways in which young women and men from the upper class (social class I) and the working class (social class III) respectively used upper secondary school.[5]

In 1989 most course programs in upper secondary school had a very uneven sex composition. Out of the five longer theoretical course programs, social science, natural science, and economics were relatively sex-integrated, while humanities and engineering course programs were markedly sex-biased. Eighty percent of the students studying the four-year engineering course program were boys, while 88 percent of the pupils studying the humanities course program were girls (U 53 SM 9001).[7] During the 1980s, however, the percentage of girls studying longer engineering course programs increased from 8 to about 20 percent. This program qualifies for continued academic studies as well as for the labor market. A somewhat higher percentage of the female pupils graduating from this course program continue on to university studies, while male pupils more easily establish themselves in permanent jobs on the labor market (U 55 SM 8901). It is even rarer that boys and girls who take practical programs at upper secondary level meet in the same classroom. There are several lines attended by at least 90 percent girls, such as social service, consumer studies, clothing manufacture, and nursing. There are a larger number of course programs attended almost exclusively by boys. Girls account for only a few percent in the following lines:

building and construction, two-year engineering, forestry, motor mechanic, metal work, electrical engineering, and production and maintenance engineering (see Table 3.2, p. 64).

Efforts have been made to equalize the socially biased recruitment to higher education. The rapid growth in the number of students in the 1960s and 1970s brought about university reform in 1977 which made some forms of post-secondary education, such as teachers' colleges and nurses' schools, an integral part of the universities. University entrance was opened up to people with no formal qualifications but with four years of gainful employment. In 1987 less than 5 percent of university freshmen had this background compared with a good half having leaving certificates from longer theoretical lines in upper secondary school, another 10 percent from the shorter theoretical lines, and 11 percent from vocational lines. The rest had other kinds of educational backgrounds (Siffror om högskolan, No. 10).

In spite of good intentions the increased number of places at university were used more by middle-class and upper-class than by working-class youth. Within the common framework 'university' three different educational routes may be defined (Gesser 1971). One route containing the most prestigious degrees in technology, business, law, and medicine is mainly filled by upper-class young people, primarily men. The bias in social background among the few women taking the most prestigious degrees is even more accentuated than among the male student population (Siffror om högskolan, No. 8). The second route consists of traditional university studies leading to a BA in arts, social science, and so on, choices made primarily by women from the upper and middle class. Women from all social classes choose the third route, which is the newly integrated programs, more often than men. Men from the middle and working class also choose teachers' education, to some extent. Women's education often leads to employment in the public sector, while men who get their degrees in technology, business, law and so forth, will generally be privately employed.

Public statistics on all Swedish school-leavers show higher average marks for girls than for boys in their upper secondary school leaving certificates, irrespective of course program (with the exception of the two-year engineering course program — see Table 3.2, p. 64). Girls have higher marks in all individual subjects except physics and in the major subjects in male dominated vocational lines (U 53 SM 9001). The average mark in the leaving certificate plays a crucial role in the selection process for nearly all kinds of university programs, and competition is naturally hardest for the most prestigious university education. In the research project referred to above, we studied the transition from upper secondary school to the three routes of university education with reference to sex, social background, and school achievement. School success measured by marks correlates very clearly with social background and sex (see Table 3.2, p. 64, and Ve 1987). Middle-class boys are most successful at school; socialization to the male role accompanied by class-specific socialization seems to function in a way which makes schooling most favorable to middle-class boys (Ve 1987).

In all other social groups girls were more successful at school than boys. In spite of their school success girls choose the most prestigious education to a lesser degree than boys. Irrespective of average marks, many of them preferred education leading to care and service occupations which means lower wages and a more uncertain position in the labor market due to cutbacks in the public sector.

Of female students with top scores, about half chose prestigious educational establishments compared with 80 percent of the boys; about as many women (17 percent) as men (20 percent) chose a traditional university education, while not a single male student chose one of the newly integrated university degrees. Such educations were chosen by about one-third of the most successful women. A very high percentage of the most successful boys (65 percent) and girls (61 percent) who continued to prestigious university education came from social class I. The proportion of students with top marks making other educational choices was considerably lower. Only a fourth of the girls choosing 'new' university education had this social background. Although these kinds of programs are also to some extent chosen by successful girls, they are to a much higher degree chosen by both girls and boys with a lower average mark. From our results one can conclude that girls, irrespective of their success at school, choose different educational routes from boys, but social background matters among girls as well as among boys. Girls from social class I continue to a much larger extent to traditional and prestigious university education than do girls from other social backgrounds (Jönsson and Arnman 1989b).[8]

The evidence on curricular choices shows that differentiation by sex is still very marked at all levels of the educational system. Since the 1970s more women than men have continued on to university studies. In the late 1980s about 60 percent of freshmen were women. The alternative to formal education might be less favourable to women; for example, women are not offered corporate training to the same extent as are men, so to reach positions equivalent to those of men, women must have higher formal education (Persson-Tanimura 1983). 'Educational advantage is thus a moving target and as girls and women cross one barrier in the direction of greater equality, the "rules of the game" change such that new barriers emerge' (OECD 1986). One must bear in mind, however, that the feminization of the Swedish universities is to a large extent due to the incorporation of traditional female training programs in 1977.

In 1987, the Swedish government reported on the measures taken to put into effect the 'Convention on the Elimination of All Forms of Discrimination against Women' (Ministry of Labour 1987). According to this report the most important outcome in the field of equal opportunities has been that women have consolidated their position in the labor market. However, women and men participate in work life on very different terms. Not only individual workplaces but entire sectors of the economy are completely dominated by one sex or the other. Women are employed in a more restricted sector of the labor market than men, and when working in the same sector they still do different jobs.[9] The ten most common occupations for women attract more than half of all working women, while the ten most common occupations for men attract only 35 percent of male employees. While only one out of every five industrial workers is a woman, the reverse is the case in the local government sector. About half of all gainfully employed women work for central and local authorities, often in jobs concerned with community care, welfare and services. Women do not normally enter male-dominated workplaces in large numbers unless there is a lack of appropriate male workers. The emergence of women in male-dominated workplaces mostly takes place in times of economic prosperity (Fürst 1987). However, it is not easy for women to break into male-dominated workplaces. When they do, they usually end up with a job of female character after a period of time (Lindgren

1982). The results from another study of women at male-dominated workplaces lead to the following conclusion:

> Women and men are sorted as if by an invisible hand to different jobs. If women approach men too much, getting too similar working conditions, it often happens that men react to recreate the established order which implies the subordination of women (Fürst 1985, p. 125).

Women and men also have different hours of work. Since women are more widely employed part-time, men on average put in about nine hours more paid work each week than women.[10] This affects women's total earnings and their chances for continuing education and promotion.[11] Women, too, in spite of being gainfully employed, still do most of the work in the home and assume most of the responsibility for caring for the children.

Ways of Understanding Class and Gender Relations in Education

How is the persistence of the fundamental features of class and gender relations to be understood in spite of all the measures taken in respect of education, working life, economic policy, family policy, and so on? Biological explanations for the reproduction of unequal gender relations have been strongly questioned by feminist researchers (e.g., Chodorow 1978). Sex-role theories and theories of reproduction and resistance attract more current interest (McDonald 1980; Berner 1984). Reproduction theories are divided according to the importance attributed to social and cultural factors in the reproduction of class and gender. Reproduction theories assign a different level of importance to patriarchy and capitalism in their interpretation of how gender and class relations are produced and reproduced. They argue that women's liberation is reached by social revolution, while the sex-role approach seeks equality with men within capitalist hierarchies. The latter sees a more equitable distribution of the sexes in the current social formation as an end in itself.

Gerson (1985) classifies theories in another way, namely the extent to which they include the role of human action. According to Gerson, reproduction theories neglect human action and overemphasize external structural constraints, while more voluntaristic approaches underestimate the influence of external economic and social factors on human action. They overstate the role of socialization in families, in schools and the mass media. Gerson suggests an alternative approach to the understanding of how women and men make decisions about their lives, specifically a developmental approach building on life stories. Esseveld (1988) used a similar approach in her study of middle-aged women. In such an approach greater consideration must be given to variations in human behavior within their social context; this implies an analysis of individuals' different resources and degrees of power over their situations as well as an analysis of contraints and possibilities in the social system.

The Sex-role Approach

The most widespread explanation of gender differences is guided by the concept of sex roles. The idea that boys and girls are socialized into complementary roles has been commonly accepted in the social sciences since Parsons' theory on complementary roles in the 1940s. Feminine character is produced by socialization into the female role, masculine character by socialization into the male role, and deviants by some kind of failure in socialization (Connell 1987, p. 49).

Since the 1960s the sex-role approach has been strongly questioned and criticized by the women's movement and feminist research, but it remains popular.

> The idea that boys and girls are socialized into different but complementary roles, which then shape their expectations of life and other people's expectations of them, is an appealing one. It fits much of common-sense knowledge of how children are treated and provides a language for describing the pressures exerted by parents, peers, mass media and schools. Perhaps, most important, it provides a strategy for change (Kessler et al. 1985, p. 34).

This approach relies on the idea that gender relations are shaped by the content of role expectations, which also influences individuals' personalities. It is primarily a psychological construction which it is considered possible to change but which overlooks the way that social institutions outside the family help to form personalities and to channel behavior. It also neglects the power dimension of male and female sex roles. In this approach, if role expectations are changed then gender relations will change. Consequently, women's liberation can be attained by changing role behaviour and role expectations.

Critics of the sex-role approach also claim that it is not a social theory as it does not relate the personal agent to social structure. The constraints of social structure are merely located in stereotyped interpersonal expectations (Connell 1987, p. 48). The larger structures are overlooked and the perspective does not take into account attitudes as responses to economic and social forces outside the individual. For example, this approach does not consider that changes in the educational system occur in connection with very definite changes in the economic structure which is in itself linked to the development of capitalism. The content and organization of the educational system are not seen as resources used in the struggles between different social classes and between men and women. Consequently, it also neglects the ways that sex roles reflect deeply entrenched material interests in society. Sex roles may be modified but not fundamentally changed without corresponding social changes (Berner 1984, p. 12). This criticism can be directed at the assumptions from which the program promoting equal opportunies between the sexes in Swedish schools started. The equal opportunity measures taken in schools were expected to have effects on the whole social and economic context in which the schools are embedded, and the power of external structural factors was underestimated.

The action program for sex equality, introduced in Swedish schools in 1977, built on experiences gained within a Sex Role Project started at the beginning of the 1970s. No less than twenty-five areas of action were defined, the project work assuming that it was possible to change girls' and boys' attitudes and behavior. Changed attitudes do not automatically imply changed behavior, however, and this was pointed out by a vocational guidance counselor commenting on the report *A Freer Choice* published in 1975:

Every girl now thinks in terms of a job. This *is* progress. They want children, but they don't pin their hopes on marriage. They don't intend to
be housewives for some future husband. But there has been no change in
their vocational choices (quoted in Scott 1985, p. 261).

Part of the reason for the action program's lack of success in promoting equality
between the sexes in schools is that the program does not question whether
girls and boys, without conflicts and reflections, assume the official goals and
intentions.

Choosing a technologically oriented education may be rational from society's
point of view because it gives access to more secure, higher paying, higher status
jobs with a larger degree of self-determination and good chance for promotion.
These kinds of training programs are to a much larger extent chosen by boys than
girls. Girls' choices of programs which prepare them for jobs in subordinate
positions with low pay are regarded as irrational. Many of the equal opportunity
measures that have been taken have aimed at changing girls' choices of education
and career to resemble more closely those chosen by men. A male choice may, in
fact, be interpreted as being contrary to female values and interests. From a girl's
point of view, choosing a traditional female education may be as rational as
choosing a non-traditional form of education.

In an analysis of female behaviour in the workplace, Sörensen (1982) found
the idea that different kinds of rationalities are shared by women and men to be
useful. This line of thought has been adopted by Scandinavian educational
researchers in their studies of the gap between policy makers and the way women
behave in the educational system (Elgqvist-Saltzman and Ve 1987). Men are more
easily supposed to share a technical, limited form of rationality originating from
paid production and the handling of goods while women more often share a
rationality originating from care work for dependent persons. The two kinds of
rationalities influence boys' and girls' educational behavior and choices of occupations (Elgqvist-Saltzman and Ve 1987).

As Kessler and his associates point out, equal opportunity programs in
education are often class-blind. However, choices of education and occupation are
very clearly bound up with both gender and class. Programs encouraging girls to
enter professional or semi-professional careers are received in quite different ways
by working-class girls and middle-class girls. Longer theoretical study programs
are to a much larger extent chosen by middle- and upper-class youth; this means
that the most non-traditional choice of education at this level, the three- or
four-year engineering course program, is made by middle- and upper-class girls.
Formal education is valued differently by different social classes. Socialization in
middle-class professional and affluent families includes expectation of achievement, meaning success in the world of public work; this is also imprinted in the
daughters of these families (Anyon 1983). When making a non-traditional choice
of education the option for a working-class girl is mostly male-dominated
vocational training. Such education implies quite different experiences both at
school and in future workplaces, compared with those encountered by middle-
class girls. The drop-out rate from the four-year engineering course program
chosen largely by women from middle-class families is substantially lower than
among the few girls choosing shorter non-traditional vocational training. The
reasons for dropping out also differ. Girls attending non-traditional vocational

education programs often feel awkward about being in a minority. Their motivation is also low, as hardly any of them are accepted into their first choice. On the longer engineering course program, school difficulties are more often mentioned (Civildepartementet 1990).

Over half of all Swedish girls finishing male-dominated vocational course programs in upper secondary school in 1984 became unemployed once or more during the following four years compared with about a third of the boys. Fewer girls than boys graduating from these course programs got jobs appropriate to their education. After graduating from male-dominated course programs about one-fifth of the girls took a second vocational course program in upper secondary school (U 55 SM 8601).

Reproduction Theories

There are various kinds of reproduction theories developed by radical feminists, Marxist feminists and socialist feminists. Among radical feminists, patriarchy is seen as the root cause of the oppression of women; this oppression is, in other words, a product of male power. The strength of this approach lies in its description of women's oppression, though it fails to show the mechanisms by which the system is created and reproduced. Neither does it carefully distinguish between causes and effects (Gerson 1985). The overemphasis on the universal existence of patriarchy has resulted in possible variations being overlooked (Esseveld 1986); class tends to be undertheorized, and it overlooks the varied subordination experienced by women in different social classes. The educational research done by radical feminists has, however, contributed to our understanding of sexist language, the social construction of femininity in the process of classroom interaction, and variation in and consequences of the varying attention given to boys and girls by teachers (Middleton 1987).

Feminist researchers have pointed out the gender-blindness of traditional educational research. However, male-female relations in education are also neglected in more up-to-date sociology of education. The 'new' sociology of education has concentrated mainly on the distribution and organization of knowledge, culture and ideology with respect to the reproduction of the class structure. Its focus is primarily on white, male working-class youth (e.g., Burton 1985; Arnot and Weiner 1987; Delamont 1989).

Social reproduction theories within a Marxist perspective overlook the gender dimension of schooling and focus mainly on the reproduction of class relations. The work of Bowles and Gintis (1975), for example, focuses primarily on the relation between schooling and the reproduction of labor in capitalist society. The reproduction of social relations found in the production process is regarded as the central function of and the determining force in the shape of schooling within capitalism. They do not, however, discuss the ways in which schools participate in the process through which sexual power relations have become integral features of capitalist work structures. Both sexes are supposed to have similar experiences at school, while the family is considered to play a crucial role in the reproduction of the sexual division in society (McDonald 1980).

Another kind of reproduction theory concentrates on how capitalist societies reproduce themselves through the interplay of a dominant culture, school knowledge, and individual biographies. Culture is used by the dominant group in society to distinguish itself from others. In western societies, overt violence and oppression are no longer accepted as methods of maintaining power; this means that the reproduction of existing power relations is carried out in more subtle ways. The educational system is an important agent in the transmission of the dominant culture, but the process is covert. The organization of the educational system and the knowledge selected for dissemination interplay with the dominant group in society in a concealed way. This means that pupils from the dominant group are, in an implicit way, more familiar with the knowledge taught. Their success at school will legitimize the reproduction of the dominant group — in other words, social hierarchies are transformed into educational hierarchies (Bourdieu 1976).

Socialist feminists have tried to broaden theories of social reproduction by including the reproduction of gender relations. Theories on patriarchy have been supplemented by Marxian analysis. In the field of education, socialist feminists have concentrated on the historical development of the provision of women's education and on its relations to women's dual situation in the family and on the labor market.

Reproduction theories are considered deterministic because of their strong emphasis on external structural factors, irrespective of whether they are patriarchical or capitalistic. People are regarded as submitting passively to the system, and subjective experiences and actions are more or less overlooked. Talking specifically about women Gerson formulates her criticism of structural theories in the following way:

> The problem of motivation, of what women want and why they want it, thus plays no independent causal role in these analyses. Women either are coerced to comply with male-dominated capitalist institutions or become victims of 'false consciousness'. Women who support the structure of female domesticity or prefer their position to that of men fail to perceive their true interest and instead maintain a mistaken allegiance to an ideology propagated by men and designed to maintain male dominance (Gerson 1985, p. 28).

In educational research the inclusion of the subjective dimension of schooling in ethnographic studies has been one way of trying to avoid the determinism of structural theories. In his study of anti-school working-class male culture, Paul Willis points out the need to consider the interplay between structural variables and individual behavior and attitudes:

> We need to understand how structures become sources of meaning and determinants on behaviour in the cultural milieu at its own level. Just because they are structural and economic determinants it does not mean that people will unproblematically obey them (Willis 1977, p. 171).

Broadening the Perspective on Women's Education

Working life and education are traditionally regarded as belonging to the public sphere, while family life, children and their upbringing are considered a private concern. When discussing women's and men's choices of education and careers, the focus must not exclusively be directed either to the public or to the private sphere; both aspects have to be considered.

In contemporary Swedish society all men and women are supposed to have the ability to maintain themselves. It is now regarded as 'natural' for all women to have paid work, and traditional housewives are very few. Most young women adhere to the idea of getting an education followed by paid work, but at the same time they do not renounce becoming mothers and having a family. For young women this 'new female role' implies a more varied life which assumes an adjustment to both family and working life. But in comparison with the 1950s, when these roles were seen as incompatible, the two roles are filled at the same time. However, in order to be able to handle the situation many Swedish women work part-time (see Note 10). For many years the issue of shorter working hours has been on the political agenda of women's organizations, though their demand has so far been turned down with the help of economic and ideological arguments. Women's and men's interests conflict. The male-dominated sectors of the labor unions wish to give priority to longer vacations rather than shorter hours when the economy permits.

Scandinavian studies on how young girls and boys perceive their future with reference to education, work and family show that girls commonly accept and wish to combine paid work with family life (Cwejman and Fürst 1988; Bjerrum-Nielsen 1988).[12] Within the framework of my own research project, an analysis was made of how 15-year-old boys and girls imagined their future with regard to education, family and working life (Malmgren 1982/1985; Esseveld and Goodman 1984).[13] Boys mentioned family and children in their essays as often as girls, but the way they expressed themselves differed markedly. Girls included in their essays future strategies which would enable them to handle both work and family life, such as working part-time or staying at home when the children were small. Such strategies were not mentioned by any of the boys. They did not imagine themselves using parental leave or working part-time. This means that already as young teenagers, girls were more mentally prepared to enter an occupation which permitted part-time work. The dilemma was not touched upon by boys who rather saw themselves as 'normal' workers, working full-time without daily responsibility for the home and children.

The age at which students imagined having a family also varied with social background. Family life was postponed until later on in life in the essays written by youths from middle- and upper-class homes. They gave priority to global traveling, careers and university studies. Most middle-class girls also imagined having a family, and only a few of them renounced children totally in favour of a career of their own. Working-class boys and girls planned to have a family at a much younger age. They gave stronger voice to a wish for security and stability in life. The girls gave very concrete descriptions of children, dogs and cats while the boys were preoccupied with cars, motorcycles and houses.

A Norwegian study of how girls' educational plans develop during their adolescence and the actual outcome confirms how young women experience the expectation of fulfilling the 'new female role' (Brock-Due and Tornes 1983).[14] In the course of upper secondary school some of these girls lowered their ambitions in order to be able to handle future family life. The double expectations to which girls and young women are exposed during their upbringing might account for how they actually behave in the educational system and on the labor market. But all girls do not behave in the same way. We have to get an idea of how motivation, goals and capacities are developed over time, as crucial choices made during the course of childhood and adolescence will have implications for choices made as adults. The influence of economic and social structure on these choices are of crucial importance, but at the same time consideration must be given to the meaning experienced by the individual.

In this article I have discussed just some of the experiences of promoting equality between the sexes in the field of education and working life in Sweden. I have argued that an understanding of equalizing efforts must be broadened beyond an explanation that emphasizes sex roles. We should also avoid, however, focusing on structural factors and ignoring individual ones. The historical development of education for women and its interplay with economic and social development in society at large must be considered. Gender (and class) relations are products of a particular time and are constantly changing. For example, the value of formal qualifications seems to change when women (and working-class students) enter the educational system in greater numbers.

To broaden our understanding of girls' and women's behavior in education and working life, we must therefore include their own reflections about their choices in the context of unequal power relations between social classes and between men and women. In addition, new insights would be gained if boys and young men were included in future studies. This would allow us to grasp their strategies and possible changes taking place with relevance to their expectations for an adult life on more equal terms with women.

Notes

1   It should be noted that this figure also includes women on parental leave, sick leave, etc. In 1990 parental insurance compensated for the equivalent of full pay during the first twelve months after a child's birth, and a reduced sum for a further three months. The parental leave period may be shared between the mother and father according to their own preferences. In 1985, 77 percent of those using parental insurance were women and 23 percent were men. However, women used 94.5 percent of the time.

2   Sweden is a small country in international terms, with only about 8.5 million inhabitants, which enables the application of a nationwide curriculum and school acts declaring the state's decisions and intentions for education. Until 1990 the Swedish school system was very centralized. Communities are now, however, permitted to arrange comprehensive and upper secondary as well as adult education in whatever ways they prefer, as long as the centrally decided goal of equal opportunity for all children to attend education of equivalent standard irrespective of sex, social background and geographical residence is observed.

3   Education as a social institution is male dominated. Only 15 percent of head teachers are women while they comprise about one-third of directors of studies. However, 63 percent of teachers in comprehensive and upper secondary school are women. In grades 1–3, 98 percent of the teachers are women compared with 67 percent in grades 4–6 and 53 percent in grades 7–9 (U 60 SM 8901).

4   According to Fürst (1990) contemporary reformers have focused on men's education in the Swedish upper secondary school and have paid less attention to women's education. The criticism also refers to the neglect of expected changes

on the labor market in general. These changes are also supposed to be of crucial importance for women's education and to affect female-dominated sectors of the labor market in particular. The proposed structure of vocational study programs in upper secondary school referred to by Fürst contains eighteen course programs, of which fifteen are in the field of manufacturing and three are in the field of service. Future changes in the labor market are expected to mean a decrease of the manufacturing sector and an increase of the service sector. Course programs for the service sector are less developed in the proposal. This part of the labor market — i.e., work in administration, social service, communication, information, leisure, and culture — is to a large extent filled by women.

5   Their proportion of the Swedish population is estimated at 10 and 50 percent respectively.

6   The figures in Table 3.1 emanate from the research project Social Segregation in Swedish Comprehensive Schools and Upper Secondary Schools. The table has also been published in Jönsson and Arnman 1989a.

In the research project about 3600 pupils in six Swedish municipalities were followed from starting school at the age of seven in 1972 until the end of upper secondary school (1983–85). In 1981 about 1700 of them wrote essays about how they imagined their future would be in respect of education, work and family life. In 1985 about 900 of the same pupils were asked about their actual and planned university studies. In 1990 another questionnaire was sent to the whole research population asking about university or other kinds of studies, work experience and family situation.

7   The Swedish upper secondary school is divided into three parts: longer (3–4 year) theoretical course programs ('lines'), shorter (2 year) theoretical course programs, and vocational course programs. Table 3.2 shows the total number of pupils, the percentage of girls and average mark of each line received in 1989.

Table 3.2

	Total Number	% Female Pupils	Average Mark* Female	Male
Longer theoretical lines				
Humanities	3261	88	3.44	3.28
Social science	5864	70	3.48	3.23
Economics	11529	63	3.30	3.16
Natural science	5933	50	3.74	3.69
Engineering (3 year)	11145	19	3.38	3.24
Engineering (4 year)	7812	19	3.31	3.20
Shorter theoretical lines				
Artistic–practical	347	80	3.41	3.15
General studies	5132	62	3.28	3.07
Music	417	59	3.57	3.31
Economics	1545	57	3.22	3.08
Engineering (2 year)	205	6	3.05	3.19
Vocational course programs				
Clothing manufacture	561	97	3.33	3.29
Social service	1618	96	2.97	2.85
Consumer studies	2082	91	3.06	2.80
Nursing	9007	91	3.25	3.06
Distributive trades and clerical work	2957	71	3.20	2.97
Commercial and clerical	4514	70	3.15	2.99
Food technology	2718	56	3.18	3.09

Table 3.2   (Cont.)

	Total Number	% Female Pupils	Average Mark* Female	Male
Gardening and landscaping	255	48	3.23	2.87
Agriculture	864	43	3.09	2.89
Process engineering	431	11	3.21	2.97
Woodwork	601	5	3.16	2.97
Production and maintenance	1418	3	3.22	3.11
Electrical engineering	5197	3	3.32	3.27
Metalwork	4346	3	3.04	2.77
Building and construction	3737	2	3.17	2.91
Motor mechanic	3486	2	3.05	2.92
Forestry	625	1	3.36	3.09

* Marks range between one and five, five being the highest and one being the lowest. Since 1981 marks have only been given in grades 8 and 9 in comprehensive school but in all grades in upper secondary school.

8   The figures in the paragraph refer to the following table published in Jönsson and Arnman 1989b, p. 23. The total number of cases in this part of the study is about 900; this sample includes only students with an average of 3.5 or more in their leaving certificate from upper secondary school in 1984 or earlier.

Table 3.3   *University education in 1985 attended by boys and girls in different achievement groups according to the leaving certificate and the proportion of social class I.*

Achievement groups/ choice of university education	Boys		Girls		Total	
	% choice	% in sc I	% choice	% in sc I	% choice	% in sc I
5.0–4.5						
Prestigious education	80	65	50	61	62	63
Traditional education	20	20	17	50	18	36
'New' education	—	—	33	25	20	25
4.4–4.0						
Prestigious education	50	47	28	36	38	42
Traditional education	47	36	44	70	45	55
'New' education	3	100	28	27	17	33
3.9–3.5						
Prestigious education	5	—	3	100	4	67
Traditional education	52	55	48	28	49	35
'New' education	43	11	49	17	48	15
Number of cases	76	34	136	51	212	85

9   For example, in 1988 men spent 31 percent of their work hours per year in manu-facturing industries compared with 14 percent of the women. Less than a fourth of the work in this sector is done by women. About 55 percent of work done in public administration, care and service jobs is done by women, compared with 19 percent done by men. Of all work hours spent in the public sector, 66 percent is done by women. The gap between the proportion of the number of female employees (75 percent) and their hours of work in the public sector (66 percent)

is explained by a widespread system of part-time work (Jonung and Persson 1990).

10   In 1985, 45 percent of all women aged 20–64 worked part-time compared with 5 percent of the men. Among women aged 25–44 with small children, about 60 percent worked part-time compared with 3 percent of the men. Part-time work also varies with position and sector of the labor market; 33 percent of the women organized in the Confederation of Professional Associations (SACO/SR) worked part-time compared with 40 percent of the female members of the Central Organization of Salaried Employees (TCO) and 53 percent of women organized in blue-collar unions (LO) (Kvinno- och mansvärlden 1986).

All parents with children younger than twelve years have the legal right to work six hours per day. They are also entitled to sickness allowances for sixty days when taking care of their sick children.

The rate of absenteeism among young women (25–34 years) are much higher (27 percent) than among men in the same age group (13 percent). About 13 percent of women's absenteeism is due to caring for children (maternity leave and care of sick children are included in this figure), while only 1 percent of male absenteeism is due to this reason (Jonung and Persson 1990).

11   In 1987 women's average incomes amounted to about 70 percent of those of men (after allowing for variations in hours of work). Women (20–64 years) earned on average S.Kr. 117,000 compared with S.Kr. 146,300 by men.

12   The results referred to in Cwejman and Fürst (1988) are so far preliminary and emanate from an exploratory study of twenty-two teenage girls from different social backgrounds. The aim was to study the strategies developed by girls in a society which is very clearly male dominated at the same time as the official policy advocates equal opportunity between the sexes. The study on sex roles and the effects of equal opportunity action programs made by Bjerrum-Nielsen and her associates (1988) took place in six classes in grade 8 comprising both girls and boys. Half of the pupils attended school in a middle-class residential area and half of them lived in a working-class area in Oslo, Norway.

13   Malmgren (1982/85) and Esseveld and Goodman (1984) depart from the essays referred to in note 6. In grade 8 about 1700 girls and boys wrote essays about how they imagined their future to be one year after leaving compulsory school, at the age of 20, and again at the age of 35, with respect to education, work and family life. In Malmgren's study a sample of 160 essays was analyzed, while Esseveld and Goodman made a quantitative analysis of the total number of essays.

14   The Norwegian study by Broch-Due and Tornes (1983) comprises a sample of thirty-two girls chosen from a larger student population (337 boys and girls) attending schools in Trondheim, Bergen and Stavanger in Norway. The design of the study makes it possible to examine the development of their educational aspirations from grade 9 in 1969 until five years after leaving upper secondary school in 1977.

References

AKU, *Arbetskraftsundersökningar 1988*, Stockholm, SBC.

ANYON, J. (1983) 'Intersections of Gender and Class: Accommodation and Resistance by Working Class and Affluent Females to Contradictory Sex-Role Ideologies', in WALKER, S. and BARTON, L. (Eds) *Gender, Class and Education*. New York, Falmer Press.

ARNMAN, G. and JÖNSSON, I. (1983) *Segregation och svensk skola: En studie av utbildning, klass och boende*, Lund, Arkiv förlag.

ARNMAN, G. and JÖNSSON, I. (1986) *Olika för olika: Aspekter på svensk utbildningspolitik,* Lund, Arkiv förlag.

ARNOT, M. and WEINER, G. (Eds) (1987) *Gender and the Politics of Schooling,* London, Hutchinson (in association with the Open University).

BERNER, B. (1982) 'Kvinnor, kunskap och makt i teknikens värld', *Kvinnovetenskaplig Tidskrift nr 3.*

BERNER, B. (1984) 'Women, Technology and the Division of Labour — What is the Role of Education?', *Nordisk Förening för Pedagogisk Forskning nr 2.*

BJARKÅ, S. (1984) *Avhopp, avbrott, linjebyten vid gymnasieskolorna i Blekinge län, årskurs 1, läsåret 1983/84,* Länsskolnämnden i Blekinge.

BJERRUM-NIELSEN, H. (Ed.) (1988) *Jenteliv og likestillingslaere: Kjönsroller og likestillingsarbeid blant ungdomar,* Oslo, J.W. Cappalans Forlag.

BOWLES, S. and GINTIS, H. (1975) *Schooling in Capitalist America: Educational Reform and the Contradictions of Economic Life,* New York, Basic Books.

BOURDIEU, P. (1976) 'Kulturell reproduktion och social produktion', in LUNDBERG, S., SELANDER, S. and ÖHLUND, U. (Eds) *Jämlikhetsmyt och klassherravälde,* Malmö, Bo Cavefors Bokförlag.

BROCK-DUE, K. and TORNES, K. (1983) 'Dualisme og ambivalens; Jenters valg av utdanning — et valg av livlop?', in SKREDE, K. and TORNES, K. (Eds) *Studier i kvinners livlop,* Oslo, Universitetsforlaget.

BURTON, C. (1985) *Subordination: Feminism and Social Theory,* Sydney, George Allen & Unwin.

CHODOROW, N. (1978) *The Reproduction of Mothering,* Berkeley, University of California Press.

CIVILDEPARTEMENTET (1990) *Yttrande över FN:s konvention om avskaffande av alla slags diskriminering av kvinnor,* Stockholm, Jämställdhetsenheten.

CONNELL, R.W. (1987) *Gender and Power: Society, the Person and Sexual Politics,* Cambridge, Polity Press.

CWEJMAN, S. and FÜRST, G. (1988) 'Tonårsflickors väg. Strategier i klyftan mellan ideologisk könsneutralitet och könssegregerande praktik', in *Kvinnors identitetsutveckling,* Rapport No. 1, August 1988, Jämfo, Stockholm.

DELAMONT, S. (1989) *Knowledgeable Women: Structuralism and the Reproduction of Elites,* London, Routledge.

ELGQVIST-SALTZMAN, I. and VE, H. (1987) 'Kvinnors livsmönster, utbildningsreformer och rationalitet', in *Nordisk Pedagogik,* 1.

ESSEVELD, J. (1986) 'Mot en kritisk feminisk. Ett sätt att förändra det olyckliga äktenskapet mellan marxism och feminism', in GANETZ, H., GUNNARSSON, E. and GÖRANSSON, A. (Eds) *Feminism och marxism: En förälskelse med förhinder,* Stockholm, Arbetarkultur.

ESSEVELD, J. (1988) *Beyond Silence: Middle-aged Women in the 70s,* Lund, Lund University.

ESSEVELD, J. and GOODMAN, S. (1984) *Students' Visions of Their Future: How a Hierarchical Society Becomes Reproduced,* Lund, Lund University.

FÜRST, G. (1985) *Reträtten från mansjobben: En studie av industriarbetande kvinnor och arbetsdelningen mellan könen på en intern arbetsmarknad,* Monografi nr 34, Sociologiska Institutionen, Göteborgs Universitet.

FÜRST, G. (1987) 'Arbersmarknadskrafter och könssegregation', in BJÖRNBERG, U. and HELLBERG, I. (Eds) *Sociologer ser på arbete,* Stockholm, Arbetslivscentrum.

FÜRST, G. (1990) *En ny gymnasieskola för flickor och pojkar: Jämställdhetsperspektiv på den nya gymnasieskolans linjestruktur,* Forskningsrapport nr 99, Sociologiska Institutionen, Göteborgs Universitet.

GERSON, K. (1985) *Hard Choices: How Women Decide About Work, Career and Motherhood,* Berkeley, University of California Press.

GESSER, B. (1971) 'Rekrytering till universitet och högskolor', in *Val av utbildning och yrke*, Rapporter från undersökningar genomförda av 1968 års utbildningsutredning, Stockholm, *SOU 1971:61*.

HAAVIND, H. (1985) 'Förändringar i förhållandet mellan kvinnor och män', in *Kvinnovetenskaplig Tidskrift 1985*, No. 3.

JONUNG, C. and PERSSON, I. (1990) 'Hushållsproduktion, marknadsproduktion och jämställdhet', in *Kvinnors roll i ekonomin*, bilaga 23 to Långtidsutredningen 1990, Stockholm, Allmänna förlaget.

JÖNSSON, I. and ARNMAN, G. (1989a) 'Social Segregation in Swedish Comprehensive Schools', in BALL, S.J. and LARSSON, S. (Eds) *The Struggle For Democratic Education, Equality and Participation in Sweden*, London, Falmer Press.

JÖNSSON, I. and ARNMAN, G. (1989b) *Högskolestudier — det är frågan*, Stockholm, UHÄ, FOU, Arbetrsrapport 1989, p. 3.

KESSLER, S., ASHENDEN, D.J., CONNELL, R.W. and DOWSETT, G.W. (1985) 'Gender Relations in Secondary Schooling', *Sociology of Education* 58, pp. 34–48.

Kvinno- och mansvärlden: Fakta om jämställdheten i Sverige 1986, Stockholm, SCB.

KYLE, G. (1979) *Gästarbeterska i manssamhället: Studier om industriarbetande kvinnors villkor i Sverige*, Stockholm, Liber Förlag.

LILJEGREN, T. (1984) *Studieavbrott i gymnasieskolan*, Stockholm, Skolöverstyrelsen.

LINDGREN, G. (1982) *Kamrater, kolleger och kvinnor: En studie av könssegregeringsprocessen i två mansdominerade organisationer*, U Sociologiska Institutionen, Umeå Universitet.

LUNDAHL, L. (1986) *Flickors utbildning för hem och yrkenågra skolpolitiska skiljelinje*, Lund, Lunds Universitet.

MALMGREN, G. (1982/85) *Min framtid: Om högstadieelevers syn på framtiden*, Lund, Symposion.

McDONALD, M. (1980) 'Socio-Cultural Reproduction and Women's Education', in DEEM, R. (Ed.). *Schooling for Women's Work*, London, Routledge & Kegan Paul.

MIDDLETON, S. (1987) 'The Sociology of Women's Education as a Field of Academic Study', in ARNOT, M. and WEINER, G. (Eds) *Gender and the Politics of Schooling*, London, Hutchinson (in association with the Open University).

MILLS, C.W. (1959) *The Sociological Imagination*, Oxford, Oxford University Press.

MINISTRY OF LABOUR (1987) *First Periodic Report by the Government of Sweden on the measures taken to give effect to the Convention on The Elimination of All Forms of Discrimination Against Women*, Stockholm, Swedish Ministry of Labour.

MYRDAHL, A. and KLEIN, V. (1957) *Kvinnans två roller*, Stockholm, Tiden.

OECD (1986) *Girls and Women in Education: A Cross-National Study of Inequalities in Upbringing and in Schools and Colleges*, Paris, OECD.

PERSSON-TANIMURA, I. (1983) 'Unga kvinnors utbildningsval och arbetsmarknadsinträde', in LUNDAHL, M. and PERSSON-TANIMURA, I. (Eds) *Kvinnan i ekonomin*, Malmö, Liber Förlag.

PERSSON-TANIMURA, I. (1988) 'The Third Dimension — Equal Status Between Swedish Women and Men', Paper presented for the symposium on *Generating Equality — The Swedish Experience* at Marienlyst, Denmark, November 24–25, 1988.

Regeringens proposition 1987/88:105, *Jämställdhetspolitiken inför 90–talet*, Stockholm.

SANDLUND, M. (1971) 'The Status of Women in Sweden: Report to the United Nations, 1968', in DAHLMSTRÖM, E. (Ed.) *The Changing Roles of Men and Women*, Appendix, pp. 209–302, Boston, Beacon Press.

SCOTT, H. (1984) 'Sweden's Efforts to Achieve Sex-role Equality in Education', in ACKER, S., MEGARRY, J.S., NISBET, S. and HOYLE, E. (Eds) *World Yearbook of Education 1984*, London, Women and Education; New York, Nichols Publishing Company.

SIFFROR OM HÖGSKOLAN (1989) *Social skiktning i utbildningsväsendet*, No. 8, Stockholm, SCB.

SIFFROR OM HÖGSKOLAN (1989) *Tio år med nya högskolan*, No. 10, Stockholm, SCB.
SÖRENSEN, B.A. (1982) 'Ansvarsrasjonalitet: Om mål — middeltenkning blant kvinner', in HOLTER, H. (Ed.) *Kvinner i fellesskap*, Oslo, Universitetsforlaget.
U 55 SM 8601 (1986) *Yrkesutbildad i gymnasieskolan*, Stockholm, SCB.
U 55 SM 8901 (1989) *Etablering på arbetsmarkanden efter gymnasieskolan*, Stockholm, SCB.
U 60 SM 8901 (1989) *Statistiska Meddelanden: Lärare 1989*, Stockholm, SCB.
U 53 SM 9001 (1990) *Statistiska Meddelanden: Avgångna och avgångsbetyg från gymnasieskolans linjer läsåret 1988/89*, Stockholm, SCB.
VE, H. (1987) 'Rasjonalitetsbegreper', *Nordisk Pedagogik*, 1.
VE, H. (1987) 'Ansvar och protest', in KRISTIANSEN, T. and SCHOU WETLESEN, T. (Eds) *Familien i endring*, Instituttet for sosiologi, Oslo, UiO/J.W. Cappenlens Forlag A.S.
WERNERSSON, I. and LANDER, R. (1979) *Män och kvinnor i barnomsorgen: En analys av könskvotering, yrkesval och arbetstrivsel*, Stockholm, Jämställdhetskommittén.
WILLIAMS, R. (1961/1975) *The Long Revolution*, Harmondsworth, Penguin Books Ltd.
WILLIS, P. (1977) *Learning to Labour: How Working-class Kids Get Working-class Jobs*, Farnborough, Eng., Saxon House.

4 Post-secondary Education of White Women in 1900

Nancy E. Durbin and Lori Kent

Introduction

Much of the controversy over the role of post-secondary education in the United States centers on the occupational-preparation function of schooling and the relationship of education to the occupational structure. Occupational preparation, however, had limited applicability to women's education, particularly women's post-secondary education, at the turn of the century. First, a minority of women were gainfully employed (18.8 percent of the women aged 10 and over). Moreover, a larger portion of single women (31.3 percent) than married women (5.6 percent) worked, which suggests that young women worked until they married and that few women pursued life-long careers (US Bureau of the Census 1904, p. ccxiii). Because marriage represented an alternative or end to gainful employment for most women, fewer women than men expected to need marketable job skills and occupational credentials. Second, most women who went to college came from social classes that disapproved of gainful employment for women; hence, women who pursued post-secondary education often had no intention of entering the labor force (Newcomer 1959; Solomon 1985). Third, other than teaching school, women had few occupational opportunities for which post-secondary educational institutions could train or certify them. Most skilled managerial, professional, and technical jobs were held by men in 1900.

It seems apparent, therefore, that occupational preparation was but one function of post-secondary education for women, and the occupational structure was but one determinant of educational participation by women at the turn of the century. Women's education, we argue, had multiple purposes and was influenced by a variety of factors.[1] In addition, the post-secondary educational institutions that women attended emphasized job preparation in varying degrees: early women's colleges, for example, placed little emphasis on professional training, but normal schools (teacher-training institutions) existed almost exclusively for this purpose. Consequently, enrollments in these different types of educational institutions probably varied in their responsiveness to characteristics of the occupational structure.

In this chapter, we contend that (1) because post-secondary education served a diversity of functions for women and society, only one of which was preparation for jobs, enrollments in various types of educational institutions responded differently to social-structural influences, depending on institutional goals and students' reasons for attending school, and (2) because post-secondary educational institutions differed in the number and variety of functions they fulfilled, analyses of total enrollments can obscure important distinctions between educational subcategories. To support these claims, we analyzed state-level data from the turn of the century.

The chapter begins with a discussion of the historical functions of post-secondary education for women in the United States. It then describes the major post-secondary educational opportunities available to women in 1900 and identifies structural influences on women's participation in post-secondary education. Correlation and regression analyses are presented to examine the impact of the social-structural characteristics of forty-six states on female enrollments in three types of post-secondary educational institutions (coeducational colleges and universities, women's colleges, and normal schools) and on the total, combined enrollments. The chapter ends by addressing the implications of the findings for future research on the social and economic functions of post-secondary education.

Historical Functions

Three important functions of post-secondary education for women were preparation for occupational roles, primarily for teaching careers but, in the West and Midwest, also for agricultural pursuits; preparation for social roles; and the acquisition of cultural capital, which was important for status maintenance and cultural transmission.

The only formal occupational role for which post-secondary education prepared a substantial number of women was teaching. The expansion of lower educational levels during the late 1800s increased the demand for schoolteachers and raised public expenditure on education; in response to these structural constraints, states recruited women to teach because women were an available and inexpensive source of labor (Richardson and Hatcher 1983; Sugg 1978). By 1900, teaching was a highly feminized occupation: nearly 74 percent of the teachers were women (US Bureau of the Census 1904, p. 1). Although initially teachers required little formal education, by 1900 the majority (81 percent) of the students who prepared to teach studied in normal schools or normal departments of colleges and universities (US Education Bureau 1900, p. 2087).

In addition to preparing women for occupational roles, post-secondary institutions prepared women for homemaking, marriage, motherhood, and social roles. This type of post-secondary education reinforced traditional female roles and, in some cases, explicitly promoted the attachment of women to the home and family. For example, at the end of the nineteenth century, the home economics movement emerged 'to combat the movement of women out of their homes' (Rury 1984, p. 22) and to prepare women for 'their roles in sustaining the central institution of modern industrial society — the family' (p. 24). Home economics education included the study of traditional female pursuits, such as cooking and sewing, plus newer 'scientific' subjects, such as household financial management, hygiene, nutrition, and family relations (Rury 1984, p. 22). Although domestic science education, as it was called, was most prevalent in the secondary schools, colleges — particularly land-grant colleges — also offered such instruction (Solomon 1985; Woody 1966b).

Post-secondary education prepared women for nonoccupational roles in other ways: by imparting social skills and graces through instruction in the fine arts, music, and foreign languages. The curricula of women's colleges, in particular, emphasized 'ornamental studies in drawing, singing, and piano playing' (Solomon 1985, p. 23). Part of the process of socializing students took place outside the classroom. At formal teas and on other social occasions, women practised the arts of proper dressing, good manners, and polite conversation (Newcomer 1959). Thus, it is not surprising that colleges have often been likened to finishing schools.

In addition to preparing women for different types of roles, post-secondary education fulfilled a status-maintenance or cultural-transmission function, making educational credentials for women valuable cultural currency in the marriage market. College-educated women were conversant in a variety of subjects and were able to perform adeptly in diverse social capacities; therefore, they made attractive wives, particularly of men of high social status (Newcomer 1959; Solomon 1985). Graduates of home economics departments, skilled in household production and management, were especially valued in rural farming areas, where self-sufficiency and economy were needed (Solomon 1985).[2] Similarly, women who were trained as schoolteachers could benefit their families with their knowledge and expertise and could tutor their children in academic subjects (Woody 1966a). It seems, then, that post-secondary education increased women's status as marital partners.[3] It also improved their prospects for marrying by introducing them to eligible men. Coeducational institutions and coordinate women's colleges (schools affiliated with elite men's schools) put men and women in close contact with one another, facilitating courtship and marriage; graduates of teaching institutions who found jobs in new communities also met potential husbands (Degler 1980; Solomon 1985).

Finally, post-secondary education filled the interim between adolescence and married adulthood with a socially respectable activity for young women, whether it was preparation for a temporary career or the pursuit of a liberal education (Solomon 1985). In 1900, the median age at first marriage for women was 21.9 years, well beyond the age at which youths graduated from high school (US Bureau of the Census 1975). College was a pleasant way to pass time before marrying, and knowledge for its own sake was frequently the only aim of women who attended (Newcomer 1959). In this sense, post-secondary institutions 'warehoused' surplus female labor by providing young women with an alternative to idleness, marriage, or gainful employment. As Walters (1984) noted, schooling that was discretionary, such as post-secondary education for women, was most apt to fulfill a warehousing function.

Educational Opportunities

The goals and functions of the three major types of post-secondary institutions were different.[4] Furthermore, the availability of each type of institution varied from region to region.

Table 4.1   Structure of Higher Education in the Northeast, West, and South Atlantic Regions,
1900

Institution	Northeast	West	South Atlantic
Colleges and Universities[a]			
Percentage of female college students in public institutions	2	62	5
Estimate tuition in schools for men and coeducational schools	$93.48	$22.07	$43.74
Estimated tuition in colleges for women[b]			
Division A schools	$163.28	—	$107.13
Division B schools	$115.37	—	$76.67
Normal Schools			
Percentage of female normal school students in public schools	95	95	76
Estimated tuition[c]			
Public schools	$12.78	$3.17	$5.13
Private schools	$88.00	$5.39	$7.27

[a] Average tuition was estimated by dividing aggregate data on tuition and fees for colleges and universities by aggregate data on enrollments separately for each region. This procedure underestimates average tuition because fewer schools reported data on tuition than on enrollment.
[b] Data are not reported for the West because the West had only three women's colleges in 1900.
[c] Average tuition was estimated by dividing aggregate data on tuition and fees for normal schools by aggregate data on enrollments separately for each region. This procedure underestimates average tuition because fewer schools reported data on tuition than on enrollment.

Coeducational colleges and universities had the most varied curricula and the greatest organizational diversity and thus fulfilled all the functions discussed earlier. These schools — including public research-oriented universities, private liberal arts colleges, and land-grant schools specializing in agricultural and industrial education — offered courses in literature, classical and modern languages, science, engineering, home economics, pedagogy, and many other subjects. Women who attended them had a variety of intentions (such as preparation for a career and enhancement of their status) and studied a variety of subjects (for example, education, home economics, liberal arts, and fine arts).

Although coeducational colleges existed in all regions, they were attended by women most frequently in the West, where there were virtually no women's colleges. Colleges attended by women were also more likely to be public than private in the West, where 62 percent of the women who attended were in public institutions. Few women attended public colleges in the Northeast (2 percent) or in the South Atlantic (5 percent) regions (see Table 4.1).[5]

Regions also differed in the cost of tuition at coeducational institutions. Tuition in the West was substantially lower than in the Northeast or the South, which suggests that men's and coeducational institutions were more accessible to a broader range of the population in the Western states. In addition, tuition was lower at men's or coeducational colleges in the Northeast and in the South Atlantic regions than at the women's colleges, most of which were private.

Women's colleges, concentrated in the South (although also found in other regions [see Appendix]), had less diverse educational goals. Their traditional and primary purpose was to turn out polished and competent ladies who could engage their husbands in intellectual discourse, transmit knowledge and culture to their children, and participate in the social and cultural affairs of their communities (Solomon 1985; Woody 1966b).

Both the quality and cost of women's colleges varied regionally. Southern colleges for women were generally less prestigious and more affordable than were their Northeastern counterparts, such as Radcliffe College in Massachusetts, Vassar College in New York, and Bryn Mawr College in Pennsylvania. The Northeast had 9 Division A women's colleges and 11 Division B women's colleges; the South had 2 Division A women's colleges and 45 Division B women's colleges.[6] Furthermore, although women's colleges were, on average, more expensive than either coeducational colleges or normal schools, Division A schools in the South ($107) were less expensive than were Division B schools in the North ($115). In 1900, women's colleges, whatever their location or division, had similar types of curricula, despite major differences in the rigor of the educational training they provided.

For a long time, women's colleges resisted the introduction of professional courses into their curricula; gainful employment was considered contrary to upper-class ideals of womanhood (Woody 1966b). Domestic sciences were similarly downplayed, reflecting, perhaps, elitist expectations that women would have help with the housework (Solomon 1985). Women's colleges subscribed to the philosophy that a liberal education was the best preparation for women's future roles as wives, mothers, homemakers, and teachers (Newcomer 1959).

Normal schools, by definition, existed to train schoolteachers. Although they offered instruction in other areas besides pedagogy (business, for instance), our focus here is on students in normal departments in normal schools whose ostensible purpose was to prepare for a career in teaching. The tuition at normal schools was lower than at women's colleges and, except for private normal schools in the Northeast, lower than at men's or coeducational institutions (see Table 4.1). Normal schools were the primary training institutions for teachers, and the availability of other forms of teacher training varied from region to region. In the West, 14 percent of the female students who were preparing to teach studied pedagogy in colleges and universities, compared with only 3.6 percent in the Northeast (US Education Bureau 1900, pp. 2072, 2080, and 2086).

Influences on Attendance

Given the diverse function of post-secondary education for women and society, several factors should have influenced the rate at which young women attended school in 1900. Moreover, since educational institutions stressed different functions and had different degrees of functional specialization, enrollments in coeducational colleges and universities, women's colleges, and normal schools should have responded differently and to different social-structural influences. This section identifies the factors that should have affected female participation in post-secondary education and suggests how these factors affected enrollments in the three types of educational institutions.

Teaching Opportunities for Women

Because schools provided skills that qualified people for occupations or conferred credentials that gave graduates access to occupations, the demand for educated female workers should have encouraged women to enroll in institutions of higher education. Previous empirical studies have supported this proposition. Fuller (1983) found, for example, that teaching opportunities for young workers increased the enrollments of women in secondary schools between 1890 and 1920, and Walters (1984) found, similarly, that professional and technical employment opportunities increased the enrollment of women in two-year and four-year colleges from 1952 to 1980.

The high rate of employment of women in teaching in 1900, in combination with the acceptability of teaching as an occupation for middle-class women (Newcomer 1959), should have increased women's participation in post-secondary education, particularly in institutions that emphasized teacher training. As was already noted, both normal schools and coeducational colleges and universities offered pedagogical instruction, and liberal arts courses could be applied to the occupation of teaching, particularly at the college level. Few women's colleges had normal departments, however, and professional preparation was a low priority in these institutions and for the students who attended them (Newcomer 1959). Teaching opportunities probably had no effect, or a negative effect, on enrollments in women's colleges.

Teaching as an employment opportunity also varied by region. Teachers represented 10 percent of the female labor force in the West, but only 5 percent in the Northeast and 3 percent in the South (Kent and Durbin 1984). Salaries for female teachers were also highest in the West, where the average monthly income for female teachers was $50.05, compared with $41.34 in the Northeast and $25.73 in the South.

The Sex Ratio

Guttentag and Secord (1983) presented considerable evidence that the ratio of men to women in a society alters sex roles and relations between the sexes. On the basis of their analysis, we propose that states with a low ratio of men to women would have shown an increase in women's pursuit of post-secondary education. First, the low ratio would have opened opportunities for college-trained women. Second, it would have decreased the prospect of marriage and encouraged women to obtain professional credentials and become self-supporting. Third, more competitive marriage markets would have compelled women to seek education that increased their status as marital partners and their opportunities to meet eligible men (Solomon 1985). Fourth, fewer opportunities for marriage would have increased the pool of young, unoccupied women who were in need of something to do; thus, warehousing increased as opportunities for marriage decreased. As Newcomer (1959) pointed out, parents often sent their less marriageable daughters to college for the lack of other alternatives. Hence, low sex ratios should have raised enrollments at all types of post-secondary institutions.

Income Levels

For a variety of reasons, the economic affluence of a state or region may have encouraged women's involvement in post-secondary education. From the perspective of the development of human resources, educating women beyond high school was less necessary than educating men: fewer women entered the labor force, fewer still remained employed throughout their lifetimes, and few occupations that required post-secondary education extensively employed women. Affluent areas could better afford the luxury of educating people whose labor they did not fully utilize in the marketplace.

The economic affluence of a state and region should also be reflected in the affluence of families and the attitudes of parents toward educating their daughters. From the parents' perspective, educating daughters was less imperative than educating sons because women, as a rule, had less need for a vocation in life, might never work, or might marry and leave the labor force. Sons typically were given preference in the competition for post-secondary education; in fact, daughters sometimes worked to help finance their brothers' schooling (Abbott 1910; Dublin 1981; Newcomer 1959; Rhine 1891). The reluctance to educate women stemmed from other considerations as well. First, daughters often cost more to educate than did sons, since fewer scholarships and fellowships were available to them (Solomon 1985), and women had greater difficulty earning enough to pay their way through school (Newcomer 1959). Second, the returns generally were lower on investments in women's than in men's education, either because women did not work after graduation or earned much lower salaries if they did work (Newcomer 1959). Third, post-secondary education did not greatly increase women's occupational status or earning power, since the white-collar occupations that women could enter from high school paid salaries similar to teaching (Newcomer 1959). For these reasons, parents, unless they were financially comfortable or valued education for its own sake, were probably reluctant to invest considerable money in the education of their daughters or to make financial sacrifices to pay for their daughters' college tuition and other expenses. Fuller's (1983) contention that the increased affluence of middle-class families encouraged the children's attendance at school and Walters's (1984) finding that unemployment, which reduced the ability of families to raise money for college tuition and expenses, decreased the growth of enrollment in post-secondary schools between 1952 and 1979 are consistent with the proposition that the affluence of an area lessened parents' concern about the cost of education and the return on their investment and, therefore, should have increased women's access to post-secondary education.

Mechanization of Farms

At the turn of the century, the organization of agriculture differed dramatically throughout the country (Wiebe 1967). Traditional agricultural economies (typical of the South) required all family members to work the land and produce goods for household consumption or distribution in local markets (Dublin 1981). Modern, capitalistic agricultural economies (typical of the Midwest and West) were less labor intensive and depended more on farm implements and machinery to plant and harvest crops. These areas produced primary goods, such as wheat and corn, for distribution in national markets, made accessible to midwestern and western farmers by improved transportation systems.

Guest and Tolnay (1985) found that the mechanization of farms was positively related to the consumption of primary education in all the states in 1900. They argued that it reduced the need for child labor, thereby freeing children to attend school, and increased the skills required to farm, which demanded greater skills by farmers. Their arguments can be applied to the involvement of women in post-secondary education.

Mechanized farming reduced women's participation in agricultural production, even more than men's (Guest 1981); women generally did not operate heavy farm machinery and equipment (compare Sachs 1983), and the secondary goods that women traditionally produced (such as butter and cheese) were centralized in factory settings. The decreased employment of women in agriculture freed women for other activities, such as attending college and teaching school. Thus, educational systems absorbed the surplus female labor by enrolling women students and employing female personnel (who first attended school to obtain teacher training and credentials).

Regional differences in the participation of women in agriculture were dramatic in 1900 and reflect differences in the mechanization of farms. Between 40 percent and 50 percent of the women in the labor force in the South Atlantic region were in agricultural work in 1900, compared with only 2 percent of the women in the Northeast and less than 8 percent of the women in the West (Kent and Durbin 1984). Since these figures do not include farmers' wives and daughters, but only wage labor, it is unlikely that any of the women working in agriculture would have been candidates for college or normal school; however, these differences reflect differences in the economic and agricultural infrastructure among the three regions.

Post-secondary education had greater relevance to women's work roles in mechanized farming regions. Women who lived on or owned a capitalist farm (usually in conjunction with their husbands) could incorporate their training into the running of the family business (keeping the books and inventory) and the efficient management of the farms (see footnote 2). As Newcomer (1959, p. 90) noted, 'If farmers could profit by scientific training, so could farmers' wives.' Specialized home economics degrees could be used to teach home economics to the daughters of the entrepreneurial farming classes, who demanded practical and relevant education for their children. Finally, the capitalist farming classes of the Midwest and West (highly mechanized farming regions) were strong advocates and consumers of post-secondary education (Carstensen 1962; Veysey 1965). Thus, the children of farmers were well represented among the students at midwestern state universities at the turn of the century (Solomon 1985).

Farm mechanization probably had the greatest influence on enrollments in coeducational colleges and universities and in normal schools for the various reasons just outlined and because these institutions taught subjects relevant to women's work roles in mechanized farming regions. Women's colleges, like other institutions, absorbed surplus labor, but they were less likely to fulfill the other functions demanded of institutions of higher education in mechanized farming regions: instruction in practical, vocational, and scientific subjects. We suspect that students who attended women's colleges were less often from farming backgrounds than were students who attended coeducational colleges and universities and, hence, were influenced less by the organization of agriculture.[7]

Method

To examine the relationships between social-structural characteristics and the participation of women in post-secondary education, we used correlation and regression analyses of data on forty-six states.[8] Since we wished to demonstrate that (1) relationships between social-structural dimensions and enrollments differed across types of post-secondary institutions and (2) analyses of total enrollments can conceal important distinctions among educational subcategories, we analyzed the total combined enrollments in addition to the enrollments in coeducational colleges and universities, women's colleges, and normal schools.

Data from 1900 were ideal for our purposes because the factors we identified as influencing women's educational participation — teaching opportunities for women, the sex ratio, income levels, and the organization of agriculture — differed dramatically at that time across states and regions. Educational enrollments and styles of post-secondary education also varied greatly, reflecting, presumably, variations in social-structural composition. Educational institutions were highly differentiated by function in 1900. The three subcategories of post-secondary education we examined became less distinctive in later decades, when women's colleges added vocational and professional courses to their curricula and collegiate institutions increasingly assumed the function of training schoolteachers (Woodring 1962).

Data and Measures

Enrollment data were obtained from the *Report of the Commissioner of Education* (US Education Bureau 1900). We computed female enrollment rates by dividing the number of female students in each type of educational institution (coeducational, women's, and normal) by the white female population, aged 18–24. We computed total enrollments by summing the three separate enrollment figures. The Appendix gives a fuller description and justification of the enrollment measures.

Other data (unless indicated) were obtained from the US Bureau of the Census (1904) and included the following measures:

1 Female teaching opportunities: the proportion of gainfully employed white females who were teachers or college professors.
2 Sex ratio: the ratio of white males, aged 15–29, to white females, aged 15–29.
3 Income per capita: estimated personal income per capita, reported in Kuznets, Miller, and Easterlin (1960).
4 Farm mechanization: the average dollar value of farm implements and machinery, per farm.
5 Proportion of foreign white females in the college-age population: foreign white females, aged 18–24, divided by total white females, aged

Table 4.2   Enrollment Rates in 1900, by Region, for White Women, aged 18–24 (per 10,000)

Region	Coeducational Colleges and Universities	Women's Colleges	Normal Schools	Total Enrollments
Northeast	23	37	103	163
South Atlantic	17	106	59	182
East North Central	69	5	109	183
East South Central	42	103	45	190
West North Central	74	14	126	214
West South Central	36	22	36	94
West	125	3	135	263

18–24. This measure was included primarily as a control variable. As Walters (1984) noted, the low involvement of immigrants in education could have depressed the combined foreign white and native white enrollments. This outcome seems especially likely at the post-secondary level, since differences in educational participation were most pronounced among older age groups, that is, those of college age (Olneck and Lazerson 1974).

Findings

Table 4.2 reports the regional enrollment rates of white women in institutions of higher learning. These figures show that the West led the nation in coeducation, the South Atlantic and East South Central regions led the nation in women's education, and the northern and western regions surpassed the southern regions in women's consumption of normal education. Total enrollments conceal these striking regional variations in educational consumption patterns. For example, the South Atlantic and East North Central regions had nearly identical total enrollment rates, yet their student populations were differently distributed across the categories of post-secondary educational institutions. In the South Atlantic region, women's colleges enrolled the majority of female students, followed by normal schools and coeducational colleges and universities. In the East North Central region, women's colleges enrolled only a small minority of stud_nts; normal schools enrolled the majority. These distinctions may be important for testing theories if different factors promoted enrollments in coeducational colleges and universities, women's colleges, and normal schools.

Table 4.3, a correlation matrix of the dependent and independent variables, shows that among the states, enrollments in different types of post-secondary institutions were either unrelated (coeducational enrollments and normal school enrollments) or negatively related (women's college enrollments and coeducational enrollments, and women's college enrollments and normal school enrollments). These correlations suggest that different types of higher education developed independently of one another or in lieu of one another. Factors promoting enrollments in one type of educational institution, therefore, need not have promoted, or may even have discouraged, enrollments in other types of educational institutions.

Table 4.3 Correlations, Means, and Standard Deviations of Dependent and Independent Variables (N=46)

	1	2	3	4	5	6	7	8	9
1. Coeducational enrollments									
2. Women's college enrollments	−.28								
3. Normal enrollments	.06	−.34							
4. Total enrollments	.62	.32	.42						
5. Teaching opportunities	.62	−.33	.28	.42					
6. Sex ratio	.31	−.29	−.06	−.01	.49				
7. Per capita income	.48	−.48	.20	.15	.26	.42			
8. Farm mechanization	.54	−.48	.26	.23	.42	.31	.86		
9. Proportion of foreign white students	−.02	−.35	.23	−.13	−.06	.10	.66	.62	
X	.006	.004	.009	.018	.099	1.08	420.22	158.75	.12
SD	.007	.006	.005	.009	.041	.18	180.56	84.91	.10

Table 4.4 presents regression results for analyses of social-structural effects on educational enrollments.[9] As predicted, several factors influenced women's enrollments in coeducational colleges and universities, since these institutions fulfilled a variety of educational functions. Opportunities for female teachers, low sex ratios, per capita income, and farm mechanization increased enrollments, and the proportion of foreign white women who were in the college-age population decreased enrollments (only three of the coefficients were statistically significant, however). The five independent variables together explained 62 percent of the variation in coeducational enrollments across the states.

Two sets of coefficients are reported for women's colleges in Table 4.4: one for an analysis of all forty-six states and the other for an analysis of the twenty-five states reporting statistics for women's colleges in 1900 (see the Appendix). The equation based on forty-six states includes a dummy variable that controls for the presence of schools: states with no women's colleges were coded 0, and states with one or more women's colleges were coded 1.

These equations show that enrollments in women's colleges had little relationship to teaching opportunities for women, farm mechanization, or the nativity of the college-age population. Low sex ratios, in contrast, increased attendance at women's colleges, but only among states that had this style of post-secondary education (the coefficient for the sex ratio was large but not statistically significant, probably because of the small number of cases).[10]

The finding that per capita income related negatively (but insignificantly) to enrollments in women's colleges was unanticipated. Economic affluence was expected to increase the participation of women in post-secondary education. Given the substantially higher costs of women's colleges, it seems particularly perplexing that higher income levels would not be associated with higher levels of attendance at women's colleges. However, given what we know about women's educational opportunities in the South, this relationship should not have been surprising. In the southern states, which scored low on per capita income, the elites possessed wealth, but the majority of the population, black and white alike, lived in poverty. This class structure should have resulted in a low per capita income, compared with states with a smaller underclass and a larger middle

Table 4.4 Standardized Regression Effects and Slopes of Social-structural Characteristics on Female Enrollments in 1900 (standard error)

Characteristics	Coeducational Colleges and Universities (46 states)		Women's Colleges (46 states)		Women's Colleges (25 states)		Normal Schools (46 states)		Normal Schools (44 states)		All Categories Combined (46 states)	
	Standard-ized	Unstan-dardized	Standard-ized	Unstan-dardized	Standard-ized	Unstan-dardized	Standard-ized	Unstan-dardized	Standard-ized	Unstan-dardized	Standard-ized	Unstan-dardized
Teaching opportunities	.42**	.07** (.02)	-.14	-.02 (.03)	.02	.004 (.06)	.45**	.06 (.02)	.48**	.07** (.02)	.47**	.10** (.04)
Sex ratio	-.17	-.006 (.005)	.07	.003 (.006)	-.46	-.09 (.05)	.08	.0025 (.005)	-.03	-.0014 (.006)	-.38*	-.02* (.008)
Per capita income	.56*	.00002** (.00001)	-.26	-.000009 (.00001)	-.60	-.00003 (.00003)	.05	.000002 (.00001)	.12	.000003 (.00001)	.37	.000019 (.00001)
Farm mechanization	.25	.00002 (.00002)	-.05	-.000004 (.00002)	.03	.000003 (.00006)	.25	.00002 (.00002)	.27	.00002 (.00002)	.05	.000005 (.00003)
Proportion of foreign white students	-.50**	-.03** (.01)	-.06	-.004 (.01)	-.005	-.0004 (.03)	.07	.003 (.01)	-.001	-.00004 (.01)	-.34	.03 (.02)
Dummy[a]	—	—	.32	.42 (.002)	—	—	.74**	1.9** (.004)	-.001	—	—	—

[a] In the second equation, states reporting women's colleges were coded 1 and those reporting no women's colleges were coded 0. In the fourth equation, the states reporting normal schools were coded 1 and those reporting no normal schools were coded 0.
* Significant at the 0.05 level.
** Significant at the 0.01 level.

class (such as the western states, which scored high on per capita income). Low levels of per capita income are also associated with traditional agricultural economies and unskilled labor markets, which may have encouraged and supported the development of education for the elites that was functionally unrelated to the occupational structure and fulfilled mainly a status-maintenance function. Women's colleges, concentrated in the South, served the elite segments of the population more than did the vocationally oriented, often public, coeducational institutions, and are associated with a form of women's post-secondary education that did not increase with a general rise in levels of income.

Table 4.4 also reports two sets of coefficients for normal school enrollments: one for all states and one for all states except Nevada and Wyoming, which reported no normal schools in 1900. The equation based on 46 cases includes a dummy variable that controls for the presence of schools. These equations show that teaching opportunities had the greatest effect on normal school enrollments, which is not surprising, given that normal schools specialized in training teachers. Farm mechanization followed in importance, but its effects were insignificant. The sex ratio had surprisingly little relationship to normal school enrollments. We argued that low sex ratios encouraged women to seek professional training and become self-supporting. High turnover among schoolteachers and prohibitions against married women teachers suggest that for most women, however, teaching was a temporary career. Perhaps women viewed this occupation more as a precursor than as an alternative to marriage, so that employment opportunities, more than marriage opportunities, influenced their pursuit of teacher training.

Per capita income also had little effect on normal school enrollments, perhaps because the training of schoolteachers was not a luxury that was contingent on economic affluence but a necessary investment by the states and because normal schools were more affordable than were colleges and universities.

Conclusions

We stated at the outset that post-secondary education fulfilled a number of functions for women and society, only one of which was job preparation, and that the three types of postsecondary institutions differed in the particular functions they emphasized and in their degree of functional specialization. We argued, accordingly, that enrollments in these institutions were differentially affected by characteristics of the social structure.

Coeducational colleges and universities performed a variety of functions and served a diversity of populations. They trained workers for the labor market, prepared women for domestic and social roles, conferred status and credentials, and warehoused surplus labor. Correspondingly, enrollments in these institutions varied with the teaching opportunities for women, the sex ratio, income levels, farm mechanization, and the nativity of the college-age population.

Women's colleges served a more elite clientele and, as their curricula indicate, prepared women for marriage, motherhood, and social roles more than for professional careers. Their enrollments responded most strongly to levels of per capita income (class and economic structures) and to the sex ratio (marriage market).

Normal school enrollments were largely a function of opportunities for female teachers. The prominence of this relationship over others reflected the highly specialized function of normal education — teacher training and certification.

We also argued that analyses of total enrollments can conceal important distinctions among educational subcategories. The analysis confirmed this contention. That is, throughout the country, regional enrollments in particular types of post-secondary institutions varied differently from total enrollments; enrollments in coeducational colleges and universities, women's colleges, and normal schools either did not vary together or varied inversely to one other; and social-structural characteristics differed in their relationship to enrollments in various types of post-secondary institutions — a fact concealed by analyses of combined enrollments. The remainder of this section discusses the implications of these findings for theory and research on the role of education in the United States.

Social and economic theories have often focused on only one aspect of the role of education, either in producing workers or in reproducing social inequality. Institutional theories of education provide a broader picture that incorporates multiple roles: the provision of socialization (into statuses, work roles, and skills), the allocation of rewards, and the legitimation of statuses (Meyer 1978). This broader institutional assessment is consistent with the picture presented in this article. Historically, post-secondary education fulfilled diverse functions for women and society, all of which were evident in the coeducational colleges. Furthermore, educational institutions varied in their degree of functional specificity (normal schools were the most specialized, and coeducational colleges and universities were the least specialized) and in the particular functions they emphasized (normal schools stressed professional training and certification, and women's colleges stressed social-skills training and status maintenance). Although institutional theory provides an important emphasis on the multiple functions that education may fulfill in society, other theories may be suited to explaining different phases or aspects of educational expansion (Tyack 1976). Conflict or status-maintenance theories, for example, may explain limitations imposed on post-secondary education for women and the development of programs (such as home economics) and curricula that focus on traditional women's roles. Technical-function theories may explain the development of specialized teacher training. A combination of the elements of competing theories may facilitate a fuller understanding of educational functions and, hence, educational expansion (Kaestle 1976).

In conclusion, future testing of theories of educational functions and expansion should consider the important distinctions that exist among subcategories. Post-secondary educational opportunities for women in 1900 were limited, but the extent and nature of these limitations varied by type of institution and by region. Coeducational colleges and universities presented a somewhat liberated view of women's roles, but home economics and the curricula of many women's colleges emphasized the role of education in maintaining narrow, traditional, and dependent roles for women. Future research that compares higher education for men with that for women should identify the mechanisms that utilized education to maintain gender segregation in work opportunities. Many post-secondary educational opportunities for women were clearly tailored toward the traditional clustering of women's roles around children and the family; we suspect that men's post-secondary educational opportunities emphasized leadership and occupational roles. Increased attention to distinctions between men's and women's education as well as among other educational subcategories (public and private education or collegiate and professional education, for example) should advance our understanding of educational processes and of the effect of these processes on the creation and maintenance of social roles.

Appendix

The numerator of the coeducational-enrollment measure includes female students in the collegiate and graduate departments of coeducational colleges, universities, and technical schools; the numerator of the women's college-enrollment measure includes female students in the collegiate and graduate departments of colleges for women (including coordinated or affiliate colleges, such as Radcliffe); and the numerator of the normal-school enrollment measure includes female students in the normal (teacher-training) departments of normal schools.

In 1900, all forty-six states included in this study reported statistics for coeducational colleges, universities, and technical schools; twenty-five reported statistics for women's colleges; and forty-four reported statistics for normal schools. We assumed that the states for which no statistics were reported had no institutions, hence no enrollments, within a given institutional category; therefore, we assigned scores of 0 to enrollment measures for these states. We believe this assumption is safe, since an examination of additional volumes of the *Report of the Commissioner of Education* indicated that states reporting no women's colleges or normal schools in 1900 generally reported none in previous or subsequent years.

We used whites in the denominator because virtually all female college students were white in 1900 (Solomon 1985). Nonetheless, to ensure comparability between the numerators and denominators of the enrollment measures, we excluded black students from the college-enrollment figures by subtracting data on the enrollment of females aggregated on black colleges from those aggregated on all colleges (college enrollments were not reported by race). Since the overwhelming majority of black students attended segregated schools in 1900 (DuBois 1900), this procedure eliminated virtually all black students. To exclude black students from the normal-school-enrollment measure, we subtracted data on black female students in normal schools (which were reported) from data on all female students in these schools.

Special reports by the US Education Bureau on the residence of college students indicated that, overall, states tended to 'export' and 'import' an equivalent number of college students, so that the mobility of college students did not seriously affect enrollment rates. Moreover, students did not travel great distances to attend school, and states within regions tended to exchange students (such states shared similar social-structural characteristics). Although state-of-residence data contained in these special reports (the annual reports did not classify students by their state of residence) were not reported by sex, we suspect that interstate mobility was lower among female students than among all students because parents were probably reluctant to send their daughters far from home.

We also suspect that normal education was even more localized than was collegiate education.

Notes

1 Certainly these arguments also apply to men's education. Only some of the occupations men entered in 1900 required advanced training and credentials; education served functions other than career preparation for men as well, and factors other than the occupational structure influenced men's participation in higher education. Nevertheless, these functions and influences, we believe, had a stronger impact on women's education than on men's education.

2 Training in home economics may also be considered occupational preparation in the Midwest, where women's involvement in raising poultry provided an important (and stable) source of income for farm families.

3 There is some evidence that college-educated women had lower marriage rates than did noncollege-educated women, but this does not mean that college decreased women's marital prospects, as some educators at the turn of the century feared (see Solomon 1985). First, college women came predominately from white professional families who already had low rates of marriage. Thus, social-class origins, rather than education per se, may have been responsible for differences in the proportions of college women and other women who were marrying. Second, the main difference between college and noncollege women was the age at which they married: college-educated women married later than did other women, perhaps because, as Newcomer (1959) pointed out, those who married early never got to college.

4 So few women attended professional schools (schools of theology, law, medicine, dentistry, pharmacy, and veterinary medicine) in 1900 that we did not consider professional schools to be a major educational opportunity for women.

5 The Northeastern states are Connecticut, Maine, Massachusetts, New Hampshire, New Jersey, New York, Pennsylvania, Rhode Island, and Vermont; the Western states are Arizona, California, Colorado, Idaho, Montana, Nevada, New Mexico, Oregon, Utah, Washington, and Wyoming; and the South Atlantic states are Delaware, Florida, Georgia, Maryland, North Carolina, Virginia, and West Virginia.

6 Division A schools were four-year schools without preparatory departments or with small preparatory enrollments; Division B schools provided a complete course of instruction from elementary school through college (US Education Bureau 1900). Many Division B schools lost their collegiate status once regional accreditation agencies established formal criteria for college accreditation.

7 We do not mean to imply, however, that agricultural organization affected the educational consumption only of farming families or that most students who attended coeducational colleges and universities came from farming backgrounds.

8 This study is part of a larger, longitudinal study of higher education that combines data on North Dakota and South Dakota into one 'Dakota' territory and excludes data on Oklahoma, which was once part of Indian Territory, to achieve consistency across time periods.

9 To test the high correlation between two of the independent variables — farm mechanization and per capita income — we entered each variable separately before entering the variables jointly to produce the equations in Table 4.4. Comparisons of the equations in Table 4.4 and equations containing either variable (not reported here) indicated that the inclusion of one or the other or both variables altered the coefficients of the other independent variables only slightly;

the coefficients for the two variables diminished somewhat, as expected, when these variables were entered jointly instead of singly. R^2 statistics were similar for the three equations. Overall, the results were stable.

10 Since the total population of the states in 1900 was used in the analysis, tests of significance are presented for heuristic purposes only.

References

ABBOTT, E. (1910) *Women in Industry: A Study in American Economic History*, New York, D. Appleton & Co.

CARSTENSEN, V. (1962) 'A Century of Land-grant Colleges', *Journal of Higher Education* 33, pp. 30–7.

DEGLER, C. (1980) *At Odds: Women and the Family in America from the Revolution to the Present*, New York, Oxford University Press.

DUBLIN, T. (1981) *Farm to Factory*, New York, Columbia University Press.

DuBOIS, W.E.B. (1900) *The College-Bred Negro*, Atlanta, Atlanta University Press.

FULLER, B. (1983) 'Youth Job Structure and School Enrollments 1890–1920', *Sociology of Education* 56, pp. 145–54.

GUEST, A.M. (1981) 'Social Structure and US Inter-state Fertility Differentials in 1900', *Demography* 18, pp. 465–86.

GUEST, A.M. and TOLNAY, S.E. (1985) 'Agricultural Organization and Education Consumption in the United States in 1900', *Sociology of Education* 58, pp. 201–12.

GUTTENTAG, M. and SECORD, P.F. (1983) *Too Many Women? The Sex Ratio Question*, Beverly Hills, Sage Publications.

KAESTLE, C.F. (1976) 'Conflict and Consensus Revisited: Notes Toward a Reinterpretation of American Education History', *Harvard Educational Review* 46, pp. 390–6.

KENT, L. and DURBIN, N. (1984) 'From Farm to Factory or from Farm to College: Female Opportunity Structures in 1900', Paper presented at the meeting of the Pacific Sociological Association, Seattle, Washington.

KUZNETS, S., MILLER, A.R. and EASTERLIN, R.A. (1960) *Population Redistribution and Economic Growth, United States, 1870–1950: Analyses of Economic Change*, Philadelphia, American Philosophical Society.

MEYER, J.W. (1978) 'The Effects of Education as an Institution', *American Journal of Sociology* 83 (2), pp. 340–63.

NEWCOMER, M. (1959) *A Century of Higher Education for Women*, New York, Harper & Bros.

OLNECK, M.R. and LAZERSON, M. (1974) 'The School Achievement of Immigrant Children: 1900–1930', *History of Education Quarterly* 142, pp. 453–82.

RHINE, A.H. (1891) 'Women in Industry', pp. 276–321, in HARPER, A.N. (Ed.) *Women's Work in America*, New York, Henry Holt & Co.

RICHARDSON, J.G. and HATCHER, B.W. (1983) 'The Feminization of Public School Teaching 1870–1920', *Work and Occupations* 10, pp. 81–99.

RURY, J.L. (1984) 'Vocationalism for Home and Work: Women's Education in the United States, 1880–1930', *History of Education Quarterly* 24, pp. 21–44.

SACHS, C. (1983) *The Invisible Farmers*, Totowa, Rowman & Allenheld.

SOLOMON, B.M. (1985) *In the Company of Educated Women*, New Haven, Yale University Press.

SUGG, R.S., Jr. (1978) *Motherteacher: The Feminization of American Education*, Charlottesville, University of Virginia Press.

TYACK, D.B. (1976) 'Ways of Seeing: An Essay on the History of Compulsory Schooling', *Harvard Educational Review* 46, pp. 355–96.

US Bureau of the Census (1904) *Special Reports. Occupation at the Twelfth Census of the United States,* Washington, DC, US Government Printing Office.

US Bureau of the Census (1975) *Historical Statistics of the United States, Colonial Times to 1970,* Washington, DC, US Government Printing Office.

US Education Bureau (1900) *Report of the Commissioner of Education,* Vol. 2, Washington DC, US Government Printing Office.

Veysey, L.R. (1965) *The Emergence of the American University,* Chicago, University of Chicago Press.

Walters, P.B. (1984) 'Occupational and Labor Market Effects on Secondary and Post-secondary Educational Expansion in the United States, 1922–1979', *American Sociological Review* 49, pp. 659–71.

Wiebe, R.H. (1967) *The Search for Order, 1877–1920,* New York, Hill & Wang.

Woodring, P. (1962) 'A Century of Teacher Education', *School and Society* 90, pp. 211, 236–42.

Woody, T. (1966a) *A History of Women's Education in the United States,* Vol. 1, New York, Octagon Books.

Woody, T. (1966b) *A History of Women's Education in the United States,* Vol. 2, New York, Octagon Books.

Diversity, Social Control, and Resistance in Classrooms

5 Race and the Schooling of Young Girls

Linda Grant

Introduction

Schools make important contributions to intergenerational transmission of gender relations. Not only does life in schools socialize students to divergent gender roles based on their combined race-gender attributes, but schools are complex, gendered environments mirroring other sectors of society (Grant and Sleeter 1986; Kessler et al. 1985; Lesko 1988; McCarthy 1990; Thorne 1985). By living in such environments students come to view differentiation by gender and race as normal in all social relationships. School experience becomes an important anticipatory socialization for inequality in society.

In this study I focus on experiences of African-American females and white females in elementary schools. I argue that school experience encourages distinctively different forms of femininity for these two groups, even when the girls sit side by side in the same classrooms. As will become apparent, the process by which this occurs is multi-layered and involves the cumulative, sometimes contradictory, influences of many forces: students' prior experiences and values, teacher actions toward students, students' orientations toward teachers, and peer interchanges.

Research on Gender, Race/Ethnicity and Schooling

Recent research suggests that race/ethnicity intersects with gender in schools, encouraging divergent forms of feminities and masculinities for students of differing attributes (L. Grant 1984, 1985; Hudson 1984; Irvine 1990; Lesko 1988; Luttrell 1989; McCarthy 1990; Moore 1983, 1988; Schofield 1982; Scott-Jones and Clark 1986). A useful starting point for analysis is Kessler et al.'s (1985, p. 184) concept of gender regimes: 'patterns of processes that construct varying forms of masculinity and femininity, array them hierarchically in terms of power and prestige, and create sexual divisions of labor within schools'.

Several components of this definition are important here. First, schools create and maintain multiple forms of masculinities and feminities that exist simultaneously, often in contest with one another. Frequently race/ethnic status is the base around which alternative forms of gender identities are articulated (Fuller

1980; Furlong 1984; L. Grant 1984, 1985, forthcoming; Moore 1988; Mullard 1983; Scott-Jones and Clark 1986). Forms of masculinity and femininity are variably supported by meaningful others, such as teachers, administrators, or student peer groups.

Second, gender regimes result from behaviors of multiple actors and are dynamically constituted. Although there are regularities in experiences of different race-gender subgroups in schools, gender relations emerge from ongoing interactions. Male and female students of varying racial groups experience what McCarthy (1990) terms 'asynchronies', or differential experience based on race in the acquisition of gender identities via schooling. Learning gender in school therefore is not a straightforward process. Students of certain race-gender configurations might be nudged toward certain forms of gender identities, but outcomes are always uncertain. Students choose among competing forms and innovate novel responses in forming gender identities and the gender regime of schools (Lesko 1988; Roman 1988; Thorne 1985 and this volume). Understanding the process and its impact requires contextual study of gender construction in schools.

Focus of this Study

Although some recent studies have probed construction of gender relations in schools, most work has been carried out at the middle or secondary school level (see, for example, Clifton et al. 1986; Connell 1986; Gaskell 1985; Eder 1985; Eder and Parker 1987; Patchen 1982). This study focuses on processes of gender in elementary schools, which have been studied less, and concentrates on girls, whose experiences have been given less attention than those of males (Eder 1985; Hudson 1984). It also explores the combined effects of race and gender on girls' experiences, extending prior research that typically considers only one race, and in doing so concentrates on schools in the United States. Many studies of classroom interaction and gender have been carried out in non-US, often English, Canadian or Australian, schools (for example, Fuller 1980; Gaskell 1985; Kessler et al. 1985). British and US schools are organized differently and have different histories of coeducation, and it is unclear whether gender relations are similar across systems. In the US there have been extensive studies of gender stereotyping in the curriculum and in teacher behavior (see Brophy 1985; Sadker and Sadker 1986 for reviews), but gendered social relations in schools and their effects have been analyzed less often.

Data and Methods

Research Settings

To explore schooling experiences of African-American and white girls, I observed desegregated first- and second-grade rooms in two regions of the country. Table 5.1 summarizes the region, grade level, and teacher race of each observed room. (All names in the table and text are pseudonyms.) The first observations took place in the early 1980s in working-class communities in the

Table 5.1   Teacher Race, Grade Level, and Region for Observed Rooms.

Teacher	Race	Grade	Region
Avery	White	1	Midwest
Maxwell	White	1	Midwest
Delby	White	1	Midwest
Todd	Black	1	Midwest
Horton	Black	1	Midwest
Douglas	Black	1	Midwest
Carson*	White	1	South
Lloyd*	White	1	South
Hilton	White	1	South
Jordan	Black	2	South
Parker	Black	2	South

* Most southern teachers were observed for two successive years. However, Carson was observed for 1988–89 and Lloyd for 1989–90, when Carson was reassigned to another grade level. Lloyd was recommended by colleagues and the principal as the teacher most similar to Carson in experience, style, and classroom organization, and had occasionally shared classroom activities with Carson the previous year.

Midwest. Six, first grades were observed over several months for a total of between twenty and thirty hours each. Three teachers (Todd, Horton and Douglas) were African-American females and three (Maxwell, Avery and Delby) were white females. When observations were complete, I interviewed teachers about the academic performance and social relationships of each child in the class. Further details about methods are provided in Grant (1984, 1985, forthcoming).

The second set of observations, carried out in the late 1980s, took place in a rural, but rapidly urbanizing, desegregated primary school in the South. I observed first- and second-grade rooms of three teachers (Hilton, Jordan and Parker) for two years. I observed the first grade class of Carson for one year and that of Lloyd for the next year when Carson was unexpectedly reassigned to another grade level. The principal and colleagues identified Lloyd as the teacher most similar to Carson in experience, style, and class organization. Hilton, Carson, and Lloyd, the first-grade teachers, were white females. Jordan and Parker, the second-grade teachers, were African-American females. Observations of each room covered several months, totaling between ten and fifteen hours in each. Teachers were interviewed each year as described above. I also attended some meetings of teacher and administrative planning teams and interviewed the principal.

All but one class (Douglas's) were in schools with African-American enrollments of 45–65 percent. Douglas's room, in a 95-percent black school, contained no white females. In all rooms, virtually all other students were white, with no other minority making up 1 percent or more of enrollment.

Data Collection and Analysis

I carried out nonparticipant observations, interacting minimally with teachers and students (Gold 1969). Most students paid little attention to me after the first few visits, casting me into common roles such as student teacher or parent visitor. Jot notes taken during observation sessions lasting 25–110 minutes were expanded into time-sequential, detailed ethnographic field notes, usually within 24 hours. Field notes from observations and interview transcripts were analyzed inductively to explore regularities and contrasts in the experiences of African-American and white females (see Glaser and Strauss 1967; Goetz and LeCompte 1984; Strauss 1987). Themes were derived separately for midwestern and southern schools, then compared across settings. Despite separations in space and time, patterns emerging for white and African-American girls in the two regions were surprisingly consistent. Also, in both regions, a teacher's race had minimal effects on the experiences of white or African-American girls, perhaps because the teachers worked in white-controlled districts, which might have reflected white cultural norms and subtly pressured African-American teachers to act in a similar fashion to their white counterparts.

As Schofield (1982) observes, searching for themes in the experiences of student subgroups focuses attention on regularities and minimizes nonconforming examples. In the remainder of this chapter the distinctive features of each racial group's experiences will be emphasized, but evidence will also be provided of variation within groups and commonalities in the experiences of females, regardless of race. These alternative forms make clear that students grapple with gender in schools, and do not simply conform with predetermined patterns advocated by teachers, school authorities, or dominant student subgroups.

Social Location and School Experience

I have argued previously (Grant 1984, 1985) that students of varying race-gender configurations occupy different social locations in classrooms. The different social locations of white and African-American females in these rooms are critical to an analysis of their position in the classroom gender order. In Goffman's terms (1959, p. 75), each racial group occupied a different 'place'. He defines place as 'not a material thing to be possessed and then displayed', but rather 'a pattern of appropriate conduct, coherent, embellished, and well articulated'. Hereafter I use the terms 'place' and 'social location' interchangeably to denote characteristic patterns of involvement and interaction of each student subgroup.

White girls were considerably more teacher-oriented than African-American females, spending more time interacting with teachers than with peers. African-American girls had more contacts, and contacts with more diverse classmates, than any other race-gender group. The different social locations of these groups in the observed classrooms contributed to their experiences in both regions. In most rooms, white girls were encouraged to develop both academic and social skills, while African-American girls received greater support for developing social rather than academic potential.

In this chapter, the place in classrooms of white and African-American females will first be contrasted, illuminating the dynamics that locate them differently in the classroom gender order. The way in which classroom social location supports differential forms of femininity by race will then be analyzed, and finally the implications of girls' school experiences for their adult roles and for all students' emerging understandings of gender relations in social life will be considered.

As will become apparent below, the research design and my attributes as a white female led to a more complete illumination of the gendered experiences of white than of African-American females. Teacher behaviors, one of the more overt and observable components of classroom social life, were more central in the experience of white as compared with African-American girls. Also, affinity of attributes and the more adult-centered orientation of white girls in comparison with African-Americans gave me greater access to peer networks of white than African-American girls. These orientations paralleled girls' behaviors toward teachers of both races (see below). Thus, as many commentators have noted (see in particular Collins 1990), my own race and gender identity necessarily influenced my angle of vision and the phenomena that were and were not observable in the setting.

Ties with Teachers

White Girls

Key elements in white girls' social location were their close ties with teachers and the insularity of their peer relations. I have reported that in the Midwest white girls in most rooms averaged more contacts with teachers than with peers (Grant 1985). Three of four southern teachers' rooms showed similar patterns.[1] The race of the teacher had only minimal effects on white girls' actions. African-American females, and males of both races, had substantially more contacts with peers than with either black or white teachers. Other pupils noted white girls' closeness to teachers, sometimes calling them 'pets' or 'teacher-lovers'. Teachers referred to some of these students privately as 'would-be pets' or 'brown-noses', terms never applied to other race-gender students.

When white girls interacted with peers they had a propensity to stick with other white girls, whatever room they were in. This pattern was very possibly strengthened by the various forms of ability grouping used in all rooms. White girls were over-represented in high-ability groups relative to their proportions of enrollment, and thus spent most academic work time primarily with other white girls. Academic groupings carried over to free time peer relations more for them than for other race-gender groups. In a pattern similar to that reported by Eder (1985) for popular white middle-school girls, students in the elementary schools referred to white girls as 'snobbish' or 'stuck-up'. Insularity was less pronounced among white southern girls from rural areas, who interacted frequently with those white boys who had been preschool playmates in isolated areas where they had limited choices of playmates.

The centrality of the teacher to white girls was apparent in daily routines. White girls in Avery's room attempted to draw her into playground activities almost every day. A group of three white girls in Maxwell's room repeatedly played 'reading group' during recess and free time, reviewing class routines and imitating Maxwell's mannerisms. The teacher role was coveted and competed for. White girls in Carson's class traded tidbits of information about the teacher's personal life. In Jordan's and Todd's rooms they closely observed and mimicked the teachers' hair and clothing styles.

As Best (1983) has noted, many white girls appeared to have entered school 'primed for the archetypal feminine role', and this might have contributed to their careful observance of, and obedience to, the teacher. However, teachers reinforced close teacher-student ties. In interviews with them, teachers offered more details about the out-of-school lives of white girls than of other pupils. In all but one room teachers chatted more frequently and longer with white girls than with others about life beyond school, offering these children more information about the teachers' lives. Delby told Christina (white) that her husband was dissatisfied with his job and seeking another. Hilton shared pictures of a relative's wedding with Marjorie and Jean (both white). Todd confessed to Gillian (white) that she was 'always nervous about what to wear' on parent visit days and smiled broadly when Gillian assured her that she looked 'lovely'. These exchanges suggested that white girls were more central to teachers than were others, and more often admitted to colleague/friend roles.

These interchanges reflected, but also reinforced, personal bonds between teachers and white girls. The girls who participated had ample opportunities to demonstrate academic skills, polish interactional skills with adults, and receive and dispense nurturance and support. As such, chats reinforced academic and social skills.

Another means by which teachers strengthened ties with white girls was by assigning them most of the high-visibility, high-responsibility 'trusted lieutenant' tasks, such as tutoring or orienting a new student. Trusted lieutenants acquired and maintained their roles by demonstrating loyalty and deference. Teachers backed their authority, when needed. Horton always chose Anna (white) to monitor classmates' behavior. She once asked Anna to watch pupils at a coloring table while Horton worked with a reading group. Horton told Anna: 'If they talk, give them one warning, then send them back to their desks.' Following directions closely, Anna first warned, then sent to his desk Matt (white male). When Matt protested to Horton, she told him: 'Anna was in charge and you should have paid attention to her.' Students of other status configurations could less reliably count on the support of teachers in Horton's room and others to back their authority with peers.

White girls also demonstrated loyalty when other students challenged teachers. With the exception of a few white girls who played a 'bad girl' role (discussed more fully below), white girls were the least likely students to challenge teachers about academic or disciplinary issues. More commonly, they aided teachers in turning back the challenges of other students. When Norris (white) and James (African-American) tried to persuade Jordan that they had already served a mandated recess detention, Ginger (white) intervened and told Jordan: 'They did not. They only stayed [in another room] ten minutes yesterday, so they still have time left.' Tricia (white) in Lloyd's room vigorously defended the teacher when Maggie (African-American) challenged her about the location of an historical marker.

White girls challenged teachers with regularity only in two black-teacher rooms in the Midwest. The girls might have been more willing to challenge an Afro-American than a white teacher, but in these two cases the African-American teachers specifically encouraged challenges around academic matters. Todd urged children to 'use their own good minds' and to 'talk with me about things you don't like or don't agree with'. Similarly, Horton told her students: 'I may mark something wrong because the answer is different from the one I had in mind, but if you think it makes sense, come and talk to me. If you can convince me that it makes sense, then I'll mark it right.' In these rooms, challenging represented conformity to rules, not defiance. The contextual effect of challenging rules was stronger for white girls than for other students. These African-American teachers, more so than other teachers, might have pressed white girls toward the autonomous learning styles not characteristic of girls but important to attainment, especially at higher levels of the educational system (Wilkinson and Marrett 1985).

White girls also were overchosen, relative to their proportions in these rooms, as exemplars of both positive and negative behavior. Parker told the class: 'I want everyone to learn math facts as fast as Janelle [white] did.' Conversely, Avery responded strongly when Maura (white) returned from lunch talking noisily. Avery told the class angrily: 'Wonderful, Maura. You've just shown everyone the *wrong* way to come back from lunch.... Walking around the room, mouth flapping. If anybody wants to break all the rules, just look at Maura.... Then we won't have any recess at all.'

White girls were in many rooms the focal students around which appropriate academic and social behavior was defined. When teachers needed an exemplar of appropriate or inappropriate academic performance or behavior, this was the student subgroup to which they turned most often. The pattern reflected and reinforced teacher-white girl contacts and also marked these students to their peers as being closely tied to teachers and class rules.

African-American Girls

African-American girls were more differentially located than white girls vis-à-vis teachers and peers. Although they did not shun contacts with teachers as many African-American males did, they approached teachers only when there were specific needs, and did not hang around to court attention or chat with teachers as many white girls did. Three teachers (Todd, Delby, and Lloyd) attempted to engage African-American girls in chats, but these chats were shorter and less personal than these teachers' informal interchanges with white girls in their classes. African-American girls spent relatively greater proportions of their time with peers rather than teachers and interacted with a more diverse race-gender group than any other students in all but Avery's and Jordan's rooms.[2] This pattern was partially supported by African-American girls' placement most typically in middle-ability instructional groups. In nearly all rooms, these groups had the most heterogeneous race and gender members, and were also the largest. Placements gave African-American girls contacts and common experience with many different pupils. Unlike white girls, they interacted with students whose relationships with teachers ranged from warm to hostile.

Unlike white girls, most African-American girls interacted with some students who were not well liked by teachers. Nor were they as fearful as were white girls of interacting with students who threatened verbal or physical hostility. African-American girls rarely provoked hostility, but defended themselves from such attacks, while white girls were more apt to retreat or appeal to the teacher for aid (Grant 1983). These patterns might have been bolstered by themes in the parental socialization of African-American girls which, as some authors note, stress taking care of others and defending oneself (Ladner 1971; Lewis 1977; Reid 1972).

Whereas white girls were perceived by their peers as loyal to teachers, and frequently operated in peer relations to convey influence from the teacher, African-American girls had more complex roles. Although they sometimes conveyed information and influence from the teacher to students with whom she had little direct contact, they also advocated with teachers on behalf of their peers. Thus, white girls transmitted information primarily from teachers to peers, but African-American girls operated as messengers and transmitted influence in both directions.

Many teacher contacts initiated by African-American girls, but virtually none by white girls, were on behalf of peers rather than self. Millie (African-American), a high-achieving and well-liked student in Horton's room, ignored Horton's warning not to interrupt her as she worked with a reading group, and approached the teacher four times in twenty minutes. Although Millie was sharply reprimanded ('Didn't I tell you to stay *put*?'), she persisted until she got academic aid needed by two male peers. Todd characterized Meredith (African-American) as a 'busybody', noting that Meredith's academic performance would improve if she concentrated on her work rather than monitoring others. Lloyd characterized Ramona (African-American) as 'our little social worker' and asked her, 'Who's got a problem now?' when the child approached her during time she should have been working on a math paper. Teachers, however, generally responded in a manner that encouraged further approaches. Lloyd chided Ramona ('You need to keep your bottom glued to that seat and not get up again or you won't finish'), but she also smiled at her and told her she was 'sweet'. Although reprimanded by Horton, Millie was thanked by the beneficiaries of her actions ('Way to go, Millie').

These contacts revealed that African-American girls had easy access to the teacher, allowing them to act as effective agents on behalf of others, but the students also took personal risks of reprimands, embarrassment, and interruption of work to aid others. Teachers responded ambivalently to such actions; even when teachers were punitive, peers were frequently grateful and provided alternative sources of rewards. Peers also pressed African-American girls to represent them in contacts with teachers.

African-American girls sometimes negotiated and took risks to settle peer disputes. Veronica (African-American), in Parker's room, settled a vigorous verbal and physical playground battle between four African-American boys and an interracial group of girls. In negotiating rules for the shared use of a play space, Veronica was punched in the ear by Leonard (African-American), told 'Your face looks ugly, real ugly now' by Denise (white), and punished with loss of recess the next day by the white teacher aide in charge. However, she ended a dispute among sixteen students, and her comment to me ('See how I did with that?') showed that she derived satisfaction from her actions.

Elsewhere (Grant 1984, forthcoming) I have provided detailed analysis of the 'go-between' role played by black girls and argued that it represents a critical, though unappreciated, integrating mechanism in desegregated classrooms. Although the role could center on academic or nonacademic issues, it usually focused on the latter; African-American girls became emotional caretakers for other students.

Go-betweens appeared in all but one midwestern room (Todd's) and in all southern rooms, and the role was invariably played by an African-American girl. The role required accessibility to teachers, yet it also required perceived independence from them so that contacts with students estranged from teachers would not be jeopardized. Since the role involved the transmission of information and influence from teachers to students, students to teachers, and among peers, it also required the particular set of social ties exhibited by African-American girls more than those shown by other students. The role derives from, but also reinforces, African-American girls' social locations: on the margins of the teacher's sphere of influence and on the margins of numerous peer subgroups, but not wholly involved in any of these.

Enforcement, another common role for African-American females, illustrated the complex location of African-American girls. Unlike trusted lieutenants, enforcers spontaneously assumed the role of gaining peer compliance with class rules. In context, African-American girls' enforcements appeared to serve many purposes: aid and loyalty demonstrations to the teacher; bids for approval; exertion of power over peers; and protection of peers. An example of the latter was Camille (African-American) in Todd's room, who admonished classmates at her work table to 'look busy' as the teacher approached to check work. White girls in middle reading groups also sometimes took on the enforcer role, but it was more prevalent among black girls. It seemed to represent one means, other than high academic achievement, of gaining the teachers' positive attention. Whatever their motivation, they assisted teachers with social control of the class.

African-American girls occasionally pressed teachers for appointments as tutors or rule enforcers, and teachers sometimes allowed them to exert authority over students who were problematic to teachers. Avery, for example, permitted Diana (African-American) to drill Jonathan (white) on printing. Jonathan was frequently unresponsive, not even attempting work assigned by Avery. Diana tapped Jonathan's knuckles sharply with a pencil whenever he ignored her orders to begin work, and was more successful than Avery in getting him to complete his assignments. When Hilton let Martha (African-American) supervise cleanup by three frequently-reprimanded African-American pupils, she told me with a wink: 'That little lady will whip them into shape faster than I can, that's for sure.'

In most midwestern and all southern rooms teachers gave less feedback, either positive or negative, to African-American girls for their academic work than to other students. Afro-American girls in most rooms fell outside the polar groups who got the most teacher feedback for work: academic superstars (usually white students) who contributed to the teachers' reputations as talented instructors, and low achievers (often African-American males) who threatened to disrupt classroom order. The average-performing African-American females fell outside these extremes and garnered little teacher notice for academic work. Other studies have also found that African-American girls receive less feedback for academic work than other students and appear to be more invisible from the perspective of their teachers (D'Amico 1986; Byalick and Bershoff 1974; Irvine 1985, 1990).

The roles played by African-American girls derived from, but also elaborated, their peripheral involvement in many class social networks. These girls had positive and negative contacts with teachers, and with a range of competing peer groups. They exercised influence, but were also frequent targets of physical and verbal abuse. While the daily experiences of white girls encouraged the development of both social and academic skills, African-American girls' experiences were less balanced and put a premium on social, rather than academic skills. They received less explicit reward or recognition for academic skill (fewer assignments as trusted lieutenants or placements in high-ability groups), but greater formal and informal encouragement to take on complex social roles that developed negotiating skills but detracted from time on the task in hand and risked criticism from teachers and peers.

Teacher Perceptions

Patterns discernible in teachers' interactions with white and African-American girls also appeared, through the teacher interviews, in the perceptions the teachers had of these students' academic and social skills. When asked to rate the reading and math performance of students as above average, average, or below average, teachers placed white girls more frequently than other students in the above average category for ability. African-American girls were most commonly placed in average categories, except by Jordan who placed them similarly to white girls in the above average category in reading both years she was interviewed.[3] Teacher race was otherwise unrelated to their assessments of the skills of students of certain race-gender groups.

Assessed Skills and Track Placements

Assessments for African-American girls were higher overall than those for African-American boys and similar to those for white boys. A notable difference in teachers' assessments of white boys and black girls were their statements that some white boys identified as average performers were bright but immature students whose performances could improve with maturity. Only Carson stated such an expectation for one African-American girl. Teachers might thus watch boys more carefully than black girls for signs of improved performance or interpret ambiguous behavior as signs of improvement.

Rarely was an African-American girl mentioned as a particularly outstanding student. Only one teacher (Horton) singled out a black female (Millie) as 'one of my best students', an accolade usually reserved for white students. Similarly, only one teacher (Hilton) singled out an African-American female (Geneva), for having a special talent (outstanding computer skills), though most teachers singled out students of other race-gender groups for outstanding skills such as artistic talent, a sharp mathematical mind, or musical aptitude.

Track placements typically followed assessments of skills, but girls of both races were advantaged over boys in doubtful cases. Maxwell placed Abigail (white) in the higher of two reading groups because 'she seemed mature, a hard worker.... And girls will often try to keep up. She had friends [in the higher group], and she really wanted to keep up with them.' Similarly, Parker placed Shirley (African-American) in the higher of two possible reading groups because 'even though she might be a little shaky [academically] she works hard, is pleasant ... is a real good example to [classmates]'. Boys whose skills were similarly rated were apt to be tracked downward, lest their 'immaturity' drag down students in higher groups.[4] In these instances, girls of both races gained academic advantages via acceptable feminine behavior.

Despite some similarities in assessments of white girls and African-American girls, there were for most teachers distinctive patterns of perceptions of academic and social skills based on students' race. These variations were apparent in teachers' responses to two open-ended questions about each child: 'Tell me about [child's name] academic skills and performance,' and 'Tell me about [child's name] relationships with other students in the class.' All teachers except Avery completed interviews for each year in which their class was observed. The open-ended questions allowed discernment of the direction of the evaluation as well as the criteria deemed relevant in assessing each group. Student's race, but not teacher's race, appeared to affect the mix of academic and nonacademic criteria used to assess the pupils' *academic* skills; the attributions made about cognitive and social maturity; and the extent to which pupils were dichotomized as good girls or bad girls.

White Girls

Criteria for assessment.   Each teacher had a distinctive skew in the extent to which she focused on academic versus nonacademic criteria in assessing *academic* skills. Academic criteria are comments about work quality, habits, or pace. Examples were: 'I can always expect a good paper from him,' or 'She works slowly, but thoroughly.' Examples of nonacademic criteria were comments such as 'She's always beautifully dressed,' or 'His family has had a lot of problems this year.' Each teacher relied on a particularistic mix of academic and nonacademic criteria as bases for evaluations, but there were nevertheless variations within students' race-gender group by teachers (see Grant, 1984, for detailed data). Horton was an exception; her assessments of academic skills of all students contained few references to nonacademic criteria.

Most teachers used relatively higher ratios of academic than nonacademic criteria in assessing skills of boys of both races. Assessments of African-American girls (see below) emphasized nonacademic criteria over academic. Assessments of white girls mixed academic and nonacademic criteria. The white girls rated most favorably were those combining intellectual skill with conforming behavior.

The mixture of academic and nonacademic criteria is apparent in Maxwell's comments about Clarissa (white):

I knew about half an hour after the year began that she was going to be a top student. She does everything neatly and on time and obeys rules and sets a good example. She reads beautifully, gets along with everybody.

Similar themes appeared in Todd's description of Gillian (white), identified as a student who 'just has it all'. Todd continued: 'Just a joy to have in the class. I know I can always count on her. She always knows what to do. I never need to remind her.' Jordan's comments about Sheila (white) were comparable:

I have no doubt that she'll stay in [gifted track classes]. She's always careful, cooperative. She works very hard and is equally strong in reading and math. Pleasant. All the students like her. All the teachers, too.

When teachers' assessments of white girls were more negative, they focused more heavily on nonacademic criteria. The implication was that the behaviorally nonconforming girls would ultimately do poorly in school, regardless of academic abilities. An example was Delby's comments about Audra (white) in response to the query about academic skill:

> All I say is that it's good that we're living in an era of women's lib. She wants to be a bronco buster, can you imagine that? She wears jeans all the time, always too big, hair a mess. I don't think I could get a comb through it even if she would stand still long enough for me to try. I just don't know what will become of her. On top of everything else, she never seems to listen to what I say.

Only after two prompts did Delby make any comment related to academics: 'She performs about average, I'd have to say. It will be a wonder if she can keep that up.'

Parker believed that Karen (white) was a capable student but would do poorly later in school, because Karen used obscene and sexually-suggestive language. Parker noted that she had thought of referring Karen for testing for gifted classes but 'wasn't all that sure about her ability, because of that mouth.' Parker did refer for gifted testing two white males whom notes showed used similar language as frequently as Karen did.

For white girls, then, inappropriate behavior was a disqualifying criterion, seen as the precursor to unacceptable outcomes of schooling even when academic skills were sound. Delamont (1983) argues that British elementary school girls are encouraged toward 'dual conformity'. Like males, girls are expected to perform well academically but also must simultaneously display behavioral conformity not required of males. These teachers' assessments suggested a similar expectation, in which white girls thought to be capable students had to display both intellectual competence and conformity. Lack of behavioral conformity was sufficient to bring academic competence into question.

Maturity expectations. Teachers expected cognitive maturity and 'readiness for school' from white females more than from other pupils. Some set performance expectations for the entire class based on enrollments of white girls. Maxwell noted that her current class performed better than her previous year's class, but added that she had 'many more girls' this year. She did not explicitly mention race, but then named five white girls whom she considered promising students. Conversely, Avery predicted she would have a difficult year when she saw 'how many boys I had on the roll'.

The phrases 'mature' and/or 'ready for school' appeared in more than one-third of the teachers' assessments of white girls, nearly twice the ratio as for any other group. Teachers also explicitly linked cognitive maturity to high performance expectations, as in Carson's comments about Tammy (white):

> She was read to a lot at home. The reading level was at least about grade two or three, I'd guess, at the beginning [of first grade]. Kept up with it. Concentrated and behaved and stuck with it in a real mature way, you know what I mean?

Jordan said that when she first met Paula (white) she questioned whether the child was older than most classmates (she was not) because:

> not just because she's bigger, but she was mature and had work habits you think of as more likely in a third or fourth grader. [I: Such as?] Oh, she put things together, like linked up programs on television and films or readings we'd done in class and talked about them with mom and dad and [older sibling] and wrote a lot, too, on her own. Very solid and mature.

Extreme judgments, good girls and bad girls. Although overall teachers' perceptions of white girls were more favorable than their views of other students, teachers placed narrower tolerance limits around judgments of white girls. They tended to characterize them dichotomously as good girls or bad girls, paralleling stereotypes applied to adult females (Fox 1977). Seventeen bad girls, all white, emerged in observed rooms. The pattern did not appear in Todd's room; she invariably made situational attributions about students' negative behavior. Other rooms had one, or occasionally two, identifiable bad girls.

Bad girls had conflictual relationships with teachers and challenged them much more often than did other white girls. They also faced substantially more verbal and physical hostility from peers than did other white girls. Teachers often used them as exemplars of inappropriate behavior, as in the example involving Maura quoted above. By contrasting their behaviors with good girls, teachers made acceptable and unacceptable forms of feminine behavior clear to all students. Moreover, bad girls and good girls conflicted with one another, and received variable support from student subgroups. These displays also illustrated alternative forms of femininity with different bases of support in classrooms.

Such an incident occurred in Avery's class, when 'bad girl' Maura (white) raised her hand to correct Avery as the teacher wrote 'lunchroom rules' on the board. Maura told her she had omitted a period. Avery scowled, but made the change. Maura then begged to add a rule of her own: 'Don't pour soup over somebody else's head.' Maura's rule amused classmates, who shouted out variations, such as 'Don't put catsup on somebody's arm.' Good girl student Maribeth (white), a favorite of the teacher, defended Avery, telling Maura: 'That's the stupidest rule I ever heard. Who would do that?' Each student had her respective groups of peer supporters, backing her role in the incident.

Maura's challenge violated teacher-defined norms about appropriate roles for white female students. Maura challenged the validity and usefulness of the exercise. The fact that some peers supported her made it more threatening to the teacher and to peers who disagreed with Maura's action. Maura offered a new definition of the situation (This is a silly exercise) to compete with the teacher's preferred definition (This is a serious lesson). Maura was reprimanded by Avery and Maribeth not for her intellectual competence but for her behavioral nonconformity.

In the southern rooms, especially the second grades, peer groups consisting mostly of behaviorally-conforming white females taunted bad girl females to their faces and behind their backs. The more-conforming girls used labels for the 'bad girls' suggestive of sexual deviance (slut, whore). The bad girls were also targets of much more verbal and physical aggression from male classmates than good white girls usually received. On occasion, teachers and peers blamed them as instigators of aggression, even when they were victims. One day in Avery's room as Maura worked on an assignment at her table Raymond (white) poked her so hard with a pencil that blood trickled through the sleeve of her sweater. When Maura cried out in pain, teacher Avery called back: 'Well, Maura, if you would just concentrate on your work, we wouldn't have any more trouble at your table.' The teacher's response implied that Maura was responsible for her victimization and that she had deserved, or failed to control, male aggression. Studies of older, nonconforming females show that those not conforming to dominant forms of femininity are seen as 'deserving' male aggression (Lesko 1988, Roman 1988), but such patterns have not been reported previously for students so young.

The emergence of the good girl/bad girl dichotomy illustrates the complexity of the classroom gender order and the influence of multiple actors on its construction and maintenance. Teachers' expectations of. greater cognitive maturity for white girls, compared with other students, led them to read these students' behaviors as reflections of stable character traits, rather than immaturity (a common attribution about white boys) or cultural deprivation or family problems (a common attribution about African-Americans of both genders). The tendency is most visible when contrasting teachers' comments about white girls and boys of either race whose behavior displeased teachers.

Incidents occurring days apart in Delby's room provided a striking example. Each involved Delby's discovery that one child possessed materials reported missing by a classmate. Delby offered strikingly different private accounts of the behavior of Ralph (African-American) and Candace (white). She described Ralph as having home problems and 'acting out, and being a little forgetful about our rules about borrowing'. In contrast, Delby described Candace as 'a very sneaky person', and said she had to 'keep my eye on her all the time'. Delby recalled, when asked, that each child had been found possessing classmates' belongings twice before.

Horton demoted two students a reading group for poor performance. She made different attributions about the causes of Patrick's (white) and Sally's (white) declining performances. She said Patrick 'had ability', but lacked support for scholarship from his family, who spent a great deal of time on karate and failed to monitor his homework. She hoped that the demotion would 'wake him up' and 'make him start working like he could be working'. She said of Sally:

> I'm not sure what it is about her. She's been a frustration to me. She's bright enough ... but she's lazy and willful. All she wants to do all day is jabber away with her friends. Sometimes she gives me the most spiteful look when I tell her to get back to work.

The account also hints that Horton viewed Sally as showing intentional resistance by performing less well than Horton thought she could. Sally's intrinsic qualities, and not her parents or home life, are seen as the root of her poor performance.

Other teachers described bad girls in ways similar to Horton's characterization of Sally, using terms such as 'willful', 'spiteful', 'a real time-waster if I ever saw one', 'a slick manipulator', or 'a real little sexpot'. Particularly striking were teachers' tendencies to use sexually related language and themes in discussing bad girls, even though these were first and second graders. These images paralleled those present in peer criticism of 'bad girl' white females. Hilton, after complaining of poor work habits and misbehavior while discussing Rochelle's (white) academic skills, added: 'I taught her two sisters. They both were pregnant by the time they were 14 or 15 and that's probably what will happen with [Rochelle].'

'Bad girl' white females did not lack intellectual competence. Only two were identified by teachers as below average achievers, with nearly half ranked as above average. Teachers were considerably less punitive with low achieving, but behaviorally conforming, white females than with the bad girls. They also were more tolerant of boys' misbehaviors. Although nearly all of them reprimanded boys of both races for behavior more often than girls, they did not make negative character attributions about many misbehaving boys. Teachers implicitly demanded intellectual competence combined with behavioral deference from white girls.

The close ties between teachers and white girls, at least partially encouraged by teachers' actions, signaled the centrality of these students in teachers' minds. Teachers expected white girls to be good students and to bolster their images of themselves as effective teachers. The capable, but nonconforming, bad girls might thus have been especially frustrating to them and therefore drew harsh responses. The dynamic created, however, magnified the nonconformity and alienation of students so labeled. By the end of the year Maura in Avery's room sat alone in a teacher-assigned desk, while classmates sat at tables of six to eight students. Maura completed less and less academic work as the year progressed, and her nonconforming behavior escalated. Toward the end of the year on three occasions she muttered under her breath: 'I hate school; I hate Miss Avery.' At the end of the term, Avery recommended her demotion from a top to a middle-ranking reading group, even though standardized tests indicated she read above the ninety-sixth percentile for students at her grade level. Avery said she 'didn't have the right work habits' to remain in the top group.

African-American Females

Academic skills. Teacher perceptions of African-American girls' academic skills had a mundane quality about them, as reflected in remarks about Carrie (African-American): 'She's about average in everything. Her work habits are good. She's very neat and quiet.... No problem at all. She usually doesn't have much to say.' Lloyd described Barbara (African-American) as 'Average, average, average, in all aspects of work. Very nice and sweet, though.'

The skew toward discussion of nonacademic, rather than academic, criteria in teacher assessments of academic skills was even more pronounced for black girls. This occurred whether evaluations were positive or negative. Thus, in response to the question about the academic skills of middle-achieving Leona (African-American), Todd praised her extensively for being a helper: 'She always picks things up, helps out other students.' In response to the same question about Doris (African-American), a low achiever, Todd described her as 'a pleasure to have in the classroom', and speculated that her sunny personality led to classmates treating her better than other low achievers and that 'that will be pretty important to her later on'. Asked about Gail's (African-American) academic work, Hilton gave a detailed, six-minute history of Gail's troubled family life, saying nothing about her academic skill.

Comments such as 'shy', 'quiet', 'no trouble at all', were common in mid-western and southern teachers' characterizations of African-American girls, more so than in their characterizations of other students. Three African-American teachers — Horton, Jordan, and Parker — gave higher ratios of attention to black girls' academic work than other teachers, especially when they discussed the higher-achieving African-American girls in their rooms.

Except for Horton, who stuck strictly to academic criteria for all students, these teachers intermingled academic and nonacademic criteria in a manner similar to that used by most teachers to describe white girls. This was one of the few effects observed that appeared to be related to race of teacher. The observation is consistent with recent work suggesting that African-American teachers more than white may be alert to 'secondary-generation discrimination', or failure on the part of teachers to recognize academic capabilities of minority students (Meier, Stewart and England 1989).

For most teachers, however, African-American girls' social deeds, rather than their intellectual ones, appeared to be central in their evaluations. Overall, this subgroup of students received more praise than any other for social and personal attributes, both in interviews and in observations. Although African-American girls overall performed as well or better than most classmates, only a few were among the students recognized by teachers as intellectual stars. Social deeds thus became the most reliable means for African-American girls in most rooms to capture their teachers' favorable attentions. This differed from patterns observed for white girls, where both intellectual skill and social deeds were noted in teachers' evaluations and feedback.

Maturity expectations. Teachers also perceived African-American girls to be mature, though, in contrast with their remarks about white girls, they emphasized social maturity rather than cognitive ability or 'readiness for school'. Furthermore, although they expressed some admiration for certain forms of social maturity shown by African-American females, they did not necessarily see this maturity as supportive or predictive of high academic achievement.

Douglas praised 6-year-old Edna (African-American) for feeding and dressing three preschool siblings each morning so that her single-parent mother, a nurse working the night shift, could get needed sleep. Douglas added, 'Of course, all that responsibility doesn't give her much time to concentrate on schoolwork.' Maxwell worried about what she termed a precocious maturity among four African-American girls in her class. During recess these children played house, enacting adult scenarios, and during show and tell they bragged of assuming adult-like responsibilities, such as babysitting or preparing a large meal. Maxwell commented:

> In one sense they are grown up, but it's not all good. Sometimes they don't have any time to be children.... When I want them to pay attention in math, they're passing around lipstick or giggling about who kissed whom on the bus yesterday.

She speculated that the girls would be better off if they played more childlike games during play time and concentrated on work in class. She hoped that their parents would encourage them to 'be children'.

Parker worried that Elena (African-American) might be 'too helpful' to her mother and speculated that in the future Elena, who now was doing well, might be pressured to work too many hours or leave school early to help with family finances. Parker added: 'And that would be a shame, because she's very smart and eager [about learning].' In reality, they prospect of an after-school paid job or early school leaving was years in the future for seven-year-old Elena, but Parker was already concerned about possible limits to her academic career. Teachers rarely expressed such concerns about white girls, regardless of their family circumstances.

Hilton referred to three African-American girls in her class as 'mini-teenagers'. They also displayed preoccupation with adult social/romantic roles. Hilton occasionally encouraged the behavior ('Who's your boyfriend this week, Teresa? Ooh, he's sure gonna like that pretty sweater'), while privately expressing distress about the effects of precocious maturity. When questioned about the apparent contradiction, she responded: 'Well, you know, you've got to make contact where they're at. Otherwise, they just tune you out.'

Thus, teachers' perceptions about African-American girls' maturity also supported disproportionate attention and reinforcement of their social rather than their intellectual attributes. Although for white girls teachers saw maturity as linked to academic success, with African-American girls maturity was seen as unrelated, or even detrimental, to academic progress. Furthermore, teachers worried that premature assumption of adult roles would limit African-American girls' academic attainment more so than white girls'. This might have led them, in subtle ways, to regard African-American girls as riskier students in whom to invest extraordinary teaching efforts.

Similarity of assessments. The good girl/bad girl dichotomy that characterized many teachers' assessments of white girls did not appear in assessments of African-American girls. Teachers' discussions of these children, with the exception of two African-American teachers (Todd and Jordan) were the briefest, including the fewest details about out-of-school life, of any students. Todd and Jordan gave fewer details about African-American than white females, but discussed as much about African-American girls as about boys of either race.[5] Only rarely did teachers make attributions about character traits of African-American girls. Interviews also suggested that these students were less central in teachers' minds than many classmates.

There were suggestions from observations that African-American girls might have been differentiated more by peers than by teachers and subjected to more extreme judgments in certain peer networks. In three midwestern and two southern classrooms a few African-American girls, invariably among the highest achievers, interacted heavily with white girls on a regular basis. Usually this involved frequent contact with a single white female friend, but in three rooms (Maxwell's, Parker's, Delby's) one or two African-American girls joined otherwise insular white female peer interactions more than those of other African-American students. These girls had favorable relationships with teachers, but experienced more hostility than most African-American girls from males of both races.

Lydia (African-American) in Maxwell's room interacted heavily with two white girls. Two African-American males in the room repeatedly called her 'white face' and wrote these words on her papers and notebooks. Although racist and sexist remarks in classrooms were rare, they were most typically delivered to these high-achieving African-American girls who interacted heavily with white females. The perpetrators were usually white males, and remarks came most frequently after the black girl had been recognized for achievement. After Cynthia (African-American) in Jordan's room answered a question that had stumped several students, Gordon (white) chanted to her repeatedly: 'You're a dark black pig.' Schofield (1982) observed a similar pattern among middle-school students. She argues that in such cases white males are appealing to their 'strong suits' of whiteness and maleness, attributes that have high status in society but ostensibly are irrelevant in the current situation, to attempt to restore their ascendancy. Analysis of the meanings of these events is speculative, since students were not interviewed systematically about their perspectives on classroom life. However, the observed patterns suggested that African-American girls' locations vis-à-vis teachers and peers affected peers' responses to them. Intellectual attainment brought white girls notice from teachers and deference from peers. African-American girls' attainment brought less notice from teachers and sometimes hostility from peers for stepping out of place.

Conclusion

Examination of everyday life in schools suggests that, even as early as the first grade, race not only influences the forms of femininity acquired by white girls and African-American girls, but also illustrates that the processes by which girls are linked to the gender order of the school differ by race. African-American girls and white girls occupy different 'places' in classrooms, and these are linked to variable experience. Intentionally or otherwise, these two groups were seemingly being channeled toward different adult social roles. Such consideration must be cautious, however, since students were not studied beyond primary school and many forces outside school influence children's gender roles and understanding of gender relations in society.

White Girls

White girls, closely tied to teachers, are encouraged to develop academic and social skills simultaneously. More specifically, these students receive pressure to combine intellectual competence with loyalty and deference. It is not the case, as some studies have argued, that girls at this level of schooling are urged to be passive or are actively discouraged from intellectual attainment. Such pressures may exist at other levels of schooling, but they were not present in these primary classrooms. From the perspectives of teachers, especially white teachers, white girls are central and African-American girls peripheral. Repetitive experiences of this sort reify the dominance of white females over African-American females and African-American females' position as 'other' (Collins 1990).

The combination of intellectual competence and deference is very consistent with private life and the occupational roles currently played by adult white women, particularly those of the middle class. As Sokoloff (1980) has explored in depth, most paid jobs held by women in advanced industrial societies demand literacy and intellectual competence in combination with loyalty. Sokoloff uses the term 'motherwork' to describe the labor women perform in and out of the home that bolsters the job performance of bosses or husbands. Clerical jobs, in which white women are heavily represented, demand such combinations of skills. Secretaries provide emotional support, nurturance, and domestic-like labor in support of the (usually male) boss (making coffee, entertaining visitors). They also perform work requiring literacy and intellectual competence that aid superiors' job performance (such as turning a rough draft into a polished report, or handling correspondence in the boss's name). These typically are gender-stratified relationships with women clericals serving male bosses (Sokoloff 1980).

Off the job, women provide similar job-supportive labor for men, like proofreading a paper or serving as a charming, literate hostess for his clients. Women typically perform these tasks for men more than men do for them. The gender order of the classroom not only encourages girls, and especially white girls, to develop skills and aptitudes for such work, but it also underpins all students' expectations that white females will perform such work. Also consistent with the adult life of middle-class white women is their expectation of dominance over women of color. As several authors have shown (Hertz 1987; Rollins 1986), many privileged white women hire women of color to perform domestic labor and even to provide them with emotional support. Potentially problematic aspects of this relationship are neutralized for many white women by years of experience during which they were more central and powerful than women of color.

African-American Girls

Classroom experiences encouraged African-American girls to emphasize social competence over intellectual attainment. These themes appeared both in relationships with teachers, who recognized their social actions more than their academic achievement, and with peers, who pressed them into service as go-betweens and couriers. Alternative forms of femininity for African-American girls seemed less apparent than those for whites, but this might be because these alternatives for African-American girls were defined and articulated more through peer networks than teacher contacts. Observations suggested such differentiation, but limitations of data (especially lack of formal interviews with students) made it impossible wholly to clarify these patterns. It also is possible that alternative forms of femininity become more prominent for African-American girls at later ages and higher grade levels.

The unbalanced attention to social rather than academic skills might encourage African-American girls to take on service-oriented jobs, the sector of the labor force in which women of color are already overrepresented. They receive less encouragement to strive toward high-pay, high-prestige occupations where women of color are grossly underrepresented. Although social and negotiation skills are undeniable assets in these high-ranking jobs, African-American girls in schools might not get the support they need to acquire the academic credentials that are the keys to access to such positions. Instead, they develop skills of serving others, keeping peace, and maintaining ties among diverse groups of persons, including relatively more advantaged white women. Dumas (1980) describes this as the 'mammy role' and sees it as a detriment to African-American women's career advancement. Emotional labor, though costly for women to perform and valuable to the smooth functioning of organizations, is rarely recognized or rewarded as real work. Furthermore, women called upon to perform such tasks might have less time and energy to devote to substantive work that leads to career success.

Elementary school classrooms show alternative forms of femininity and gender regimes. Two distinctive forms of femininity are developed and maintained among white girls, one clearly ascendent over the other. African-American femininity is distinguished from these. Teacher actions and perceptions elevate white girls as more central than African-Americans, laying a subtle groundwork to make such a relationship normative in social life. This theme is not particularly prevalent in peer interactions, since girls' peer networks were usually racially divided, but some peers responded negatively to African-American girls who took on roles usually reserved for whites.

School experience thus does more to perpetuate status quo social relationships based on race and gender than to transform them. Although possibilities for variable outcomes exist and sometimes occur, classroom experience differs for white and African-American girls in ways that encourage re-creation rather than transformation of current gender and race relationships. Girls learn skills consistent with, and ideologies supportive of, status quo gender relations, including the greater centrality and power of white women than African-American women in social organizations. All students learn subtle, but powerful, lessons about what white girls and African-American girls are like, how they should relate to one another and to others, and what can be expected of them in all social relations.

Notes

1 The two exceptions were Delby's room in the Midwest and Carson's in the South. Both teachers used more student-group-oriented, multi-task instructional forms (in contrast to other observed teachers in their respective districts), the instructional formats that most encourage peer interaction (Bossert 1979).
2 Jordan's room was an exception to the pattern each year it was observed. During both years Jordan's room was skewed toward high-attainment students. The African-American girls enrolled were likely to have come from predominantly white neighborhoods, interacted frequently with white children out of school, and behaved more similarly to white girls than did African-American girls in most other rooms.
3 In year one, Jordan taught a class consisting solely of high-aptitude students, so the ratings were not surprising. However, she showed the same pattern of assessments the following year, when she taught a heterogeneous-ability class.
4 Maxwell sometimes referred to her second-highest reading group as her 'playpen', noting that she placed in it several bright but immature boys whose behavior might disrupt 'my good workers'.

5   These comparisons were derived from point-by-point comparisons of the number of themes or details introduced in teachers' discussions of each pupil. For example, statements such as 'Her parents just bought a new house and she takes music lessons after school' would be counted as offering two details about the student.

General Note
Portions of this research were supported by a predoctoral fellowship in Sociology and Social Policy from the National Institute for Mental Health and a small grant from the Spencer Foundation, entitled 'Tracking and Detracking: Social and Academic Consequences of School Organizational Change'. Neither funding agency bears any responsibility for the interpretations presented here. I am grateful to Layne A. Simpson for aid in data collection, Carl Glickman for aid in locating research sites, and teachers, paraprofessionals, and administrators who permitted me access to classrooms and took part in interviews. The paper has benefited from critiques by Donna J. Eder, Judith Preissle Goetz, Kathryn B. Ward, and Julia Wrigley.

References

BEST, RAMONA (1983) *We've All Got Scars*, Bloomington, Indiana University Press.

BOSSERT, STEVEN (1979) *Tasks and Social Relationships in Schools*, New York, Oxford University Press.

BROPHY, JERE (1985) 'Interactions of Male and Female Students with Male and Female Teachers', in WILKINSON, L.C. and MARRETT, C.B. (Eds) *Gender Influences in Classroom Interaction*, pp. 115–42, New York, Academic Press.

BYALICK, R. and BERSHOFF, D. (1974) 'Reinforcement practices of black and white teachers in integrated classrooms', *Journal of Educational Psychology* 66, pp. 473–80.

CLIFTON, R., PERRY, R., PARSONSON, K. and HRUYNIUK, S. (1986) 'Effects of ethnicity and sex on teachers' expectations of junior high school students', *Sociology of Education* 59, pp. 58–67.

COLLINS, PATRICIA HILL (1990) *Black Feminist Thought*, New York, Allen & Unwin.

CONNELL, ROBERT (1986) *Gender and Power*, Stanford, Stanford University Press.

D'AMICO, SANDRA (1986) 'Cross-group opportunities: Impact on interpersonal relationships in desegregated middle schools', *Sociology of Education* 59, pp. 113–23.

DELAMONT, SARA (1983) 'The conservative school? Sex roles at home, at work, and at school', in WALKER, S. and BARTON, L. (Eds) *Gender, Class, and Education*, pp. 93–105, London, Falmer Press.

DUMAS, RHEATAUGH (1980) 'Dilemmas of black females in leadership', in ROGERS-ROSE, LAFRANCES (Ed.) *The Black Woman*, pp. 203–16, Beverly Hills, Sage.

EDER, DONNA J. (1985) 'The cycle of popularity: Interpersonal relations among female adolescents', *Sociology of Education* 58, pp. 154–65.

EDER, DONNA and PARKER, STEVE (1987) 'The cultural production and reproduction of gender: The effects of extracurricular activities on peer group culture', *Sociology of Education* 60, pp. 200–33.

FOX, GREER LITTON (1977) 'Nice girls: Social control through a value construct', *Signs* 2, pp. 805–17.

FULLER, MARY (1980) 'Black girls in a London comprehensive', in DEEM, ROSEMARY (Ed.) *Schooling for Women's Work*, London, Routledge & Kegan Paul.

FURLONG, JOHN (1984) 'Black resistance in the liberal comprehensive', in DELAMONT, SARA (Ed.) *Readings on Interaction in the Classroom*, 2nd ed., pp. 212–36, London, Methuen.

GASKELL, JANE (1985) 'Course enrollment in the high school: The perspective of working-class females', *Sociology of Education* 58, pp. 48–59.

GLASER, BARNEY G. and STRAUSS, ANSELM L. (1967) *The Discovery of Grounded Theory*, Chicago, Aldine.

GOLD, RAYMOND (1969) 'Roles in sociological field observations', pp. 30–9, in McCALL, G. and SIMMONS, J.L. *Issues in Participant Observation*, New York, Random House.

GOFFMAN, ERVING (1959) *The Presentation of Self in Everyday Life*, Garden City, NY, Anchor Doubleday.

GOETZ, JUDITH P. and LeCOMPTE, MARGUERITE D. (1984) *Ethnography and Qualitative Design in Educational Research*. Orlando, Academic Press.

GRANT, CARL A., and SLEETER, CHRISTINE (1986) *After the School Bell Rings*, Philadelphia, Falmer Press.

GRANT, LINDA (1983) 'Gender roles and statuses in elementary school children's peer relationships', *Western Sociological Review* 14, pp. 58–76.

GRANT, LINDA (1984) 'Black females' "place" in desegregated classrooms', *Sociology of Education* 57, pp. 98–111.

GRANT, LINDA (1985) 'Race-gender status, classroom interaction, and children's socialization in classrooms', in WILKINSON, L.C. and MARRETT, C.B. (Eds) *Gender Influences in Classroom Interaction*, pp. 57–77, New York, Academic Press.

GRANT, LINDA (forthcoming) 'Helpers, enforcers and go-betweens: black girls in elementary schools', in ZINN, M.B. and DILL, B.T. (Eds) *Women of Color in America*, Philadelphia Temple University Press.

HERTZ, ROSANNA (1987) *More Equal Than Others: Women and Men in Dual-Career Families*, Berkeley, University of California Press.

HUDSON, BARBARA (1984) 'Femininity and adolescence', in McROBBIE, A. and NEVA, M. (Eds) *Gender and Generation*, pp. 31–53, London, Macmillan.

IRVINE, JACQUELINE JORDAN (1990) *Black Students and School Failure: Policies, Practices, and Prescriptions*, New York, Greenwood Press.

IRVINE, JACQUELINE JORDAN (1985) 'Teacher-student interactions: Effects of student sex, race, and grade level', *Journal of Educational Psychology* 78, pp. 14–21.

KESSLER, S., ASHENDEN, D.J., CONNELL, R.W. and DOWSETT, G.W. (1985) 'Gender relations in secondary schooling', *Sociology of Education* 58, pp. 34–47.

LADNER, JOYCE (1971) *Tomorrow's Tomorrow: The Black Woman*, Garden City, NY, Doubleday.

LESKO, NANCY (1988) *Symbolizing Society: Stories, Rites and Structure in a Catholic High School*, New York, Falmer Press.

LEWIS, DIANE (1977) 'A response to inequality: Black women, racism, and sexism', *Signs* 3, pp. 331–7.

LUTTRELL, WENDY (1989) 'Working-class women's ways of knowing: Effects of gender, race, and class', *Sociology of Education* 62, pp. 33–46.

McCARTHY, CAMERON (1990) *Race and Curriculum: Social Inequality and the Theories and Politics of Difference in Contemporary Research on Schooling*, London, Falmer Press.

MEIER, KENNETH J., STEWART, JOSEPH and ENGLAND, ROBERT E. (1989) *Race, Class, and Education: The Politics of Second-Generation Discrimination*, Madison, University of Wisconsin Press.

MOORE, HELEN A. (1988) 'Effects of gender, ethnicity, and school equity on students' leadership behaviors in a group game', *Elementary School Journal* 88, pp. 515–27.

MOORE, HELEN A. (1983) 'Hispanic women: Schooling for conformity in public education', *Hispanic Journal of Behavioral Science* 5, pp. 45–63.

MULLARD, CHRIS (1983) 'Multiracial education in Britain: From assimilation to cultural pluralism', in BARTON, L. and WALKER, S. (Eds) *Race and Gender: Equal Opportunities in Education*, pp. 39–52, Oxford, Pergamon.

PATCHEN, M. (1982) *Black-White Contact in Schools*, W. LAFAYETTE, Ind., Purdue University Press.

REID, INEZ (1972) *'Together' Black Women*, New York, Emerson Hall.

ROLLINS, JUDITH (1986) *Between Women: Domestic Workers and Their Employers*, Philadelphia, Temple University Press.

ROMAN, LESLIE E. (1988) *Becoming Feminine: The Politics of Popular Culture*, Philadelphia, Falmer Press.

SADKER, MYRA and SADKER, DAVID (1986) 'Sexism in the Classroom of the 80s', *Psychology Today*, March.

SCHOFIELD, JANET (1982) *Black and White in Schools: Trust, Tolerance, or Tokenism?* New York, Praeger.

SCOTT-JONES, DIANE and CLARK, MAXINE (1986) 'The schooling experience of black girls: The interaction of gender, race, and socioeconomic status', *Phi Delta Kappan* 67, pp. 520–6.

SOKOLOFF, NATALIE (1980) *Between Money and Love: The Dialectics of Women's Home and Market Work*, New York, Praeger.

STRAUSS, ANSELM L. (1987) *Qualitative Analysis for Social Scientists*, New York, Cambridge University Press.

THORNE, BARRIE (1985) 'Girls and boys together … but mostly apart: Gender arrangements in elementary schools', in HARTRUP, WILLARD and RUBIN, ZICK (Eds) *Relationships and Development*, pp. 167–84, Hillside, NJ, Erlbaum.

WILKINSON, LOUISE CHERRY and MARRETT, CORA B. (1985) *Gender Influences on Classroom Interaction*, New York, Academic Press.

6 Girls and Boys Together ... But Mostly Apart: Gender Arrangements in Elementary Schools

Barrie Thorne

Throughout the years of elementary school, children's friendships and casual encounters are strongly separated by sex. Sex segregation among children, which starts in preschool and is well established by middle childhood, has been amply documented in studies of children's groups and friendships (e.g., Eder and Hallinan 1978; Schofield 1981) and is immediately visible in elementary school settings. When children choose seats in classrooms or the cafeteria, or get into line, they frequently arrange themselves in same-sex clusters. At lunchtime, they talk matter-of-factly about 'girls' tables' and 'boys' tables'. Playgrounds have gendered turfs, with some areas and activities, such as large playing fields and basketball courts, controlled mainly by boys, and others (smaller enclaves like jungle-gym areas and concrete spaces for hopscotch or jumprope) more often controlled by girls. Sex segregation is so common in elementary schools that it is meaningful to speak of separate girls' and boys' worlds.

Studies of gender and children's social relations have mostly followed this 'two worlds' model, separately describing and comparing the subcultures of girls and of boys (e.g., Lever 1976; Maltz and Borker 1983). In brief summary: Boys tend to interact in larger, more age-heterogeneous groups (Lever 1976; Waldrop and Halverson 1975; Eder and Hallinan 1978). They engage in more rough and tumble play and physical fighting (Maccoby and Jacklin 1974). Organized sports are both a central activity and a major metaphor in boys' subcultures; they use the language of 'teams' even when not engaged in sports, and they often construct interaction in the form of contests. The shifting hierarchies of boys' groups (Savin-Williams 1976) are evident in their more frequent use of direct commands, insults, and challenges (Goodwin 1980).

Fewer studies have been done of girls' groups (Foot, Chapman and Smith 1980; McRobbie and Garber 1975), and — perhaps because categories for description and analysis have come more from male than female experience — researchers have had difficulty seeing and analyzing girls' social relations. Recent work has begun to correct this skew. In middle childhood, girls' worlds are less public than those of boys; girls more often interact in private places and in small groups or friendship pairs (Eder and Hallinan 1978; Waldrop and Halverson

1975). Their play is more cooperative and turn-taking (Lever 1976). Girls have more intense and exclusive friendships, which take shape around keeping and telling secrets, shifting alliances, and indirect ways of expressing disagreement (Goodwin 1980; Lever 1976; Maltz and Borker 1983). Instead of direct commands, girls more often use directives which merge speaker and hearer, such as 'let's' or 'we gotta' (Goodwin 1980).

Although much can be learned by comparing the social organization and subcultures of boys' and of girls' groups, the separate worlds approach has eclipsed full, contextual understanding of gender and social relations among children. The separate worlds model essentially involves a search for group sex differences, and shares the limitations of individual sex difference research. Differences tend to be exaggerated and similarities ignored, with little theoretical attention to the integration of similarity and difference (Unger 1979). Statistical findings of difference are often portrayed as dichotomous, neglecting the considerable individual variation that exists; for example, not all boys fight, and some have intense and exclusive friendships. The sex difference approach tends to abstract gender from its social context, to assume that males and females are qualitatively and permanently different (with differences perhaps unfolding through separate developmental lines). These assumptions mask the possibility that gender arrangements and patterns of similarity and difference may vary by situation, race, social class, region, or subculture.

Sex segregation is far from total, and is a more complex and dynamic process than the portrayal of separate worlds reveals. Erving Goffman (1977) has observed that sex segregation has a 'with-then-apart' structure; the sexes segregate periodically, with separate spaces, rituals, and groups, but they also come together and are, in crucial ways, part of the same world. This is certainly true in the social environment of elementary schools. Although girls and boys do interact as boundaried collectivities, an image suggested by the separate worlds approach, there are other occasions when they work or play in relaxed and integrated ways. Gender is less central to the organization and meaning of some situations than others. In short, sex segregation is not static, but is a variable and complicated process.

To gain an understanding of gender which can encompass both the 'with' and 'apart' of sex segregation, analysis should start not with the individual, nor with a search for sex differences, but with social relationships. Gender should be conceptualized as a system of relationships rather than as an immutable and dichotomous given. Taking this approach, I have organized my research on gender and children's social relations around questions like the following: How and when does gender enter into group formation? In a given situation, how is gender made more or less salient or infused with particular meanings? By what rituals, processes, and forms of social organization and conflict do 'with-then-apart' rhythms get enacted? How are these processes affected by the organization of institutions (different types of schools, neighborhoods, or summer camps, for example), varied settings (such as the constraints and possibilities governing interaction on playgrounds versus classrooms), and particular encounters?

Methods and Sources of Data

This study is based on two periods of participant observation. In 1976–7 I observed for eight months, in a largely working-class elementary school in

California, a school with 8 percent black and 12 percent Chicana/o students. In 1980 I did fieldwork for three months in a Michigan elementary school of similar size (around 400 students), social class, and racial composition. I observed in several classrooms (a kindergarten, a second grade, and a combined fourth-fifth grade) and in school hallways, cafeterias, and playgrounds. I set out to follow the round of the school day as children experience it, recording their interactions with one another, and with adults, in varied settings.

Participant observation involves gaining access to everyday, 'naturalistic' settings and taking systematic notes over an extended period of time. Rather than starting with preset categories for recording, or with fixed hypotheses for testing, participant-observers record detail in ways which maximize opportunities for discovery. Through continuous interaction between observation and analysis, 'grounded theory' is developed (Glaser and Strauss 1967).

The distinctive logic and discipline of this mode of inquiry emerges from: (1) theoretical sampling — being relatively systematic in the choice of where and whom to observe in order to maximize knowledge relevant to categories and analysis which are being developed: and (2) comparing all relevant data on a given point in order to modify emerging propositions to take account of discrepant cases (Katz 1983). Participant observation is a flexible, open-ended and inductive method, designed to understand behavior within, rather than stripped from, social context. It provides richly detailed information which is anchored in everyday meanings and experience.

Daily Processes of Sex Segregation

Sex segregation should be understood not as a given, but as the result of deliberate activity. The outcome is dramatically visible when there are separate girls' and boys' tables in school lunchrooms, or sex-separated groups on playgrounds. But in the same lunchroom one can also find tables where girls and boys eat and talk together, and in some playground activities the sexes mix. By what processes do girls and boys separate into gender-defined and relatively boundaried collectivities? In what contexts, and through what processes, do boys and girls interact in less gender-divided ways?

In the school settings I observed, much segregation happened with no mention of gender. Gender was implicit in the contours of friendship, shared interest, and perceived risk which came into play when children chose companions — in their prior planning, invitations, seeking-of-access, saving-of-places, denials of entry, and allowing or protesting of 'cuts' by those who violated the rules for lining up. Sometimes children formed mixed-sex groups for play, eating, talking, working on a classroom project, or moving through space. When adults or children explicitly invoked gender (and this was nearly always in ways which separated girls and boys) boundaries were heightened and mixed-sex interaction became an explicit arena of risk.

In the schools I studied, the physical space and curriculum were not formally divided by sex, as they have been in the history of elementary schooling (a history evident in separate entrances to old school buildings, where the words *Boys* and *Girls* are permanently etched in concrete). Nevertheless, gender was a visible marker in the adult-organized school day. In both schools, when the *gender division*

public address system sounded, the principal inevitably opened with 'Boys and girls ...' and in addressing clusters of children, teachers and aides regularly used gender terms ('Heads down, girls'; 'The girls are ready and the boys aren't'). The forms of address made gender visible and salient, conveying an assumption that the sexes are separate social groups.

Teachers and aides sometimes drew upon gender as a basis for sorting children and organizing activities. Gender is an embodied and visual social category which roughly divides the population in half, and the separation of girls and boys permeates the history and lore of schools and playgrounds. In both schools (although through awareness of Title IX, many teachers had changed this practice) one could see separate girls' and boys' lines moving, like caterpillars, through the school halls. In the fourth-fifth grade classroom the teacher frequently pitted girls against boys for spelling and math contests. On the playground in the Michigan school, aides regarded the space close to the building as girls' territory, and the playing fields 'out there' as boys' territory. They sometimes shooed children of the other sex away from those spaces, especially boys who ventured near the girls' area and seemed to have teasing in mind.

In organizing their activities, both within and apart from the surveillance of adults, children also explicitly invoked gender. During my fieldwork in the Michigan school, I kept a daily record of who sat where in the lunchroom. The amount of sex segregation varied: it was least at the first-grade tables and almost total among sixth-graders. There was also variation from classroom to classroom within a given age, and from day to day. Sometimes, particular actions heightened the gender divide. In the lunchroom, when the two second-grade tables were filling, a high-status boy walked by the inside table, which had a scattering of both boys and girls, and said loudly, 'Oooo, too many girls,' as he headed for a seat at the far table. The boys at the inside table picked up their trays and moved, and no other boys sat at the inside table, which the pronouncement had effectively made taboo. In the end, that day (which was not the case every day), girls and boys ate at separate tables.

Eating and walking are not sex-typed activities, yet in forming groups in lunchrooms and hallways children often separated by sex. Sex segregation assumed added dimensions on the playground, where spaces, equipment, and activities were infused with gender meanings. My inventories of activities showed similar patterns in both schools: boys controlled the large, fixed spaces designated for team sports (baseball diamond, grassy fields used for football or soccer); girls more often played closer to the building, doing tricks on the monkey bars (which, for sixth-graders, became an area for sitting and talking) and using cement areas for jumprope, hopscotch, and group games like four-square. Lever (1976) provides a good analysis of sex-divided play. Girls and boys most often played together in kickball and group (rather than team) games like four-square, dodgeball, and handball. When children used gender to exclude others from play, they often drew upon beliefs connecting boys to some activities and girls to others. A first-grade boy, for example, avidly watched an all-female game of jumprope. When the girls began to shift positions, he recognized a means of access to the play and he offered, 'I'll swing it.' A girl responded, 'No way, you don't know how to do it, to swing it. You gotta be a girl.' He left without protest. Although children sometimes ignored pronouncements about what each could or could not do, I never heard them directly challenge such claims.

When children had explicitly defined an activity or a group as gendered, those who crossed the boundary — especially boys who moved into female-marked space — risked being teased: 'Look! Mike's in the girls' line!'; 'That's a girl over there,' a girl said loudly, pointing to a boy sitting at an otherwise all-female table in the lunchroom. Children, and occasionally adults, used teasing, especially the tease of 'liking' someone of the other sex, or of 'being' that sex by virtue of being in their midst, to police gender boundaries. Much of the teaching drew upon heterosexual romantic definitions, making cross-sex interaction risky, and increasing the social distance between boys and girls.

Relationships Between the Sexes

Because I have emphasized the 'apart' and ignored the occasions of 'with' in this analysis of sex segregation, I have perhaps falsely implied that there is little contact between girls and boys in daily school life. In fact, relationships between girls and boys (which should be studied as fully as, and in connection with, same-sex relationships) are of several kinds:

1 'Borderwork', or forms of cross-sex interaction which are based upon and reaffirm boundaries and asymmetries between girls' and boys' groups;
2 Interactions which are infused with heterosexual meanings;
3 Occasions where individuals cross gender boundaries to participate in the world of the other sex; and
4 Situations where gender is not predominant, and girls and boys interact in more relaxed ways.

Borderwork

In elementary school settings boys' and girls' groups are sometimes spatially set apart. Same-sex groups sometimes claim fixed territories such as the basketball court, the bars, or specific lunchroom tables. However, in the crowded, multi-focused, and adult-controlled environment of the school, groups form and disperse at a rapid rate and can never stay totally apart. Contact between girls and boys sometimes lessens sex segregation, but gender-defined groups also come together in ways which emphasize their boundaries.

'Borderwork' refers to interaction across, yet based upon and even strengthening, gender boundaries. I have drawn this notion from Fredrik Barth's (1969) analysis of social relations which are maintained across ethnic boundaries without diminishing dichotomized ethnic status.[1] His focus is on more macro, ecological arrangements; mine is on face-to-face behavior. But the insight is similar: groups may interact in ways which strengthen their borders, and the maintenance of ethnic (or gender) groups can best be understood by examining the boundary that defines the group, 'not the cultural stuff that it encloses' (Barth 1969, p. 15). In elementary schools there are several types of borderwork: contests or games where gender-defined teams compete; cross-sex rituals of chasing and pollution; and group invasions. These interactions are asymmetrical, challenging the separate-but-parallel model of 'two worlds'.

Contests

Boys and girls are sometimes pitted against each other in classroom competitions and playground games. The fourth-fifth grade classroom had a boys' side and a girls' side, an arrangement that re-emerged each time the teacher asked children to choose their own desks. Although there was some within-sex shuffling, the result was always a spatial moiety system — boys on the left, girls on the right — with the exception of one girl (the 'tomboy' whom I'll describe later), who twice chose a desk with the boys and once with the girls. Drawing upon and reinforcing the children's self-segregation, the teacher often pitted the boys against the girls in spelling and math competitions, events marked by cross-sex antagonism and within-sex solidarity.

The teacher introduced a math game, for example; she would write addition and subtraction problems on the board, and a member of each team would race to be the first to write the correct answer. She wrote two score-keeping columns on the board: 'Beastly Boys' and 'Gossipy Girls'. The boys yelled out, as several girls laughed, 'Noisy girls!' 'Gruesome girls!' The girls sat in a row on top of their desks; sometimes they moved collectively, pushing their hips or whispering 'Pass it on.' The boys stood along the wall, some reclining against desks. When members of either group came back victorious from the front of the room, they would do the 'giving five' hand-slapping ritual with their team members.

On the playground a team of girls occasionally played against a team of boys, usually in kickball or team two-square. Sometimes these games proceeded matter-of-factly, but if gender became the explicit basis of team solidarity, the interaction changed, becoming more antagonistic and unstable. On one occasion, two fifth-grade girls played against two fifth-grade boys in a team game of two-square. The game proceeded at an even pace until an argument ensued about whether the ball was out or on the line. Karen, who had hit the ball, became annoyed, flashed her middle finger at the other team, and called to a passing girl to join their side. The boys then called out to other boys, and cheered as several arrived to play. 'We got five and you got three!' Jack yelled. The game continued, with the girls yelling, 'Bratty boys!' 'Sissy boys!' and the boys making noises — 'weee haw' 'ha-ha-ha' — as they played.

Chasing

Cross-sex chasing dramatically affirms boundaries between girls and boys. The basic elements of chase and elude, capture and rescue (Sutton-Smith 1971) are found in various kinds of tag with formal rules, and in informal episodes of chasing which punctuate life on playgrounds. These episodes begin with provocation (taunts like 'you can't get me!' or 'Slobber monster!', bodily pokes, or the grabbing of possessions). A provocation may be ignored, or responded to by chasing. Chaser and chased may then alternate roles. In an ethnographic study of chase sequences on a school playground, Christine Finnan (1982) observes that chases vary in number of chasers to chased (for example, one chasing one, or five chasing two); form of provocation (a taunt or a poke); outcome (an episode may end when the chased outdistances the chaser, or with a brief touch, being wrestled to the ground, or the recapturing of a hat or a ball); and in use of space (there may or may not be safety zones).

Like Finnan (1982), and Sluckin (1981), who studied a playground in England, I found that chasing has a gendered structure. Boys frequently chase one another, an activity which often ends in wrestling and mock fights. When girls chase girls, they are usually less physically aggressive; they less often, for example, wrestle one another to the ground.

Cross-sex chasing is set apart by special names — 'girls chase the boys'; 'boys chase the girls'; 'chasers'; 'chase and kiss'; 'kiss chase'; 'kissers and chasers'; 'kiss or kill' — and by children's animated talk about the activity. The names vary by region and school, but contain both gender and sexual meanings (this form of play is mentioned, but only briefly analyzed, in Finnan 1982; Sluckin 1981; Parrott 1972; and Borman 1979).

In 'boys chase the girls' and 'girls chase the boys' (the names most frequently used in both the California and Michigan schools) boys and girls become, by definition, separate teams. Gender terms override individual identities, especially for the other team ('Help, a girl's chasin' me!'; 'C'mon Sarah, let's get that boy': 'Tony, help save me from the girls'). Individuals may call for help from, or offer help to, others of their sex. They may also grab someone of their sex and turn them over to the opposing team: Ryan grabbed Billy from behind, wrestling him to the ground. 'Hey girls, get 'im,' Ryan called.

Boys more often mix episodes of cross-sex with same-sex chasing. Girls more often have safety zones, places like the girls' restroom or an area by the school wall, where they retreat to rest and talk (sometimes in animated post-mortems) before new episodes of cross-sex chasing begin.

Early in the fall in the Michigan school, where chasing was especially prevalent, I watched a second-grade boy teach a kindergarten girl how to chase. He slowly ran backwards, beckoning her to persue him, as he called, 'Help, a girl's after me.' In the early grades chasing mixes with fantasy play, like a first-grade boy who played 'sea monster', his arms out-flung and his voice growling, as he chased a group of girls. By third grade, stylized gestures — exaggerated stalking motions, screams (which only girls do), and karate kicks — accompany scenes of chasing.

Names like 'chase and kiss' mark the sexual meanings of cross-sex chasing, a theme to which I shall return later. The threat of kissing (most often girls threatening to kiss boys) is a ritualized form of provocation. Cross-sex chasing among sixth-graders involves elaborate patterns of touch and touch avoidance, which adults see as sexual. The principal told the sixth-graders in the Michigan school that they were not to play 'pom-pom', a complicated chasing game, because it entailed 'inappropriate touch'.

Rituals of Pollution

Cross-sex chasing is sometimes entwined with rituals of pollution, as in 'cooties', where specific individuals or groups are treated as contaminating or carrying 'germs'. Children have rituals for transferring cooties (usually touching someone else and shouting 'You've got cooties!'), for immunization (such as writing 'CV' for 'cootie vaccination' on their arms), and for eliminating cooties (saying 'no gives', for example, or using 'cootie catchers' made of folded paper, which is described in Knapp and Knapp, 1976). While girls may give cooties to girls, boys do not generally give cooties to one another (Samuelson 1980).

In cross-sex play, either girls or boys may be defined as having cooties, which they transfer through chasing and touching. Girls give cooties to boys more often than vice versa. In Michigan, one version of cooties is called 'girl stain'; the fourth-graders whom Karkau (1973) describes used the phrase 'girl touch'. 'Cootie queens' or 'cootie girls' (there are no 'kings' or 'boys') are female pariahs, the ultimate school untouchables, seen as contaminating not only by virtue of gender, but also through some added stigma such as being overweight or poor.[2] That girls are seen as more polluting than boys is a significant asymmetry, which echoes cross-cultural patterns, although in other cultures female pollution is generally connected with menstruation, and not applied to pre-pubertal girls.

Invasions

Playground invasions are another asymmetric form of borderwork. On a few occasions I saw girls invade and disrupt an all-male game, most memorably, a group of tall sixth-grade girls who ran on to the playing field and grabbed a football which was in play. The boys were surprised and frustrated and, unusual for boys this old, finally tattled to the aide. In the majority of cases, however, boys disrupt girls' activities rather than vice versa. Boys grab the ball from girls playing four-square, stick feet into a jumprope and stop an ongoing game, and dash through the area of the bars, where girls are taking turns performing, sending the rings flying. Sometimes boys ask to join a girls' game and then, after a short period of seemingly earnest play, disrupt the game. Two second-grade boys, for example, begged to 'twirl' the jumprope for a group of second-grade girls who had been jumping for some time. The girls agreed, and the boys began to twirl. Soon, without announcement, the boys changed from 'seashells, cockle bells' to 'hot peppers' (spinning the rope very fast), and tangled the jumper in the rope. The boys ran away laughing.

Boys disrupt girls' play so often that girls have developed almost ritualized responses: they guard their ongoing play, chase boys away, and tattle to the aides. In a playground cycle which enhances sex segregation, aides who try to spot potential trouble before it occurs sometimes shoo boys away from areas where girls are playing. Aides do not anticipate trouble from girls who seek to join groups of boys, with the exception of girls intent on provoking a chase sequence. Indeed, if they seek access to a boys' game, girls usually play with boys in earnest rather than breaking up the game.

A close look at the organization of borderwork, or boundaried interactions between the sexes, shows that the worlds of boys and girls may be separate, but they are not parallel, nor are they equal. The worlds of girls and boys articulate in several asymmetric ways:

1   On the playground, boys control as much as ten times more space than girls, when one adds up the area of large playing fields and compares it with the much smaller areas where girls predominate. Girls, who play

closer to the building, are more often watched over and protected by the adult aides.

2 Boys invade all-female games and scenes of play much more than girls invade boys. This, and boys' greater control of space, correspond with other findings about the organization of gender, and inequality, in our society: compared with men and boys, women and girls take up less space, and their space, and talk, are more often violated and interrupted (Greif 1982; Henley 1977; West and Zimmerman 1983).

3 Although individual boys are occasionally treated as contaminating (like a third-grade boy who both boys and girls said was 'stinky' and 'smelled like pee'), girls are more often defined as polluting. This pattern ties to themes that I shall discuss later. It is more taboo for a boy to play with (as opposed to invade) girls, and girls are more sexually defined than boys.

A look at the boundaries between the separated worlds of girls and boys illuminates within-sex hierarchies of status and control. For example, in the sex-divided seating in the fourth-fifth grade classroom, several boys recurrently sat near 'female space': their desks were at the gender divide in the classroom, and they were more likely than other boys to sit at a predominantly female table in the lunchroom. These boys (two nonbilingual Chicanos and an overweight 'loner' boy who was afraid of sports) were at the bottom of the male hierarchy. Gender is sometimes used as a metaphor for male hierarchies; the inferior status of boys at the bottom is conveyed by calling them 'girls'. Once, when seven boys and one girl were playing basketball, two younger boys came over and asked to play. While the girl silently stood, fully accepted in the company of the players, one of the older boys disparagingly said to the younger boys, 'You girls can't play.'[3]

In contrast, the girls who more often travel in the boys' world, sitting with groups of boys in the lunchroom or playing basketball, soccer, and baseball with them, are not stigmatized. Some have fairly high status with other girls. The worlds of girls and boys are asymmetrically arranged, and spatial patterns map interacting forms of inequality.

Heterosexual Meanings

The organization and meanings of gender (the social categories 'woman/man', 'girl/boy',) and of sexuality vary cross-culturally (Ortner and Whitehead 1981) and, in our society, across the life course. Harriet Whitehead (1981) observed that in our (Western) gender system, and that of many traditional North American Indian cultures, one's choice of a sexual object, occupation, and one's dress and demeanor are closely associated with gender. However, the 'center of gravity' differs in the two gender systems. For Indians, occupational pursuits provide the primary imagery of gender; dress and demeanor are secondary, and sexuality is least important. In our system, at least for adults, the order is reversed: heterosexuality is central to our definitions of 'man' and 'woman' ('masculinity' 'femininity') and the relationships that obtain between them, whereas occupation and dress/demeanor are secondary.

Whereas erotic orientation and gender are closely linked in our definitions of adults, we define children as relatively asexual. Activities and dress/demeanor are more important than sexuality in the cultural meanings of 'girl' and 'boy'. Children are less heterosexually defined than adults, and we have nonsexual imagery for relations between girls and boys. However, both children and adults sometimes use heterosexual language — 'crushes', 'like', 'goin' with', 'girlfriends', and 'boyfriends' — to define cross-sex relationships. This language increases through the years of elementary school; the shift to adolescence consolidates a gender system organized around the institution of heterosexuality.

In everyday life in the schools, heterosexual and romantic meanings infuse some ritualized forms of interaction between groups of boys and girls (such as 'chase and kiss') and help maintain sex segregation. 'Jimmy likes Beth', 'Beth likes Jimmy' is a major form of teasing, which a child risks in choosing to sit by or walk with someone of the other sex. The structure of teasing, and children's sparse vocabulary for relationships between girls and boys, are evident in the following conversation which I had with a group of third-grade girls in the lunchroom. Susan asked me that I was doing, and I said I was observing the things children do and play. Nicole volunteered. 'I like running, boys chase all the girls. See Tim over there? Judy chases him all around the school. She likes him.' Judy, sitting across the table, quickly responded, 'I hate him. I like him for a friend.' 'Tim loves Judy', Nicole said in a loud, sing-song voice.

In the younger grades, the culture and lore of girls contains more heterosexual romantic themes than that of boys. In Michigan, the first-grade girls often jumped rope to a rhyme which began:

> Down in the valley where the green grass grows,
> There sat Cindy [name of jumper], as sweet as a rose.
> She sat, she sat, she sat so sweet.
> Along came Jason, and kissed her on the cheek ...
> First comes love, then comes marriage,
> Then along comes Cindy with a baby carriage ...

Before a girl took her turn at jumping, the chanters asked her 'Who do you want to be your boyfriend?' The jumper always proffered a name, which was accepted matter-of-factly. In chasing, a girl's kiss carried greater threat than a boy's kiss; 'girl touch', when defined as contaminating, had sexual connotations. In short, starting at an early age, girls are more sexually defined than boys.

Through the years of elementary school, and increasing with age, the idiom of heterosexuality helps maintain the gender divide. Cross-sex interactions, especially when children initiate them, are fraught with the risk of being teased about 'liking' someone of the other sex. I learned of several close cross-sex friendships, formed and maintained in neighborhoods and church, which went underground during the school day.

By the fifth grade a few children began to affirm, rather than avoid, the charge of having a girlfriend or a boyfriend; they introduced the heterosexual courtship rituals of adolescence. For example, in the lunchroom in the Michigan school, as the tables were forming, a high-status fifth-grade boy called out from his seat at the table: 'I want Trish to sit by me.' Trish came over and, almost like a king and queen, they sat at the gender divide — a row of girls down the table on her side, a row of boys on his. In this situation, which inverted earlier forms, it was not a loss but a gain in status publicly to choose a companion of the other sex. By affirming his choice, the boy became unteasable (note the familiar asymmetry of heterosexual courtship rituals: the male initiated). This incident signals a temporal shift in arrangements of sex and gender.

Traveling in the World of the Other Sex

Contests, invasions, chasing, and heterosexually-defined encounters are based upon and reaffirm boundaries between girls and boys. In another type of cross-sex interaction, individuals (or sometimes pairs) cross gender boundaries, seeking acceptance in a group of the other sex. Nearly all the cases I saw of this were tomboys, girls who played organized sports and frequently sat with boys in the cafeteria or classroom. If these girls were skilled at activities central in the boys' world, especially games like soccer, baseball, and basketball, they were pretty much accepted as participants.

Being a tomboy is a matter of degree. Some girls seek access to boys' groups but are excluded; other girls limit their 'crossing' to specific sports. Only a few (such as the tomboy I mentioned earlier, who chose a seat with the boys in the sex-divided fourth-fifth grade) participate fully in the boys' world. That particular girl was skilled at the various organized sports which boys played in different seasons of the year. She was also adept at physical fighting and at using the forms of arguing, insult, teasing, naming, and sports-talk of the boys' subculture. She was the only black child in her classroom, in a school with only 8 percent black students; overall that token status, along with unusual athletic and verbal skills, may have contributed to her ability to move back and forth across the gender divide. Her unique position in the children's world was widely recognized in the school. Several times, the teacher said to me, 'She thinks she's a boy.'

I observed only one boy in the upper grades (a fourth-grader) who regularly played with all-female groups, as opposed to 'playing at' girls' games and seeking to disrupt them. He frequently played jumprope and took turns with girls doing tricks on the bars, using the small gestures (for example, a helpful push on the heel of a girl who needed momentum to turn her body around the bar) which mark skillful and earnest participation. Although I never saw him play in other than an earnest spirit, the girls often chased him away from their games and both girls and boys teased him. The fact that girls seek and have more access to boys' worlds than vice versa, and the fact that girls who travel with the other sex are less stigmatized for it, are obvious asymmetries, tied to the asymmetries previously discussed.

Relaxed Cross-sex Interactions

Relationships between boys and girls are not always marked by strong boundaries, heterosexual definitions, or by interacting on the terms and turfs of the other sex. On some occasions girls and boys interact in relatively comfortable ways. Gender is not predominant nor explicitly invoked, and girls and boys are not organized into boundaried collectivities. These 'with' occasions have been neglected by those studying gender and children's relationships, who have emphasized either the model of separate worlds (with little attention to their articulation) or heterosexual forms of contact.

Occasions where boys and girls interact without strain, where gender wanes, rather than waxes in importance, frequently have one or more of the following characteristics:

1   The situations are organized around an absorbing task, such as a group art project or creating a radio show, which encourages cooperation and lessens attention to gender. This pattern accords with other studies finding that cooperative activities reduce group antagonism (e.g., Sherif and Sherif, 1953, who studied divisions between boys in a summer camp; and Aronson et al. 1978, who used cooperative activities to lessen racial divisions in a classroom).

2   Gender is less prominent when children are not responsible for the formation of the group. Mixed-sex play is less frequent in games like football, which require the choosing of teams, and more frequent in games like handball or dodgeball which individuals can join simply by getting into a line or a circle. When adults organize mixed-sex encounters — which they frequently do in the classroom and in physical education periods on the playground — they legitimize cross-sex contact. This removes the risk of being teased for choosing to be with the other sex.

3   There is more extensive and relaxed cross-sex interaction when principles of grouping other than gender are explicitly invoked — for example, counting off to form teams for spelling or kickball, dividing lines by hot lunch or cold lunch, or organizing a work group on the basis of interests or reading ability.

4   Girls and boys may interact more readily in less public and crowded settings. Neighborhood play, depending on demography, is more often sex and age integrated than play at school, partly because with fewer numbers one may have to resort to an array of social categories to find play partners or to constitute a game. And in less crowded environments there are fewer potential witnesses to 'make something of it' if girls and boys play together.

Relaxed interactions between girls and boys often depend on adults to set up and legitimize the contact.[4] Perhaps because of this contingency (and the other, distancing patterns which permeate relations between girls and boys) the easeful moments of interaction rarely build to close friendship. Schofield (1981) makes a similar observation about gender and racial barriers to friendship in a junior high school.

Implications for Development

I have located social relations within an essentially spatial framework, emphasizing the organization of children's play, work, and other activities within specific settings, and in one type of institution, the school. In contrast, frameworks of child development rely upon temporal metaphors, using images of growth and transformation over time. Taken alone, both spatial and temporal frameworks have shortcomings; fitted together, they may be mutually correcting.

Those interested in gender and development have relied upon conceptualizations of 'sex-role socialization' and 'sex differences'. Sexuality and gender, I have argued, are more situated and fluid than these individualist and intrinsic models imply. Sex and gender are differently organized and defined across situations, even within the same institution. This situational variation (for example, in the extent to which an encounter heightens or lessens gender boundaries, or is infused with sexual meanings) shapes and constrains individual behavior. Features which a developmental perspective might attribute to individuals, and understand as relatively internal attributes, unfolding over time, may, in fact, be highly dependent on context. For example, children's avoidance of cross-sex friendship may be attributed to individual gender development in middle childhood. But attention to varied situations may show that this avoidance is contingent on group size, activity, adult behavior, collective meanings, and the risk of being teased.

A focus on social organization and situation draws attention to children's experiences in the present. This helps correct a model like 'sex-role socialization' which casts the present under the shadow of the future, or presumed 'endpoints' (Speier 1976). A situated analysis of arrangements of sex and gender among those of different ages may point to crucial disjunctions in the life course. In the fourth and fifth grades, culturally defined heterosexual rituals ('goin' with') begin to suppress the presence and visibility of other types of interaction between girls and boys, such as nonsexualized and comfortable interaction, and traveling in the world of the other sex. As 'boyfriend/girlfriend' definitions spread, the fifth-grade tomboy I described had to work to sustain 'buddy' relationships with boys. Adult women who were tomboys often speak of early adolescence as a painful time when they entered puberty and the rituals of dating; that is, when they became absorbed into the institution of heterosexuality (Rich 1980). When Lever (1976) describes best-friend relationships among fifth-grade girls as preparation for dating, she imposes heterosexual ideologies on to a present which should be understood on its own terms.

As heterosexual encounters assume more importance, they may alter relationships in same-sex groups. For example, Schofield (1981) reports that for sixth- and seventh-grade children in a middle school, the popularity of girls with other girls was affected by their popularity with boys, while boys' status with other boys did not depend on their relations with girls. This is an asymmetry familiar from the adult world; men's relationships with one another are defined through varied activities (occupations, sports), while relationships among women (and their public status) are more influenced by their connections with individual men.

A full understanding of gender and social relations should encompass cross-sex as well as within-sex interactions. 'Borderwork' helps maintain separate gender-linked subcultures, which, as those interested in development have begun to suggest, may result in different milieus for learning. Daniel Maltz and Ruth Borker (1983), for example, argue that because of different interactions within girls' and boys' groups, the sexes learn different rules for creating and interpreting friendly conversation, rules which carry into adulthood and help account for miscommunication between men and women. Carol Gilligan (1982) fits research on the different worlds of girls and boys into a theory of sex differences in moral development. Girls develop a style of reasoning, she argues, which is more

personal and relational; boys develop a style which is more positional, based on
separateness. Eleanor Maccoby (1985), also following the insight that because of
sex segregation, girls and boys grow up in different environments, suggests
implications for gender-differentiated prosocial and antisocial behavior.

This separate worlds approach, as I have illustrated, also has limitations. The
occasions when the sexes are together should also be studied, and understood
as contexts for experience and learning. For example, asymmetries in cross-sex
relationships convey a series of messages: that boys are more entitled to space and
to the nonreciprocal right of interrupting or invading the activities of the other
sex; that girls are more in need of adult protection, and are lower in status, more
defined by sexuality, and may even be polluting. Different types of cross-sex
interaction — relaxed, boundaried, sexualized, or taking place on the terms of the
other sex — provide different contexts for development.

By mapping the array of relationships between and within the sexes, one
adds complexity to the overly static and dichotomous imagery of separate
worlds. Individual experiences vary, with implications for development. Some
children prefer same-sex groupings; some are more likely to cross the gender
boundary and participate in the world of the other sex; some children (for
example, girls and boys who frequently play 'chase and kiss') invoke heterosexual
meanings, while others avoid them.

Finally, after charting the terrain of relationships, one can trace their development over time. For example, age variation in the content and form of
borderwork, or of cross- and same-sex touch, may be related to differing cognitive, social, emotional, or physical capacities, as well as to age-associated cultural
forms. I earlier mentioned temporal shifts in the organization of cross-sex
chasing, from mixing with fantasy play in the early grades to more elaborately
ritualized and sexualized forms by the sixth grade. There also appear to be
temporal changes in same- and cross-sex touch. In kindergarten, girls and boys
touch one another more freely than in fourth grade, when children avoid relaxed
cross-sex touch and instead use pokes, pushes, and other forms of mock violence,
even when the touch clearly couches affection. This touch taboo is obviously
related to the risk of seeming to 'like' someone of the other sex. In fourth grade,
same-sex touch begins to signal sexual meanings among boys, as well as between
boys and girls. Younger boys touch one another freely in cuddling (arm around
shoulder) as well as mock violence ways. By fourth grade, when homophobic
taunts like 'fag' become more common among boys, cuddling touch begins to
disappear for boys, but less so for girls.

Overall, I am calling for more complexity in our conceptualizations of
gender and of children's social relationships. Our challenge is to retain the
temporal sweep, looking at individual and group lives as they unfold over time,
while also attending to social structure and context, and to the full variety of
experiences in the present.

Notes

1 I am grateful to Frederick Erickson for suggesting the relevance of Barth's analysis.
2 Sue Samuelson (1980) reports that in a racially mixed playground in Fresno,

California, Mexican-American, but not Anglo children gave cooties. Racial, as well as sexual, inequality may be expressed through these forms.

3   This incident was recorded by Margaret Blume, who, for an undergraduate research project in 1982, observed in the California school where I earlier did fieldwork. Her observations and insights enhanced my own, and I would like to thank her for letting me cite this excerpt.

4   Note that in daily school life, depending on the individual and the situation, teachers and aides sometimes lessened and at other times heightened sex segregation.

General Note

I should like to thank Jane Atkinson, Nancy Chodorow, Arlene Daniels, Peter Lyman, Zick Rubin, Malcom Spector, Avril Thorne, and Margery Wolf for comments on an earlier version of this paper. Conversations with Zella Luria enriched this work.

References

ARONSON, E. et al. (1978) *The Jigsaw Classroom*, Beverly Hills, Sage.

BARTH, F. (Ed.) (1969) *Ethnic Groups and Boundaries*, Boston, Little, Brown.

BORMAN, K.M. (1979) 'Children's Interactions in Playgrounds', *Theory into Practice* 18, pp. 251–7.

EDER, D. and HALLINAN, M.T. (1978) 'Sex Differences in Children's Friendships', *American Sociological Review* 43, pp. 237–50.

FINNAN, C.R. (1982) 'The Ethnography of Children's Spontaneous Play', in SPINDLER, G. (Ed.) *Doing the Ethnography of Schooling*, pp. 358–80, New York, Holt, Rinehart & Winston.

FOOT, H.C., CHAPMAN, A.J. and SMITH, J.R. (1980) *Friendship and Social Relations in Children*, pp. 1–14, New York, Wiley.

GILLIGAN, C. (1982) *In a Different Voice: Psychological Theory and Women's Development*, Cambridge, Harvard University Press.

GLASER, B.G. and STRAUSS, A.L. (1967) *The Discovery of Grounded Theory*, Chicago, Aldine.

GOFFMAN, E. (1977) 'The Arrangement Between the Sexes', *Theory and Society* 4, pp. 301–36.

GOODWIN, M.H. (1980) 'Directive-Response Speech Sequences in Girls' and Boys' Task Activities', in MCCONNELL-GINET, S., BORKER, R. and FURMAN, N. (Eds) *Women and Language in Literature and Society*, pp. 157–73, New York, Praeger.

GREIF, E.B. (1982) 'Sex Differences in Parent-Child Conversations', *Women's Studies International Quarterly* 3, pp. 253–8.

HENLEY, N. (1977) *Body Politics: Power, Sex, and Nonverbal Communication*, Englewood Cliffs, Prentice-Hall.

KARKAU, K. (1973) *Sexism in the Fourth Grade*, Pitsburgh, KNOW, Inc. (pamphlet).

KATZ, J. (1983) 'A Theory of Qualitative Methodology: The Social System of Analytic Fieldwork', in EMERSON, R.M. (Ed.) *Contemporary Field Research*, pp. 127–48, Boston, Little, Brown.

KNAPP, M. and KNAPP, H. (1976) *One Potato, New Potato, The Secret Education of American Children*, New York, W.W. Norton.

LEVER, J. (1976) 'Sex Differences in the Games Children Play', *Social Problems* 23, pp. 478–87.

MACCOBY, E. (1985) 'Social Groupings in Childhood: Their Relationship to Prosocial and Antisocial Behavior in Boys and Girls', in OLWEUS, D., BLOCK, J. and

RADKE-YARROW, M. *Development of Antisocial and Prosocial Behavior*, pp. 263–84, San Diego, Academic Press.

MACCOBY, E. and JACKLIN, C. (1974) *The Psychology of Sex Differences,* Stanford, Stanford University Press.

MALTZ, D.N. and BORKER, R.A. (1983) 'A Cultural Approach to Male–Female Miscommunication', in GUMPERZ, J.J. (Ed.) *Language and Social Identity*, pp. 195–216, New York, Cambridge University Press.

McROBBIE, A. and GARBER, J. (1975) 'Girls and Subcultures', in HALL, S. and JEFFERSON, T. (Eds) *Resistance Through Rituals*, pp. 209–23, London, Hutchinson.

ORTNER, S.B. and WHITEHEAD, H. (1981) *Sexual Meanings*, New York, Cambridge University Press.

PARROTT, S. (1972) 'Games children play: Ethnography of a second-grade recess', in SPRADLEY, J.P. and McCARTHY, D.W. (Eds) *The Cultural Experience*, pp. 206–19, Chicago, Science Research Associates.

RICH, A. (1980) 'Compulsory Heterosexuality and Lesbian Existence', *Signs* 5, pp. 631–60.

SAMUELSON, S. (1980) 'The Cooties Complex', *Western Folklore*, 39, pp. 198–210.

SAVIN-WILLIAMS, R.C. (1976) 'An Ethological Study of Dominance Formation and Maintenance in a Group of Human Adolescents', *Child Development* 47, pp. 972–9.

SCHOFIELD, J.W. (1981) 'Complementary and Conflicting Identities: Images and Interaction in an Interracial School', in ASHER, S.R. and GOTTMAN, J.M. (Eds) *The Development of Children's Friendships*, New York, Cambridge University Press.

SHERIF, M. and SHERIF, C. (1953) *Groups in Harmony and Tension*, New York, Harper.

SLUCKIN, A. (1981) *Growing Up in the Playground*, London, Routledge & Kegan Paul.

SPEIER, M. (1976) 'The Adult Ideological Viewpoint in Studies of Childhood', in SKOLNICK, A. (Ed.) *Rethinking Childhood*, pp. 168–86, Boston, Little, Brown.

SUTTON-SMITH, B. (1971) 'A Syntax for Play and Games', in HERRON, R.E. and SUTTON-SMITH, B. (Eds) *Child's Play*, pp. 298–307, New York, Wiley.

UNGER, R.K. (1979) 'Toward a Redefinition of Sex and Gender', *American Psychologist* 34, pp. 1085–94.

WALDROP, M.F. and HALVERSON, C.F. (1975) 'Intensive and Extensive Peer Behavior: Longitudinal and Cross-Sectional Analysis', *Child Development* 46, pp. 19–26.

WEST, C. and ZIMMERMAN, D.H. (1983) 'Small Insults: A Study of Interruptions in Cross-Sex Conversations between Unacquainted Persons', in THORNE, B., KRAMARAE C. and HENLEY, N. (Eds) *Language, Gender and Society*, Rowley, Newbury House.

WHITEHEAD, H. (1981) 'The Bow and the Burden Strap: A New Look at Institutionalized Homosexuality in Native America', in ORTNER, S.B. and WHITEHEAD, H. (Eds) *Sexual Meanings*, pp. 80–115, New York, Cambridge University Press.

7 Responding to Differences in the Classroom: The Politics of Knowledge, Class, and Sexuality

Saundra Gardner, Cynthia Dean, and Deo McKaig

A contemporary challenge to women's studies, as well as to the feminist movement, is to recognize and appreciate the diversity of women's experience (Baca Zinn et al. 1986; Bunch 1985; Cole 1986; Cruikshank 1982; Hooks 1984; Lorde 1984; Moraga and Anzaldua 1981). This shift from an emphasis on commonalities among women to a perspective that also includes differences among them has necessitated a rethinking of feminist theory and has forced many women to explore critically how they and others respond to the issue of difference in their daily lives, including the classroom.

This chapter examines the personal and interpersonal struggles that arise when differences in knowledge, class, and sexuality become visible in the feminist classroom.[1] We assume, as have others (Bunch and Pollack 1983; Culley and Portuges 1985; Fisher 1982; Geiger and Zita 1985), that the goals and dynamics of such a classroom are to encourage nonhierarchical, mutually supportive, and empowering modes of thought and behavior. However, the patterns of interaction that emerge often conflict with this ideology. This schism is intricately tied to how students and faculty members respond to differences that often reinforce patriarchal values rather than those commonly associated with feminism.

Framework

Our analysis of this classroom dynamic is based on Lorde's (1984) framework for redefining differences. In essence, Lorde argued that all people learn to respond to differences out of what may be called a patriarchal consciousness. This mode of thinking is dualistic and hierarchical. Specifically, it 'conditions us to see human differences in simplistic opposition to each other: dominant/subordinate, good/bad, up/down, superior/inferior' (Lorde 1984, p. 114). As a consequence, people respond to differences with fear and often deny or distort the meaning of them. Those who are different, become outsiders whose experiences are devalued and often ignored or erased.

Thus, for Lorde, it is not differences that divide people but how differences are conceptualized and responded to. To homogenize differences or pretend that everyone is alike will not alter this patriarchal dynamic or create bonds of sister-hood among women. Such changes depend, instead, on the ability to reclaim and redefine differences, which entails learning to view difference as a source of strength, creative energy, and personal power. Only then will women be able to appreciate their differences, learn from them, and use them as a source of collective power for creating social change. However, women must first learn to relate as equals to others who are different. To do so requires that patriarchal consciousness and oppression, both external and internal, be challenged. To root out these internalized patterns of oppression, women must be willing to name and struggle with that 'piece of the oppressor which is planted deep within each one of us' (Lorde 1984, p. 123).

The following sections represent our responses to Lorde's challenge. To preserve the differences among us, we wrote the article in three voices. The first section, on differences in knowledge, was written by the first author, who is a faculty member; the second and third sections, on differences in social class and sexuality, were written by the second and third authors respectively, who are an undergraduate student and a graduate student. The author of each section describes and analyzes her experiences with differences in feminist classrooms. She also recommends changes that will foster new patterns of relating across differences and that will strengthen the integration of theory and practice in these classrooms.

Differences in Knowledge

As teachers, we often find that students vary in their familiarity with the subject of or specific issues presented in a course. My initial experience teaching an intro-ductory course on women's studies was no exception. The class consisted of thirty-five students, the majority of whom had a strong background in feminism and women's issues. Most had taken two or more women-centered courses, many had been reading about feminism for a number of years, and several were political activists.[2] Although many might think (and, indeed, I did) that teaching a class in which the majority of students are feminists is a dream come true, it soon became painfully clear that this was yet another illusion. Instead of creating excitement and enthusiasm among students, this skewed distribution of feminist knowledge created divisions. However, my expectations for the course, as well as how I initially defined my role in the classroom, were equally responsible for the problems that arose.

I entered the course relieved that I did not have to spend a significant part of the semester explaining why it was legitimate and important to study women's experiences. Since I assumed that the students would offer little, if any, resistance to feminism, I envisioned the class as a semester-long discussion of women's lives characterized by mutual excitement and support. In addition, because this was my first officially designated women's studies course, I thought it had to be 'truly feminist' in content and form. Consequently, I was more concerned than usual with the structure and dynamics of the classroom. Even though I had always strived to create a classroom environment that empowered students, I began to view these efforts as only approximations of the 'real thing'.

The more I contemplated what a 'truly feminist' classroom environment might entail, the more my thoughts began to mirror the dualistic thinking so accurately described by Lorde (1984). For example, if professional authority and expertise were emphasized in the traditional classroom, then these qualities would be devalued or absent in a 'truly feminist' classroom. Instead of being *the* source of knowledge and socially distant, I would become a peer and facilitator of knowledge. Thus, I perceived, as have others (Friedman 1985; Kaye 1972; Mumford 1985), that the 'truly feminist' classroom is one in which I would give up my official trappings, merge with the class, and, in the classic sense of 'instructor', become invisible.

By playing such a passive role, I helped set the stage for the following dynamic that emerged early in the semester. The feminist majority, or those students with a strong background in feminism, began to use their knowledge as a source of power. As a group, they were articulate and dominated the class discussions. They often talked *at* rather than *with* the other students and, as a consequence, effectively silenced the nonfeminist minority. Thus, rather than sharing ideas and learning from each other, the students used differences in knowledge to create a distinct hierarchy in the classroom, with knowledge being a source of power *over* others. In other words, the feminist majority defined the class as *their* class and soon became the new caste of 'men', while the remaining 'women' sat passively, accepting their subjugation (Kaye 1972, p. 70). These dynamics polarized the class.

My initial response of these patterns of interaction was confusion. Given my idealized expectations of the course, I had not anticipated such behavior and hence was not prepared to deal with it. Having abdicated my professional authority, I was uncertain about whether or how I should intervene. On the one hand, I was hesitant to 'take control', since doing so would have been inconsistent with my conceptualization of a feminist classroom. In addition, I did not want to silence or put down those students who had finally found a safe place to speak their 'feminist truths' (Geiger and Zita 1985; Kaye 1972). On the other hand, I knew that my passivity was contributing to the problem and could not continue. The question was, How could I intervene without taking control? Ideally, I wanted all of us to discuss and analyze the patterns of classroom interaction that had emerged. However, given the polarization of the class, I thought such a discussion could not take place unless I created a way for the students to express their concerns 'safely'. Thus, I asked the students to write about their perceptions of the overall dynamics of the class, as well as my role in the classroom. The following comments were typical:

> There seems to be a definite division within the class with one group not daring to say anything, yet either opposing or at least questioning many of the comments being made. I'm sure they feel intimidated in class. As for myself, some of the comments in class make me furious because of their judgmental edge, yet others make me reevaluate my opinions.
>
> . . . . .
>
> We are all on different levels with regard to feminism. Some of us have been into the movement for years, some since this class began. Sometimes I have a very difficult time understanding, let alone relating to,

what is being said. I feel some women in the class are very condemning of the other women who aren't quite as 'into' it as they are. It is turning me off from the movement (and the class) more than encouraging me.

. . . . .

Class dynamics? It appears to be a case of the 'haves' and 'have-nots', those who are free, able, and willing to speak and others (me included) who can't or *won't*. In my view, the class reflects many aspects of the dominant culture. Those who have the education and self-confidence to speak to the concepts and course content do not realize that they achieved this with a lot of help from many people and resources. We say we want to learn from women's diversity, yet when we discussed Alice Walker's definitions of womanism, she was labeled divisive. The dominant group has to realize that the world is defined from their viewpoint and if they *really* want to learn from other races, classes, etc. they will have to take a look at where they are and *how* they got there. I believe that feminists have a big job to do within their ranks. Theory without practice is useless.

. . . . .

I never feel like I belong. Even though we all talk about appreciating difference and diversity. I don't feel as if we act on it. Especially 'the feminists' in the class. I'd often see them in the Union and they wouldn't even acknowledge me — they'd kind of look right past me. Well, so much for sisterhood.

It is clear that many students were acutely aware of the disparity between theory and praxis in what they defined as a 'feminist classroom'. In sum, many felt angry, alienated, devalued, and silenced by others. The patterns of domination that had become an integral part of the classroom interaction caused many of the students to perceive themselves as 'outsiders' rather than peers. Furthermore, the students suggested that I become 'more visible' and assertive and that I provide more structure, synthesize ideas and comments more often, and 'wrap things up more tightly'. Thus, they wanted me to reclaim my professorial authority and share my expertise, or, as one member of the class commented, 'You need to act more like a teacher and less like one of us.'[3]

To initiate what Butler (1985, p. 236) referred to as a 'pressure-valve-release' discussion,[4] I shared these comments with the class. The more traditional students expressed relief at finally having their reality validated, but the feminist majority initially responded with strong feelings of guilt. They had not been aware of how their behavior had affected others in the class or the ways in which it reinforced the patriarchal dynamics they were so committed to changing. Although these responses could have polarized the class even more, by suggesting that one group of students (the feminist majority) was solely responsible for what had occurred, they did not. By taking an active role in the discussion and highlighting our collective responsibility for group dynamics, I managed to avoid such scapegoating. Thus, we were able to acknowledge how we had each contributed to the classroom dynamics that now divided us: the traditional students by their silence, the feminist majority by their dominance, and me, by abrogating my power and thus my responsibility (Geiger and Zita 1985).

After much discussion and brainstorming about what might be done to alter our patterns of interaction, we decided to incorporate several changes. The first, suggested by a student, was to have the class form two concentric circles. The smaller or inner circle consisted of 3–4 students who would discuss their reactions to a specific reading assignment. Each student was allotted 5–10 minutes in which to speak.[5] During that time, members of the larger or outer circle were not permitted to interrupt or ask questions; their task was to concentrate on what was being said. After each member of the inner circle had spoken, others were invited to comment on their remarks. However, such comments had to be directed to the substantive content of what had been said in the small circle. This 'rule' was designed to discourage the pontificating that had earlier plagued the class.

The second change was in my role in the classroom. I provided more structure for the class by contributing concise introductions to new material or sections of the course and periodically 'pulling together' or synthesizing ideas that emerged from the discussion, as well as illustrating how these ideas were directly linked to other key themes of the course. Initially, I also acted as a bridge among the students. When I sensed that some members of the class were confused or did not understand what another student was saying, I would ask the speaker to clarify or explain her ideas more fully. Often the speaker would have to define a particular concept that she had assumed everyone understood (such as compulsory heterosexuality) or identify a particular person (Mary Daly or Ellie Smeal, for example), or describe a specific event (the Nairobi conference, for instance).[6]

The effects of these changes were remarkable. The 'legitimated silence' created by the small-circle concept broke the cycle of verbal domination by the feminist majority. The students realized they could *learn from each other*, regardless of how much they 'knew'. They also discovered that knowledge could be a means of empowerment, rather than a source of *power over* others. My more active role in the classroom also produced some positive results. Students reported feeling less confused and lost. They thought that my introductory comments or mini-lectures provided a foundation that increased not only their understanding of the material but their willingness to speak in class. By pulling together seemingly disparate ideas and comments during class discussions, I increased their ability to make important theoretical connections or to see 'how the pieces of the puzzle fit together'. The greater self-confidence and altered perceptions of difference induced by these changes (particularly among the nonfeminist minority) initiated another change: the students began to make an active effort to ensure that their comments were accessible to others in the class. This change was crucial if the students were to speak with, rather than at, each other. For successful communication to occur, it was also imperative that the listeners ask questions or seek clarification when they did not understand what was being said. As each student assumed these reciprocal responsibilities, my role as a bridge among the students became obsolete.

The mutual respect engendered by the restructuring of the classroom enabled all the students to take more responsibility for their learning and, perhaps what was more important, to appreciate and respond to differences in a radically new way. By exposing and challenging hierarchical modes of responding to differences and by confronting that 'piece of the oppressor within [them]' (Lorde 1984,

p. 123), the students developed a new pattern of relating to each other as equals — at least for the remainder of the semester. They were able to do so, in part, because the feminist majority began to realize that

> it is as important for feminists to learn to listen as to be heard — to understand the complexity of traditional women's lives as to present the alternatives of their own. Otherwise, no one is 'advanced', we are still in first grade (Hillyer Davis 1985, p. 248).

The shifts in my role also afforded some valuable insights. I learned that to define a 'truly feminist' classroom as one devoid of any authority is a great disservice to the instructor as well as to the students. As Culley (1985, p. 207) pointed out:

> It is only in accepting her authority — by this I mean the authority of her intellect, imagination, passion — that the students can accept the authority of their own like capacities. The authority the feminist teacher seeks is authority with, not authority over.

It took me some time to realize *experientially* what Culley meant. 'Authority' can, indeed, be a source of empowerment. As I learned to accept mine within the classroom, the students learned to accept theirs, and we all benefited. Our learning experience was richer, and we managed to create a new pattern of relating across the hierarchical differences imposed by the structure of higher education.

Differences in Class

Divisions among women because of their social-class background have been prevalent in the feminist movement. Even though feminism is frequently thought to include the experiences of all women, the experiences with which it deals are often those of white middle-class heterosexual women (Baca Zinn et al. 1986; Cruikshank 1982; Dill 1983). In the feminist classroom, which is a microcosm of the feminist movement, the lives of working-class women have been ignored or treated as far removed from the lives of the students. This section explores how the issue of social class becomes visible in the classroom, the students' and instructor's responses to it, and the possible reasons for these reactions. Since my background frames my analysis, I will briefly summarize it as well as the assumptions with which I first entered feminist classrooms.

I grew up in a French, Catholic, working-class family in rural Maine. Both my parents worked in local factories, and their employment was fairly stable, except for occasional layoffs and labor strikes. We were what Rubin (1976) referred to as a 'settled living' working-class family. I was always conscious that my environment was different from that of my middle-class friends — that I was, indeed, an 'outsider'.

As a child, I was not exposed to art, literature, or music. My parents did not read much — other than the Bible and *Reader's Digest* — or value education. Thus, although my grades were high, I received no encouragement or support from them to continue my education beyond high school. Fortunately, someone outside my family saw my potential and urged me to apply to the state university.

The letter of acceptance to the university signified more than just acceptance into school. I was now 'good enough' and no longer the 'other' (Lorde 1984). My class background was erased; I had suddenly become middle class. However, I discovered, much to my disappointment, that the reality of the university was not much different from what I had left behind. Divisive class lines were still drawn. I was, once again, the 'other' and felt that I did not belong. Inside the classroom, these feelings intensified.

It was within a traditional course on introductory sociology that I first heard my class background discussed. In the class, 'the working-class experience' was presented as an object to be studied, rather than as a possible experiential reality for students in the room. I felt not only invisible but dehumanized. Rather than remain passive, I decided to share some of my experiences as a member of the working class. When I did, a curious silence fell over the room. It became clear that I had broken two unspoken rules of this middle-class academic setting: I had spoken experientially in an environment that values 'objective knowledge' and I had revealed my class background. Since the students and the professor did not respond to my comments, I was silenced. I did not speak again in that class or share my personal experience in another class until I started taking women's studies courses.

When I first entered a women's studies class, I expected it to be different. I assumed that since women's studies is concerned with the lives of all women, my experiences would matter and be heard. However, once again, I found that the experiences of working-class women were often invisible or invalidated.

When the lives of working-class women were discussed, three approaches were used. The first was to include social class as a separate, 'special' topic, rather than a topic that was integral to the course. This approach is much like the 'add women and stir' approach discussed by McIntosh (1984). The second approach was to incorporate a social-class analysis of each topic, thereby making students cognizant that social-class issues are an integral part of women's experience. The third approach was for students, usually working-class students, to challenge the middle-class assumptions made in class by the instructor or the other students.

Of these three methods, the third created the most resistance among the students and the instructor. Here the patriarchal consciousness described by Lorde (1984) was most evident and the responses to differences in social class included silence, distancing, guilt, and fear. In contrast, the method that produced responses more closely associated with feminism, such as validation, support, and mutual learning, was the inclusion of a class analysis in each topic. The following example illustrates how partiarchal consciousness operates with respect to social-class differences among women.

The instructor of one women's studies course presented issues, both for discussion and throughout the readings, that involved only the concerns of white middle-class heterosexual women. These issues included dual careers for women, career advancement for professional women, and the 'new' issues of child care and housework for women who work outside the home. When I challenged the instructor about her failure to present an analysis of social class and racial issues, she replied that she would love to incorporate these perspectives but they were beyond her students! Although she was unwilling to include these perspectives, she encouraged me and several other concerned students to add such analyses to the discussions in class. She even went so far as to say that we were responsible for teaching the others about these issues. Thus, she implied that it was the responsibility of the subordinate or oppressed group to teach or raise the consciousness of those who are more privileged than themselves. This pattern also allows the privileged to maintain their position and evade responsibility for their actions (Lorde 1984).

During one disturbing discussion about the lack of good child care and the fears about the sexual abuse of children in day care centers, which ignored the realities of working-class women, one student stated that she did not consider these issues to be a social problem, since one could just hire a nanny. In following the instructor's suggestion, I challenged the student's assumption that all working women can afford to hire a nanny and asked her to consider who is supposed to take care of the nannies' children. Both the instructor and the students responded with an uncomfortable silence. They may have felt uncomfortable for a variety of reasons. Given the low level of class consciousness in American society (Mantsios 1988), any comment that highlights class differences (regardless of how it is presented), will challenge both middle- and working-class students' assumptions about the world. Thus, the middle-class students may have felt uncomfortable (and perhaps guilty) because my remarks directly challenged their biases and privilege. Although this would account for the silence of the middle-class students, I believe that the working-class students were silent for different reasons.[7] If they had publicly agreed with me or raised working-class issues, they would have risked being exposed as working class and hence defined as outsiders.

The silence served to invalidate my point and exacerbate the differences between me and the other students. Over time, the students came to define class issues as 'my issue or problem'. By individualizing an issue that affects millions of women, they were able to discount the social significance of class.

In another women's studies course, the response to social-class differences among women was more congruent with my expectations of a feminist classroom. Instead of fear and silence, there was validation, encouragement, and mutual learning. Many self-identified middle-class students acknowledged their class privilege and the wide range of feelings (including guilt) this awareness provoked. By doing so, *all* the students felt free to share their experiences and ideas openly. I credit this atmosphere to the way in which the instructor presented social-class issues. She incorporated a social-class analysis into every topic and continually emphasized and affirmed the importance of diversity. This approach created an environment that enabled the working-class students to express themselves and the middle-class students to recognize their privilege.

My experience suggests that a number of factors account for the negative responses to social-class issues described here. They include the denial of one's working-class background, guilt associated with class privilege, and the fear of difference. Working-class students who have internalized middle-class values often view their class background as a source of shame or personal inadequacy and, as a consequence, frequently deny their heritage. For them, silence is the safest, and perhaps the only, response that will ensure their anonymity. In contrast, middle-class students are more likely to express guilt once they realize that their privileged status depends on the exploitation and oppression of others. Guilt about class privilege often keeps people paralyzed. They try to relieve their guilt by ignoring and denying class differences or by refusing to accept their own privilege. Both denial and guilt reinforce the fear of difference. However, as long as women fear those who are different from themselves, that fear will be a barrier to understanding. Instead, all women need to become aware of the assumptions they make about others and then challenge those assumptions. If we allow our fear of differences to divide us, we shall not be able to work together to change the social conditions that oppress us all.

Differences in Sexuality

Sexual preference is one of the most emotionally charged areas of difference in this society. Usually, it remains hidden through denial and repression by heterosexuals and homosexuals alike. When the subject of lesbianism does emerge, however, reactions are typically judgmental and dualistic. For example, heterosexuals often characterize lesbianism as inferior, bad, sick, disgusting, dangerous, and sinful, while lesbians may be more likely to view their sexual preference as superior, highly evolved, visionary, and a source of pride. Such patterns of polarization and denial not only alienate women from each other, but reinforce a way of thinking about differences that has historically contributed to the oppression of all women.

In a university, these responses to difference in sexual preference are perhaps most evident in the traditional classroom. Given the androcentric assumptions and hierarchical structure of such classrooms, it is not surprising that assumptions about sexual preference are rarely addressed. But what about the feminist classroom? Instructors and students have different expectations about the visibility of differences here. It is tacitly assumed that the nontraditional structure and emphasis on process found in the feminist classroom will encourage the exploration of theoretical and experiential differences among women. In this woman-centered environment, surely sexual preference will be one of the differences that is critically examined. How well are these expectations met? What are the responses to differences in this context?

The feminist classroom would seem to be a safe place for students to challenge lifelong assumptions. But challenging assumptions, especially about lesbianism, can be frightening and unsettling. The lesbian who contemplates 'coming out' in the classroom may fear rejection or reprisal. The other students, many of whom may have been upset by feminist challenges to their taken-for-granted patriarchal world view, may perceive the subject of lesbianism as an additional threat. They may worry, Is lesbianism a disease? Can I catch it? If I listen to or agree with any of these new ideas, will my life have to change? Will I still like men? Other responses may include disinterest, curiosity, silence, approval, defensiveness, deference, bonding, and envy (Beck 1982; Bulkin 1982; McDaniel 1985; McNaron 1982).

The variety of responses are as disparate as the individuals who express them. However, some factors can minimize or exacerbate the fear of differences. For example, if the instructor is comfortable with the subject, she is more likely to create a climate that facilitates open discussion. If the class is small, it is easier to establish the climate of trust so necessary for honest sharing. Another important factor is whether the lesbians in the class are also feminists. Those who are not may send out nonverbal messages of discomfort, maintain a rigid silence, or try to change the subject, thus increasing the others' fear of differences. To clarify these issues, I shall discuss some of my experiences regarding lesbianism in feminist classrooms.

In the first feminist class I attended, the subject of lesbianism was introduced through the readings. For the most part, the discussions were theoretical; the students agreed or disagreed with the lesbian authors on intellectual grounds but had few experiential referents. We personally distanced ourselves from the topic, communicating primarily with the instructor rather than with each other. However, in the class discussions, some of the students' enthusiasm for the readings seemed personal as well as academic. Others communicated their fear and dislike of the theories and the personal implications associated with them. Though potentially divisive, these differences did not create a schism in the classroom, since neither the lesbians nor the heterosexuals bonded into groups.

A different dynamic emerged in my second feminist course. Although lesbianism was not explicitly part of the syllabus, it became a topic of discussion as the semester progressed, mainly because of the climate of acceptance and exploration in the class. Lesbians came out of the closet and challenged the heterosexist assumptions in the class discussions as well as in the reading materials. In doing so, of course, they clearly reinforced the patriarchal dynamic referred to by Lorde (1984): that of the oppressed group (lesbians) taking responsibility for raising the consciousness of those defined by society as the superordinate group (heterosexuals). Initially, this dynamic took the form of an 'us' versus 'them' mentality among some of the lesbians. Their unspoken assumption that lesbianism is a politically correct lifestyle, coupled with their greater knowledge of feminism, helped to create this divisive dynamic. It is ironic and unfortunate that in breaking the silence of denial and invisibility, so characteristic of lesbian life, some lesbians contributed to the silencing of other classmates.

Once the issue of difference in relation to lesbianism became an explicit topic of discussion, the heterosexual students began to express defensiveness. They had a difficult time moving beyond the security of their attachments to specific males in their lives to a more global vision of the possible value of women-centered lives. Gradually, this response gave way to a greater curiosity about and a greater awareness of lesbian experiences. As the mutual sharing of heterosexual and homosexual lived experiences increased, the importance of differences in formal feminist knowledge diminished. All the students were learning about difference and trust through open discussions of sexual preference, race, and class.

My experience in another course was a vivid demonstration that even in a classroom with a self-identified feminist instructor who espoused a feminist approach to the course content, a dualistic and hierarchical consciousness can still operate. As was similar to the case of the students in the course on introductory women's studies discussed in the first section, the lesbian students in the class had a more formal knowledge of feminism. However, unlike the instructor in the introductory course, this instructor exploited the us-versus-them potential. She gave undue deference, and therefore more power, to the lesbians in the class for two reasons. First, I suspect that she was entranced at meeting real out-of-the-closet lesbians. Second, she held the naive belief that all lesbians are highly evolved feminists. By deferring to us as true feminists and enlisting our help as teachers of the others, she reinforced the initial tension and conflict in the class.

These hierarchical dynamics were established at the beginning of the semester and would have continued if personal journals were not used as a pedagogical tool. The lesbians in the class used their journals to vent their impatience with the attitudes of the other students and the instructor; the nonlesbians used them to express their discomfort with the gap in knowledge and their reactions to the presence of lesbians in the class.

This acknowledgment of feelings by all members of the class, albeit in a private communication, led to a breakthrough. In the midst of all the theoretical analysis, the class discussions became experiential. Heterosexuals expressed their curiosity about lesbian stereotypes, and lesbians spoke of the joys of lesbian life and the pain of living as outsiders. This sharing culminated in a small-group presentation that focused on the lesbian continuum discussed by Rich (1980). The participants were three lesbians and two women who were in heterosexual primary relationships yet were deeply cognizant of the depth of their feelings for other women. This panel enhanced the ability of class members to move from their narrow vision of sexism and heterosexism to a broader vision of these forms of oppression as manifestations of patriarchy.

In my current seminar on women's studies, the topic of lesbianism was introduced in a combination of ways: by the instructor, by the students, and through the reading list. The students' responses have ranged from fear to interest to approval. From the first session, all patriarchal assumptions were challenged, and differences were acknowledged through discussions of many isms: sexism, classism, racism, ageism, and heterosexism.

The underlying fear of differences was addressed, primarily through a discussion of Rich's (1980) article on 'Compulsory Heterosexuality'. In the present seminar, theory was combined with feelings, and resistance was examined — resistance to change, feelings of threat to one's heterosexual assumptions and lifestyle, the fear that strong emotional bonds to women may really mean one is a latent lesbian, the fear of becoming a more conscious feminist and still not being as 'legitimate' as is a lesbian if one continues to relate to men sexually, and the discomfort of questioning the concept of choice. These issues were examined from a micro and a macro perspective and validated all our selves and our places along the woman-identified continuum discussed by Rich (1980).

I believe that the more openly the issue of differences is dealt with in the classroom, the greater the opportunity for clearer and more in-depth analyses of feminist issues and women's experiences. Initially, the discussion of differences may cause students to distance themselves from the material, both emotionally and intellectually. Later, it may create a maelstrom of feelings and reactions. However, out of all this potential conflict, students and faculty members alike can gain the clarity necessary for growth, increased understanding, and new feminist visions of the world and our classrooms. The probability of their doing so will increase significantly if the following changes are incorporated (for additional suggestions, see Bulkin 1981; Fontaine 1982; Haney 1985):

1 Include a separate unit on lesbianism in the class syllabus and incorporate the subject throughout the course. This change will make differences and responses to differences integral to all the discussions in the course.
2 In the required reading list, include some first-person accounts by lesbians, especially about the process of coming out. The best stories are graphic dramatizations of the experience of being different.

3 Schedule a lesbian to speak with the class about her life (preferably one who is articulate, intelligent, and humorous). There's nothing like a dose of reality to undermine the fear of the unknown and counteract stereotypical thinking and reactions.

4 Form a panel of women of various beliefs and behaviors to encourage bonding within and across groups in the classroom and to take the pressure to perform off any one person or group. If the students are not willing or able to speak about their experiences, assign various roles to them, such as lesbian, bisexual, or feminist, that they must research and present to the class. As an extension of the panel, ask class members to spend a day acting as if they were black, native American, lesbian, working class, and so on and report on their experiences.

5 Structure a panel discussion to cover the most prevalent theories of feminism, emphasizing the groups that are likely to subscribe to each. Such a panel would ensure that the radical lesbian separatist position would be presented, as well as the involvement of lesbians in liberalism, socialist feminism, and other movements.

6 Assign students to write journals, encourage personal communication, and promise confidentiality. Journal writing frees the students to examine their thoughts and feelings in safety and encourages them to assume responsibility for their intellectual and emotional growth.

7 Since the openness of the instructor sets the tone of the classroom, check your attitude and that of other instructors who will be involved in the course. Are all willing to question and challenge their homophobia? In addition to creating an atmosphere in which students will feel free to explore differences and their responses to differences, the openness of the instructors will create a safe space for lesbian students in the class who decide to come out.

Conclusion

We have examined responses to difference within a variety of feminist classrooms. Regardless of whether our focus was on differences in knowledge, class, or sexuality, hierarchical modes of responding to the diversity of women's lives emerged. Differences were used by the superordinate group to gain power over others or were ignored or denied. Each of these responses divided the women in the class. As a consequence, their ability to acknowledge, respect, appreciate, and learn from differences was radically reduced. These classroom dynamics were, in large part, the part of a patriarchal consciousness that 'conditions us to see human differences in simplistic opposition to each other' (Lorde 1984, p. 114). In an effort to create new patterns of relating, we offered specific suggestions for transforming how we think about as well as respond to differences in the classroom.

Such changes also have significant implications for the women's movement. Teachers, as well as students, are or will be among those who work to change women's lives. To be an effective agent of social change, one must be aware of both the commonalities and differences among women. An awareness of commonalities enables us to recognize women's oppression as a class, but it is only through an acknowledgment of differences that we learn that all women do not experience this oppression in the same way. By discussing our differences and our responses to them, we are forced to confront our oppressive attitudes and behaviors. Such a confrontation is the beginning of change and a necessary prerequisite if we, as women, are to move beyond a patriarchal conceptualization of differences that views us all as 'the other'. According to Lorde (1984), such a transformation is essential for our future survival.

As teachers and students, we can contribute to this process by working to create a classroom environment in which differences among women are not only acknowledged but valued. Only then will it be possible to 'devise ways to use each others' difference to enrich our visions and our joint struggles' (Lorde 1984, p. 122). As Conlon, da Silva, and Wilson (1985, pp. 11–12) noted:

> The things that divide us can define us and help us claim ourselves; they can also be used against us, as ways of keeping us separate from each other and powerless. Only by writing and talking of our differences can we begin to bridge them.

Notes

1 These differences were chosen because they were most salient to our experiences in the classroom. We do not consider them to be more significant or less significant than are other differences among women, such as race, ethnicity, age, and religion.

2 Given the introductory nature of this course, one might have expected students with a strong background in feminism to be in the minority. However, since the University of Maine does not have a formal women's studies program, relatively few women-centered courses are available. Consequently, students often enroll in every such course that is offered, regardless of their background in feminism.

3 This desire for a more 'traditional' teaching style is frequently expressed by students in feminist classrooms (Friedman 1985; Kaye 1972; Mumford 1985).

4 Once divisions have emerged in the classroom, Butler (1985) advised making such issues the focus of class discussions. Doing so works best when 'the teacher directly acknowledges and calls attention to the tension in the classroom' (p. 236). After 'naming' the problem, the class discusses why it occurred, possible solutions, and the like.

5 Students could discuss their intellectual and emotional responses to the material. All reactions were considered legitimate, and great care was taken to emphasize that there was no 'politically correct' response to the readings.

6 Hillyer Davis (1985) described a similar technique for fostering more effective communication in this regard. She suggested the teacher function as a 'simultaneous translator', 'giving back in other words what another person has just said, and presenting an explanation in another language which will illuminate the issue for a second group without alienating the first' (p. 250). A key difference between this role and the one described here is that the *students* are expected to assume responsibility for the 'translation'.

7 Since a significant proportion of those enrolled at the University of Maine are first-generation college students, I suspect that there were others in the course who shared my class background. However, I was not sure just how many there were, since working-class students often attempt to deny their class background by 'passing' as middle class.

References

BACA ZINN, M., CANNON, L.W., HIGGINBOTHAM, E. and DILL, B.T. (1986) 'The Costs of Exclusionary Practices in Women's Studies', *Signs* 11, pp. 290–303.

BECK, E.T. (1982) 'Teaching About Jewish Lesbians in Literature: From *Zeitl and Rickel to The Tree of Begats*', in CRUIKSHANK, M. (Ed.) *Lesbian Studies: Present and Future*, pp. 81–7, Old Westbury, Feminist Press.

BULKIN, E. (1981) 'Heterosexism and Women's Studies'. *Radical Teacher* 17, 25–31.

BULKIN, E. (1982) 'Kissing/Against the Light': A Look at Lesbian Poetry', in CRUIK-SHANK, M. (Ed.) *Lesbian Studies: Present and Future*, pp. 32–54, Old Westbury, Feminist Press.

BUNCH, C. 1985. *Bringing the Global Home*, Denver, Antelope Publications.

BUNCH, C. and POLLACK, S. (Eds) (1983) *Learning Our Way: Essays in Feminist Education*, Trumansburg, Crossing Press.

BUTLER, J.E. (1985) 'Toward a Pedagogy of Everywoman's Studies', in CULLEY, M. and PORTUGES, C. (Eds) *Gendered Subjects: The Dynamics of Feminist Teaching*, pp. 230–9, Boston, Routledge & Kegan Paul.

COLE, J.B. (Ed.) (1986) *All American Women: Lines That Divide, Ties That Bind*, New York, Free Press.

CONLON, F., DA SILVA, R. and WILSON, B. (1985) *The Things That Divide Us*, Seattle, Seal Press.

CRUIKSHANK, M. (Ed.) (1982) *Lesbian Studies: Present and Future*, Old Westbury, Feminist Press.

CULLEY, M. (1985) 'Anger and Authority in the Introductory Women's Studies Classroom', in CULLEY, M. and PORTUGES, C. (Eds) *Gendered Subjects: The Dynamics of Feminist Teaching*, pp. 209–17, Boston, Routledge & Kegan Paul.

CULLEY, M., and PORTUGES, C. (Eds) (1985) *Gendered Subjects: The Dynamics of Feminist Teaching*, Boston, Routledge & Kegan Paul.

DILL, B.T. (1983) 'Race, Class and Gender Prospects for an All-Inclusive Sisterhood', *Feminist Studies* 9, pp. 131–50.

FISHER, B. (1982) 'What is Feminist Pedagogy?' *Radical Teacher* 18, pp. 20–4.

FONTAINE, C. (1982) 'Teaching the Psychology of Women: A Lesbian Feminist Perspective', in CRUIKSHANK, M. (Ed.) *Lesbian Studies: Present and Future*, pp. 70–80, Old Westbury, Feminist Press.

FRIEDMAN, S. (1985) 'Authority in the Feminist Classroom: A Contradiction in Terms?' in CULLEY, M. and PORTUGES, C. (Eds) *Gendered Subjects: The Dynamics of Feminist Teaching*, pp. 203–8, Boston, Routledge & Kegan Paul.

GEIGER, S. and ZITA, J.N. (1985) 'White Traders: The Caveat Emptor of Women's Studies', *Journal of Thought* 20, pp. 106–21.

HANEY, E.H. (1985) 'Incorporating Lesbian and Other Woman-Identified Perspectives into Courses', in FRITSCHE, J. (Ed.) *Toward Excellence and Equity: The Scholarship on Women as a Catalyst for Change in the University*, pp. 144–9, Orono, University of Maine Press.

HILLYER DAVIS, B. (1985) 'Teaching the Feminist Minority', in CULLEY, M. and PORTUGES, C. (Eds) *Gendered Subjects: The Dynamics of Feminist Teaching*, pp. 245–52, Boston, Routledge & Kegan Paul.

HOOKS, B. (1984) *Feminist Theory: From Margin to Center*, Boston, South End Press.

KAYE, M. (1972) '"Diving into the Wreck": The Woman Writer in the Twentieth Century', in HOFFMAN, N., SECOR, C. and TINSLEY, A. (Eds) *Female Studies VI*, pp. 68–78, Old Westbury, Feminist Press.

LORDE, A. (1984) 'Age, Race, Class, and Sex: Women Redefining Difference', in LORDE, A. *Sister Outsider*, pp. 114–23, Trumansburg, NY, Crossing Press.

MANTSIOS, G. (1988) 'Class in America: Myths and Realities', in ROTHENBERG, P. (Ed.) *Racism and Sexism*, pp. 56–68, New York: St Martin's Press.

McDaniel, J. (1985) 'Is There Room for Me in the Closet? Or, My Life as the Only Lesbian Professor', in Culley, M. and Portuges, C. (Eds) *Gendered Subjects: The Dynamics of Feminist Teaching*, pp. 130–5, Boston, MA, Routledge & Kegan Paul.

McIntosh, P. (1984) 'Interactive Phases of Curricular Revision', in McIntosh, P. *Toward a Balanced Curriculum*, pp. 25–34, Cambridge, Schenkman Publishing Co.

McNaron, T.A.H. (1982) 'A Journey into Otherness: Teaching the Well of Loneliness', in Cruikshank, M. (Ed.) *Lesbian Studies: Present and Future*, pp. 88–92, Old Westbury, Feminist Press.

Moraga, C. and Anzaldua, G. (Eds) (1981) *This Bridge Called My Back: Writings by Radical Women of Color*, Watertown, Persephone Press.

Mumford, L.S. (1985) ' "Why Do We Have to Read All This Old Stuff?" Conflict in the Feminist Theory Classroom', *Journal of Thought* 20, pp. 88–96.

Rich, A. (1980) 'Compulsory Heterosexuality and Lesbian Existence', *Signs* 5, pp. 631–60.

Rubin, L.B. (1976) *Worlds of Pain: Life in the Working Class Family*, New York, Basic Books.

Section 3

Gender and Knowledge

8 Why Does Jane Read and Write so Well? The Anomaly of Women's Achievement

Roslyn Arlin Mickelson

The evidence is in and the conclusion is clear: Women can and do achieve academically as well as men. The myth of female underachievement has been exposed by many studies that have indicated that women's behavior and motivation to achieve not only equal but often surpass that of men (Klein 1985; Maccoby and Jacklin 1974; National Center for Educational Statistics 1986; Stockard 1985; Stockard and Wood 1984; US Bureau of the Census 1987). Today, as in the past, more girls than boys graduate from high school and more women than men receive baccalaureate degrees,[1] and nationwide women now outnumber men in master's degree programs. More men than women are enrolled only in professional and Ph.D. programs but, even here, the gaps between women and men are closing (National Center for Educational Statistics 1986; Stockard et al. 1980). Fields of specialization continue to be gender linked — mathematics, engineering, and the physical and biological sciences are dominated by males, and the social sciences and humanities are dominated by females — but evidence from a study of undergraduates indicates that differences are disappearing here, too (Hafner and Shaha 1984).

If the picture of women's achievement and attainment is so positive, why do educators and researchers pay so much attention to the subject? One obvious answer lies in the different areas of achievement. Because high-paying careers (those with the best pay, benefits, working conditions, and career ladders) usually require strong backgrounds in mathematics and science, the fact that women continue to lag behind men in these areas is important. A second answer involves the links among schooling, work, and income. Even though women have all but closed the overall gap in educational attainment between the sexes, the occupational world fails to reward women equitably for their accomplishments. Research suggests strongly that the inequalities faced by women in the occupational world cannot be linked, except in the most tenuous ways, to differences in educational achievement and attainment (Stockard 1985, p. 320).

The issue of structural inequality in the work world raises another question that is the focus of this chapter: in view of the limited rewards that women are likely to receive from education, why do they do as well and attain as much education as they do? In our society, in which educational credentials purportedly are linked to jobs, promotions, wages, and status, women's educational accomplishments appear anomalous because women continue to receive far fewer rewards for their educational credentials than do men with comparable credentials. One might expect that if women knew of the diminished opportunities that lay ahead, they would put less effort into school, because those efforts are likely to yield smaller returns to them than to males who make similar efforts. Yet this is not the case. This chapter explores why gender stratification in the opportunity structure appears to be of little relevance to young women's academic achievement and attainment. It examines the anomaly of females' achievement in the light of four hypotheses, and presents empirical evidence to assess each hypothesis. Finally, drawing on emerging feminist theory, it suggests directions for future research.

Basis of the Anomaly

The academic achievement of female students is a curious reversal of a dynamic found among minority and working-class students. A study conducted by the author in 1983 indicated that both working-class and minority youths underachieve, in part, because of the poor returns they are likely to receive from education (Mickelson 1984, 1990). This research was inspired largely by the work of Ogbu (1978), which examined the American opportunity structure and its possible influence on the scholastic achievement of minority students. Ogbu argued that members of a social group that face a job ceiling know that they do so, and this knowledge channels and shapes their children's academic behavior. The term 'job ceiling' refers to overt and informal practices that limit members of castelike minority groups (such as blacks and Chicanos) from unrestricted competition for the jobs for which they are qualified. Members of these groups are excluded from or not allowed to obtain their proportionate share of desirable jobs and hence are overwhelmingly confined to the least desirable jobs in the occupational structure. Ogbu contended that because the job ceiling faced by black adults prevents them from receiving rewards that are commensurate with their educational credentials, education is not the same bridge to adult status for blacks as it is for whites. Black children see that efforts in school often do not have the same outcomes for them as do similar efforts for members of socially dominant groups, such as middle-class white men. Thus, they tend to put less effort and commitment into their schoolwork and hence perform less well, on average, than do middle-class white youths. As Ogbu (1979, p. 193) stated:

> I think their perception of the job ceiling is still a major factor that colors [minority] attitudes and school performance.... Given the premise that what motivates Americans to maximize their achievement efforts in school is their belief that the better education one has, the more money and more status [one will acquire] ... is it logical to expect Blacks and Whites to exert the same energy and perform alike in school when the job ceiling consistently underutilizes the black talent and ability and underrewards Blacks for their education?

The author's study tested Ogbu's thesis on minority underachievement but expanded the research to include class and gender (two additional social forces that are strongly related to differential occupational returns on education) by examining students' attitudes toward education in relation to their high school grades. In 1983, 1193 seniors in nine comprehensive public high schools in the Los Angeles area completed a questionnaire that ascertained their attitudes toward education, family background, and educational and occupational aspirations, as well as various measures of school outcomes. The results showed that all students hold two sets of attitudes toward education, but only one set predicts their achievement in school. The first set of attitudes is composed of beliefs about education and opportunity, as found in the dominant ideology of US society. These attitudes, which the author calls *abstract* attitudes toward education, embody the Protestant Ethic's promise that schooling is a vehicle for upward mobility and success (for example, 'Education is the key to success in the future'). These beliefs are widely shared and vary little at this level of abstraction. Abstract attitudes, therefore, cannot predict achievement behavior. The second set of beliefs about education consists of *concrete* attitudes, which reflect the diverse material realities that people experience with regard to returns on education from the opportunity structure ('Based on their experiences, my parents say people like us are not always paid or promoted according to our education'). Agreement or disagreement with statements of concrete attitudes closely follow class and racial divisions in society. The overall findings indicate that concrete attitudes, not abstract ones, predict achievement in high school (see Mickelson 1990 for a complete presentation of the research).

This research demonstrates that the effort that students put into their schoolwork and their academic achievement is influenced by students' accurate assessments of the class- and race-linked occupational returns their education is likely to bring them as they make the transition to adulthood. It suggests that middle-class white youths correctly interpret their parents' experiences in the labor market as evidence that they, too, can expect returns commensurate with their educational attainment; therefore, it is not surprising that they generally earn high grades and are likely to attend college. Following this same logic, working-class and black youths put less effort into their schoolwork because they judge that, for people like themselves, the payoffs for schooling are limited; hence, they receive lower grades and go to college less often than do middle-class whites (Mickelson 1984, 1990).

Consequently, individuals who are reasonably aware of the realities of the opportunity structure that lie ahead should put more effort or less effort into schoolwork, depending on the occupational returns they are likely to receive. It is in this context that the achievement and attainment of females appear anomalous. If occupational opportunities help shape students' educational goals and achievements, as Ogbu and this author believe, women should not achieve as well or attain as much education as do men in comparable racial and class subgroups. Yet women do not achieve as one might predict on the basis of gender inequalities in the opportunity structure. In other words, the relatively poor occupational return on educational investments does not appear to depress either their school performance or their willingness to earn advanced degrees. The anomaly considered in this chapter, then, is not 'Why can't Jane read and write?' because she certainly does, but 'Why does Jane read and write so well?'

Extent of the Anomaly

To capture the anomalous quality of women's educational achievement in the light of the gender-linked job ceiling women face, the following discussion reviews the research on women's educational and occupational outcomes, with special attention to racial and class variations in each. It is important to note that most sociological studies, including those that compare the educational attainment of blacks and whites, tended, until recently, either to ignore women or to treat them as persons whose social status was a function of their father's or husband's positions (Acker 1973, 1980; Bernard 1981; Oakley 1974). Turner's (1964) was a classic study in this tradition; it measured women's goals and ambitions by the occupation they expected their husbands to attain. During the past two decades, however, many social scientists have turned their attention to women's unique experiences in achievement, education, and the labor market. It is these studies that are reviewed in this section.

Academic Achievement

Differences in the academic achievement of males and females involve issues of both performance and motivation. Differences in performance are mediated by age and by type of cognitive activity (Kaufman and Richardson 1982). For example, girls generally do better in school until puberty (Klein 1985). The new learning climate of the junior high school, which is more competitive and more individualistic than is the elementary school, works against girls' strengths, such as working cooperatively in groups (Eccles and Hoffman 1985; Steinkamp and Maehr 1984). Although the grade-point averages of boys and girls are comparable in high school, girls tend to outperform boys in verbal tasks, while boys do better in visual-spatial and quantitative activities. Boys and girls differ, however in the kind of elective courses they choose in high school (there are few gender differences in the enrollment in mandatory high school courses). These gender differences appear particularly in vocational education, where the sex segregation of the work world is mirrored in the students' enrollment. Thus, boys are still more likely than are girls to enroll in higher level mathematics and science courses (National Center for Educational Statistics 1984). Many researchers have attributed the gender differences in quantitative achievement to the different courses in which boys and girls enroll (Berryman 1983; Pallas and Alexander 1983).[2] Although the domains of academic achievement continue to differ by gender, once-popular stereotypes of girls as under- or nonachievers are now considered more mythical than factual (Stockard and Wood 1984).

Gender differences in the motivation to achieve are complex. Earlier research attributed differences in attainment and alleged achievement to girls' lower motivation to achieve. More recent studies, however, have confirmed Maccoby and Jacklin's (1974) conclusions that levels of motivation to achieve among women, including intellectual achievement, continue to equal or surpass those of men (Klein 1985; Lueptow 1980, 1984; Stockard 1985; Stockard and Wood 1984).[3]

Educational Attainment

Until recently, men and women differed in how much schooling they acquired. Alexander and Eckland (1974) showed that female status depressed educational attainment. Nevertheless, today, more women than men graduate from high school (National Center for Educational Statistics 1986; Stockard et al. 1980; US Bureau of the Census 1987). Differences in the subjects in which women and men major at the undergraduate level contribute to differences at the graduate and professional levels (Berryman 1983). On the graduate level, gender differences in attainment appear both in the types of degrees that are sought (women are less likely to be found in science departments and professional schools) and in the completion of advanced degree programs (Astin 1969; Berryman 1983; Klein 1985). Structural factors, such as curricular placement and counseling practices in elementary and high schools, are likely contributors to these patterns in higher education. For example, Hallinan and Sorensen (1987) reported that among equally able girls and boys in elementary school, boys are more likely than girls to be placed in high-ability mathematics groups. However, in a personal communication (1987), Jeannie Oakes noted that she found no systematic evidence of gender differences in track placement among secondary students; girls are just as likely as boys to be found in academic tracks, although they are less likely to choose additional mathematics and science courses when they have fulfilled the minimum requirements for entrance into college.

Racial and Class Differences

Historically, white working-class women generally did not seek education beyond high school because they thought that the home and family were their careers and that their husbands' 'family wage' would provide them with a decent life (Rubin 1976). Bernard (1981) noted that among working-class women, the lack of a job was evidence of their husbands' abilities as providers. Today, when working-class women work outside the home, they do so in the secondary labor market, in which advanced educational credentials are not necessary (Howe 1977; Rubin 1976). Nevertheless, they often have more education than their husbands because when they work, they sometimes work in clerical or service occupations that require writing, typing, and spelling skills. Although white middle-class women often went to college in the past, most of those who sought a higher education did not necessarily plan careers because work outside the home was not intrinsically desired or financially necessary. However, they might attempt to start careers after the children left home (Bernard 1981). Only since the 1970s, with the decline of the 'family wage', have middle- and working-class white women faced the economic and social realities that make employment and the concomitant educational credentials seem necessary.

The case of black women is strikingly different from that of white women. Black women from all classes have always worked outside their homes (Davis 1981). Because the labor market was highly segregated by gender and class, the vast majority of black women were excluded from all but the most menial domestic and service jobs. Nevertheless, black women were more likely than were black men to obtain an education, especially a higher education. This gender pattern of educational achievement represents a reversal of the pattern found historically among whites.

Consequently, the small cadre of educated middle-class blacks was composed primarily of women. Middle-class black women did not view their education as a credential for a desirable marriage or as 'social finishing', as did many of their white counterparts. Instead, they believed that education was a bona fide credential for entry into the middle-class occupational structure. Although the vast majority of these women were confined to careers in teaching and, to a lesser degree, nursing or social work, they worked in their chosen occupations for which they were trained, albeit their careers were constrained severely by a race- and sex-segregated occupational structure. Black women today, unlike white women, do not face the relatively new experience of having to work to survive; they have always had to do so (Davis 1981; Simms and Malveaux 1987; Wallace 1980).

Today, class differences in black women's educational attainment remain. Teenage motherhood, epidemic among poor blacks, has a devastating effect on educational outcomes (Children's Defense Fund 1985, 1988; Rumberger 1983).[4] Black women from working- and lower-class backgrounds continue to attain less schooling than any ethnic group except Hispanics and Native Americans (Children's Defense Fund 1988; US Bureau of the Census 1987).

Differences in Returns on Education

Members of the working class, women, and minorities continue to receive lower returns on their education than do middle-class white men. In 1982, the US Commission on Civil Rights reported that at every level of training, blacks, Hispanics, and women receive lower pay and have higher levels of under- and unemployment than do middle-class men. Moreover, in many instances, the disparities are greater among female and minority workers with the most education (Treiman and Hartman 1981).

Treiman and Hartman (1981, p. 16) reported that 'minority males employed full time earned 75.3 percent of the salary of similarly employed majority males; majority females earned 58.6 percent and minority females 55.8 percent'. These disparities were present even after the authors controlled for differences in seniority, education, age, specific vocational training, local pay rates, average number of hours worked, number of weeks worked per year, and other characteristics.

A primary reason for the persistence of unequal returns is that men and women continue to work in sex-segregated labor markets that have different career ladders (Sewell, Hauser and Wolf 1980). Rosenfeld (1980) examined career trajectories (the job histories of socioeconomic status and income over an individual's work life) by sex and race. She found that white men have a general advantage over all other groups in many aspects of their careers, including wages and status, and that women and nonwhite men have similar career profiles. Kanter (1977) described the problems faced by women in the corporate world: white men gain more status than does any other group and nonwhite women gain the least, and the differences between white men and other groups increase over time. The exception to this trend is the small number of black women with extremely high levels of education (Carrigan 1981; Jones 1987; Rosenfeld 1980; Wilkerson 1987). Among black women managers with MBAs, the evidence is mixed. Although their career mobility rates were nearly identical to those of men, personal and institutional factors affected their promotions differently than they did for men (Nkomo and Cox 1987). For example, mentors were more available to men than to women and men were more likely to be promoted if they had line positions, while women were more likely to be promoted if they worked in large, rather than small, firms.

Why do women continue to achieve and value education in the face of limited potential returns on their efforts? A review of the literature reveals at least four hypotheses as possible explanations for this anomaly. The following sections discuss these hypotheses and assess each in the light of some relevant research.

Differential Reference Groups

The first hypothesis is drawn from reference-group theory, which Nilson (1982, p. 1) summarized as follows:

> 'Mentally healthy' individuals realistically assess their statuses in comparison to others who are perceived to be fairly similar on at least one important, visible dimension of actual or expected rewards or resources. It is only within a range of meaningful comparison that satisfaction or dissatisfaction is felt.

From reference-group theory, one can deduce that women are aware of their diminished status in relation to men, but when they evaluate what a fair and just return on education might be they look to other women, not to men, as a point of reference. Women's evaluations of whether returns on schooling are equitable are based on their awareness that there are two occupational structures, one for them and one for men (Treiman and Terrell 1975).[5] In this context, women are likely to believe that their education is rewarded. Empirical research indicates that women's incremental return on education is similar to men's, but the intercept of the regression equation is lower for women than for men. That is, year for year and credential for credential, both men and women receive more returns on more education but they start in different places in the opportunity structure. In addition, the internal career ladders in the female occupational structure are much more limited than are those in the male sector (England et al. 1988; Sewell, Hauser and Wolf 1980).

Reference-group theory may explain why women do not consider their mothers', aunts', and older sisters' poor returns on education to be unfair. The returns are fair in terms of a sex-segregated occupational structure, particularly if a woman sees that her role model's education enabled her to move from an unskilled, tedious, dangerous laboring position to a higher-status, clean, pink-collar job. This is exactly what educational credentials have done for many women in the past twenty years: with education, a woman can move from cafeteria worker to secretary, from secretary to teacher, and from clerk to registered nurse.[6]

The author's survey of high school seniors' occupational aspirations, conducted as part of the research described earlier (Mickelson 1984; Mickelson 1990), offers an indirect test for the reference-group hypothesis. If reference-group theory is correct, the occupational aspirations of the young women in the sample should have reflected the sex-segregated occupational structure, as they seemed to do (Table 8.1).

The types of occupations to which males and females aspire offer tentative support for this hypothesis. First, differences in class, rather than gender,

Table 8.1   Percentage of Selected Occupational Goals by Gender/Class Cohort

Occupational Goal	Middle-class Female	Middle-class Male	Working-class Female	Working-class Male
Accountant	3.4	1.8	4.7	2.8
Architect	0.6	1.8		1.6
Computer scientist	6.7	5.7	14.1	10.9
Engineer	0.9	6.8	0.9	6.0
Lawyer	4.3	5.7	3.4	2.8
Registered nurse	5.8		7.7	
Psychologist	6.5	1.8	3.4	0.4
Social worker	2.8	0.4	0.9	
Teacher	4.4		2.0	
Musician	1.2	3.9		3.2
Fashion designer	3.4		3.9	
Writer	1.8	2.9		
Broadcaster	3.1			2.0
Business executive	9.8	8.6	5.6	2.4
Manager	1.2	2.1	3.4	2.0
Clerical worker	3.5	0.4	9.5	1.0
Fire/Police officer	0.3	5.3	0.8	4.0
Computer technician	0.9	1.3	3.0	5.6
Beautician	1.5		3.9	
Carpenter				2.0
Electrician				2.4
Athlete				2.8

Modal Category

First	Business executive	Business executive	Computer scientist	Computer scientist
Second	Computer scientist	Engineer	Clerical	Engineer
Third	Psychologist	Lawyer Computer scientist	Registered nurse	Computer technician

Source: Mickelson 1984.

distinguish students' modal choices. As Table 8.1 shows, the most popular occupation of the middle-class boys and girls was business executive, while the most popular choice of both the male and female working-class students was computer scientist. (This category includes the choices of some working-class girls who indicated that they wanted a 'career working with computers', a statement that often meant that they wanted to use a word processor for clerical work.) The difference in the career aspirations of middle-class and working-class students supports O'Shea's (1984) argument that working-class people tend to choose technical and engineering occupations as vehicles for upward mobility.

In addition, when nonmodal choices are examined, one finds the traditional patterns of the sex-segregated occupational structure, although they are less sex stereotyped than are those that actually exist among current members of the work force. Thus, the occupations of teacher, fashion designer, clerical worker (the few boys who chose this category aspired to be mail carriers), beautician, and registered nurse were chosen exclusively by female students, and those of social worker and psychologist attracted a majority of female aspirants. Conversely, the occupations of athlete, electrician, and carpenter had only male working-class aspirants, and those of architect, engineer, computer technician, musician, and police officer were chosen more often by boys than by girls. Traditional gender stereotyping, however, did not occur with respect to the occupations of lawyer, computer scientist, accountant, and business executive.

The data in Table 8.1 show that although gender differences in occupational aspirations may have narrowed, they still persist. Women are moving away from traditional jobs, as the narrow differences in the choices of the male and female students indicate with regard to the professional and business-executive positions. Below the higher reaches of the occupational structure, however, traditional gender patterns are evident: Most girls in the study chose 'women's work'.

The Pollyanna Hypothesis

According to this explanation, the typical young woman who graduates from high school is likely to be optimistic about her future. Although she may be aware of the sexism that her mother and aunts experienced in the workplace, she interprets it as the problem of the 'older generation', which the women's movement has already addressed. Such a view is likely to be a product of this historical moment and of the limited world of high school seniors. Young women today have been exposed to fifteen years of rhetoric from the women's movement. They have heard of affirmative action and Title IX. They see that society is changing; women can run for the vice-presidency of the United States. The major social institutions that they experience beyond the nuclear family are the mass media and the high school, where women appear to be moving toward gender equity. The rhetoric and the reality of the world outside their family converge into a picture in which women seemingly can achieve their potential, largely unencumbered by sexism.

Adolescent girls have not yet faced situations that conflict with the rhetoric of equal opportunity for women. They are not yet in the job market, and they have yet to enter into close relationships with men in which they may face the choice of subordinating their goals and ambitions to save the family unit. It will be two or three years before these young women achieve adult status and face these possibilities. In the Pollyanna-ish world of adolescent girls, their education will be treated just like a man's and their careers will not be compromised by family responsibilities because their husbands will be equal partners in a dual-career marriage. For these Pollyannas, sexism is a thing of the past; they need not worry about it because the battle for equality has been won.

Indirect support for this hypothesis may be seen in the attitudes of young women surveyed in Johnston, Bachman and O'Malley's (1975, 1985) longitudinal study of approximately 18,000 American high school seniors. The study ascertains the attitudes and behaviors of adolescents on a number of issues, including women's roles, marriage, and career and family. A comparison of attitudes in 1975 and in 1985 would indicate the change in the degree to which women believe that gender equity is possible and desirable. If the Pollyanna hypothesis is true, young women would be optimistic about the prospects for gender equality

equality

Table 8.2   Attitudes toward Marriage, Familly, Work, and Gender Roles among Selected High School Youths, 1975 and 1985[a]

	1975		1985	
	Males	Females	Males	Females
1. How important to your life is having a good marriage and family life?	86.0[b]	92.1[b]	86.0	93.2
2. Being a mother and raising children is one of the most fulfilling experiences a woman can have.	60.2	63.8	49.6	66.9
3. I expect my work to be a central part of my life	67.0	62.7	76.8	72.3
4. Parents should encourage just as much independence in their daughters as in their sons.	67.1	89.7	66.1	92.9
5. Men and women should be paid the same money if they do the same work.	86.2	96.6	88.8	97.8
6. It is usually better for everyone involved if the man is the achiever outside the home and the woman takes care of the family.	54.7	35.7	42.7	31.0
7. The husband should make all the important decisions.	32.5	22.2	30.3	9.5
8. In a family with no preschool children, husband and wife both work full time.	53.2	73.5	62.0	78.5
9. In a family with preschool children, husband works full time and wife works half time.	40.5	53.2	60.4	72.8
10. In a family with preschool children, husband and wife both work full time.	22.4	23.4	38.6	48.8
11. A working mother can establish just as warm and secure a relationship with her children as a mother who does not work.	30.2	52.5	46.4	76.5

[a] Percentages reflect the total of 'mostly agree' and 'agree' response categories.
[b] The item did not appear in 1975; percentages are from the 1982 survey.
Sources: Johnston, Bachman and O'Malley 1975, 1982, 1985.

in the family and workplace and about the possibilities of combining the traditional roles of wife and mother with a career. Table 8.2 presents the percentage of male and female respondents who agreed with eleven selected statements about equality, families, and work in 1975 and 1985.

As Table 8.2 shows, the attitudes of the young women changed substantially from 1975 to 1985 about careers, sex roles, and gender equality. However, there was little change in attitudes toward marriage, which was still important to most women, and no decrease in the proportion who believed that having children is one of the most fulfilling experiences a woman can have (although only two-thirds of the young women agreed with this statement). At the same time, these young women planned careers. In 1985, approximately 72 percent of them, up from 63 percent in 1975, stated that they believed their work would be a central part of their lives, and 98 percent believed in equal pay for equal work.

Other items reflect changes in views regarding gender equality in the family and the workplace. In 1985, for example, more women than in 1975 agreed that parents should encourage independence in daughters as much as in sons. However, there was a marked decrease in those who favored a patriarchal power structure in the nuclear family, from 36 percent in 1975 to 31 percent in 1985. Similarly, far fewer women in 1985 than in 1975 agreed that the husband should make all the important decisions.

Perhaps the issue that causes the most role conflict for young women is whether to work when they have young children. As Table 8.2 indicates, more young women in 1985 than in 1975 would accept work outside the home, even if they had small children. Furthermore, 77 percent of the young women in 1985, as compared with 53 percent in 1975, agreed that a woman who works outside the home can be just as good a mother as one who is a housewife.

Taken together, these findings suggest that today's female high school graduates want a family and a career, think that both are important, and believe that they will be able to have both without sacrificing the quality of either. The attitudinal changes from 1975 to 1985 support the argument that, although today's adolescent girls may be aware of the sexist barriers their mothers faced, they do not anticipate encountering the same ones.

Fox and Hesse-Biber (1984, pp. xi–xii) made essentially the same point:

> Compared to their peers of even ten years ago, young women today feel more secure about their chances for active and full participation in areas that have been male domains.... When [our] students were asked to predict their lives ... at age 40 ... a young woman said, 'At age 40 I can see myself as a wife and mother and as a successful lawyer working in a well-established firm.' ... [Few] expect any difficulty in combining working and family demands ... they accept the fact that they must work hard, and they assume that, in doing so, they will be rewarded with rank and earnings commensurate with their education, training and ability. In short, they accept the American creed about equality of opportunity, advancement, and reward for performance.

The Pollyanna hypothesis suggests that today young women believe they have 'come a long way', that barriers to successful careers in both the marketplace and the home have fallen by the wayside. This belief may explain the anomaly of women's achievement: Women do well in school because they have no doubt that they will be able to take their rightful places in industry and the professions next to their comparably educated brothers. To explode the myth that the battle has been won, more comparable-worth cases must make the headlines and more Elizabeth Hishons, Christine Crafts, and Theda Skocpols may have to sue their employers for sexism.[7] Perhaps young women must encounter the gender-segregated occupational structure, the gap in the salaries of men and women, and the problems that most women face in 'happily integrating' the career-husband-children 'triad' before their attitudes toward education, career, and family reflect, to a greater degree, the realities of modern society.

Social Powerlessness

Theories of the social powerlessness of women are the basis of the third explanation for the apparent failure of sexism in the opportunity structure to affect women's motivations to achieve in school. This explanation posits that marriage is a consciously sought alternative to a career. Aware of the structural inequalities in the occupational world, women know that they cannot expect equitable returns on their education, no matter how well they have done in school, and realize that they must seek a husband if they wish to be socially and financially secure. In addition, they are aware of the economic plight of those who attempt to be independent of a male partner (breadwinner) or of those who are left to support young children alone. Thus, young women strive for future status and success by choosing a 'promising' husband rather than by focusing on a career. Education still has a role: it is essential for acquiring an appropriate husband.

Educational achievement in high school allows a woman to attend college, where she can meet men who are likely to have suitable futures as breadwinners. Accordingly, the primary evaluation of social returns on her educational achievement and attainment will not be made in the labor market, but in marriage. This hypothesis applies to the middle-class woman who must marry a college-educated man simply to maintain the social status and lifestyle of her childhood and to the working-class woman who aspires to upward mobility.

Studies of middle-class white women show that many continue to go to college for the same reasons that the daughters of the elite attended in previous decades: to obtain a liberal arts 'finishing' and to find appropriate husbands (Bernard 1981; Finley 1983; Mickelson 1989; Ostrander 1984). Educational achievement in high school is necessary for middle-class women to gain access to college. Therefore, for some middle-class women, occupations and careers may not be the critical measure of a return on their education; for them, finding an appropriate husband means that the education has 'paid off'. For upper-class women, this dynamic is slightly different. Ostrander (1984) reported that elite women rarely work outside the home but consider their roles to be those of society volunteer and hostess, helpmate to their husbands, and primary socializing parent for their children. They view higher education as essential to fulfilling these roles.

Marriage is also an alternative to a career for working-class white women but for different reasons. Rubin (1976) stated that working-class women choose early marriage when their childhood illusions of glamorous occupations dissolve. These women in particular believe that staying married is an economic necessity, rather than an option (Richardson 1981). Finley (1983) noted that working-class adolescents choose early marriage as a way out of oppressive home situations of powerlessness and poverty. This author (Mickelson 1989) found that many white working-class women who married immediately after high school did so consciously to leave the poverty of their single mothers' homes. Although many of these young women reported that they believed in the value of education and planned to attend college eventually, the immediacy of their poverty over-powered any other social forces in their lives. Thus, many working-class white women may choose early marriage instead of the much more time-consuming and risky route out of poverty — college and a professional husband or a career of their own. Both Finley (1983) and this author (Mickelson 1989) also found that some white working-class women consciously chose to do well in high school so they would have the opportunity to go to college where they would meet middle-class men. Often their mothers explicitly encouraged their academic achievement in these terms.

The case of black women is more complicated. Black women, especially educated black women, have always been able to gain employment (in a sex- and race-segregated occupational structure) more reliably than have black men. The complex gender and class patterns of educational and occupational attainment among black Americans are certainly rooted in historical differences between opportunity structures for men and for women and for blacks and for whites. Today, black women from middle-class families are the most likely to achieve and attain academically. Those with high levels of educational attainment (five or more years of college) are more likely to have jobs commensurate with their education than are white women (Jones 1987; Wilkerson 1987). Middle-class black women do not necessarily perceive marriage as a route to upward mobility or out of poverty. Although many hope to marry a man who will keep them in the lifestyle to which they have become accustomed, they expect to work as well. Because black families have historically been characterized by flexible gender roles, middle-class black women are familiar with the role of breadwinner. Perhaps black parents, more than white, fear the precarious position of women who do not have occupational resources of their own. Education is crucial, 'just in case something happens', one black middle-class mother cautioned her daughter and her daughter's friends (Mickelson 1989).

Many working-class black women are highly motivated to succeed in an occupation. Even if they are married, they know their husbands are unlikely to earn enough to take care of their families. For certain black women, especially in the lower class, marriage may be a liability. Poor women build mutual support networks from which they draw resources for survival (Stack 1974), and husbands may be a threat to these networks, since they inhibit a woman's ability to rely on these diverse resources. For such women, the avoidance of marriage may help them to survive financially. The precarious condition of black men as breadwinners is reflected in the advice that one black father gave his two daughters: 'Get yourself an education so you won't have to stay with no sorry man' (Mickelson 1989).

For both middle- and working-class women, black and white, education and marriage have different meanings for potential social status. Arguably, white adolescent girls are aware of the less-than-favorable occupational options that await them and know that for most women (at least for white women), the safest and most reliable route to high status as an adult may be through a good marriage. Although the situation is more ambiguous for young black women, marriage remains important to the economic survival of black families. Wilson (1988) made this point as well in his discussion of the structural origins of the underclass.[8] As Featherman (1978, p. 53) commented, 'Vicarious achievement (through a spouse) remains a major mechanism for intergenerational continuity or change in status for women, supplementing or complementing the opportunities for achievement through independent pursuits outside marriage and the home economy.'

Sex-role Socialization

The fourth hypothesis with regard to the anomaly of women's achievement comes from the literature on sex-role socialization. According to the asymmetry model described by Kaufman and Richardson (1982), boys' achievement is motivated by the desire for mastery and other intrinsic rewards, while girls' achievement is directed toward winning social approval and other extrinsic rewards. Little girls want to please and be 'good' so they will earn love and approval. Women's motivation for achievement, it is suggested, evolves from early childhood needs for love and the approval of others, more than for mastery and self-reliance, which underlies the motivation of men. Clearly, this distinction is rigidly simplistic. Marciano (1981) suggested a subtler explanation: the 'center of gravity' of women's motivation to achieve is an orientation to others, while the 'center of gravity' of men's motivation is a desire for mastery and self-gratification. Girls perform well in school because good performance is compatible with affiliative motives and consistent with the "good girl" role into which they are socialized (Kaufman and Richardson 1982; Maccoby and Jacklin 1974; Weitzman 1979, 1984).

The sex-role socialization hypothesis actually has two aspects. First, girls do well in school because they are socialized to be good. Being a 'good girl' in school means dutifully following orders and instructions from teachers, being decorous and compliant, and accepting rules with little protest. This is the kind of behavior that is more compatible with female than with male sex roles. Weitzman (1984, p. 172) explained how girls' early sex-role socialization produces a particular kind of motivation to achieve that is not found in boys:

> The dependence and affection-seeking responses seen as normal for both boys and girls in early childhood become defined as feminine in older children.... [Girls] are not separated from their parents as sources of support and nurturance, and they are therefore not forced to develop internal controls and an independent sense of self. Instead, the self they value is the one that emanates from the appraisals of others. Consequently, girls develop a greater need for the approval of others ... than do boys.

The second part of this argument revolves around the male sex role and achievement. Although the female sex role demands that girls be good and do well in school, the male sex role, particularly among working-class white boys, requires a degree of resistance to authority figures like teachers and a certain devaluation of schoolwork because it is 'feminine' (Stockard et al. 1980; Willis 1981). The lived culture of working-class men glorifies manual labor, which involves physical strength, a willingness to get dirty, and an attitude of rebellion against and independence from superiors, as distinguished from the attitudes of submission and appeasement associated with women (Bologh 1986). Thus, the high achievement of female students may be due to two separate sex-role processes: girls do well because they are socialized to be good, and they do better than some boys because the sex-role socialization of boys requires a degree of academic underachievement. As Stockard et al. (1980) noted, good students display behavior that is generally sex typed as feminine. Therefore, it is understandable if boys do not conform to the role of good student because being a good student would mean acting feminine. Boys do not refuse to learn, but they may not reflect learning in the ways that are required for high grades. Until this century, even elite white men tempered their achievement in college to receive a 'gentleman's C'.[9]

Table 8.3   Means of Grade-Point Averages, by Subgroup (Frequencies are in Parentheses)

	Black Males[a]	Black Females	White Males	White Females[b]
Middle class[c]	2.185	2.363	2.714	2.805
	(56)	(8.4)	(224)	(241)
Working class	2.096	2.293	2.415	2.738
	(138)	(140)	(110)	(93)

[a] Race, p<.0001; [b]Gender, p<.0001; [c]Class, p<.0005
Source: Mickelson 1984

Indirect support for this hypothesis appeared in two studies. Stockard and Wood's (1984) investigation of underachievement among Oregon secondary school students revealed that underachievement was much more common among boys than among girls. This author's study (Mickelson 1984) offered limited support for this hypothesis in a comparison of students' grade-point averages. Data in Table 8.3 reveal that in all instances the achievement of the female students surpassed that of the male students (p<.0001). Moreover, working-class gender differences in grade-point averages were almost three times greater than the middle-class differences, especially when one compares white working-class male and female students. The gender differences in grades are in the directions one might expect if the sex-role socialization hypothesis is correct. Finally, in response to a question about the importance of getting an education relative to going to work, white working-class male students more than any other race-by-gender-by-class subgroup, reported that going into family businesses (which were overwhelmingly in the skilled crafts or services) was more important than getting good grades (Mickelson 1984, p. 144). Taken together with the significant class and gender differences in grade-point averages, this attitude toward work vis-à-vis education lends indirect support to the sex-role socialization hypothesis.

Discussion

The anomaly with which this article began remains essentially unresolved. Why do women do so well in school when they can expect only relatively limited returns on their educational achievements? The rationale underlying the educational attainment of most men (gaining credentials that will bring higher pay, better jobs, and promotions) is, in many ways, inadequate for women. The academic achievement and attainment of women defy this logic because women continue to match (and often surpass) men without the same occupational returns from schooling that men receive.

The four hypotheses explored in the previous section offered a variety of perspectives on the question of why women achieve in school. The first three hypotheses examined how young women view the connection between education and the occupational structure, while the fourth ignored structure altogether. Although these hypotheses offer some insight into the question of women's achievement, all four hypotheses suffer from certain problems:

1 Reference-group theory assumes that women are aware of the greater returns from education that men receive but do not care. This idea requires a major leap of faith.

2 If one accepts the reference-group premise that young women are aware of a sex-segregated occupational structure, one must deny the Pollyanna and the social powerlessness hypotheses. The Pollyanna theory presumes that the basis of the reference-group hypothesis — a sex-segregated occupational structure — is a thing of the past. The social powerlessness hypothesis denies the direct relevance of occupational returns on education for women's decisions and proposes that good marriages, not careers, are the fundamental motivation behind women's educational attainment. If this is true, then a sex-segregated occupational structure is less relevant than is women's primarily dependent status in society.

3 Furthermore, the Pollyanna theory and the social powerlessness theory are mutually exclusive. One denies that young women perceive sexism as a factor in the status-attainment process, but the other identifies sexism as such a prominent component of the status-attainment process that marriage appears to be the most reasonable alternative for women who seek social and financial security.

4 The sex-role socialization hypothesis focuses completely on the individual and her early socialization experiences. It fails to link her behavior in school to such broad social-structural phenomena as those discussed in the other hypotheses. Any account of social behavior that fails to incorporate structure is limited in its explanatory power.

A final shortcoming of all the hypotheses discussed in this article is the uneven ability of the theories to explain the achievement and attainment behavior of women from diverse racial and class backgrounds. It is likely, for example, that the Pollyanna phenomenon is more characteristic of middle-class women, while reference group is a more likely explanation of working-class experiences. Social-powerlessness theory is also relevant mainly to middle-class white women; it is especially inadequate for poor and working-class black women.

Directions for Future Research

Although the four hypotheses offer some insight into the anomaly of women's achievement, none truly explains it. One important reason for the theoretical shortcomings of sociology concerning women's lives stems from the tendency to generalize from the experience of white highly educated middle-class men to all people in society (Acker 1973, 1980; Bologh 1986; Gilligan 1983; Richardson 1981). Such generalizations impose inappropriate categories on a woman's definition of the situation (Berg 1987) and they ignore race and class differences among women's experiences (Higginbotham 1991; Baca Zinn 1991). Future research can benefit from the emerging body of feminist theory that argues that a social theory which accounts for the male experience will not necessarily describe the female experience successfully. A number of feminist scholars have attempted to break out of this androcentric paradigm, but theories and empirical work that capture the female experience in education and in the opportunity structure remain incomplete. For instance, the assumption that women evaluate returns from education through the same system of meaning as do men leads one to conclude that women's achievement is anomalous. Yet if women's achievement and attainment are understood from an alternative feminist paradigm that is built on women's lived experiences, they may not be anomalous.

For example, recent feminist scholarship has challenged the division between public and private worlds found traditionally in social science, and has offered a potentially useful framework for understanding women's lived experience in relation to education and occupations. Bologh (1986) suggested that the boundaries between the private world (domestic life, home and family, and communal relations) and the public world (economy and polity) are demarcated less clearly for women than for men. A continuum, rather than a dichotomy, captures more accurately the public and private dimensions of women's lives.

Women's experience is characterized by systems of interdependencies, relationships, and networks. Women are not as likely as men to see family responsibilities as distinct from and competing with professional responsibilities. For women, the two are part of one reality and must be accommodated simultaneously. This is not to say that women are ignorant of the tensions and crosspressures (such as role conflicts) between public and private demands. Rather, they recognize the internal tension between individual and community because the two are linked irrevocably and inextricably in their experience (Bologh 1986). Gilligan (1983, p. 19) noted, for example, that women's resolution of moral problems relies on 'conflicting responsibilities rather than ... competing rights and requires for their resolution a mode of thinking that is contextual and narrative rather than formal and abstract'. This idea suggests that women approach their lives by weaving diverse elements into a single tapestry of public and private roles. A world view such as this inevitably will affect the way women evaluate the meaning and significance of education in their lives. This perspective suggests that returns from education are refracted not only through the lens of income, status, and career ladders but through familial and community roles.

Aspects of this argument may appear similar to human capital theory's explanations of the sex-segregated occupational structure and the lower status and monetary returns from education that accompany traditionally female jobs. Both emerging feminist theory and human capital theory propose that women take their familial roles into account when making occupational choices. But the theories are fundamentally different. Central to human capital theory is the notion of actors who maximize individual self-interest in the marketplace and that all people define self-interest in the same way. Accordingly, women, like men, choose careers that will maximize their market value. Women accept the lower pay and limited career ladders of jobs in the female occupational structure because these are the quid pro quo that permit serial entries and exits with fewer penalties than jobs in the male sector.[10] In contrast, emerging feminist theory proposes that many women have a different notion of value that is related to human relationships. From this perspective, the concept of individual self-interest that is based on the highest rate of economic return from educational investment loses its explanatory power. If women operate from this other set of values, they may ask, 'What is useful to people, to my family, to my community?' Although both explanations of women's occupational choices take family issues into account, the underlying models of human capital theory and emerging feminist theory are different.

The structural arguments with which this article began offer a partial account of the way social forces affect women's educational accomplishments. As Ogbu (1979) and Mickelson (1984, 1990) have shown, there is a link between the opportunity structure and educational outcomes. Historically, women responded to new labor market opportunities by getting more education. For example, Olneck and Lazerson's (1974) study of immigrant children during the early part of the twentieth century found that girls were more likely than boys to be in high school because the employment opportunities for men without high school diplomas were greater than those for untrained women. The growing sectors of the economy that were open to women — secretarial and office work and especially teaching — required specific skills for which women had to be prepared. It thus made more economic sense, at least in the short run, for boys to take jobs and girls to continue in school.

Now that a wider range of occupations is opening up to women, primarily in the professions (and, to a much lesser degree, in the shrinking, skilled blue-collar sector), women are responding and obtaining the educational credentials they must have if they are to have any chance to enter these jobs. Overall, women's educational profiles respond to the race- and class-specific opportunities that are there; however, women fail to respond to the 'job ceiling' they face because of their gender. It is in this way that the structural explanations are incomplete. Although these explanations account for the role of the race- and class-linked job ceiling in depressing the achievement of minority and working-class students, they do not explain why the gender-linked job ceiling fails to depress women's achievement net of race and class. Arguments that connect school outcomes to the opportunity structure must be broadened to account for the anomaly of women's achievement and the various racial and class patterns within that social landscape.

To this end, future researchers might consider the perspective of women's lived culture in which public and private spheres are more likely to be interwoven than dichotomized, as they are in the male world. Although a call for incorporating women's experience into research designs may sound banal, it is necessary because so little feminist research exists in the social sciences. It will be difficult to understand the anomaly of women's achievement or any other aspect of women's lives without such a feminist perspective. Until this perspective is adopted, it is unlikely that social scientists will capture more completely the ways in which gender contributes to the organization and structure of social life.

Notes

1 Recently, a member of the Board of Trustees of the University of North Carolina at Chapel Hill, the state's flagship institution, publicly expressed alarm that unless the university's admissions formula was changed, the school could become a predominantly female institution, given the current levels of qualified female and male candidates.

2 Whether gender differences in quantitative achievement are due to sociobiological or environmental factors, such as socialization and exposure to different curricula, remains controversial. However, recent work by Professor Harold Stevenson and his colleagues in the Department of Psychology, University of Michigan, Ann

Arbor (personal communication 1987), strongly supports the idea that gender differences in the performance of American students in mathematics are due to socialization and experiences in school. These researchers compared the mathematics achievement of American schoolchildren with that of children from Japan, Taiwan, and China. They found that there are no significant gender differences in mathematics achievement among Asian students.

3 Although gender differences exist in vocational tracks, they are rooted in differences in the lived cultures of adolescent boys and girls, as well as in certain structural aspects of schooling, such as counseling practices. Valli's (1986) research on clerical education and Lee and Bryk's (1986) study of girls' achievement and attitudes in single-sex secondary schools suggest the importance of lived cultures for the achievement of females.

4 The 'epidemic' is not confined to the black community; the rate of increase in teenage pregnancies is higher among white girls than among black girls (Children's Defense Fund 1985, 1988).

5 Waite (1981) confirmed that 75 percent of women work in occupations whose incumbents are more than 50 percent female and that 32 percent are in occupations whose incumbents are more than 90 percent female.

6 Popular magazines offer insights into the contemporary popular female culture and women's career choices. Some of the fiction found in the 'seven sisters' (*Better Homes and Gardens, Family Circle, Good Housekeeping, Ladies' Home Journal, McCalls, Redbook,* and *Woman's Day*) support the differential reference-group hypothesis (Bernard 1981, p. 165). For example, an article in *Ladies' Home Journal* told the story of a housewife who decides to return to college as a solution to her midlife crisis. 'So I decided to finish up my BA in English and then maybe learn word processing' ('I Had an Affair' 1984, p. 18). Yet, it is not clear to what extent these magazines reflect or create women's culture.

7 Elizabeth Hishon is the lawyer who won permission from the US Supreme Court to sue her former employer, Atlanta's prestigious law firm King and Spalding, for sex discrimination because it failed to grant her or any other woman partnership in the 100-partner firm. Christine Craft is the television anchor who was fired because her employers thought she was not sufficiently attractive to report the news. Theda Skocpol is the sociologist at Harvard University who won a sex-discrimination suit against the university which originally failed to grant her tenure. The many instances of working-class women who face sex discrimination do not generate as much publicity as those of professional women.

8 Wilson (1988) has been criticized by those who interpret his discussion of the unavailability of marriageable men for underclass women as an argument that poor women are but a husband away from economic insolvency. Although he denies that this was his intent, the relative absence of a detailed discussion of the effects of the sex-segregated occupational structure in his book lends support to his critics.

9 An interesting twist on this was reported by Fordham and Ogbu (1986), who described how some able black students consciously hide their ability and temper their achievement lest they be labeled as 'acting white'. The similarities and differences between labeling achievement as either feminine or white behavior, an implication of pariahlike status in both cases, need further exploration.

10 Recent research challenged human capital theory's explanation of the sex-segregated occupational structure and its accompanying wage differentials. England et al. (1988) demonstrated that the human capital model does not hold up under empirical scrutiny. Their analysis offers indirect support for structural factors like 'the multiple feedbacks between gender-role socialization, discrimination, and institutional practices' (p. 554) as the primary reasons for the poor returns that women tend to receive from education.

General Note
An earlier version of this chapter was presented at the 1986 Annual Meeting of the American Sociological Association, New York City. The author's research was supported by a US Department of Labor Grant from the Social Science Research Council. The author wishes to thank Judy Aulette, Iris Carlton-LaNey, Doug Davidson, Thomas Forrest, Leslie Hill-Davidson, Stella Nkomo, John U. Ogbu, Carol A. Ray, Stephen S. Smith, Jean Stockard, and Janice Stroud, for their helpful comments on an earlier draft, and Doris Carter for her assistance in the preparation of the manuscript.

References

ACKER, J. (1973) 'Women and Social Stratification: A Case of Intellectual Sexism', *American Journal of Sociology* 78 (4), pp. 936–45.

ACKER, J. (1980) 'Women and Stratification: A Review of Recent Literature', *Contemporary Sociology* 9, pp. 25–39.

ALEXANDER, K.L. and ECKLAND, B.K. (1974) 'Sex Differences in the Educational Attainment Process', *American Sociological Review* 39, pp. 668–82.

ASTIN, H. (1969) *The Female Doctorate in America*, New York, The Russell Sage Foundation.

BACA ZINN, M. (1991) 'Race and the Reconstruction of Gender', Paper presented at the Annual Meeting of the American Sociological Association, Cincinnati.

BERG, E. (1987) 'Feminist Theory: Moving Sociology from the "Malestream"', *Footnotes* 15 (3), pp. 5–11.

BERNARD, J. (1981) *The Female World*, New York, Free Press.

BERRYMAN, S.E. (1983) *Who Will Do Science?* New York, Rockefeller Foundation.

BOLOGH, R.W. (1986) 'Dialectical Feminism: Beyond Marx, Weber, and Masculine Theorizing', Paper presented at the Annual Meeting of the American Sociological Association, New York.

CARRIGAN, S.P. (1981) 'Income Variation: A Comparison of Determinants for Men and Women', Unpublished doctoral dissertation, Los Angeles, University of California.

CHILDREN'S DEFENSE FUND (1985) *Black Children, White Children*, Washington, DC, Children's Defense Fund.

CHILDREN'S DEFENSE FUND (1988) *Children's Defense Fund Budget FY 1989*, Washington, DC, Children's Defense Fund.

DAVIS, A. (1981) *Women, Race, and Class*, New York, Random House.

ECCLES, J.S. and HOFFMAN, L.W. (1985) 'Sex Roles, Socialization, and Occupational Behavior', in STEVENSON, H.W. and SIEGEL, A.E. (Eds) *Research in Child Development and Social Policy*, vol. 1, pp. 367–420, Chicago, University of Chicago Press.

ENGLAND, P., FARKAS, G., KILBOURNE, B. and DOU, T. (1988) 'Explaining Occupational Sex Segregation and Wages: Findings from a Model with Fixed Effects', *American Sociological Review* 53 (4), pp. 528–43.

FEATHERMAN, D.O. (1978) 'Schooling and Occupational Careers: Constancy and Change in Worldly Success', Madison, Center for Demography and Ecology, University of Wisconsin.

FINLEY, M. (1983) 'Transition from School to Work: The Education and Careers of Working Class Women', Unpublished manuscript, Los Angeles, University of California.

FORDHAM, S. and OGBU, J.U. (1986) 'Black Students' School Success: Coping with the Burden of "Acting White"', *Urban Review* 18, pp. 176–206.

FOX, M.F. and HESSE-BIBER, S. (1984) *Women at Work*, Palo Alto, Mayfield Publishing Co.

GILLIGAN, C. (1983) *In a Different Voice*, Cambridge, Harvard University Press.

HAFNER, A.L. and SHAHA, S. (1984) 'Gender Differences in the Prediction of Freshman Grades', Paper presented at the Annual Meeting of the American Educational Research Association, New Orleans (April).

HALLINAN, M.T. and SORENSEN, A.B. (1987) 'Ability Grouping and Sex Differences in Mathematics Achievement', *Sociology and Education* 60 (2), pp. 63–73.

HIGGINBOTHAM, E. (1991) 'Gender, Race, Ethnicity, and Social Mobility', Paper presented at the Annual Meeting of the American Sociological Association, Cincinnati.

HOWE, L.K. (1977) *Pink Collar Workers*, New York, Avon Books.

'I HAD AN AFFAIR' (1984) *Ladies Home Journal*, April, pp. 18–25.

JOHNSTON, L., BACHMAN, J.G. and O'MALLEY, P.M. (1975) *Monitoring the Future*, Ann Arbor, Survey Research Center, Institute for Social Research.

JOHNSTON, L., BACHMAN, J.G. and O'MALLEY, P.M. (1982) *Monitoring the Future*, Ann Arbor, Survey Research Center, Institute for Social Research.

JOHNSTON, L., BACHMAN, J.G. and O'MALLEY, P.M. (1985) *Monitoring the Future*, Ann Arbor, Survey Research Center, Institute for Social Research.

JONES, B.A.P. (1987) 'Black Women and Labor Force Participation: An Analysis of Sluggish Growth Rates', in SIMMS, M.C. and MALVEAUX, J. (Eds) *Slipping Through the Cracks: The Status of Black Women*, pp. 11–32, New Brunswick, Transaction Books.

KANTER, R.M. (1977) *Men and Women of the Corporation*, New York, Basic Books.

KAUFMAN, D.R. and RICHARDSON, B. (1982) *Achievement and Women: Challenging the Assumptions*, New York, Free Press.

KLEIN, S. (Ed.) (1985) *Handbook for Achieving Sex Equity through Education*, Baltimore, Johns Hopkins University Press.

LEE, V.E. and BRYK, A.S. (1986) 'Effects of Single-Sex Secondary Schools on Student Achievement and Attitudes', *Journal of Educational Psychology* 78 (5), pp. 381–95.

LUEPTOW, L.B. (1980) 'Social Change and Sex Role Change in Adolescent Orientation toward Life, Work, and Achievement: 1967–1975', *Social Psychology Quarterly* 43 (1), pp. 48–59.

LUEPTOW, L.B. (1984) *Adolescent Sex Roles and Social Change*, New York, Columbia University Press.

MACCOBY, E. and JACKLIN, C. (1974) *The Psychology of Sex Differences*, Palo Alto, Stanford University Press.

MARCIANO, T.D. (1981) 'Socialization and Women at Work', *National Forum* 71, pp. 24–5.

MICKELSON, R.A. (1984) 'Race, Class, and Gender Differences in Adolescent Academic Achievement Attitudes and Behaviors', Unpublished doctoral dissertation, Los Angeles, University of California.

MICKELSON, R.A. (1989) 'The Logic and Structure of School Achievement and Failure', Unpublished manuscript, Charlotte, University of North Carolina.

MICKELSON, R.A. (1990) 'The Attitude-Achievement Paradox among Black Adolescents', *Sociology of Education* 63 (1), pp. 44–61.

NATIONAL CENTER FOR EDUCATIONAL STATISTICS (1984) 'Science and Mathematics Education in American High Schools: Results from the High School and Beyond Study', *Bulletin of the US Department of Education*, Washington, US Government Printing Office.

NATIONAL CENTER FOR EDUCATIONAL STATISTICS (1986) *Earned Degrees Conferred, Department of Education*, Washington, US Government Printing Office.

NILSON, L.B. (1982) 'The Perceptual Distortions of Social Distance: Why the Underdog Principle Seldom Works', Paper presented at the Annual Meeting of the American Sociological Association, San Francisco.

NKOMO, S.M. and COX, T. (1987) 'Gender Differences in the Upward Mobility of Black Managers', Paper presented at the meeting of the National Academy of Management, New Orleans.

OAKLEY, A. (1974) *The Sociology of Housework*, New York, Pantheon Books.

OGBU, J.U. (1978) *Minority Education and Caste*, New York, Academic Press.

OLNECK, M.R. and LAZERSON, M. (1974) 'The School Achievement of Immigrant Children 1900–1930', *History of Education Quarterly* 14 (4), pp. 453–82.

O'SHEA, D.W. (1984) 'The Impact of College Curriculum and Sector of Employment on Earnings', Paper presented at the Annual Meeting of the American Educational Research Association, New Orleans (April).

OSTRANDER, S.A. (1984) *Women of the Upper Class*, Philadelphia, Temple University Press.

PALLAS, A.M. and ALEXANDER, K. (1983) 'Sex Differences in Quantitative SAT Performance: New Evidence on Differential Course Work Hypothesis', *American Educational Research Journal* 20 (2), pp. 165–82.

RICHARDSON, L.W. (1981) *The Dynamics of Sex and Gender*, Boston, Houghton Mifflin Co.

ROSENFELD, R. (1980) 'Race and Sex Differences in Career Dynamics', *American Sociological Review* 45, pp. 583–609.

RUBIN, L. (1976) *Worlds of Pain*, New York, Basic Books.

RUMBERGER, R. (1983) 'Dropping Out of High School: The Influence of Race, Sex, and Family Background', *American Educational Research Journal* 20 (2), pp. 199–220.

SEWELL, W., HAUSER, R. and WOLF, W. (1980) 'Sex, Schooling, and Occupational Status', *American Journal of Sociology* 86 (3), pp. 551–83.

SIMMS, M.C. and MALVEAUX, J. (1987) *Slipping Through the Cracks: The Status of Black Women*, New Brunswick, Transaction Books.

STACK, C. (1974) *All Our Kin*, New York, Harper Touchstone.

STEINKAMP, M.W. and MAEHR, M.L. (1984) 'Gender Differences in Motivational Orientation toward Achievement in School Science: A Quantitative Synthesis', *American Educational Research Journal* 21 (1), pp. 39–59.

STOCKARD, J. (1985) 'Education and Gender Equality: A Critical View', in *Research in Sociology of Education and Socialization* vol. 5, pp. 299–326, Greenwich, JAI Press.

STOCKARD, J., SCHMUCK, P.A., KEMPNER, K., WILLIAMS, P., EDSON, S.K. and SMITH, M. A. (1980) *Sex Equity in Education*, New York, Academic Press.

STOCKARD, J. and WOOD, J.W. (1984) 'The Myth of Female Underachievement: A Reexamination of Sex Differences in Academic Underachievement', *American Educational Research Journal* 21 (4), pp. 825–38.

TREIMAN, D.W. and HARTMAN, H. (1981) *Women, Wages, and Work: Equal Pay for Equal Value*, Washington, National Academy Press.

TREIMAN, D.W. and TERRELL, K. (1975) 'Sex and the Process of Status Attainment: A Comparison of Working Men and Women', *American Sociological Review* 40 (20), pp. 174–200.

TURNER, R. (1964) *The Social Context of Ambition*, San Francisco, Chandler Publishing Co.

US BUREAU OF THE CENSUS (1987) 'Educational Attainment in the United States: March 1982–1985', *Current Population Reports*, Series P-20, No. 415, Washington, DC, US Department of Commerce.

US COMMISSION ON CIVIL RIGHTS (1982) *Unemployment and Underemployment Among Blacks, Hispanics, and Women*, Clearinghouse Publication 74, Washington, DC, US Government Printing Office.

VALLI, L. (1986) *Becoming Clerical Workers*, Boston, Routledge & Kegan Paul.

WAITE, L.J. (1981) *US Women at Work*, Santa Monica, CA: The RAND Corp.

WALLACE, P.A. (1980) *Black Women in the Labor Force*, Cambridge, MIT Press.

WEITZMAN, L.J. (1979) *Sex-Role Socialization*, Palo Alto, Mayfield Publishing Co.

WEITZMAN, L.J. (1984) 'Sex-Role Socialization: A Focus on Women', in FREEMAN, J. (Ed.) *Women. A Feminist Perspective*, pp. 157–237, Palo Alto, Mayfield Publishing Co.

WILKERSON, M.B. (1987) 'A Report on the Educational Status of Black Women During the UN Decade of Women: 1976–85', in SIMMS, M.C. and MALVEAUX, J. (Eds) *Slipping Through the Cracks: The Status of Black Women*, pp. 83–96, New Brunswick, Transaction Books.

WILLIS, P. (1981) *Learning to Labor: How Working-class Kids Get Working-class Jobs*, New York, Columbia University Press.

WILSON, W.J. (1988) *The Truly Disadvantaged*, Chicago, University of Chicago Press.

9 Working-Class Women's Ways of Knowing: Effects of Gender, Race, and Class

Wendy Luttrell

Well, I'm not schoolwise, but I'm streetwise and motherwise and housewifewise. I think there are two kinds of intelligence-streetwise and schoolwise. I don't know much facts about things I learned in school, but I know a lot about life on the streets. I guess I someday might be schoolwise if I stick to it long enough. But what I have now, what I know already, nobody can take away.

— *Doreen*

You don't need an education to be smart. I know people who can read and write and do their figures. They are smart but they just never finished school. Like me and my husband. We've learned a lot along the road — in that school of hard knocks. We've got what you call common sense.

— *Beatrice*

The two women just quoted above come from distinctly different cultural backgrounds. Doreen, a student in a community-based adult education program, was born and raised in a white, ethnic working-class community in a northeastern city; she characterized her early school experiences as 'uncomfortable' and explained that she could not wait until the day she could quit and go to work in the local box factory. Beatrice, a student in a workplace-based adult education program, was born and raised on a farm in the southeast; she described going to school as a luxury — something she could only do on rainy days, along with all the other black children she knew who worked for white farmers. Despite their differences, these women share some similar ideas about knowledge and a common framework for evaluating their claims to knowledge. They both distinguish between knowledge produced in school or in textbooks by authorities and knowledge produced through experience. They also have some similar ideas about their 'commonsense' capabilities to take care of others. Their ways of knowing are embedded in community, family, and work relationships and cannot be judged by dominant academic standards. Most important, their commonsense knowledge cannot be dismissed, minimized, or 'taken away'.

This article describes and analyzes how black and white working-class women define and claim knowledge. It is based on participant observation in classrooms and in-depth interviews outside school with 30 women who enrolled in adult basic education programs. The article argues that although these womens' conceptions about knowledge overlap, they are not the same and can be traced to differences in their lives. Both the similar and contrasting meanings that the women attached to their knowledge provide us with unique lenses through which to examine the development of gender, race and class identities and consciousness.

The article begins with a brief discussion of the relevant literature and a description of the research methodology. It then examines the women's shared views of intelligence and common sense, exploring the conflicting working-class interests and values that are promoted through these self-perceptions. This section is followed by a description of hidden gender asymmetries and inequalities in working-class women's ways of knowing and how these asymmetries surface differently for black and white working-class women. The article ends with a discussion of how dominant ideologies of knowledge undermine women's collective identities, claims to knowledge, and power and the consequences for the adult education of working-class women.

Relevant Literature

Although the literature has not specifically addressed working-class women's ways of knowing, several bodies of theoretical and empirical scholarship framed my study. First are ethnographic accounts that described the schooling process as an arena of struggle in which dominant and subordinate cultures, values, and knowledge collide, producing both resistance to and compliance with dominant social relationships (Apple and Weiss 1983; Connell et al. 1982; Eisenhart and Holland 1983; Fuller 1980; Gaskell 1985; Holland and Eisenhart 1988, 1990; McRobbie 1978; Valli 1983; Willis 1981). These accounts form the basis of a critical theory of education in their focus on the experiences of teenagers and young adults in secondary, vocational, or post-secondary education but do not address the issues that adults face when returning to school. This literature argues that working-class girls prepare for their future identities as wives, mothers, and workers through school. However, the women I interviewed seek to change their lives as women through education; their identities are already firmly embedded in cultural, community, family, and work relationships, yet their desire to expand, perfect, or contradict the work they do as women underlies their participation in school. An understanding of how they think they learn and know enables us to appreciate better how people negotiate external constraints and internal meanings in and outside school.

A second body of literature addresses the subjective experiences of adult learners. What is strikingly absent is a critical theory of adult learning that analyzes the production of meanings and class, racial, and gender identities through resistance to imposed knowledge and adult education practices. Although Freire (1970, 1972, 1973, 1978) outlined such a theoretical approach in his work on adult literacy, he minimized gender issues.

Only a handful of researchers have approached the issue of women's adult basic education or literacy practices from a critical perspective, exploring the dilemmas and double-binds that working-class women face as they pursue an education (Luttrell 1984; McLaren 1985; Rockhill 1987). Their accounts suggest that working-class women feel a deep conflict between self and others, placing their needs last either by choice or by force. Therefore, if learning is to engage working-class women, it must be presented not only as an individual self-development process but as one that is rooted in family and community relationships (Luttrell 1984). In her study of Hispanic women learners, Rockhill (1987) argued that women participate in literacy education as part of the work of the family — a way to serve their children and husbands better and to comply with the dominant values of the middle class, femininity, and Anglo-ethnocentrism — but that women's participation in school also challenges Hispanic patriarchal family relations by threatening men's power and control. Despite her compelling analysis of what Hispanic women must risk to become literate and what is at stake when they are denied this basic right, Rockhill did not address the effects of those social, cultural, and political realities on how women learn and understand the world.

This is not to say that feminist questions have not surfaced in research on adult education. Some researchers have examined women's and men's differential access to adult education (McLaren 1981; Scott 1980), and others have explored the psychological, social, and economic impact of education on women's lives (Robinson, Paul, and Smith 1973, 1978). Although scholars generally agree that women's self-perceptions may improve as a result of adult education, some have found women's economic and occupational gains to be negligible (Lovell 1980; McLaren 1985). Still others have focused on the content and pedagogy of adult education courses, suggesting that women's lives and concerns are being minimized or neglected by adult education theory and practice, which further promote unequal gender relations (Hootsman 1980; Thompson 1983). But overall, the field has not provided a comprehensive approach to the understanding of power relations and resistance in women's learning and knowing.

Relevant to this issue is the burgeoning, yet controversial, feminist scholarship about 'women's ways of knowing' (Belenky et al. 1986; Chodorow 1978; Gilligan 1982; Keller 1978, 1982), which is the third body of literature to frame my study. The literature claims that through unconscious psychodynamic processes, cognitive development, and gender-role socialization, women develop propensities toward self and knowing that are less linear, separate, and hierarchical than are men's. It also suggests that women's more continuous and connected sense of self-knowledge is embedded in their social relationships and sustained and reproduced by patriarchal Western conceptions of rationality. Both men and women internalize these concepts of rationality and knowledge that falsely dichotomize emotion and thought, objectivity and subjectivity, mind and body, masculinity and femininity (Bordo 1968; Fee 1983; Rose 1983; Smith 1979). Yet, although patriarchal impositions on knowledge may be said to exist, not all women experience them in the same way. Despite the call of feminist scholars for a more comprehensive discussion of differences among women and an examination of the construction of gender in specific historical and social contexts (Dill 1983; Jaggar 1983; Rosaldo 1980; Stack 1986; Thorne 1986), we still know little about the multiple meanings that women attach to the knowledge they have or are seeking and its relationship to the concrete conditions of their lives.

Finally, to understand the cultural and political significance of working-class women's ways of knowing, I drew on Thompson's (1963) analysis of class, culture, and consciousness as ways of living within certain relationships of power. These relationships are formed and change when people articulate and identify their class interests, capabilities, or concerns as being common to others like themselves and against those whose interests are different from (and usually opposed to) theirs. Applying Thompson's framework, I examined how black and white working-class women define their knowledge and capabilities in this way. Cognitive processes are usually understood as individual or psychological, not as part of class, racial, or gender culture and consciousness. Yet a focus on women's claims to knowledge can help expand the parameters for explaining how consciousness develops in the context of political struggle.

Methodology

The findings reported in this article are from a study of the educational experiences and perceptions of black and white working-class women attending two programs: an urban, northeastern, community-based program serving a white ethnic working-class population, and an adult basic education program serving predominantly black maintenance and housekeeping employees of a southeastern university. I chose these programs because they provide a unique access to working-class women learners. The community-based program, with its emphasis on supportive services for women, particularly day care, has made it possible for white working-class women, who otherwise would not have had or considered the opportunity, to continue their education. The workplace literacy program, with its four-hour-a-week work-release arrangement, makes adult education accessible to people whose family responsibilities and transportation problems seriously limit their participation in classes held at night. Both programs attract students who do not feel comfortable in formal academic settings, such as high schools or community colleges. In the classroom observations and in-depth interviews, the black women identified their workplace and the white women identified the local settlement house in which the program is housed as hospitable sites for adult learning.

I was involved in both programs as an adult educator, teaching classes, training teachers, and developing learner-centered curriculum materials. Later, I returned to the programs to conduct research. I informed the women in each program that I was studying working-class women's experiences with and perceptions of education. I collected data in classrooms at different levels of instruction (zero to fourth-grade reading level, fifth- to eighth-grade level preparatory classes for the high school equivalency examination, and community college preparatory classes), and conducted unstructured interviews with over 200 women. I took notes openly during observations and the initial unstructured interviews. Field notes included descriptions of conversations before, during, and after classes. Notes from the unstructured interviews and classroom observations were coded on a variety of dimensions that emerged as persistent themes, including past school experiences, past and present family experiences and relations, self-concept and self-esteem, educational values, and future aspirations. These themes became the focus of the in-depth interviews.

I selected fifteen women from each program to interview in depth. The stratified, selective samples represent the basic demographic profile of women in each community: their marital status, occupation, income, educational level, and religion. The samples also reflect the basic profile of women in each program: their age, past attendance and type of school, number of children living at home, and community (active and inactive).

The fifteen white women who were interviewed all grew up in a tightly knit, ethnic working-class urban community (mostly Polish and Irish) that has suffered from industrial relocation, inadequate social services, and neglect by officials for the past two decades. Like the subjects of other studies of white working-class communities (Kohn 1977; Rubin 1976), the majority of adults in this neighborhood drop out of or have no education beyond high school, are employed in skilled or semiskilled occupations, are paid an hourly wage, and experience periodic unemployment. All the women attended neighborhood schools (two-thirds attended public school and one-third attended Catholic schools) and since then have moved in and out of the workforce as clerical workers, factory workers, waitresses, or hospital or teachers' aides. Two women were displaced homemakers when the study began in 1980.

The black working-class women all grew up in southern rural communities and attended segregated schools. Their work histories are more homogeneous than the white women's in that they all work as housekeepers on the university campus, and some have done so for as many as twenty years. More than half have done domestic work in white people's homes either full time or to supplement their incomes, and most picked cotton or tended tobacco during their youth. Some women have split their work between service and farm labor in an effort to hold on to the land, a practice that is common among southern black working-class people (Stack and Hall 1982). Even though these women reside in different neighborhoods near the university, they share a common heritage in and identity with black rural communities.

The women in both groups shared one basic characteristic: all were mothers, aged 25–50, with children still living at home. The two groups differed, however, in which stage of the life cycle they were in, income, and marital history. Thus, black women of the same age as white women tended to be grandmothers and to have older children or grandchildren living at home. In addition, the family incomes of the white women were higher than those of the black women. More white women were married at the time of the interviews; the proportion of never-married women with children was higher among black women than among white women, but the same number of black women and white women had dropped out of school because they were pregnant.

The final interview took place in the women's homes, and lasted from two to four hours, with a follow-up interview over the course of a year. In the first interview, I asked each woman to tell me what she remembered about being in school, to describe what she liked and disliked and what kind of student she had been. As part of these accounts, the women also talked about their early work and family experiences. In the second interviews, I asked the women to talk about their current school experiences and what caused them to participate and to evaluate themselves as learners now. These discussions led to an exploration of the women's concepts of intelligence and knowledge. Although I had not included questions about intelligence or common sense in the original guide for the in-depth interviews, each woman inevitably brought up the issue of intelligence in response to the question, 'How would you describe yourself as a student?' Definitions of intelligence and common sense, who possesses them, and how they are acquired focused the women's reflections about their capacities as learners. In these final interviews I followed up on earlier discussions, asking the women to clarify their life histories or to respond to my interpretations of their experiences. This last interview was especially important for me because, as a white middle-class researcher, I felt hesitant in interpreting experiences that were so vastly different from my own.

The interviews were tape-recorded and then transcribed. The interviews with the white working-class women were analyzed and written up as part of my doctoral dissertation (Luttrell 1984) before I began interviewing black women, in order to deepen and expand my understanding and analysis of working-class women's ways of knowing. In analyzing all the interviews, I tried to balance between identifying persistent themes across the interviews and treating each woman's narrative as a unique text. Translating working-class women's ways with words into sociological analysis is problematic but, as other feminist researchers have argued, it is also the task at hand (McRobbie 1982; Oakley 1981; Smith 1987).

Intelligence and Common Sense

Individually, the women expressed diverse and wide-ranging definitions of intelligence, but as a whole they distinguished between intelligence and common sense. Common sense was most often described as a category of 'smarts' attained outside school, a form of knowledge that stems from experience and is judged by people's ability to cope with everyday problems in the everyday world:

> Jim considers himself stupid. He's very good at what he does at his job, but he was never good in school. He has a kind of street smarts — he's the commonsense type. I don't know, I'm not sure that intelligence can be measured.

> Intelligence is knowing how to use what you know — it's knowing how to do things. I think being intelligent means coping with things in life. Even people with high IQs or with college degrees don't know how to do the simplest, everyday things or cope with everyday problems — that takes *real* intelligence; it takes common sense.

'Real intelligence', or common sense, is a highly valued capacity that flourishes outside school. It is not measured by what school authorities teach you, but what you can teach yourself or what you learn in the 'school of hard knocks':

> My brother is very intelligent — he's self-educated, not school educated. He reads a lot and has taught himself how to play musical instruments. I consider him one of the most intelligent people I know.

> My father is *really* intelligent. He loves to read everything and is interested in all sorts of things. He graduated high school, but he did really lousy. But he's by far one of the most intelligent people around and what he knows he taught himself.

The women usually contrasted common sense with school intelligence and indicated that common sense can be ruined by too much education or formal schooling:

> I don't think that intelligence has anything to do with schooling. Schools only make you know more. Education is not a sign of intelligence. But people who are well schooled always seem intelligent. I suppose they might not be any more intelligent than me. My husband has this idea that people with a lot of schooling don't have common sense. It is like the more schooling you have, the less common sense you have.

> I used to beg my mother to let me go to school. She would say, 'Girl, you have no common sense.' Or when I would want to read instead of doing my chores she would say, 'You're never going to learn anything like that — you've got to have common sense in this world.'

Common sense has been characterized as a cultural form of knowledge, a way to apprehend the world as familiar and knowable, and as concrete knowledge to inform action (Fingeret 1983a, 1983b; Geertz 1983). The women's definitions of common sense confirm these characterizations by identifying the knowledge that grows out of people's lived experiences. For these women, common sense is accessible; it requires no specialized training or credentials.

Common sense is a way of assessing or judging the truth on the basis of what people have seen and know to be true. The black women especially believed that you can assess the truth more reliably if you know the person or if the person is known by someone within the community. As Barbara said:

> The people I know have common sense. Like my grandmother. She's seen it all and I believe what she says because she's been there. Like she knows about slavery, she didn't read about it, like all of us young folk.

In addition to its cultural base, common sense is also a class-based form of knowledge, a way that the women distinguished themselves from 'professionals' and identified themselves as working class:

Interviewer: So who do you consider to be intelligent?
Debra: I don't know. I know a lot of people who are very intelligent but they are fruity; I wouldn't want to be one. I have common sense. Maybe I have more intelligence than I'm aware of in some areas, but I am not an academic, learned person, and I don't think I'll ever be. I'm not the professional type. I can work with those kind of intelligent people, but I don't want to be like them.
Dottie: I have just never thought about average people like myself being intelligent. People like me have common sense.

According to these women, common sense is not simply an individual characteristic or possession; it reflects working-class capabilities. Common sense affirms and validates working-class experiences and is a way to identify oneself with others who share problems and potentials, creating common bonds and a sense of community. This affirmation came across most strongly in the interviews when the women described how they solved everyday problems through common sense. To them, common sense means relying on family and friends who 'know the ropes' to help you learn how to negotiate bureaucracies (schools, welfare agencies, and hospitals), and seeking advice from people who can be trusted, not because they are professional experts but because they share the same problems. The claim of common sense recognizes and validates working-class solutions, despite the power of scientific knowledge. Common sense supports working-class judgments about what is relevant to everyday life and assessments about what one social historian referred to as 'really useful knowledge' in educational practice (Johnson 1979).

Unlike common sense, which is easily defined and acquired through daily life experiences as part of working-class cultures, intelligence, which is acquired through schooling, cannot be so clearly defined and is in potential conflict with working-class cultures. For example, the women thought that although school-wise intelligence can enhance one's life, it can also interfere with one's ability to meet the demands of working-class existence; they suggested that the *more* schooling one has, the *less* common sense one is likely to have. Similarly, 'real intelligence' that is gleaned from books that people teach themselves to read can benefit working-class life, but schoolwise intelligence that is gleaned from textbooks or school authorities can come into conflict with working-class, especially black working-class, experiences and values.

By distinguishing between common sense and schoolwise intelligence, the women came to believe that a certain type of intelligence, rather than class, separates people and that intelligence, rather than class, determines a person's place in the social structure:

> Intelligence has to do with how people accept life, how life comes to them, and how they deal with it. My boys don't use their intelligence. I don't use half my intelligence. If I did, why would I be here?

The women's shared notions of intelligence embraced the dominant ideology of meritocracy in a capitalist society: people's class position is not fixed but is determined by their individual efforts and ambitions:

> There are a few people who make it. They are the ones that are blessed or that has intelligence. The rest of us just have to make do.

> The important point is that the system is not working. People's mobility is very limited. People really need education to get out of their ruts. The system keeps people in their place, in their class. You need intelligence to get out of your place.

When I responded, 'I know a lot of intelligent people living here,' one woman replied, 'Yeah, but if they were more ambitious, like me — what I'm trying to do here is use my intelligence — then at least they'd have half a chance of getting out of their ruts.'

The ideology of intelligence is a filter through which these women think about and express themselves as adult learners, denying the actual experience and knowledge they have in their everyday lives. The dichotomy they make between intelligence and common sense reflects the disjuncture between the world they know and experience directly and the dominant ideas and images that are fabricated externally, provide a way to understand the everyday world, and serve as a means of social control (Smith 1987). For this reason, although working-class women can claim commonsense knowledge, they are distanced from their intellectual capacities, as is Mary:

> When I was in grade school, one of my teachers said I was smart, so they put me in the advanced class. Now I didn't think of myself as smart until the teacher pointed it out. I would say I have common sense, but then maybe I am smart, maybe I'm intelligent, and I don't know it. But it's been my common sense that has gotten me by in life — how I get along with people — not my grades in school. You can bet on that.

In the end, the women accepted class stratification and relations of domination through the false dichotomy of common sense and intelligence and through class-based notions of 'real intelligence'.

Gender-based Knowledge

When the women discussed commonsense knowledge and how it is gained, they revealed their belief that common sense is not a genderless concept. Instead, they indicated that men's claims to knowledge are superior to women's and affirmed the idea that men are more powerful by virtue of their knowledge, not the privilege they have as men. However, the pattern of this gender asymmetry and its impact on each group of women was not the same and thus requires careful examination.

When talking about people they knew who were intelligent, the white working-class women gave only men as their examples. Although they described their mothers, aunts, or sisters as having common sense, they saw only certain aspects of common sense as 'real intelligence' — those that are associated with men's work and their activities.

The differences are most evident in the women's distinction between mental and manual work and ways of knowing. Throughout the interviews, the white working-class women reiterated that intelligence is required to do manual work:

> The most intelligent person I know is my brother — he can fix anything. And when you get right down to it, what's more important than being able to make things work? Not everybody can do that, you know.

> Now just because we're going to school and getting educated, we shouldn't forget that people, like my husband, who work with their hands are just as important as college professors and just as smart.

But when the white working-class women defined manual ways of knowing as 'real intelligence', they always referred to skilled manual work performed by *men*, not to the manual work required of women in factory jobs. Similarly, they equated men's physical common sense, the ability to work with their hands, with 'real intelligence', never discussing women's ability to work with their hands, as in sewing.

In the same spirit, the women also equated men's self-learned activities, such as reading or playing a musical instrument, with intelligence, ignoring the wide range of activities that women teach themselves, including reading and helping children with homework. Instead, the white working-class women described themselves as 'housewife-wise', 'motherwise', 'good problem-solvers', or 'always balancing a lot of things, if that counts'. They associated commonsense abilities with activities in the family or the community and considered them trivial.

Not only did the white women value men's common sense more than their own, they described the different ways that working-class men and women acquire common sense. White working-class men learn common sense that translates into 'real intelligence' through a set of collective, work-related experiences, including apprenticeships, as sons or employees, or as participants in vocational training programs that teach them what might be called 'craft' knowledge. This 'craft' knowledge, the ability to work with one's hands and muscles, belongs to the work group; it is not individualized as a character trait and cannot be learned from books. It also identifies one as masculine, capable of performing traditionally sex-stereotyped manly tasks. Men acquire this masculinity and 'craft' knowledge not by nature or instinct, but through some public, collective experience. In contrast, working-class women acquire common sense naturally, as intuition. They describe this knowledge as simply a part of being a woman. As Anne explained:

> There are lots of things I know — what you might call woman's intuition or mother's intuition. Taking care of a child with a chronic disease teaches you this. You can begin to predict what the doctors are going to tell you and then you go home and deal with it on your own. That's just common sense; in the end, you do what you have to do as a mother.

For women, common sense stems from relational activities that are embedded in the care of and affiliation with others. They do not recognize these activities as learned but associate them with feelings and intuition. Women's common sense comes in flashes, precipitated by an event such as childbirth or divorce. It can also develop over the years, as women evaluate their ability to cope with extenuating circumstances. The learning process is invisible because this intuitive knowledge is individualized and personal. It is not collective or public, even though it identifies women as feminine and able to fulfill sex-stereotyped roles as mothers and wives, and is seen as affective rather than cognitive. As Cheryl explained:

> Common sense is a feeling, really. Like being a mother. You do things that seem right at the time. Nobody ever tells you to do this or do that. Although my sister, she just had a baby, drives me crazy always calling

me up, saying, 'What do I do?' You'd think she would have a little more common sense than that.

The black working-class women also located their commonsense knowledge in a variety of caretaking and domestic skills done for the benefit of others. Like the white working-class women, they referred to their common sense as intuitive and stemming from feelings and most often focused on the common sense that it takes to raise children:

Interviewer: Where did you get the common sense you have to raise your children?

Lois: I was born with it. Now I didn't always use it, like with my boys, but then I was young and running all the time. But you get older, you experience things, you know what's right to do for them and what they need. You're their mother and you stay close to them; you can just feel it.

The women's classification of their knowledge as 'affective', not 'cognitive', as 'intuitive', not 'learned', or as 'feelings', not 'thoughts', all reflect an acceptance of dominant conceptions of knowledge and ultimately diminish women's power. Feminist critics of dominant conceptions of knowledge have challenged these ideological dimensions of women's ways of knowing (Rose 1983; Smith 1979). They have argued that just as the nature of women's domestic work makes it impossible to distinguish what is 'love' from what is 'labor', the nature of women's knowledge makes it impossible to distinguish what is emotional from what is objective or rational. They also noted that the false dichotomy between emotional versus objective labor promotes relations of authority and the domination of men (who are exempt from personal service work) over women (who perform unpaid domestic work as part of their gender role); this false dichotomy is translated into a distinction between feelings and thoughts. Women are then falsely associated with feelings, while men are falsely associated with thoughts (Fee 1983).

Because society does not view women as sources of official, legitimate, or rational knowledge (nor do women), the women who were interviewed associated their commonsense knowledge with feelings and intuitions. As class relations shape attitudes toward schoolwise versus commonsense knowledge, gender relations influence attitudes toward rational versus intuitive knowledge, thus constraining societal expectations of women's intellectual capabilities.

White and black working-class women are drawn to common sense and intuition because both forms of knowledge allow for subjectivity between the knower and the known, rest in women themselves (not in higher authorities), and are experienced directly in the world (not through abstractions). But both classifications (common sense and intuition) place women in less powerful positions vis-à-vis men (both black and white) and white middle-class professionals (men and women). They do so not simply because women are fooled or seduced into believing in the ideological split between feelings and rationality, the false dichotomy of mental and manual work, or the promise of meritocracy, but because the real nature of women's knowledge and power is hidden from view and excluded from thought.

How Race Makes a Difference

Women do not experience their exclusion in the same way, however; their daily experiences of maintaining a household, raising children, and sharing a life with men vary according to race and class and create different imperatives for women's ways of knowing. Race affects how women claim knowledge, which is reflected in how the black women differentiated common sense from 'real intelligence'. First, they did not make the same distinctions between mental and manual ways of knowing or emphasize the intelligence required to do manual work, perhaps because black men have historically had limited access to the 'crafts'. Instead, they viewed common sense, most often referred to as 'motherwit', as encompassing everything from solving family disputes to overcoming natural disasters. It was not uncommon for black women to identify both men and women relatives who possess common sense capabilities that stem from keeping families together. As Lois said, 'I got my common sense from my momma and daddy. They worked real hard to keep us, and they would always be there to help anyones that needed it.'

Second, unlike white women, black women did claim 'real intelligence' for themselves and their experiences in doing domestic, caretaking work. This 'real intelligence' is based on their ability to work hard and get the material things they and their children need and want, with or without the support of a man:

> I got a sister I think she is smart, real intelligent. All of them is smart, but this one is special and she do the same kind of work I do but she's smart. She can hold on to money better than anyone. It look like anything she want she can get it. She bought her a car, this was in the 60s. Then after that she bought her a trailer. She don't buy that many cars, but anytime she or her childrens need something, she can go and get it. But she has a husband that help her, not like my other sisters or me. Her husband is nice to her and both of them working. But even that, it takes a lot of intelligence.

> I would say my sister is the most intelligent person I know. She knows how to get what she wants and she has done it on her own, her kids and working; she ain't never been on welfare or nothing.

Black women are central in keeping black families together — swapping resources and child care and adapting to adverse economic constraints through extended-kin networking and mutual support (Jones 1985; Ladner 1972; Stack 1974). As a result, their work as women is also the work of black survival and, therefore, is not as easily diminished or trivialized as that of the white women.

The ability to deal with racism (another type of 'real intelligence') is also something black women learn through doing domestic work in the service of others.

Kate: I'll tell you what takes real intelligence — dealing with people's ignorance. One day, I was at the department store, you know, maybe it was Belk's. I was getting on the escal-

> ator and there was this little white boy pointing at me
> saying to his daddy, 'Look there at that nigger.' Now you
> should have seen the look on his daddy's face; he looked
> scared, like I was going to start a race riot or something. He
> pushed this boy along trying to get out of my way fast. But
> I know children and they don't mean what they say. He
> was just saying what he hears at home. But people are
> ignorant, and it takes real intelligence to know that it's not
> that little boy's fault.
>
> *Interviewer*: And how did you get that kind of intelligence?
> *Kate*: Oh, well, you live and learn. You see a lot and watch
> people. It's a feeling you have to have because not all white
> people are the same. I sure know that 'cause I worked for
> different ones, you know, taking care of their children, and
> I've seen different things.

This 'real intelligence' is acquired by virtue of being a black woman in a white world. It is also a knowledge that black women share equally with black men. It is collective, learned through extended-kin relations, and practiced in daily interactions with white people.

Class-based concepts of intelligence and common sense pit experience against schooling and working-class people against middle-class people; race-based concepts of 'ignorance' and 'real intelligence' pit whites against blacks. But the invisible gender-based concept that pits collectivity against individuality and autonomy against dependence is the basis for unequal power relations between working-class men and women. The craft knowledge of white working-class men, like scientific knowledge, which is acquired through collective experience and consensual agreement on what constitutes a 'fact', is seen as more legitimate and therefore more powerful in the hierarchy of knowledge. White working-class women's knowledge, which is acquired through individual or private experience, seems to provide no basis for consensual agreement to legitimate the 'facts' of caretaking. The particulars of meeting individual needs make it impossible to universalize this knowledge and thus make women's collective claims to the knowledge of relationships unthinkable. Therefore, women's knowledge and power are structurally excluded from thought. Similarly, because intuitive common sense comes from domestic responsibilities that are not recognized as work, it appears that white working-class women do not initiate their knowledge but must be receptive when it comes; thus, the actual hard work, mastery, and collective nature of their activities in acquiring knowledge are concealed. It also appears that white working-class men seek autonomy through knowledge and that white working-class women preserve relationships through theirs; this false notion undermines women's claims to authority or power.

Black women, however, claim knowledge not only through gender, but through racial identity and relations. Their intuitions and claims to the knowledge of relationships are part of a collective identity as black women. This knowledge is a particular, not a universal, kind in that one must be black to have real knowledge about the world of white people, who are often 'ignorant' (prejudiced). Both black men and black women collect and disseminate their knowledge within extended-kin and community relationships and through hard

manual work. The result is that black women are not distanced from their knowledge and power. The daily reminder of their collective identity as working-class
blacks mitigates the daily reminder of their individual identity as women.

Knowledge: Paradox or Power?

The women's images, concepts, knowledge, and ways of knowing must be seen
as integral to the practice of power. To understand how claims to knowledge
become empowering, one can apply Thompson's (1963) analysis of how class
identities and interests get defined in opposition to ruling-class interests, and see
that when women define and claim their knowledge they articulate class and race
relations the most clearly. All the women acquire common sense in opposition to
middle-class professional people, and black women acquire 'real intelligence' in
opposition to white people. This 'real intelligence' poses whites, who lack the
knowledge of racism or who behave in racist ways, as 'ignorant' (regardless of
their education, status, income, or power) against blacks who 'know better'. In
the struggle to maintain dignity and self-respect in a world that judges people
according to white middle-class standards, the 'real intelligence' and knowledge
of blacks and the common sense of working-class people suggests the possibility
of collective autonomy and power, because women's knowledge is not acquired
as a group in opposition to men but appears to be individually intuited. Thus, the
gender conflicts that exist are made invisible.

At the same time, black and white working-class women express these
gender conflicts differently. White working-class women express a gender
conflict when they talk about going to school to be 'better' in relation to their
husbands:

> I'm coming back to school to show my husband that he isn't the only
> one in the family who can carry on an intelligent conversation.

> I can't wait to wave my diploma in his face and say, 'Listen here, I know
> what I'm talking about.'

They also acknowledge a conflict when they identify the catalyst for enrolling in
school as their separation or divorce. Ironically, white working-class women seek
school knowledge to empower themselves. Since it is clear that their intuitive
commonsense knowledge is valued less than is men's learned common sense,
they turn to school knowledge to legitimate their opinions, voices, and needs: to
be 'better' in relation to their children, family members, and jobs.

Pursing schoolwise knowledge puts white working-class women in a paradoxical situation and creates in them considerable ambivalence. Schooling puts a
strain on working-class women's ties with the working-class culture, a culture
that values commonsense knowledge and working-class men's 'real intelligence'
more than it does book learning and mental work. Yet schooling is perceived as
one of the few avenues by which working-class women can achieve upward
mobility. Consequently, working-class women must seek legitimation from the
same source that undermines their knowledge and sense of identity (as women
and as part of the working class). Nevertheless, working-class women's access to

school learning and to white-collar jobs gives them an edge in the balance of power. If their common sense is inevitably valued less than is the common sense of husbands, brothers, or fathers, having schoolwise *and* motherwise intelligence is perhaps their only chance. In the end, white working-class women embrace the dominant concepts of knowledge because doing so not only promises them class mobility but gives them their sole legitimate form of power vis-à-vis working-class men.

Black working-class women express this gender conflict differently. Although they do not embrace the dominant white male value of knowledge, they attribute black men's power to black men's superior knowledge. In addition to all the many skills that black men have developed to survive, the black women mentioned that black men's 'real intelligence' is getting black women to 'take leave of their senses'. Black men have the ability to convince black women to do the very things they have sworn they will not do. Thus, black women see black men's knowledge as the power to dominate black women and black women's lack of intelligence or common sense as their willingness to accept domination:

> I lose my common sense when it comes to men. I don't know how it happens. They're just so smart getting you to listen to them and what they want. I should have learned that lesson by now, but I haven't — it's just plain stupidity on my part.

> There's lots of intelligence. It's not so easy to say. And sometimes I have it and sometimes I don't, you know the commonsense type. I can get myself into some trouble when I don't. I sure need more, but not the kind we get here in school. I mean John, you know, he can get me to do just what he wants, just like that. And that takes real intelligence, it takes something to get me to do things I know's not good for me.

In the end, unequal gender relations are concealed through the women's notion that men's power lies in their intelligence or knowledge and not in their culturally sanctioned license to dominate women in many ways, including sexually.

The paradox for black working-class women vis-à-vis adult education is complex, reflecting the multiple layers of their oppression in American society. Although black working-class women do not seem to need schoolwise knowledge to legitimate their power within black communities, they do need ways to balance and legitimate their power with black men and with white men and women. They have been denied entrance to the pathways to legitimation with whites, however, through their systematic exclusion from schooling and jobs that provide the social and economic resources for upward mobility. So black women may appear less ambivalent about their ways of knowing and less willing to embrace dominant white middle-class values of knowledge, but the arenas in which their knowledge, intelligence, and common sense can be developed and disseminated have been severely limited.

In addition to this discrimination, some 'scientific studies' have suggested that blacks are genetically inferior to whites in intelligence. These studies have had devastating effects on public educational policy and practice with regard to blacks, warping the expectations of both blacks and whites about what black people can achieve. Another erroneous finding that educators commonly believe is that black women are genetically more intelligent than are black men (Reid 1975). In this context, black women's claims to schoolwise intelligence are problematic and may be destructive to the relationships of black men and women. Furthermore, although there has been a parallel system of black education, which historically has provided for the development of black identities, interests, and knowledge (Giddings 1984), black working-class women have not always been its beneficiaries.

That black women's pursuit of adult education is embedded in all these contexts necessarily casts schoolwise intelligence and book learning in a vastly different light for them than for white working-class women. White working-class women's antagonism toward schoolwise intelligence is grounded in their class consciousness, but black women's conflict stems from their 'dual consciousness' of being black and working class. Although the ways in which these multiple constraints are manifested in classroom learning are beyond the scope of this chapter, it should be emphasized that, ultimately, black women's claim to 'real intelligence' cannot be easily translated into perceptions of academic skill or competence.

Conclusion

The differences between white and black working-class women's claims to knowledge reveal that women do not have a common understanding of their gender identities and knowledge. What they *do* have in common is the organization of knowledge as a social relation that ultimately is successful in diminishing their power as they experience the world. To understand women's exclusion requires an examination of the similarities and differences in the object-ive conditions of women's lives, as well as an analysis of how ideologies of knowledge shape women's perceptions and claims to knowledge. Since women do not all experience the work of being a women in the same way, it is imposs-ible to identify a single mode of knowing. To understand why certain forms of knowledge appear more amenable to women, we must look more closely at the ethnic-, class-, and race-specific nature of women's experiences, as well as the values that are promoted in each context.

In the end, the paradox and the challenge of education for all women under patriarchy are to confront the balance of power as they pursue new and different kinds of knowledge. What is important to emphasize, however, is the *ideological* nature of the knowledge women seek. The universality and rationality of school-wise knowledge conceal its opposite: that credentials and instrumental reason are not answers to asymmetrical and unequal social relationships. If women are to *claim* rather than simply *receive* an education, an act that 'can literally mean the difference between life and death' (Rich 1979, p. 232), we feminists, sociologists, and educators must be prepared to untangle both the ideologies and objective con-ditions in women's lives that render our work, knowledge, and power invisible.

Note

This chapter is a revised version of a paper presented at the 1988 Annual Meetings of the American Sociological Association. The author would like to thank Jean O'Barr for her encouragement and Martha Dimes Toher, Rachel Rosenfeld, Robert Shreefter, Jean Stockard, John Wilson, and Julia Wrigley for their perceptive comments on earlier versions. The author is also indebted to the women who participated in the study (whose names have been changed to protect confidentiality) for their patience, openness, and critical insights. Address all correspondence to Dr Wendy Luttrell, Sociology Department, Duke University, Durham, North Carolina 27706.

References

APPLE, M.W. and WEISS, L. (1983) 'Ideology and Practice in Schooling', in APPLE, M. and WEISS, L. (Eds) *Ideology and Practice in Schooling*, pp. 3–33, Philadelphia, Temple University Press.

BELENKY, M.F., CLINCHY, B.M., GOLDERGER, N.R. and J.M. TARULE, J.M. (1986) *Women's Ways of Knowing: The Development of Self, Voice and Mind*, New York, Basic Books.

BORDO, S. (1986) 'The Cartesian Masculinization of Thought', *Signs* 11 (3), pp. 439–56.

CHODOROW, N. (1978) *The Reproduction of Mothering: Psychoanalysis and the Sociology of Gender*, Berkeley, University of California Press.

CONNELL, R.W., ASHENDEN, D.J., KESSLER, S. and DOWSETT, G.W. (1982) *Making the Difference: Schools, Families and Social Division*, London, George Allen & Unwin.

DILL, B.T. (1983) 'On the Hem of Life: Race, Class and Prospects for Sisterhood', in SWARDLOW, A. and LESSINGER, H. (Eds) *Class, Race and Sex: The Dynamics of Control*, Boston, G.K. Hall & Co.

EISENHART, M. and HOLLAND, D. (1983) 'Learning Gender from Peers: The Role of Peer Groups in the Cultural Transmission of Gender', *Human Organization* 42 (4), pp. 321–32.

FEE, E. (1983) 'Women's Nature and Scientific Objectivity', in LOWE, M. and HUBBARD, R. (Eds) *Women's Nature: Rationalizations of Inequality*, New York, Pergamon Press.

FINGERET, A. (1983a) 'Common Sense and Book Learning: Cultural Clash?' *Lifelong Learning: the Adult Years* 6 (8).

FINGERET, A. (1983b) 'Social Network: A New Perspective on Independence and Illiterate Adults', *Adult Education Quarterly* 33 (3), pp. 133–46.

FREIRE, P. (1970) *Pedagogy of the Oppressed*, New York, Seabury Press.

FREIRE, P. (1972) *Cultural Action for Freedom*, Harmondsworth, Penguin.

FREIRE, P. (1973) *Education for Critical Consciousness*, New York, Continuum.

FREIRE, P. (1978) *Pedagogy-in-Process*, New York, Continuum.

FULLER, M. (1980) 'Black Girls in a London Comprehensive School', in DEEM, R. (Ed.) *Schooling for Women's Work*, London, Routledge & Kegan Paul.

GASKELL, J. (1985) 'Course Enrollment in the High School: The Perspective of Working-class Females', *Sociology of Education* 58, pp. 48–57.

GEERTZ, C. (1983) *Local Knowledge: Further Essays in Interpretive Anthropology*, New York, Basic Books.

GIDDINGS, P. (1984) *When and Where I Enter: The Impact of Black Women on Race and Sex in America*, New York, William Morrow & Co.

GILLIGAN, C. (1982) *In a Different Voice: Psychological Theory and Women's Development*, Cambridge, MA, Harvard University Press.

HOLLAND, D. and EISENHART, M. (1990) *Educated in Romance: Women, Achievement, and College Culture*, Chicago, University of Chicago Press.

HOLLAND, D. and EISENHART, M. (1988) 'Women's Ways of Going to School: Cultural Reproduction of Women's Identities as Workers', in WEISS, L. (Ed.) *Class, Race, and Gender in American Education*, Buffalo, State University of New York Press.

HOOTSMAN, H. M. (1980) 'Education and Employment Opportunities for Women: Main Issues in Adult Education in Europe', *Convergence* 13 (1–2), pp. 79–89.

JAGGAR, A. (1983) *Feminist Politics and Human Nature*, Totowa, NJ, Rowman & Allenheld.

JOHNSON, R. (1979) ' "Really Useful Knowledge": Radical Education and Working-class Culture, 1790–1848', in CLARKE, J., CRITCHER, C. and JOHNSON, R. (Eds) *Working Class Culture: Studies in History and Theory*, New York, St Martin's Press.

JONES, J. (1985) *Labor of Love, Labor of Sorrow: Black Women, Work, and the Family from Slavery to the Present*, New York, Basic Books.

KELLER, E.F. (1978) 'Gender and Science', *Psychoanalysis and Contemporary Thought* 1, pp. 409–33.

KELLER, E.F. (1982) 'Feminism and Science', *Signs* 7 (3), pp. 589–602.

KOHN, M. (1977) *Class and Conformity*, Chicago, University of Chicago Press.

LADNER, J. (1972) *Tomorrow's Tomorrow: The Black Woman*, Garden City, NY, Doubleday Anchor.

LOVELL, A. (1980) 'Fresh Horizons: The Aspirations and Problems of Intending Mature Students', *Feminist Review* 6, pp. 93–104.

LUTTRELL, W. (1984) 'The Getting of Knowledge: A Study of Working-class Women and Education'. Unpublished PhD dissertation, University of California at Santa Cruz.

McLAREN, A.T. (1981) 'Women in Adult Education: The Neglected Majority', *International Journal of Women's Studies* 4 (2), pp. 245–58.

McLAREN, A.T. (1985) *Ambitions and Realizations: Women in Adult Education*, London, Peter Owen.

McROBBIE, A. (1978) 'Working Class Girls and the Culture of Femininity', in Women Studies Groups CCCS (Eds) *Women Take Issue: Aspects of Women's Subordination*, London, Hutchinson.

McROBBIE, A. (1982) 'The Politics of Feminist Research: Between Talk, Text and Action', *Feminist Review* 12, 46–57.

OAKLEY, A. (1981) 'Interviewing Women: A Contradiction in Terms', in ROBERTS, H. (Ed.) *Doing Feminist Research*, London, Routledge & Kegan Paul.

REID, I. (1975) 'Science Politics, and Race', *Signs* 1 (2), pp. 397–422.

RICH, A. (1979) 'Claiming an Education', in *On Lies, Secrets and Silence*, New York, W.W. Norton.

ROBINSON, J., PAUL, S. and SMITH, G. (1973) *Project Second Start: A Study of the Experience of a Group of Low-Income Women in Adult Programs at Brooklyn College*, New York, John Hay Whitney Foundation.

ROBINSON, J., PAUL, S. and SMITH, G. (1978) *Second Start Revisited*, New York, John Hay Whitney Foundation.

ROCKHILL, K. (1987) 'Literacy as Threat/Desire: Longing to Be Somebody', in GASKELL, J. and McLAREN, A.T. (Eds) *Women and Education: A Canadian Perspective*, Calgary, Detselig Enterprises.

ROSALDO, M. (1980) 'The Use and Abuse of Anthropology', *Signs* 8, pp. 389–417.

ROSE, H. (1983) 'Hand, Brain, and Heart: A Feminist Epistemology for the Natural Sciences', *Signs* 9 (1), 73–90.

RUBIN, L.B. (1976) *Worlds of Pain: Life in the Working-Class Family*, New York, Basic Books.

SCOTT, N.A. (1980) *Returning Women Students: A Review of Research and Descriptive Studies*, Washington, DC, National Association for Women Deans, Administrators, and Counselors.

SMITH, D. (1979) 'A Sociology for Women', in SHERMAN, J. and BECK, E. (Eds) *The Prison of Sex: Essays in the Sociology of Knowledge*, Madison, University of Wisconsin Press.

SMITH, D. (1987) *The Everyday World as Problematic: A Feminist Sociology*, Boston, Northeastern University Press.

STACK, C. (1974) *All Our Kin: Strategies for Survival in the Black Community*, New York, Random House.

STACK, C. (1986) 'The Culture of Gender: Women and Men of Color', *Signs* 11 (2), 321–4.

STACK, C. and HALL, R. (1982) *Holding on to the Land and Lord: Kinship, Ritual, Land Tenure and Social Policy in the Rural South*, Athens, University of Georgia Press.

THOMPSON, E.P. (1963) *The Making of the English Working Class*, New York, Vintage Books.

THOMPSON, J. (1983) *Learning Liberation: Women's Responses to Men's Education*, London, Croom Helm.

THORNE, B. (1986) 'Girls and Boys Together, But Mostly Apart: Gender Arrangements in Elementary Schools', in HARTUP, W. and RUBIN, Z. (Eds) *Relationships and Development*, pp. 167–84, Hillsdale, NJ, Lawrence Erlbaum.

VALLI, L. (1983) 'Becoming Clerical Workers: Business Education and the Culture of Feminity', in APPLE, M. and WEISS, L. (Eds) *Ideology and Practice in Schooling*, pp. 213–34, Philadelphia, Temple University Press.

WILLIS, P. (1977) *Learning to Labor: How Working-class Kids Get Working-class Jobs*, New York, Columbia University Press.

10 Opportunity and Performance: A Sociological Explanation for Gender Differences in Academic Mathematics

David P. Baker and Deborah Perkins Jones

Searching for and explaining gender differences in mathematics performance fascinates researchers and the general public alike. Renewed debate occurs with each major finding. In the early 1980s, two psychologists, Camellia Benbow and Julian Stanley, touched off a still-reverberating controversy when they published several studies on the mathematics performance of American middle-school students. They reported that among the middle-school students who earned top scores on the math portion of the Educational Testing Service's Scholastic Achievement Test (the SAT), males outnumbered females (Benbow and Stanley 1980, 1983). These findings renewed the debate about whether, as these researchers and others claimed, there are not some inborn differences in mathematical ability between males and females which accounted for the male testing advantage.

During the decade or so prior to Benbow and Stanley's entry into the debate, a relatively standard view of gender differences in mathematics had emerged which was quite different from that which the two psychologists were suggesting. Starting with the extensive review of empirical research by Maccoby and Jacklin (1974) and running through more recent socialization research, the standard set of conclusions went as follows: gender differences in mathematics abilities were small; there was some evidence, none of it overwhelming, which indicated that males did better than females; and what differences there were were probably caused by social factors embedded within the family and school (e.g., Brophy and Good 1974; Brophy 1985; Fennema 1980; Baker and Entwisle 1987; Fox et al. 1979).

Benbow and Stanley challenged each of these conclusions. They claimed that there are gender differences in mathematics favoring males, that large differences can be found at the higher end of the male and female performance distributions, and that the causes are most probably not due to socialization factors but rather stem from innate differences. Benbow and Stanley's claims gained credibility because they reported on differences in a very large sample, restricted the issue to advanced mathematics, focused on the performance of young students (who presumably had been less subject to socialization than older students would have been) on a standardized test developed for much older students, and, last but certainly not least, reported their findings in the pages of *Science*, America's premier journal of general scientific research.

Benbow and Stanley chose to interpret their findings as reinforcing an older biological perspective on gender and cognitive ability (see Hubbard and Lowe 1979 for a review and critique of this perspective), although their findings could have been interpreted in other ways. Their study does not actually test their biological argument; rather, they use their results as a springboard to raise, once again, the issue of internal differences between males and females. Reasoning that most seventh-graders in the US sit in classes together and thus receive the same mathematical training, Benbow and Stanley claim that their findings show that males have superior mathematics abilities 'which may in turn be related to greater male ability in spatial skills' (1980, p. 1264).[1]

Later, there were other findings in the area of gender differences and mathematics that further stirred the debate. First, in the early 1980s, some researchers of comparative education began to report that gender differences in school mathematics were not always the same size and direction (male superior to females) in all societies (e.g., Finn 1980; Harnish 1984). Second, by the end of the 1980s, other researchers reported that gender differences between American students had narrowed over the preceding ten-year period (Kolata 1989). Both sets of findings run counter to Benbow and Stanley's biological interpretation: one suggests that cross-national forces affect gender differences and the other suggests that such differences are not necessarily immutable.

These are diverse findings, each leading to a different conclusion about the origins of gender differences. On one hand, the standard literature suggests that there are numerous social factors which could produce gender differences, while on the other hand, the biological perspective suggests that this is not the case. For different reasons neither literature incorporates the emerging cross-national findings. The standard approach tends to examine only why American females sometimes perform less well than males without expanding the argument to explain where and when differences of all types emerge. The biological approach assumes cross-national invariance because inborn causes of gender differences are endogenous to all humans regardless of society. Even the cross-national researchers themselves have generally offered little interpretation of their findings, leaving an intriguing pattern to stand without explanation. Finally, none of these perspectives yields a clear argument about why gender differences should change over time within a society.

The remainder of this chapter attempts to provide a sociological interpretation of gender differences and mathematics performance, tying together some of the diverse findings into one common argument. We then summarize our past research which examines our argument using data on mathematics achievement from over 77,000 eighth-graders in nineteen nations (Baker and Jones 1991; Jones and Baker 1991).

Opportunities and Performance

The basic premise of our sociological explanation of gender differences and mathematics performance is that opportunities are tied to performance. In other words, if individuals, in this case students, see that important future opportunities are linked to current performance, their attempts to improve their performance will generally intensify. Schools and schooling provide this link for students. They send students a clear and strong message that current achievement is a kind of currency that can be spent in the future; the teacher or parent admonishes the student to 'do well now and you will be granted access to some opportunity in the future'.

When sociologists of education think of future opportunities that motivate people to perform academic tasks, they think chiefly of two kinds: advanced educational opportunities and occupational opportunities. Most students understand both that more schooling is generally better than less, and that the labor market uses forms of certificates of academic performance to help judge between job applicants. Advanced education and the credentials it yields are clearly seen as connected with adult opportunities. This is a fundamental part of the logic behind the participation of students in the long and at times difficult enterprise of schooling.

A sociological interpretation of why one group of students, such as males, do better than another group, such as females, can stem from thinking of differences in opportunities offered to the groups. If males are afforded the possibility of greater future educational and occupational opportunities as a function of their mathematics performance, they may try harder, teachers may encourage them more, and parents and friends may help them see that mathematics is a domain of performance that they should take very seriously. On the other hand, female students faced with less opportunity may tend to see mathematics as less important for their futures and they may be told so in a number of ways by teachers, parents, and friends.

Thus, one way to explain gender differences in academic mathematics is to examine if educational and occupational opportunities are stratified by gender. A sociological position would predict that the more opportunities are stratified by gender, the more performance will also be stratified by gender. A similar argument has been used to explain why minority students have lower motivation to achieve academic success than do their white counterparts (Ogbu 1978; Mickelson 1990).

Educational and occupational opportunities are stratified by gender in most societies, but the degree of inequality varies considerably across nations. Women's access to advanced educational and labor market opportunities are quite different in different nations (Benavot 1989; Boserup 1970; Boulding 1977; Goode 1963; Ramirez and Weiss 1979; Smith 1979; Smock 1981; Solomon 1985). Although there is evidence to suggest that gender stratification is decreasing worldwide, there is still variation among nations (Duverger 1955; Mincer 1985; Semyonov 1980; Youssef and Hartley 1979; Youssef 1972, 1974).

A sociological argument suggests that if opportunities and performances are linked, there should be a relationship between large-scale trends in gender stratification of opportunities and gender differences in the mathematics performance of students who are preparing for a particular opportunity structure within a country. Understanding shifting opportunities for males and females may help us to understand the origins of the diverse set of findings that have recently been reported on gender differences in mathematics.

Analysis

In the light of the above framework, we have attempted in recent research reports (Baker and Jones 1991; Jones and Baker 1991) to answer four questions related to a sociological explanation of gender differences in mathematics.

We first asked: Is there cross-national variation in the size and direction of sex differences in mathematics performance? It is important to establish this first since cross-national variation in sex differences is necessary in order to explore a connection between gender stratification and mathematics performance. In addition, arguments which do not consider social factors, such as those made by Benbow and Stanley, assume that the pattern of sex differences will be mostly invariant across societies (in other words, that males will outperform females everywhere). Although few who argue from a biological perspective would fully embrace 'biological determinism', most of these researchers would consider social factors as trivial or subordinate by comparison with dominant biological processes and thus predict cross-national invariance (Benbow and Stanley 1980, 1983; Bock and Kolakowski 1973; Broverman et al. 1968; Kinsbourne 1978; Levey 1976; Stafford 1961; Waber 1979).[2]

If we find cross-national variation, we then ask: Is national gender stratification of opportunities correlated with national sex differences in mathematical performance? This question goes to the heart of our sociological perspective by examining the two central institutional domains that have increased women's social status in many societies: the educational system and the labor market (Chafetz 1984; Mincer 1985; Semyonov 1980). Since early mathematical performance is important for further schooling and occupational placement, countries in which women have gained access to these institutional domains should exhibit smaller sex differences in mathematics among students. More opportunities for adult women will reshape socialization, motivations, and other social factors that will lessen sex differences in mathematical performance among students. The answer to this question may help us understand why there is cross-national variation in gender differences and also how large-scale social changes can influence student behavior.

If less gender stratification is associated with smaller sex differences, we ask next: Have sex differences in mathematics performance declined over time? The literature on gender stratification indicates that the status of women has generally improved in most societies (e.g., Boserup 1970; Chafetz 1984; Goode 1963; Semyonov 1980; Smock 1981) and, as we indicated above, there have been reports of declining gender differences in mathematics performance in the USA. We should find, then, a decline over time in sex differences in mathematical performance in those countries which have developed the greatest female access to education and the labor market.

Lastly, we ask: Are national sex differences in access to mathematical instruction and parental encouragement for achievement related to national variation in the status of women, and, if so, are sex differences in instruction and encouragement related to sex differences in performance? A sociological explanation assumes a connection between opportunities and performance, and one way to demonstrate this is to see if gender stratification of opportunities influences either access to mathematics training in middle school, or parental encouragement. If such differences are found, one then needs to show that these influences are transformed into gender differences in performance.

Our analysis relies on a complex string of cause and effect that is not well described by the kind of survey data we used but, as a first step to understanding how gender stratification could affect sex differences, we can determine if school and home influences on academic performance vary by national differences in the status of women. Then we can determine the degree to which sex differences in school and home influences are related to sex differences in performance.

We used data from a large comparative study of mathematics in over twenty countries conducted in 1982 by the International Association for the Evaluation of Educational Achievement (IEA). Along with similar studies carried out over the past twenty years on different academic subjects, the IEA conducted a study of middle-school mathematics in 1982 called the Second International Mathematics Study (SIMS). For SIMS, the IEA drew nationally representative samples of middle-school mathematics classrooms in each country and administered the identical mathematics test to all the students in all the classrooms in the sample.

Here we used the score from SIMS's forty-item test to calculate a gender difference by subtracting the female mean score from the male mean score in each country.[3] In addition to the test, SIMS collected information about students' access to the curriculum and their perceptions of parental encouragement to learn mathematics. From published sources we collected for each participating country in SIMS a number of indicators of the gender stratification of advanced education and the labor market in a period prior to the collection of the SIMS data (Kent, Huab and Osaki 1985; Sivard 1985; OECD 1983). These included indicators such as: the percentage of females in higher education, the ratio of female university students to female students in non-university programs, and the percentage of females in the full labor forces and various economic sectors.

To see if gender differences vary cross-nationally we calculated the mean differences and list the countries by type of difference in Table 10.1. There is considerable cross-national variation; national sex differences fall into three distinct categories. In the first and largest category are the eight systems in which there is no statistically significant difference between the sexes; in the second category are seven systems in which males do better than females; and in the last category are four systems in which females do better than males. When we averaged the differences together to form a full sample mean (at the system level), we found no overall difference between males and females in middle-school mathematics. But, at the same time, when we compared the average size of difference in male-advantage countries with the same for female-advantage countries, we found that the former is twice the size of the latter, indicating that where there are differences male advantages tend to be larger than female advantages.[4] Overall, though, these data suggest that differences are not outstandingly large nor consistently in favor of either gender; in fact, the majority of systems show no difference and, most importantly, there is a fair amount of variation in the direction of differences in this group of national systems. We next examine if there is a systematic pattern to these differences in regard to gender stratification.

When we calculated the association between the various indicators of gender stratification in each system and the size of the gender difference in mathematics performance, we found that, as females gain more access to advanced training

Table 10.1   Summary of Gender Differences in Eighth-grade Mathematics, Using FIMS, 1964, and SIMS, 1982.

	Changes in Gender Differences 1964–82
National Systems without Gender Difference in 1982:	
British Columbia	—
England/Wales	M:ND
Hong Kong	—
Japan	M:ND
Nigeria	—
Scotland	—
Sweden	M:ND
USA	M:ND
National Systems with Male Advantage in 1982:	
France	M:M
Israel	F:M
Luxembourg	—
Netherlands	M:M
New Zealand	—
Ontario	—
Swaziland	—
National Systems with Female Advantage in 1982:	
Belgium	M:ND
Finland	M:F
Hungary	—
Thailand	—

Key: M:ND = Male advantage 1964 to No difference 1982
      M:M = Male advantage remains or increases 1964–82
      M:F = Male advantage in 1964 is replaced by female advantage 1982
      F:M = Female advantage in 1964 is replaced by male advantage in 1982.
Source: Compiled from analyses reported in Baker and Jones (1991).

and to the workplace (in other words, as gender stratification decreases), sex differences in middle-school mathematics performance decreases. For instance, in countries with large proportions of women in higher education, sex differences in eighth-grade mathematics performance are smaller (or move away from a clear male advantage). In addition, as women are channelled less into non-university training, sex differences decrease, although this association is not statistically significant.[5]

Similarly, we found that the occupational status of females is related to the size of the sex difference in test performance among that society's eighth-grade students.[6] In systems with higher percentages of women working in the formal workforce, girls are more likely to perform as well as or better than boys in mathematics.[7] There is a sector effect as well; female participation in lower-status agricultural work is less related to sex differences than female participation in higher-status industrial work.[8] This type of sector effect is suggested in earlier research on the negative impact of agricultural work on women's status (Boserup 1970). All these associations remain stable even after controlling for general economic development of the country (GNP) (Jones 1989).

The second column in Table 10.1 shows what changes have occurred in gender differences in mathematics between 1964 and 1982. To determine this we examined national gender differences for the nine national systems that participated in the First International Mathematics Study (FIMS) (Husen 1967) in 1964 with the 1982 SIMS results. Overall there has been a large drop from a male advantage in 1964 to no clear advantage for either gender in 1982. Individual country means show how this has happened. In 1964, all but one of the countries had a distinct male-advantage mean difference. By 1982 four of these countries had moved substantially toward parity between the sexes. Two countries (Belgium and Finland) actually replaced a male advantage with a female advantage.

We also found that those countries with the largest increase in women's access to advanced education and the labor market over this period had the largest declines in male advantage in school mathematics.

Lastly, we examined if the increase in women's access to opportunities increased both female students' access to middle-school mathematics curriculum and parental encouragement for daughters to learn mathematics. In both cases this is true. Not all national systems have open mathematics curricula and in some (the Netherlands, for example) more girls than boys sit in classrooms where less mathematics is taught (Jones and Baker 1991). Like gender differences in achievement, there is cross-national variation (although less variation than is to be found in achievement differences), and this variation is related to gender stratification of opportunities. Furthermore, in systems in which opportunities are more open to females, female students report as often as males that their parents encourage them to learn mathematics. Both smaller gender differences in access to mathematics curricula and parental involvement appear related to smaller gender differences in achievement.

Discussion

A sociological explanation of the origin of gender differences in mathematics is supported by our analysis of the SIMS data. First, there is variation in the size and direction of sex differences in mathematical performance among a sample of countries. It is not the case that on average males do better than females everywhere. Second, this cross-national variation correlates with cross-national variation in women's access to higher education and the labor market; countries which approach equal opportunities for males and females show smaller sex differences in mathematical performance among students. Third, there has been a general decline in gender differences in mathematics, and the decline appears to be associated with an expansion of opportunities for females. Last, the SIMS data suggest that boys and girls are granted equal access to mathematical instruction and are equally encouraged by their parents to learn mathematics in countries with lower levels of gender stratification of opportunities.

These results show a connection between the opportunity structure for men and women and their behaviors. Parity in opportunity yields parity in performance.

How then does this conclusion help explain the seemingly divergent set of findings we described at the beginning of this chapter? Let us start with the findings of Benbow and Stanley (1980, 1983). How should we interpret their findings in the light of our own research? First, we should point out that we did not investigate the higher ends of the performance distribution and that this should be done cross-nationally. It may be, however, that even here performance differences between the genders is shaped by opportunities.[9] We did find, however, a large amount of variation across national systems in the size and direction of gender differences. This is a difficult fact for a general biological perspective to account for without admitting the existence of important social influences such as opportunities. An admission of this sort runs against a central biological assumption of invariance in gender differences across females and males everywhere.[10] In other words, if a difference is found in one place, it should be found elsewhere, since the biological forces that are alleged to cause differences are part of females and males everywhere. A biological approach does not necessarily preclude cultural or social forces, but it relegates them to a lower, sometimes trivial, theoretical position. The pattern of cross-national differences that is evident in the SIMS data suggests that it would be unwise quickly to dismiss social factors as trivial.

Our results also provide an explanation of why there are cross-national gender differences in mathematics performance. The associations we find between gender stratification and gender differences in performance point to the link between the structure of opportunities and group differences in performance. As national systems differ in the degree to which they grant females access to future opportunities (at least in part based on proven mathematics skills) so do they differ in the degree to which females learn mathematics in school.

While our findings support the general conclusions from the standard socialization literature, they do broaden this perspective considerably. We suggest that the many socialization factors identified in this literature are part of the transmission between opportunities and performances. We show evidence of two of these — parental encouragement and access to instruction. What our results suggest further, however, is that socialization patterns are at least associated with (if not influenced by) the gender stratification of opportunities. Socialization follows social structure. This is, for example, one reason why Maccoby and Jacklin (1974) find very few reports of large gender differences in a range of performances among Americans. The relative low gender stratification of opportunity in the USA (particularly over the past two decades) works against large gender effects on performance.

Lastly, our results indicate that gender differences in mathematics performance are fading in much of the world. This trend appears rooted in several social processes that are related to decreasing gender stratification in societies in general. First, concern over gender equality is increasingly incorporated into many organizations. Governments, schools, armies, political parties, and cultural associations are all examples of organizations which can (and do) promote gender equality. Reducing gender stratification, particularly in terms of equal access to opportunity, is a source of legitimation that organizations cannot ignore. Consider, for example, recent charges that the American Boy Scouts organization should change its membership rules to allow females to join; or the strong public belief that intercity, public academies for disadvantaged students should not only be for males as was originally planned. Differential treatment of one gender versus the other in organizations is diminishing in many societies.

Second, our results point to an even larger social process that goes beyond organizational change. Across the world, there is institutional change in the definition of the individual that leads to reduced gender inequalities (e.g., Lenski 1966; Ramirez and Weiss 1979) and possibly, as we have shown, to smaller performance differences. Along with gender, traditional characteristics used for social stratification, such as race, ethnicity, and age, are replaced by a more general and abstract notion of a modern individual (Meyer 1988). A profound change in gender roles is a result; there is a shifting away from roles based solely on a belief in biological differences toward roles based on a belief in general social equality (Goffman 1977). This is a highly reinforcing process; beliefs in gender similarity underpin further social production of equality. The very forces that drive increased opportunities for women in education and the economy are themselves intensified by 'new discoveries' of performance equality between the sexes.

Notes

1 There are many criticisms of this conclusion, not the least of which is whether or not to believe the 'same classrooms thus all things equal' assumption.
2 Recently others have attempted to integrate both biological and social factors (Rossi 1985). Our data cannot examine these kinds of hypotheses.
3 This test was the core test made up of forty multiple-choice items (no form scores were used here). We corrected the scores for guessing; see Baker and Jones (1991) for technical details.
4 For countries with statistically significant mean differences between the sexes the effect size of the differences is modest. There is more variation in effect size among male-advantage systems, ranging from a high of 0.4 (d value, see Hyde 1981) for France to a low of 0.07 for Ontario, Canada. The effect size for the female advantage systems are all close to 0.2.
5 The significant correlation coefficients between indicators of gender stratification and performance differences are in the 0.5 range with a sample size of nineteen systems.
6 Since there is a slight tendency for countries with female advantage to have higher overall means, we also did this analysis by controlling for overall mean differences between countries. This did, as would be expected, attenuate the correlation coefficients somewhat, but exactly the same pattern of associations and statistical significance remained.
7 Similar associations to these were also found for other domains of female participation, such as the numbers of females in the national legislature.
8 We have considered two of the three dimensions of women's incorporation into the labor force (participation and segregation); the third that is often suggested is earnings. We were only able to collect the ratio of female to male earnings for a small group of countries. The pattern of results followed that of the participation indicators.
9 Jones (1989) did examine gender differences on the most difficult items of the SIMS test. She found cross-national variation, but more male advantage than in the full test. She presents some evidence that this may be associated with opportunities as well.
10 We do not wish to imply that a biological perspective would assume that all males perform differently from all females, rather that the difference between the male and female performance distributions should be found in all sizable samples of humans.

References

BAKER, D. and ENTWISTLE, D. (1987) 'The Influence of Mothers on Academic Expectations of Young Children: A Longitudinal Study of how Gender Differences Arise', *Social Forces* 65, pp. 670–94.

BAKER, D. and JONES, D. (1991) 'Creating Gender Differences: A Cross-national Assessment of Gender Inequality and Sex Differences in Mathematics Performance', Unpublished paper, Washington, DC, Department of Sociology, Catholic University of America.

BENAVOT, A. (1989) 'Education, Gender, and Economic Development: A Cross-national Study', *Sociology of Education* 62, pp. 14–32.

BENBOW, C.P. and STANLEY, J.C. (1980) 'Sex Differences in Mathematical Ability: Fact or Artifact?' *Science* 210, pp. 1262–4.

BENBOW, C.P. and STANLEY, J.C. (1983) 'Sex Differences in Mathematical Reasoning Ability: More Facts', *Science* 222, pp. 1029–31.

BOCK, R. and KOLAKOWSKI, D. (1973) 'Further Evidence of Sex-linked Major-gene Influence on Human Spatial Visualizing Ability', *American Journal of Human Genetics* 25, pp. 1–14.

BOSERUP, E. (1970) *Women's Role in Economic Development*, New York, St Martin's Press.

BOULDING, E. (1977) *Women in the Twentieth-century World*, New York, Halsted Press.

BROPHY, J. (1985) 'Interactions of Male and Female Students with Male and Female Teachers', in WILKINSON, L. and MARRETT, C. (Eds) *Gender Influences in Classroom Interaction*, Orlando, Academic Press.

BROPHY, J.E. and GOOD, T.L. (1974) *Teacher-Student Relationships*, New York, Holt, Rinehart & Winston.

BROVERMAN, D.M., KLAIBER, E.L., KOBAYASHI, Y. and VOGEL, W. (1968) 'Roles of Activation and Inhibition in Sex Differences in Cognitive Abilities', *Psychological Review* 75, pp. 23–50.

CHAFETZ, J. (1984) *Sex and Advantage: A Comparative, Macro-structural Theory of Sex Stratification*, Totowa, NJ, Rowman & Allanheld.

DUVERGER, M. (1955) *The Political Role of Women*, Paris, Unesco.

FENNEMA, E. (1980) 'Sex-related Differences in Mathematics Achievement: Where and Why?' in Fox, L. (Ed.) *Women and the Mathematical Mystique*, Baltimore, Johns Hopkins University Press.

FINN, J. (1980) 'Sex Difference in Educational Outcomes: A Cross-national Study', *Sex Roles* 6, pp. 9–28.

FOX, L.H., TOBIN, D. and BRODY, L. (1979) 'Sex-role Socialization and Achievement in Mathematics', in WITTIG, M. and PETERSON, A. (Eds) *Sex-related Differences in Cognitive Functioning: Developmental Issues*, p. 303, New York, Academic Press.

GOFFMAN, I. (1977) 'The Arrangement between the Sexes', *Theory and Society* 4, 3, pp. 301–32.

GOODE, W.J. (1963) *World Revolution and Family Patterns*, New York, Free Press.

HARNISCH, D. (1984) 'Females and Mathematics: A Cross-national Perspective', *Advances in Motivation and Achievement* 2, pp. 73–91.

HUBBARD, R. and LOWE, M. (Eds) (1979) *Genes and Gender*, vol. II, New York, Gordian Press.

HUSEN, T. (1967) *International Study of Achievement in Mathematics: A Comparison of Twelve Countries*, vols I and II, Stockholm, Almqvist and Wiksell.

JONES, D. (1989) 'Gender Differences in Mathematics Achievement: A Cross-national Analysis'. Unpublished Doctoral Thesis, Washington, DC, The Catholic University of America.

HYDE, J. (1981) 'How Large are Cognitive Gender Differences: A meta-analysis using W^2 and d', *American Psychologist* 36, 8:892–901.

JONES, D. and BAKER, D. (1991) 'Effective Mathematics Instruction for All: Gender Differences in Access to Curriculum and Achievement', in BAKER, D., ETHINGTON, B., SOSNICK, L. and WESTBURY, I. (Eds) *In Search of More Effective Mathematics Education*, New York, Ablex Publishing.

KENT, M., HUAB, C. and OSAKI, K. (1985) *The World's Women: A Profile*, Washington, DC, Population Reference Bureau, INC.

KINSBOURNE, M. (1978) *Asymmetrical Function of the Brain*, London, Cambridge University Press.

KOLATA, G. (1989) 'Gender Gap in Standard Tests is Narrowing, Experts Find', *New York Times* 1.

LEVY, J. (1976) 'Cerebral Lateralization and Spatial Ability', *Behavior Genetics* 6, pp. 171–88.

LENSKI, G. (1966) *Power and Privilege*, New York, McGraw-Hill.

MACCOBY, E.E. and JACKLIN, C.N. (1974) *The Psychology of Sex Differences*, Stanford, CA, Stanford University Press.

MEYER, J. (1988) 'Society without Culture: A Nineteenth-century Legacy', in RAMIREZ, F. (Ed.) *Rethinking the Nineteenth Century*, New York, Greenwood Press.

MICKELSON, R. (1990) 'The Attitude-Achievement Paradox among Black Adolescents', *Sociology of Education* 63, 1, pp. 44–61.

MINCER, J. (1985) 'Intercountry Comparisons of Labor Force Trends and Related Developments', *Journal of Labor Economics* 3, s1–s32.

OECD (1983) *Policies for Higher Education in the 1980s*, Paris, OECD.

OGBU, J. (1978) *Minority Education and Caste*, New York, Academic Press.

RAMIREZ, F. and WEISS, J. (1979) 'The Political Incorporation of Women', in MEYER, J. and HANNAN, M. (Eds) *National Development of the World System*, Chicago, University of Chicago Press.

ROSSI, A. (1985) 'Gender and Parenthood', in ROSSI, A. (Ed.) *Gender and the Life Course*, Hawthorne, NY, Aldine.

SEMYONOV, M. (1980) 'The Social Context of Women's Labor Force Participation: A Comparative Analysis', *American Journal of Sociology* 86, pp. 534–50.

SIVARD, J. (1985) *Women — A World Survey*, Washington, DC, Population Reference Bureau, INC.

SMITH, R. (Ed.) (1979) *The Subtle Revolution: Women at Work*, Washington, DC, Urban Institute.

SMOCK, A.C. (1981) *Women's Education in Developing Countries*, New York, Praeger.

SOLOMON, B.M. (1985) *In the Company of Educated Women: A History of Women and Higher Education in America*, New Haven, CT, Yale University Press.

STAFFORD, R.E. (1961) 'Sex Differences in Spatial Visualization as Evidence of Sex-linked Inheritance', *Perceptual and Motor Skills* 13, p. 428.

YOUSSEF, N. (1972) 'Differential labor force participation of women in Latin America and Middle Eastern countries: The influence of family characteristics', *Social Forces* 51, pp. 135–53.

YOUSSEF, N. (1974) *Women and Work in Developing Societies*, Berkeley, CA, Institute of International Studies.

YOUSSEF, N. and HARTLEY, S. (1979) 'Demographic indicators of the status of women in various societies', in LIPMAN-BLUMEN, J. and BERNARD, J. (Eds) *Sex Roles and Social Policy*, Beverly Hills CA, Sage.

WABER, D.P. (1979) 'Cognitive Abilities and Sex-related Variations in the Maturation of Cerebral Cortical Functions', in WITTIG, M.A. and PETERSEN, A.C. (Eds) *Sex-related Differences in Cognitive Functioning*, New York, Academic Press.

Section 4

Families and Schools

11 Gender Differences in Parent Involvement in Schooling

Annette Lareau

There is no question that children's life chances are influenced by the social class position of their parents. The higher the social class, the more likely children are to have high scores on achievement tests, enroll in college preparatory classes in high school, attend college, and graduate from college (Sewell and Hauser 1980; Sewell and Shah 1977; Karabel and Halsey 1977; Shavit and Featherman 1988). Even in the early years of elementary school, social class has an important influence on children's academic abilities, thereby shaping their placement in reading groups and math groups (Eder 1981; Kerckhoff 1976). There are questions, however, about how parents transmit school success to their children. Some social scientists have argued that parents transmit different levels of educational aspirations to children, and it is these varying desires for educational success, enacted by children in school, that influence children's life chances. Others have suggested that parents value education equally across social classes but that social class provides parents with unequal resources to assist their children in schooling.

The French sociologist Pierre Bourdieu, for example, has argued that 'cultural capital' is unequally available. Bourdieu maintains that cultural capital includes linguistic aptitude, informal knowledge about school, manners, personal style, and taste used in social selection (Bourdieu 1977, 1984; Bourdieu and Passeron 1977; Lamant and Lareau 1988). He suggests that children of professionals are familiar with schools, particularly the curriculum of schools, in a way lower-status children are not. For example, exposure at home to classical music and rap music varies by social class; music appreciation courses, however, build only on some children's home experiences and not others'. Similarly, sociolinguistic patterns vary by social class: upper-middle-class children's experience with turn-taking and information questioning is closely aligned with the structure of school discourse (Heath 1982; Bernstein 1977; Mehan 1979). This familiarity is an advantage not available to working-class and lower-class children raised with different sociolinguistic patterns of interaction (Heath 1982, 1983; Bernstein 1977).

Researchers study children's educational aspirations and cultural capital as a means of understanding the mechanisms through which social class inequality in educational success is sustained across generations. Yet, these research programs have been characterized by important flaws. For example, the emphasis on educational aspirations (Sewell and Hauser 1980) ignores the role of parents, especially mothers, in managing their children's school careers. Some children are highly motivated, but other children are not. Mothers can work to request teachers with good reputations, request additional homework, suggest their children be placed with the reading resource teacher, and take other steps to supplement, intervene, and shape the character of their children's school experiences (Baker and Stevenson, 1986; Becker and Epstein 1982; Epstein 1986, 1987a; Epstein and Becker 1982). These small, and often invisible, steps by parents need to be taken into account by researchers. Research on cultural capital does focus on the role of parents in transmitting advantages to children, but the attention to cultural capital has been blind to the ways in which parents use, or fail to use, cultural resources. Notably, it ignores the role of gender in shaping the activation of cultural capital. Women and men may take on very different burdens in attempting to transmit social class advantages to their children. Although both parents may believe in the importance of school success as a pathway to occupational rewards, gender roles may shape the ways in which adults work to promote this success. Some researchers have pointed to the unequal benefits of cultural capital for children, with males gaining more privileges than females (DiMaggio and Mohr 1985). The role of gender in shaping parents' efforts to transmit privilege, however, has been neglected.

This chapter examines the day-to-day dynamics of class transmission through education. I argue there are important social class differences in how parents manage their children's school careers, and, moreover, I show that the actions of parents are heavily shaped by traditional gender roles. In a study of families of first-graders, I found working-class families had a pattern of separation between home and school. Parents turned over responsibility for education to higher-status teachers. Although they read to their children and helped their children with school work from time to time, working-class parents reacted to school requests and rarely initiated contacts with teachers. As high school dropouts or high school graduates, parents felt they lacked the requisite skills and resources (in other words, cultural capital) to help their children properly. Class and gender interacted here, however. Fathers were almost entirely absent from the process; mothers were responsible for overseeing their children's education. Mirroring studies of housework, working-class women and men appear to engage in a clear division of responsibility by gender (Hochschild 1989).

By contrast, in upper-middle-class families, parents were more heavily involved in monitoring, supervising, and intervening in their children's schooling. Rather than a pattern of separation, there was a pattern of interconnectedness between home and school. Parents supplemented the curriculum at home, made requests to have their children placed in school programs, publicly and privately criticized teachers, and collected detailed information about teachers' reputations and their children's academic progress. Armed with a college education and other cultural resources (cultural capital again), parents felt capable of assisting their children with school and of critically assessing the performance of educators. As I show below, gender heavily structured parents' actions. The routine activities of supervising schooling overwhelmingly fell to mothers. Fathers expressed a belief that they should be involved but generally pleaded off from monitoring children's education, often citing the demands of their careers. When fathers were involved, however, they made important decisions and often took an assertive and con-

Table 11.1   The Occupational Distribution of Parents at Colton and Prescott Schools

Parental Occupation	Colton %	Prescott %
Professionals, executives, managers	1	60
Semi-professionals, sales, clerical workers and technicians	11	30
Skilled and semi-skilled workers	51	9
Unskilled workers (and welfare)	23	1
Unknown	20	—

Note: The data for Colton School are from *California Assessment Program, 1981–1982*, California State Department of Education, Sacramento, California, 1983, which is based on teachers' estimates. The data for Prescott School are based on the principal's estimate.

trolling role in their interactions with female teachers. In general, husbands appeared to depend upon their wives for transmitting class advantages to their children. The activation of cultural capital was heavily shaped by gender, and this helps to illuminate the mechanisms leading to the reproduction of social inequality.

Taken together, this suggests that models of the transmission of social class privileges from parents to children need to consider the importance of gender in shaping parents' actions. Although fathers do have important authoritative roles, particularly in upper-middle-class families, the labor of managing children's school careers (and marshalling their own cultural capital to comply with teachers' requests for educational assistance) follows other aspects of childcare. Despite changes in women's labor force participation and shifts in ideology regarding proper roles for men and women, mothers rather than fathers are overwhelmingly responsible for caretaking, including shaping their children's school careers.

Research Methodology

The research presented here involved participant-observation in two first-grade classrooms found in two different communities. In-depth interviews were also carried out while the children were in first and second grade. Following other studies of social class differences in family life (Rubin 1976; Kohn 1977), I chose one working-class and one upper-middle-class community. I sought a working-class community in which the majority of the parents were high school graduates or dropouts, employed in skilled or semiskilled occupations, paid an hourly wage, and periodically unemployed. For the upper-middle-class school, I sought a community in which a majority of the parents were college graduates and professionals who had strong career opportunities and who were less vulnerable to changes in the economy. The two communities chosen met these criteria.

Colton School (a pseudonym) is located in a working-class community. Most of the parents of Colton students are employed in semiskilled or unskilled occupations (Table 11.1). School personnel report that most of the parents have a high school education; many are high school dropouts. The school has about 450 students in kindergarten, first grade, and second grade. Slightly over one-half of the children are white, one-third are Hispanic, and the remainder are black or

Asian, especially Vietnamese immigrants. About one-half of the children qualify for free lunches under federal guidelines.

Prescott School (a pseudonym) is in an upper-middle-class suburban community about a 30-minute drive from Colton. Most of the parents of Prescott students are professionals (Table 11.1). Both parents in the family are likely to be college graduates, and many of the children's fathers have advanced degrees. The school enrolls about 300 students from kindergarten to fifth grade. Virtually all the students are white, and the school does not offer a lunch program, although the Parents' Club sponsors a Hot Dog Day once a month.

For a six-month period, January to June 1982, I visited one first-grade classroom at each school. My visits averaged once or twice a week per school and lasted around two hours. During this time, I observed the classroom and acted as a volunteer in the class, passing out papers and helping the children with math and spelling. At the end of the school year, I selected six children in each class for further study. The children were selected on the basis of reading-group membership; a boy and a girl were selected from the high, medium, and low reading groups. To avoid the confounding factor of race, I chose only white children. I interviewed a single mother in each school; the remaining households selected had two parents. In both of the schools, three of the mothers worked full time. All of the Colton mothers, however, had worked in recent years. The Prescott mothers had worked prior to the birth of their children but had not been in the labor force since that time.

When the children finished first grade, I interviewed their mothers individually. When they finished second grade, I interviewed their mothers a second time, and in separate sessions I interviewed most of their fathers. I also interviewed the first- and second-grade teachers, the school principals, and a resource specialist at one of the schools. All of the interviews were semi-structured and lasted about two hours. The interviews were tape-recorded and all participants were promised confidentiality.

The Impact of Gender

There is considerable evidence that mothers and fathers have radically different experiences in family life. Bernard (1982) argued that there are two marriages: a 'his' marriage and a 'her' marriage. It also appears that there are two types of parent-school relationships: 'his' and 'hers'.

In the working-class families at Colton school, there was a clear division of labor by gender. Overseeing the children's school experience was seen primarily as 'her' job. This was most clear in parent-teacher conferences: almost all were attended exclusively by mothers. For example, Laura's mother did not drive. Her husband, a high school dropout, did shift work at a local plant and was usually home in the afternoon. During parent-teacher conferences, he drove his wife to the school, but he never went into the classroom to talk to the teacher. He waited in the car.

Colton mothers and fathers reported that mothers were more involved in the schooling process; they woke the children in the morning, got them to the bus stop on time, and monitored their day-to-day emotional states and experiences at school. For example, as one mother said, although her children brought papers home from school almost every day, their father only looked at their schoolwork periodically: 'It was not every day. It was more if they wanted to show him something particular or else if I wanted to show him something. He didn't go through it every day.'

The definition of parent involvement in schooling as women's work was also apparent in the language parents used: mothers almost always said 'I' rather than 'we' when discussing their perceptions of their children's school experience. Fathers were an important source of authority. If mothers felt that the children were not 'minding' them, they would arrange for the father to become involved. Children would tell their fathers about their school day, particularly at dinner time. Fathers occasionally read to their children or helped them with their spelling words. Fathers also attended Open House nights at school; mothers and children saw this as a special event. One mother, Mrs Morris, told Mrs Thompson that she was angry with her son Tommy because he had not cleaned up his desk 'for his father' for Open House night. Throughout the year, fathers talked with their wives about important changes in their children's schooling, including promotion and retention decisions. But they had little detailed information about their children's schooling (one father had trouble remembering what grade his child was in). Nor did fathers routinely monitor their children's schooling. Mothers, fathers, and children in the working-class families in Colton appeared to define parent involvement as mothers' involvement.

In upper-middle-class families it was also mothers rather than fathers who shouldered the burden of parent involvement in schooling. For example, Prescott mothers were the first to meet children when they came home from school, to look at their papers, and to talk to them about their day. Mothers sometimes read to children in the afternoon or in the morning, before school. They also determined in what spelling, reading, or math activities their children needed help; they also decided when supplementing their children's schooling with private tutors might be advisable. Finally, as volunteers and schedulers, they generally informed their husbands of key school dates, including parent–teacher conferences and Open House nights.

In the lower grades especially, the Prescott fathers' role in the routine events of schooling was a more peripheral one. Fathers did spend time on their children's schooling, just as they spent some time on other aspects of child rearing, and some fathers read to their children every night for about twenty minutes. More often, however, fathers read to their children at bedtime two or three times a week and talked to their children about their papers once a week. They also discussed their children's school day with them at dinner and visited the school periodically. Involvement by fathers in schooling was often organized, coordinated, and monitored by mothers. It was mothers rather than fathers who took the lead in deciding how much school work would be done at home; in hiring tutors; in scheduling special conferences with the teachers; and in monitoring improvements in the classroom performance of low achievers. As part of that process, mothers asked fathers to help them.

For example, Jonathan Roy was in special education and his mother and father regularly worked with him at home. As a nurse, his mother sometimes worked the swing shift at the hospital and so was gone in the early evening. By volunteering in the classroom and having a series of mini-conferences with the teacher, Mrs Roy accurately anticipated when Jonathan would be bringing work home. His father, on the other hand, admitted that he had no idea when to expect homework:

> [His] mother seemed to know prior to his getting homework what he was going to get. She seemed to, I don't know how. But maybe she had an idea of what was going on in class, with his spelling and the spelling lists. She knew that he had one a week. She knew the schedule of the homework. She was able to keep up on that.

Jonathan's mother worked with him when she was at home in the afternoon, but two or three times a week Jonathan's father would work with him at home, reading to him, helping him with his math, spelling, or other school work. Still it was Jonathan's mother who decided what work needed to be done and told Jonathan's father what areas to work on with Jonathan. Mr Roy explained what he and his son did with spelling words:

> Well, you got the list every week. The only time I did it is when his mother told me he had to do his homework. She worked. Then [I tried to do it and help him with it]. He did sentences, but only within the structure of the homework. He had to use a certain word in every sentence. Having him do it, not telling him how. Which I did a lot [laughs]; you know, it is hard not to. You know, give them ideas.

In addition to keeping track of the curriculum at school, Jonathan's mother also scheduled all his lessons. As his father acknowledged:

> She had control as far as knowing what he was doing or where he was at in school. She seemed to have a fairly good idea of where he was in regards to the class. She tried to improve his ability. It didn't always work. See, she scheduled everything. The piano lessons, the karate lessons, swim team, the soccer practice. She looked it up. She found the schedule.

In summarizing his role in schooling, Jonathan's father said he was 'supportive but not what you would call active'. Instead, his wife took an active role in overseeing and supplementing their son's schooling.

Other Prescott families described similar patterns. Fathers attended school conferences, Open House nights, reviewed papers, and read to children at night. But it was mothers who 'kept on top' of the children's schooling, who knew the names of children's friends in the class, who were at school during the day, and who monitored the day-to-day changes in their children's school lives. Other research findings suggest a similar pattern of mothers spending more hours supervising children's lives than fathers (Berk 1985; Coverman 1985; Coverman and Sheley 1986).

The coordination and supervision of their children's educational activities often demanded a major portion of mothers' waking hours. This was particularly the case for upper-middle-class mothers whose children were doing poorly in school. One mother reported that she was 'consumed' by the process during her daughter's first-grade year. During the spring, she spent some time almost every day calling tutors, arranging testing, visiting the school, and talking with family and friends about her daughter's poor school performance. She reported that, for a period of six months, she and her husband talked about her daughter's school problems on a daily basis.

Other mothers' lives were also significantly influenced by their role as guardian and booster of their children's cognitive development. As part of their family lives, mothers spent time reading to their children and driving them to lessons; time talking to adult friends about the quality of their children's educational program at school; and time consulting with teachers and other professionals. In addition, they spent time volunteering in the classroom twice a month, and many mothers were active in the Mothers Club, particularly in the annual fund-raising event. Some mothers spent over ten hours per week in school-site activities at different times of the year, in addition to their educational activities with family members.

As with studies of housework, mothers' labor-force participation appeared to reduce, but not eliminate, the number of hours they devoted to promoting children's cognitive development (Benin and Agostinelli 1988; Coverman and Sheley 1986). For example, one single mother worked full time outside the home. Because of this, she was unable to volunteer in the classroom. She did, however, alter her work schedule to be able to attend parent–teacher conferences, Halloween parade, and Holiday program. In addition, in the evening she read to her daughter, took her to the library, and encouraged her to spend time reading to younger children in the neighborhood. Thus, her labor-force participation reduced — somewhat — the amount of time she spent on educational activities. Other mothers showed a similar pattern. Working outside the home reduced the hours they devoted to classroom volunteering and school fund-raising, but had a less dramatic influence on time spent reading to children or promoting their verbal development.

Disruption and Protection from Disruption

One consequence of mothers' more intensive involvement in schooling is that it is mothers' lives rather than fathers' that are disrupted when changes occur in the regular school schedule. Such disruptions are an inevitable, if unpredictable, part of children's school experiences. Children become sick at school, forget their lunch, need to be taken out of school for a medical appointment, or come home early because of a temporary change in the school schedule. Some of the parents surveyed reported that they found these disruptions irritating.

For example, once a month, Prescott school would have a shortened day to allow teachers to attend a workshop, have parent–teacher conferences, or prepare for an evening event. This infuriated Mr Harris — even though it was his wife, not he, who had to adjust to these schedule changes:

> He would get upset about the screwy schedules that they would have. I would say to him, 'I don't know why you get upset because you don't have to deal with it. I am the one who deals with it. I am the one with the revolving front door. I am the one who has to remember that they all go to school at 8.30 today and they are all coming home at 12.30 or

whatever. So why are you getting upset about it?' Then he [would go]
into a tirade about how they had all of this time off ...

Sometimes the children's reading-group schedules were very inconvenient.
While fathers were consulted about their children's reading placement, it was
mothers who were responsible for shepherding children back and forth to school.
For example, a family with two girls, one in kindergarten and one in first grade,
lived a ten-minute drive from school, but it was too far for the girls to walk. Mrs
Walters, the first-grade reacher at Prescott, put the first-grader in the later reading
group, which did not coincide with the kindergarten schedule. This reading-
group assignment forced the girls' mother to make four round trips to school
each day. Mrs Walters noted that it was the father who called her to talk about
the inconvenience:

> The father called me and talked to me at the beginning of the year. I sent
> assignments home, their reading times, and I talked about the differences
> that I would be doing with the two groups. And they went for the
> option which was right for her, really. But it was kind of hard for her
> [the mother]. I mean, think of your day being broken up by driving....
> The mom was really sort of put out of her way for a whole lot of time.

Mothers also bore the brunt of an inconvenient classroom volunteering
schedule, particularly if they had more than one child. Allen's mother finally
offered to coordinate the schedule for classroom volunteers after having her day
broken up in bits and pieces:

> As the mother of more than one, I didn't want to be going back and
> forth. I wanted to be able to say that Thursday morning from 9.30 until
> 1.30 I was going to be at school. In the past I personally had been frus-
> trated. Last year my volunteer days were the first and third Tuesdays
> and the second and fourth Thursdays. It was very difficult. I was meet-
> ing myself coming and going.

In not having to chauffeur their children to school, coordinate child care after
school, or volunteer in the classroom, fathers' lives were often exempt from the
disruptions caused by changes in children's schedules.

The division of responsibility between mothers and fathers in these Prescott
homes mirrors the research findings on the sexual division of labor in child
rearing and household duties. Upper-middle-class fathers expressed the belief that
they had a responsibility to share these roles, but said that their work obligations
precluded them from spending more time on these tasks. For example, all the
fathers interviewed said that, had they more time, they would like to spend some
of it in the classroom: 'I didn't have the time to actually participate in activities at
school, to be a parent volunteer or something like that.'

Working with children generally, and in elementary schools in particular,
is a low-status task which, historically, has been allocated to women, and the
gender-segregated character of volunteering may contribute to the lack of fathers'
involvement in this area. When asked if he volunteered in the classroom, Allen
Harris's father's first response was the same as the other fathers': 'I would have
liked to, but I didn't have the time.' He then paused for a moment, and added:

I never thought of it, but if it was something I wanted to do, like skiing,
I would find the time. It never crossed my mind. I guess I thought that it
was women's work. It was not manly — was that too much of a male
chauvinist thing to say? I would have rather do the soccer than sit around
with the little kids cutting out paper.

Mr Harris felt he could not justify the expense of hiring a substitute at his work
so that he could volunteer in the classroom. As he acknowledged, however, he
thought the work 'was not manly'. He justified the expense of finding a substitute for other tasks, such as soccer practice with the boys.

In fact, parent involvement in schooling often includes tasks that are not
gender-neutral. The lack of upper-middle-class (and working-class) fathers' involvement is not simply a question of time. It is linked to their definition of their
proper role. The existence of gender segregation is further supported by
comments made by fathers who expect to become more involved as their children
get older and have more courses in math and science.

In Prescott homes, as in most intact families, the fathers' role as economic
provider was central; their child-rearing activities were supplemental (Bernard
1982). Although many mothers were employed, they tended to have 'jobs' rather
than 'careers' and thus viewed child rearing as a central part of their lives. These
different relationships to the labor market and child rearing seemed to shape
parents' roles in schooling and the kinds of interactions concerning schooling they
had with their children. For example, all the fathers reported emphasizing the
significance of school success. They stressed to their children the importance of
studying hard in school in order to get an interesting job. Emily said that she
wanted to be a cheerleader someday:

'Well, Emily,' I would say, 'the cheerleaders have to get good grades. It
is important that you give yourself a good foundation to be able to do
those things.' I viewed my role as providing support to the children in
explaining to them what the educational process was for. And why it
was important.

Children are not always receptive to this form of encouragement. Donald's
father notes, for example, that his children do not appreciate his sermons on the
importance of schooling for later success: 'My kids didn't like to be told that it
was a good experience. This is an opportunity that you will never have again.
You will look back on [it] and you'll wish that you had taken greater advantage
of it.'

By contrast, Prescott mothers were preoccupied with the micro-details of
their children's classroom life, including their performance in specific subjects,
their friendship networks, and their overall emotional state.

Upper-middle-class Fathers and Authority

While upper-middle-class fathers were less involved in the schooling process than
were their wives, they were not uninvolved. In fact, as studies of power dynamics in marriage would predict, there are indications that Prescott fathers made

fewer decisions but that these decisions were more important than the typical decisions of mothers (Blood and Wolfe 1960; Safilios-Rothschild 1970; Steil 1984). For example, mothers decided which drawings would be hung up on the refrigerator and which would be thrown away, if children would purchase books with a class mail order, and what objects from home children would take to school for 'Sharing' time. Mothers also interviewed tutors, arranged tutoring schedules, and made transportation arrangements for these lessons. Fathers, however, were involved in decisions to hire a tutor or change children's academic programs (such as moving children from one reading group to another), to retain children for a school year, and to complain formally to school officials.

In addition, when fathers participated in routine school events, they appeared to take on a more authoritative role than mothers. Because of mothers' more intimate involvement in schooling, couples reported that mothers talked more in conferences than did fathers. For example, Mr Harris said:

> I am the one that showed up for moral support. I was not the one who was the least bit bashful about talking but because she was in the classroom she could come out with all kinds of things that I heard second-hand from her. She was the more knowledgeable speaker of the two of us. I would do like you are doing, nod my head [laughter]. I had my two cents' worth but really relied on Joanie to do the talking because she was the more knowledgeable of the two. Something [i.e., talking] I didn't know if she would have done ten years ago herself. But she was very familiar with the situation and she really got herself involved.

Still, his wife felt that he played a critical role in the process. Her husband had a college degree; she did not. She keenly felt her lack of education at certain moments and was very grateful for his attendance at conferences:

> I was nervous because I was not well educated in the collegiate sense. I felt that I didn't ask the right questions. I was glad when Tim went with me because he always seemed to ask the right questions. He always went with me.

Moreover, her husband also admitted that he felt he played a more assertive role in the conference than his wife: 'I thought I asked the more penetrating questions. Such as, "Look, what are these three books down here if that is the third level or the highest level, and how come Allen has already read this book?"'

The teachers also commented on the tendency of fathers to be more inquisitive in conferences, particularly regarding school success. Mrs Walters remarked:

> The man would be more interested in [the] detail of the lessons, or what things their child has to know ... like the blue sheet that tells all the math skills that you want at the end of year, things like that; fathers are very interested in that kind of information. And the moms tended to be more interested in [their children's friends], other friends, and did they get along, and did people like their child.

A few fathers spoke explicitly about the problems they had in deferring to teachers' control of the classroom. Mr Smith had a Ph.D. in physics and taught at a local university. His wife volunteered in the classroom bimonthly, but he had only been in the classroom twice over the previous year. In our interview, he said that he wanted to volunteer more but that his schedule didn't permit it. For example, when asked if he considered going to school more often he said:

I did and I really intended to. It was the same old thing of being torn in five thousand directions. I don't know. I was doing about ten things over at the place where I [worked]. The schedule wasn't uniform. It was not 8 to 5 or anything. So I was back and forth so much it was hard to guarantee that next week I could be there Tuesdays at 10. On occasion, in fact the occasions that I went over there, I think they occurred because I was available, and so I said to Claire, 'Why don't I go instead of you?'

At first, he attributed his lack of involvement to his own lack of discipline:

Part of it was probably just not getting up and doing it. I should probably have just pushed myself to do it more. I don't know. It was like any habit if you didn't do it enough. But it was hard for me to set up a schedule in advance because things were always popping and things just didn't jar well.

On further questioning, however, it became clear that he was uncomfortable both about deferring to the teacher's expertise and his inability to control the situation. For example, when asked about the disadvantages of volunteering in the classroom, he replied:

Well, if I went regularly ... I would probably have gotten into it too much. I would probably have begun to have gotten some control feelings about it. I would probably have overdone it. I didn't want to rock the boat.

Mrs Cates was really great. Mrs Walters was really good. And I had confidence in them and I had confidence in the class. The children seemed to work together well. [pause] It was funny because everything was such a mixed bag. On the one hand, I felt like going once or twice. I got probably all I needed in terms of insight as to what was going on as far as what I felt I needed to get. I think I should have gone more for the girls' sake because they liked me going very much. They enjoyed that. So I should have. But I thought I might have begun to have gotten a little control in there.

In his visits to the classroom, Mr Smith observed that the math curriculum was organized around memorization. A proponent of hands-on learning, this was like 'nails scratching down a blackboard'. The role of the parent volunteer, however, was to be the teacher's helper. Since Mr Smith found it difficult to fulfill that role, his solution was to stay out of the classroom.

Parents' efforts to control classroom activities and/or be critical of teachers also show some evidence of gender differences. For example, mothers were more likely than fathers to reveal doubts and anxiety about their right to challenge teachers' decisions. As Emily's mother fretted:

It was hard for a mother to judge. You know, as I had told David so many times: We were not professionals in teaching. How did I know? I walked into a classroom and I knew the way I would like to see it run. But who was I? I did not know whether that was right. I was just a mother who came and observed. Unless I saw my child's work being affected and then that made a difference.

Similarly, Allen's mother was anxious when she confronted teachers:

I had to get up my nerve, like the day I went to ask Mrs Walters for the math packets for Allen. I made up my mind that I was going to be friendly but firm. I got what I wanted. I was friendly and firm again [the next year] and it didn't get me any place [laughs].

Allen's mother attributed her nervousness in dealing with teachers to a general problem of non-assertiveness:

I was a chicken. I was asking someone to do something for me and for my children. That was never a comfortable position for me in any area. Any area, whether it was the baby-sitter or anything. It was very difficult for me to ask someone to do something for me. Other people it just flows right off. Not me. It was very hard.

Prescott fathers did not express similar feelings of anxiety about their interactions with teachers. Some said plainly that teachers did not intimidate them. Nor did fathers appear anxious or withdrawn in their visits to the school. Some, in fact, felt very free to give teachers ideas and criticism. Mrs Smith was embarrassed by her husband's behavior in the parent–teacher conference: 'He came into the parent conference the first time and he spent half the time telling her all these ideas on how to teach math!' Mrs Smith had different expectations for the conference:

I felt that we had a few minutes with the teacher.... I went with the expectation that she would be talking fifty miles an hour for the entire time telling us where Carol was.... I really went with the attitude of listening to her tell us about what Carol had been doing.

Mrs Smith did not try to hush her husband:

I figured it was her show, and if she didn't like it then she had to say, 'Well, could you make an appointment tomorrow after school to talk about this but right now I feel the need to get on with this agenda.' And I thought, well, she didn't say that and it wasn't my place to say it. So I just sat back and enjoyed it.

Hence, mothers appeared to experience more doubts than fathers about the legitimacy of criticizing teachers. Mothers did, in fact, criticize and challenge Prescott teachers, but they did so by overriding their own internal doubts and fears. Prescott fathers did not appear to be plagued by such concerns. As a result, fathers were present, and often took a leadership role, when parents confronted school staff about problems in their children's schooling. In keeping with traditional gender role socialization, it appears that fathers brought their training in assertiveness, leadership, and direct confrontation to their interactions with female teachers and administrators.

Social Class and Parent Involvement

Gender was not the only force shaping parent involvement in schooling. Social class also made a difference. Overall, upper-middle-class parents were far more active than working-class parents in school site activities such as Open House and parent–teacher conferences, in responding to teachers' requests for help, and in reading to their children at home. For example, few mothers and fathers at Prescott school missed Open House night, while about 60 percent of parents did so at Colton. For parent–teacher conferences, all of the Prescott mothers attended while 60 percent of Colton mothers came to school for their fifteen-minute meeting with the teacher. There were also disparities in other areas. Requests for particular teachers were rare at Colton (two per year for the entire school) and more common at Prescott (five per classroom), although the principal vigorously discouraged parents from making such requests. There was also evidence that Prescott parents read to their children at home more regularly than did Colton parents, where only a handful of children completed more than eight hours of reading at home during the school year.

These differences in parent involvement by parents' social class did not appear to be linked to how much parents valued educational success in the first grade. Working-class parents did appear to value educational success in the first grade, however: they admonished their children to do well in school, they regretted their own lack of education, and reported that they 'desperately' wanted their children to graduate from high school. Nor could the differences be traced to variations in how teachers treated parents in the two communities. Teachers in the working-class school made as many, if not more, requests for parent involvement as in the upper-middle-class school. Colton teachers sponsored a 'Read-at-Home' program which gave children a free book for every eight hours of reading at home, and made repeated statements to parents about the importance of reading at home in parent–teacher conferences, Back-to-School night, and informal visits with parents after school.

Instead, parent involvement was linked to the class-based resources parents possessed, or, put differently, their cultural capital. For example, working-class parents (even high school graduates) felt that they lacked the educational knowledge to help their children accurately with their spelling, math, and other school work. They were afraid they would give their children incorrect advice. These parents were disposed to treat teachers as 'educated people' with specialized training and expertise which they, as parents, lacked. Located below teachers in the social hierarchy, few Colton parents were predisposed to treat teachers as social equals or to question the professional judgment of educators. As a result, working-class parents defined education as within the teacher's control. They did not believe that they were capable of systematically helping their children improve their educational performance; they depended upon the teacher.

The social networks (or social capital) of parents also varied by social class. Colton parents lived in a world of working-class people. They did not generally have friends, relatives, or co-workers who were teachers, principals, or professional educators to turn to if their children had a problem in school. Nor were they friends with other parents in the school; their strongest social ties were with relatives. Taken together, Colton parents appeared to turn over responsibility for education to the school, viewing schooling as something which took place on the school site. There was a separation between home and school which was linked to cultural and social capital, particularly parents' educational knowledge, their disposition to defer to teachers, and their social networks.

By contrast, upper-middle-class parents felt that, armed with their college educations, they were completely capable of helping their young children with their school work. As professionals themselves, they viewed teachers as equals, rather than superiors, and were disposed critically to evaluate the performance of the teacher. Upper-middle-class parents also had considerable social capital; the parents had educators among their relatives, friends, and neighbors. Their social networks provided them with access to supplemental information about schooling, programs to increase school success, and strategies for improving the performance of low achievers. Overall, Prescott parents defined education as a partnership and, rather than turning responsibility over to teachers, monitored, supervised, and intervened in their children's education. There was an interconnectedness between home and school among these families, which was linked to the use of cultural and social capital, particularly educational knowledge, parents' definition of their proper relationship with teachers, and their social relationship with educators.

These differences by social class intersected with gender roles in a complex fashion. In working-class marriages, many couples experience a segregation of gender roles (Bott 1971; Rubin 1976). Women and men believe in a gender-based division of labor where women are responsible for expressive roles in the family as well as child care. This predisposes working-class parents in Colton to an asymmetrical relationship with the school: mothers rather than fathers are responsible for supervising their children's activities. Some working-class fathers did end up picking their children up from school or helping with homework, but they saw themselves as 'helping' their wives rather than enacting their proper role. Upper-middle-class men and women are more likely to espouse beliefs in an egalitarian marriage, with shared responsibility for parenting and expressive duties. In most aspects of family life, upper-middle-class wives carry out far more of the parenting duties and housework than their husbands. Nevertheless, fathers and mothers are likely to believe in fathers' symbolic participation in childrearing activities (for a similar pattern in housework see Hochschild 1989).

These social class differences in gender roles are important, as they shape the likelihood of parents complying with teachers' definitions of the proper role of parents in school, regardless of parents' desires to see their children succeed. Teachers sought parent involvement in schooling, but were more likely to be successful with upper-middle-class parents than working-class ones. More importantly, teachers revealed a gender bias in their assessment of parent involvement in schooling. Just as fathers are often given praise for carrying out household chores that mothers carry out routinely, Prescott teachers admired fathers' involvement in schooling, involvement that they expected routinely from mothers. In their conversations at school, teachers treated the appearance of a father differently from that of a mother. Prescott teachers talked more about a father volunteering in the classroom than about mothers coming to school. Mothers' volunteering was routine; fathers' visits were newsworthy.

Teachers also revealed in interviews that they interpreted fathers' involvement differently from that of mothers. Mrs Walters, for example, took fathers' attendance as an indication of the interest parents had in education:

> If the father came, you got biased in a particular way that that family really was interested in [education]; and, in fact, nearly all Prescott fathers come still. I think as they go up the grades, sometimes ... the fathers drop out a bit ... they felt that things are on the road. But the first grades were real busy.

Implicitly and explicitly, teachers' different reactions to mothers and fathers suggest that teachers see fathers' time as more valuable than mothers' time. It also raises the possibility that teachers' expectations are heightened by fathers' attendance at school events. The potential benefits that children and parents gain from impressing teachers, however, differ by social class. With norms for segregated gender roles in working-class families, Colton parents were less likely to comply with teachers' expectations than Prescott parents embracing an ideology of egalitarian gender roles in marriage.

Conclusion

Many studies of gender have focused on the differential treatment of children in the classroom, as well as the way in which encouragement to pursue academic success in math and science is directed more to boys than girls. Researchers have also pursued the feminization of the profession and inequity by gender in the proportion of female administrators in higher education. In this chapter I suggest that we need to see gender as operating in another important (and neglected) dimension of education: the role of parents in helping their children in school. As I have shown, 'parents' clearly means 'mothers', especially in working-class communities. Although fathers sometimes play an important symbolic role at school sites in upper-middle-class communities, mothers, not fathers, carry the burden of supervising children's day-to-day school experiences in the early grades. It has been a mistake to discuss 'parent involvement' in schooling rather than offering gender-specific terms. The current debate in the literature aimed at increasing parent involvement in education (Epstein 1987b; Rich 1987; Bergen 1983) implies that parents are equally likely to assist in the educational process. This is inaccurate.[1]

Moreover, the study points to the mechanisms of the reproduction of inequalities by social class. Upper-middle-class mothers invest substantial amounts of time and energy monitoring their children's school experiences. They were more likely than working-class mothers to comply with teachers' requests for assistance, particularly reading to their children and attending school events. The failure of working-class parents to be as closely involved in their children's schooling cannot be persuasively seen as linked to low values placed on educational success. As I have shown elsewhere, working-class parents in Colton placed a very high value on school success and were deeply disappointed by school failure (Lareau 1989). Instead, class differences appear to reflect the lack of educational competence and the relatively low social status of parents compared with teachers. Working-class parents accepted a notion of professional expertise; they deferred to teachers for the education of their children and reported feeling uncomfortable and intimidated by teachers. Upper-middle-class parents did not face such problems. They usually had as much education as teachers, if not more, and were in occupations of equal or higher prestige. These class resources, or cultural capital, were invested by upper-middle-class parents and sometimes yielded substantial educational profits for children, especially children of average intelligence with low motivation to work hard in the classroom (Lareau 1989). Thus, parents' social class position provided substantially different resources to comply with teachers' requests for parent involvement in schooling.

Nevertheless, in a society with powerful divisions of labor by gender, the task of monitoring children's schooling was heavily influenced by gender. In working-class homes, mothers handled schooling; fathers were absent from the process. Although the rhetoric changed by social class, the disproportionate involvement of mothers compared with fathers is striking in upper-middle-class families. Even when fathers were involved, their activities were generally initiated and coordinated by their wives. This suggests that the reproduction of crucial aspects of social inequality falls heavily to women. In this context, studying gender roles in parents' management of children's education is important. It offers the opportunity to provide a more dynamic and accurate portrayal of the impact of 'parents' on children's school success, by illustrating the importance of women as well as men in the process. With such radically different roles for mothers and fathers in managing school careers, it is a mistake to ignore the influence of gender. Social class differences are important, but they are mediated in crucial ways by gender.

In the end, the study of the role of parents in children's school careers stands as a reminder of the powerful and complex interaction between social-structural forces and biography (Mills 1959). Class and gender were critical in shaping the character of children's school careers, yet there were differences among upper-middle-class mothers in the ways in which they negotiated the school year. For example, some mothers, of comparable social class positions, were shrewder and more skillful than others in getting teachers to do what they wanted. Each family was unique, yet the broader social pattern of gender and class shaping the actions of parents is clear. By infusing models of the reproduction of social class inequality with more developed notions of gender roles, social scientists stand to improve the accuracy and sophistication of their research models in education, as well as social stratification. Improving these conceptual models, and their understanding of the intersection between social structure and biography, remains one of the most pressing problems facing social scientists.

Notes

1 There are some indications that mothers' involvement in schooling may also be gender biased. One study, for example, found that mothers spend more hours

overseeing and helping to improve boys' educational performance than that of girls (Stevenson and Baker 1987). Overall, low levels of academic performance triggered maternal activity. Nevertheless, at the same (poor) level of performance, mothers were more likely to attend school events, help with homework, and contact the teacher for boys than girls. This suggests that in the social construction of school careers, mothers and fathers make many decisions — to reward, complain about, demand improvement, or accept their children's level of school performance. Mothers and fathers may be less willing to tolerate a mediocre school performance from boys than from girls. Since parent involvement in children's education is associated with higher levels of school performance, girls may not gain the same academic benefits available to some boys of having their mothers intensely supervise their schooling.

General Note

I am grateful to Julia Wrigley, Eun Mee Kim, Kathryn Ward, Hugh Mehan, Aaron Cicourel, Amy Wharton, and Nicole Biggart for comments on an earlier version of this chapter. Portions of this chapter have appeared in *Home Advantage: Social Class and Parental Intervention in Elementary Education*, London, Falmer Press, 1989.

References

BAKER, D. and STEVENSON, D. (1986) 'Mothers' Strategies for School Achievement: Managing the Transition to High School', *Sociology of Education* 59, pp. 156–67.

BECKER, H.J. and EPSTEIN, J.L. (1982) 'Parent Involvement: A Survey of Teacher Practices', *The Elementary School Journal* 83 (2), pp. 85–102.

BENIN, M.H. and AGOSTINELLI, J. (1988) 'Husbands' and Wives' Satisfaction with the Division of Labor', *Journal of Marriage and the Family* 50, May, pp. 349–61.

BERGER, E.H. (1983) *Beyond the Classroom: Parents as Partners in Education*, St Louis, C.V. Mosby.

BERK, S.F. (1985) *The Gender Factory*, New York, Plenum.

BERNARD, J. (1982) *The Future of Marriage*, New Haven, Yale University Press.

BERNSTEIN, B. (1977) *Class, Codes, and Control*, vol. 3, 2nd ed., London, Routledge & Kegan Paul.

BLOOD, R. Jr. and WOLFE, D.M. (1960) *Husbands and Wives*, New York, Free Press.

BOTT, E. (1971) *Family and Social Networks*, New York, Free Press.

BOURDIEU, P. (1977) 'Cultural Reproduction and Social Reproduction', in KARABEL, J. and Halsey, A.H. (Eds) *Power and Ideology in Education*, pp. 487–511, New York, Oxford University Press.

BOURDIEU, P. (1984) *Distinction: A Social Critique of the Judgment of Taste*, trans. NICE, R. (Ed.), Cambridge, Harvard University Press.

BOURDIEU, P. and PASSERON, J. (1977) *Reproduction in Education, Society, and Culture*, Beverley Hills, Sage.

COVERMAN, S. (1985) 'Explaining Husbands' Participation in Domestic Labor', *Sociological Quarterly* 26 (1), pp. 81–97.

COVERMAN, S. and SHELEY, J.F. (1986) 'Changes in Men's Housework and Child-Care Time, 1965–1975', *Journal of Marriage and the Family* 48, May, pp. 413–22.

DIMAGGIO, P. and MOHR, J. (1985) 'Cultural Capital, Educational Attainment, and Marital Selection', *American Journal of Sociology* 90, pp. 1231–61.

EDER, D. (1981) 'Ability Grouping as a Self-fulfilling Prophecy: A Micro-Analysis of Teacher-Student Interaction', *Sociology of Education* 54, July, pp. 151–62.

EPSTEIN, J.L. (1986) 'Parents' Reactions to Teacher Practices of Parent Involvement', *The Elementary School Journal* 86 (3), pp. 277–94.

EPSTEIN, J.L. (1987a) 'Parent Involvement: What Research Says to Administrators', *Education and Urban Society* 19 (2), pp. 119–36.

EPSTEIN, J.L. (1987b) 'Toward a Theory of Family-School Connections: Teacher Practices and Parent Involvement', in HURRELMANN, K., KAUFMAN, F. and LOSEL, F. (Eds) *Social Interventions: Potential and Constraints*, pp. 121–36, New York, Walter de Gruyter.

EPSTEIN, J.L. and BECKER, H.J. (1982) 'Teachers' Reported Practices of Parent Involvement: Problems and Possibilities', *Elementary School Journal* 83, November, pp. 103–13.

HEATH, S.B. (1982) 'What No Bedtime Story Means: Narrative Skills at Home and School', *Language in Society* 11 (2), pp. 49–76.

HEATH, S.B. (1983) *Ways with Words*, New York, Cambridge University Press.

HOCHSCHILD, A.R. (with MACHUNG, A.) (1989) *The Second Shift*, New York, Avon.

KARABEL, J. and HALSEY, A.H. (1977) 'Educational Research: A Review and Interpretation', in KARABEL, J. and HALSEY, A.H. (Eds) *Power and Ideology in Education*, pp. 1–86, New York, Oxford University Press.

KERCKHOFF, A.C. (1976) 'The Status Attainment Process: Socialization or Allocation', *Sociology of Education* 51 (6), pp. 842–58.

KOHN, M.L. (1977) *Class and Conformity: A Study of Values,* 2nd ed., Chicago, University of Chicago Press.

LAMONT, M. and LAREAU, A. (1988) 'Cultural Capital: Allusions, Gaps, and Glissandos in Recent Theoretical Developments', *Sociological Theory* 6, Fall, pp. 153–68.

LAREAU, A. (1989) *Home Advantage: Social Class and Parental Intervention in Elementary Education*, London, Falmer Press.

MEHAN, H. (1979) *Learning Lessons*, Cambridge, Harvard University Press.

MILLS, C.W. (1959) *The Sociological Imagination*, New York, Free Press.

RICH, D. (1987) *Teachers and Parents: An Adult-to-Adult Approach*, Washington, DC, NEA Press.

RUBIN, L.B. (1976) *Worlds of Pain*, New York, Basic Books.

SAFILIOS-ROTHSCHILD, C. (1970) 'The Study of Family Power Structure: A Review 1960–1969', *Journal of Marriage and the Family* 31, November, pp. 539–50.

SEWELL, W.H. and HAUSER, R.M. (1980) 'The Wisconsin Longitudinal Study of Social and Psychological Factors in Aspirations and Achievements', in KERCKHOFF, A.C. (Ed.) *Research in Sociology of Education and Socialization*, vol. 1, pp. 59–100, Greenwich, JAI Press.

SEWELL, W.H. and SHAH, V.P. (1977) 'Socio-economic Status, Intelligence and the Attainment of Higher Education', in KARABEL, J. and HALSEY, A.H. (Eds) *Power and Ideology in Education*, pp. 197–214, New York, Oxford University Press.

SHAVIT, Y. and FEATHERMAN, D.L. (1988) 'Schooling, Tracking, and Teenage Intelligence', *Sociology of Education* 61 (1), pp. 42–51.

STEIL, J.M. (1984) 'Marital Relationships and Marital Health: The Psychic Costs of Inequality', in FREEMAN, J. (Ed.) *Women: A Feminist Perspective*, pp. 113–23, Palo Alto, Mayfield.

STEVENSON, D.L. and BAKER, D.P. (1987) 'The Family–School Relation and the Child's School Performance', *Child Development* 58, pp. 1348–57.

12 The Educational Contest for Middle- and Working-class Women: The Reproduction of Inequality

Merrilee Krysa Finley

Introduction

Most American youth stay in high school through graduation. Their common compulsory presence behind school walls and daily rounds in classrooms give an institutional sameness to their lives for many years. Yet this shared school existence gives little hint of the enormous divergence shortly to come in their lives. Educational studies have shown that, in fact, young people have quite different experiences in school (Carnoy and Levin 1985; Metz 1978), but it is not until they leave school behind that their different destinies, suddenly highly visible, are played out. They make choices which lead them in very different directions. They are no longer found in the same institutional settings. Some go away to college and live the privileged life of the campus; some shuttle between community college classes and night-time jobs, trying to get skills for jobs above minimum wage; and some (a large proportion) immediately put student life behind them and take on the full burdens of adult life. This sudden divergence in young people's lives is most pronounced among young women. While some merely continue their adolescence in college and the protective family home, others almost immediately take on the adult burdens of work, marriage, and motherhood. Those with the fewest resources take on the greatest burdens, since the divergence between young women's paths is by no means random. Their lives are shaped by their class positions. Because middle- and working-class women's lives diverge so greatly in this period when adult choices can be made, it is a crucial period to analyze and to understand.

Through a series of interviews over a period of nearly five years, this study examines the lives of young women of middle- and working-class backgrounds as they made the important transition from school to work and/or college. Research already tells us that middle- and working-class women will have lives more like their own mothers' lives than like each others', but it does not tell us how these differences come about. Sociologists know more about what decisions these women make than how they make them. This study focuses on the decisions working- and middle-class women make and why they decide as they do. I investigated how their decisions about education, occupation, marriage, and motherhood were shaped by the differing circumstances they faced, focusing on the complex process by which women of different class backgrounds came to have different lives.

Young women on the brink of maturity decided whether to go to college or to work full time; whether to leave the family home or to stay with their parents; whether to remain single or to marry and start families of their own. The study demonstrated that women had some freedom of action, with their own values and determination affecting their choices and their ability to realize their goals; more broadly, the study also showed that the choices these women made were shaped by their class backgrounds. For most, their own individually made decisions contributed to a large and impersonal process of social class reproduction, with inequalities being reinforced anew in their generation. The women's futures were shaped in countless small, but often decisive, ways by the resources they could command. My study sheds light on how seemingly minor circumstances, such as access to transportation, or ability to count on parents for some college costs, add up to a set of critical advantages for the women from middle-class backgrounds and critical disadvantages for their working-class peers.

The women in the study were affected by their gender as well as by their class. Throughout, I analyze how gender and class interacted in shaping the women's transition to adulthood. In various concrete ways the middle-class women had more opportunity to operate in male arenas, or at least in parallel arenas, than did the working-class women. While most of the middle-class women were still maintaining the status of college students, a significant proportion of the working-class women had become mothers and had experienced full induction into a decisively gendered adult role. Once they became mothers, the working-class women usually lost all means of pursuing their education. My study, by tracing the interwoven educational, work, and family choices of young women as they become adults, treats class and gender as equally powerful forces in shaping women's lives. The women do make choices, but they do not make them without constraint.

For most of the working-class women in my sample, the five-year span of the study covers a period in which they relinquished their early aspirations. Some, while still young themselves, transferred their hopes to their children. Many of the women interviewed dropped out without getting even two-year associate of arts degrees. They ended their schooling with no vocational skills and no means of cracking job markets dominated by those with higher credentials. Instead of attributing their hardships or the denial of their hopes to any systemic bias, they emphasized their individual difficulties. They did not find it hard to nurture hopes for children even while adjusting their own expectations downward. They contrast with the working-class English youth studied by Paul Willis (1981), who scorned the official culture of the schools. The forces that press young women back into their class milieus suppress individual ambition but not individual belief in education. My study illustrates how the 'cooling out' (Clark 1960) of one generation of women can coexist with a transfer of hope to the next generation.

My research question focuses on social reproduction, how inequalities are reproduced across generations. As such, it both falls within a traditional area of inquiry in the social sciences and addresses a gap in that tradition. Although the study focuses on women, the large literature on class reproduction is relevant. This literature broadly divides between individualistic and structural perspectives on educational inequality. For those with an individualistic perspective, the key question has been why working-class children do not achieve in school and obtain educational credentials and occupational advantages equal to those of the middle class. Explanations have usually centered on individual differences. Researchers argue that individuals' abilities, values, traits, and aspirations are acquired in the family. Children are thus viewed as 'programmed' to behave in certain ways, some of which, in working-class children, produce school and occupational underachievement. Sociologists and psychologists have looked at child-rearing practices, personality traits, values, aspirations, and such perceptions as sense of control over the environment to explain differences in school performance. They have found systematic differences between children from different social classes, and have assumed that such differences are the causes of inequality in education, if not in life (Coleman et al. 1966; see also Jencks et al. 1972). Such research is unable to offer any explanation as to why children and their families should vary systematically in these ways, however, since it does not place them in their material, social, and cultural contexts.

The individualistic perspective has been challenged by writers favoring a structural approach. Researchers in this perspective have improved upon the individualistic conception of educational success by locating individuals in their social groups, which in turn are structurally determined and share common material, social, and cultural conditions. Structuralists emphasize the importance of group differences in power and resources in the reproduction of inequality and the underlying structure of the economy which requires certain occupational positions and creates different job markets (Bluestone 1972; Bowles and Gintis 1976). Most theorists also add the concept of class culture and posit a relationship between structure and culture (Willis 1977).

Those in the structuralist tradition have long argued that educational systems in Western democracies help reproduce social classes through the unequal distribution of skills, knowledge, and credentials (Bowles and Gintis 1976; Bourdieu and Passeron 1970; Collins 1979). Education helps legitimate social inequality by leading the dispossessed to blame themselves for their class position. The notion of equality of opportunity through public education masks the class biases at work in distribution of educational credentials through a seemingly 'objective' selection based upon merit. Dominant groups determine the standards for selection based upon their power within institutions (Bourdieu and Passeron 1970; Sennet and Cobb 1972; Karabel 1977). As many researchers have suggested, however, cultural domination through the educational system is never complete and subordinate group consciousness remains mixed (Giroux 1983). Class experiences and solidarity produce subcultural variations in dominant values, norms, and ideologies. Mingled dominant and subordinate elements in the subcultures of subordinate groups inhibit the development of a fully structural explanation for social reproduction (Mann 1970; Parkin 1971; Sennet and Cobb 1972; Willis 1977).

Researchers investigating women's subordinate position in society have found parallels between education's role in producing class and gender inequality. Women acquire less education and less valuable credentials than men; they are differentially socialized in skills and attitudes in the education process; their aspirations are limited by their lesser share of family resources, as well as by job ceilings which limit their chances in the opportunity structure. As with class reproduction, the experiences of subordination produce a mixed consciousness, with women from birth being exposed to sex-role socialization which prepares them to focus primarily on their families and secondarily on their educational or job ambitions.

The recent research on women's place in the stratification system has documented pervasive gender inequality, but it has obscured the importance of social class inequality among women. Compared with men, women's educational attainment has historically been more class-biased (Alexander and Eckland 1974; Sewell and Shah 1967). Education helps reproduce class differences among women, as academic credentials have helped some women secure access to professional jobs, while other women, with lesser credentials, remain mired in women's clerical and factory ghettos (Blau 1978; Roby 1975). This suggests that if gender equality were to become a reality, class polarization would actually increase among working- and middle-class households. With equal representation of women in high-prestige, previously male occupations, middle-class women would end up contributing more to their families' resources than working-class women to theirs. Such a tendency has already been observed in the growing polarization between two-career middle-class families and those with either one career, two jobs, or one job (Currie et al. 1980). In families where both partners bring in substantial incomes, couples have shown little inclination to support collective solutions for social problems, instead relying on their market power to buy housecleaning and child-care services (Hertz 1986). Thus, not only in material, but also in ideological terms, increased gender equality could have the paradoxical effect of strengthening class biases and inequalities.

My study aims to integrate class and gender perspectives. The working- and middle-class women in my sample experienced gendered modes of schooling and of occupational choice. Their treatment within their families of origin also depended in significant part on their gender. The consequences for all women were not the same, however, with gender being more of a disadvantage for low-resource working-class women than for their middle-class counterparts. Middle-class women have family-based economic and educational assets which can help them make their way in what remains a male-dominated world. They can turn class assets to account even when they continue to suffer gender disadvantages. For working-class women, class and gender interact to keep them in socially subordinate positions. They receive fewer family resources than their brothers, but have less means of acquiring their own because they operate within sex-segregated labor markets where they earn low wages. This diminishes their ability to pursue higher education, which further restricts their opportunities.

Women of different social classes experience 'cooling out' (Clark 1960) in the educational system in different ways and in different places. In class reproduction, the crucial point in the educational 'contest' is where people drop out of the educational system. Working-class women, buffeted by economic pressures and lack of social support, typically drop out between high school and college or before college graduation. Middle-class women are not subjected to class 'cooling out' but to gender 'cooling out'. Their choice of college, choice of major, and professional and graduate education differentiate them from men, but they have a basic ability to remain in the educational contest abandoned far earlier by their working-class counterparts. My study explores the interplay between class and gender and how it affects women in the educational arena.

Research Method

To analyze the process by which women of different backgrounds come to have different occupational and educational destinies, I followed a group of young middle- and working-class women through their first six years out of high school, conducting intensive interviews with them as they made the transition to adulthood. The study's long time line enabled me to gauge outcomes in the light of the women's early expectations. The detailed nature of the interviews allowed integration of material on many different aspects of the women's social environments, from the emotional tone of their households to the women's ability to secure resources. The initial sample contained sixty women from a high school in Southern California. The school was chosen because of the social class variation in its students, with the school serving two distinct communities in a large metropolitan area. One community, 'Flatlands', is a lower-middle-class/working-class suburb, and the other, 'Woodlands', is upper-middle-class. The women in the sample had the common experience of attending one high school, but the institutional similarity of their experiences changed once they graduated, with the women's paths beginning to diverge. It is the nature of that divergence that I explore.

The school's class variation was not matched by ethnic variation. Among the whites in this urban enclave, there are few or no divisions based upon ethnicity, for in this Southern California city, class is not interrelated with ethnicity as it is so powerfully in many older Eastern and Midwestern cities. Rubin (1976) suggests that such communities may be increasingly representative of the American working-class population.

The sample has the limitation of including only whites. While there is a sizeable minority population in the working-class area, the inclusion of African-American, Asian-American, and Latina women would have introduced a new source of complexity into the study. In this community, there are few middle-class minority families; thus, if I had included minority women in the study, the class comparison would have been a racial comparison as well, since the middle-class group would be predominantly white, while the working-class group would include both whites and minorities. The interaction of race and class divisions is of great importance in American society, and the particular experiences of women of color in the processes of race, gender, and class reproduction deserve careful attention in their own right; however, for the purposes of class comparisons in this study, minority women were not included.

The sixty young women were interviewed for the first time in the spring of 1983 (during the first year after their high school graduation in 1982). They were interviewed for a second time in the fall of 1983, at the start of their second year out of high school. Their school records were also examined, including their grades and course programs. Those in the sample who could be located five years later, forty-four women, were interviewed again in the spring of 1988, nearly six years after high school. Each of the semi-structured, lengthy, tape-recorded interviews covered the broad areas of family relationships, family resources,

Table 12.1   *Type of Schooling Begun during the First Three Semesters after High School by Class Background*

Type of Schooling	Middle Class %	Working Class %
None*	5	34
Vocational School	0	17
Community College	63	29
Four-year College/University	32	20
Total	100	100
Number	19	41

* Counted among those with no schooling are one middle-class and five working-class women who dropped out of a community college before completing a single semester.

schooling experiences, work experiences, and romantic relationships. In the first interviews, the women were asked about their educational and occupational hopes and plans. In the last interviews, they were asked to describe what had become of those and to interpret their own lives.

Inequality in Educational Attainment

The middle- and working-class young women in the sample differed most visibly in their levels of post-secondary educational attainment. The interviews provided revealing information on the origins of these broad differences in the amount and quality of schooling the young women received after high school. Post-secondary schooling differences were closely related to the resources available in the women's families. The Horatio Alger myth in the United States celebrates those who achieve success despite initial lack of resources. Such triumphs sometimes occur, but more often educational careers are truncated as would-be students find they cannot surmount the undramatic and yet real problems of assembling resources on their own, with little or no help from their families. In this final leg of the educational contest, families' resources proved especially crucial. Even those young women who had been encouraged by their high school teachers could not translate an illustrious high school career into further success without family resources. Table 12.1 illustrates how middle- and working-class women differed in their patterns of enrollment in post-secondary educational institutions.

As Table 12.1 shows, there were important differences in the destinations of these two groups of young women immediately after high school, but the differences were greater in the women's final destinations. The outcomes for those who began at the same types of institutions also differed by class.

The role of family resources is shown by examining the category of women who did not pursue any kind of schooling after high school. Twenty-four percent of the working-class women fell into this category, and an additional 10 percent began the first semester at a community college but dropped out before even completing that semester. There was only one middle-class woman in this category. The young women who received the least schooling after high school had the least family resources. Over half had a problem regarding their living arrangements after high school. Not only did they receive no financial assistance from their parents, they could not count on 'in kind' aid through receiving room and board from parents. Some were asked to leave home after high school by parents who could not or would not support their daughters further. One young woman, Barbara, had been told by her mother while still in high school that she and her siblings would have to move out when they turned eighteen. Barbara's father had deserted the family when she was six and her mother had struggled to support three children. The mother remarried while Barbara was in high school, but made it plain she wanted a clearly demarcated end to her financial responsibility for her children. Another young woman, Jennifer, lost access to what limited family resources there might have been when her parents separated during her senior year in high school. Both her father and mother, struggling to reestablish themselves financially and emotionally, left their daughter to manage on her own.

Others in this group of young working-class women who had no further schooling after high school moved out of their parents' home because of difficult family relationships. For these women, pursuing schooling from the independence of a dormitory was not possible; if they wanted to go to school, they had to live at home. For some, this was too great a cost. One young woman, Shelley, came from a family with two working parents, which allowed for a modest affluence. She reported she could not draw upon this resource, however, because her father had been 'physically abusive' toward her since she was young. Her goal was to be self-supporting and not to have to ask her father for aid. She dropped out of community college during her first semester, left home about a year after graduation, had a series of abusive boyfriends, and finally married a young man in the Navy. She had had her first child shortly before the last interview was conducted.

Other women without post-secondary schooling came from families with the material resources and family relations to enable their daughters to remain dependent for a period, but they lacked the means to provide their daughters with transportation. In Southern California the automobile reigns supreme, with an almost complete absence of efficient mass transit, and the heavy expenses of buying and maintaining a car cripple the budgets of the poor. A car might represent a luxury to a middle-class college student ensconced on a college campus, but it borders on a necessity for young women whose homes, community colleges, and work places can be far apart. Those women who could not secure transportation from their families often postponed further schooling. When first interviewed, they said they were 'concentrating on getting a car first', and that they would not go to school until after they had worked full time to secure one. The women's low wage rates in practice made it hard for them to save, and for many the goal of further schooling receded from year to year. The larger inequalities of society penetrate these women's lives not only in terms of their access to direct resources, but in terms of the limited availability of socially provided goods such as mass transit.

For those women who did not receive post-secondary education, the reasons for not attending college were multiple and overlapping. Most had insufficient material resources. A few probably had sufficient material resources in some objective sense, but they did not have access to them because of difficult family relationships. The case of Cindy showed how problems could be compounded:

Cindy, a young working-class woman who wanted to be a lawyer, borrowed money from her father for a used car after high school graduation, with an agreement that she would give him monthly payments and save up for quarterly insurance payments from a part-time job in retail sales. During her first semester at the neighborhood community college branch, her car needed a major repair. Cindy's parents could not loan her the money. She tried unsuccessfully to get more hours at her job, had to rely upon her boyfriend for evening transportation, and walked everywhere during the day. She dropped out of school that semester, planning to go back when finances permitted. In addition, Cindy fought with her father, who was extremely restrictive and accused her of promiscuity when she came home late. Cindy was desperate to get away from home. She soon became pregnant and married a young man in the Navy. Five years later, Cindy was struggling as a single mother to raise her daughter on her own, working in a dental office. Six years after high school graduation, she was further than ever from a college education.

Attending Vocational School

No middle-class women enrolled in vocational school after school, but seven working-class women, 17 percent of the sample, did. Of these, the majority went to cosmetology schools to become hairdressers or manicurists. Two went to schools offering training in medical assistant fields. All remained within highly gender-defined forms of vocational training. These women had more resources than the group who went straight out to work after high school. They either had the opportunity to live at home or had some funds available to pursue training. These resources were limited, however, so they chose private vocational training as the least expensive, quickest way to obtain job skills. Beth provides an example of a young woman who pursued a vocational route. Long interested in hairdressing, for which she felt she had a flair, she joined several relatives doing similar work. Beth was able to live at home and her father drove her to school every day for ten months. She borrowed the $5000 tuition through the student loan program, and was working in a neighborhood salon shortly after her graduation from vocational school. Five years later, she was still working in the field, though only part time because she had an eight-month-old daughter to care for.

As Beth's experience illustrates, the small proportion of working-class women who attended private vocational schools had somewhat better circumstances than those who received no schooling. They had access to living arrangements which cost nothing or some funds for schooling expenses. With their short time line, they were in the workforce full time in a year or less after high school graduation.

Beginning at a Community College

A number of middle- and working-class women enrolled in community colleges immediately after high school. A large proportion of middle-class women (63 percent) began at a community college, while a smaller proportion (29 percent) of working-class women did. The majority of middle-class women went to the main campus of the city's community college system, while most of the working-class women began at the small, very limited local branch campus. Many of the working-class women selected this branch campus because they had no cars or because they worked long hours and had to consider proximity in selecting the campus they would attend. This peripheral campus is decidedly vocational and working-class in character and has none of the campus life of the main campus which most of the middle-class women selected.

Middle-class women and working-class women had different reasons for attending community colleges. The middle-class community college women were in one of two situations: some had been reluctant scholars in high school who had either made only mediocre grades or had disliked academic work were but under parental pressure to go to college, while others were women whose families were in difficulty due to divorce or other hardship. The working-class women, on the other hand, tended to choose community colleges mainly for financial reasons, although they had often had mediocre high school careers as well.

The class groups also differed in the outcome of their community college experiences. The middle-class women attended community colleges longer, earned more credits, and transferred to four-year colleges more often than did the working-class women. The most common outcome for the middle-class women was transfer to a university. For the working-class women, however, it was dropping out before completing their general education requirements or receiving an associate of arts degree. Only one working-class woman transferred from a community college to a four-year university.

The common experience for the working-class women attending a community college was to begin with one foot in the world of school and one foot in the world of work, and to move quickly over totally into the world of work. Jody, for example, began at the main community college campus and carried twelve units in her first semester. By the second semester, she had moved to the local branch campus and was carrying only six units in the evenings because of work. By the second year, she had quit entirely and did not return. She found a full-time job in an office and spent money on a car. By the time of the last interview, she was married, hoping to have a child, and had little prospect of further college attendance. Another working-class woman dismissed her early community college ambitions as having been 'just a dream', put aside when she took a full-time job in a retail shop.

The working-class women typically made slow progress toward vague goals. Going to school only part time lengthened the time they were in the student role, sacrificing their time and money for education. If they attended half time, they faced an eight-year commitment to evening classes and homework. If they attended full time, they faced at least four years without a car or spending money or any freedom from their families. If they had to take remedial courses to make up for academic deficiencies, the path before them stretched out endlessly.

Beginning at a Four-year College

Even those young women who began at four-year colleges differed in the types of institutions they attended and how they fared at them, depending partly on their class background and ability to mobilize resources. First, a smaller proportion of working-class women attended the more selective of the two public universities in the city. More importantly, only the middle-class group was actually able to leave the four-year colleges with degrees. All the middle-class women graduated, while very few of the working-class women did. There were, however, rare instances of success by the working-class women. Tammy, the only college graduate in the sample with a typical working-class background, graduated from the local state university with an 'A' average. She had not been an academic standout while in high school, but she had attracted the attention of some of her teachers by her perseverance, earnestness, and likeable personality. They encouraged her to go to college. So did her father, with whom she lived after her parents' divorce. She made many sacrifices to work her way through college. For the first year, she took the bus across town two hours each way to attend classes. In the second year, she and her father bought a car for $100 each, which he repaired. She broke up with her high school boyfriend after a year in college, when she realized that he would soon want to marry and did not value her educational aspirations. By the time of the last interview, she had been teaching for two years and was planning to join the Peace Corps. Her success arose from her ability to stick to long-range objectives and to win support from those around her, including, critically, her high school teachers and her father. Most working-class women had vaguer goals and less support. It is worth noting that Tammy also came from a family with no sons in which to invest the family resources.

Inequality in Educational Attainment

Six years after high school graduation, half of the middle-class women had bachelor's degrees, a few were in graduate school, and one was completing a law degree. The half who did not have degrees had completed between two and three years of college and were still attending or back attending after dropping out. In contrast, among the working-class women, only two of the thirty located for the final interview had received bachelor's degrees. Another two were within a year of a degree. Most who had begun college had attained about a year's worth of units at a community college and had quit. Only one transferred from a community college to a four-year university, compared with about half of the middle-class women who began at community colleges.

Middle-class women were also much more successful when beginning at a university. One hundred percent graduated, compared with only 25 percent of the working-class women who had begun at universities. The disadvantage of working-class women follows them at every stage in the attainment process: they are less likely to enroll at all, less likely to enroll at or transfer to a university, and less likely to graduate even if they do enroll at a university.

Comparing Middle- and Working-Class Experiences

Financing College

Patterns of educational attainment clearly reflect class differences, but these differences also show up concretely in the ability of middle- and working-class

Table 12.2   Educational Attainment Six Years after High School by Class Background

Years of College	Middle Class %	Working Class %
None	7	57
One Year	7	17
Two Years	29	7
Three Years	14	13
Four-year Degree	43	7
Total	100	101*
Number	14	30

* Total is more than 100 percent due to rounding error.

parents to finance their daughters' college educations. While theoretically in the United States the doors of college are ever open, with community colleges being either free or charging very low tuition fees, in practice the economic costs of even community colleges are high. Students must forgo wages and, in addition, attendance at any kind of college entails a variety of large indirect costs. Because the community college system and state universities available locally are relatively inexpensive, tuition, books, and supplies make up only a small part of the costs of college for those attending. The biggest expense is room and board, the second is transportation (car payments, insurance, maintenance, and gasoline), the third is tuition and books. The middle-class and working-class women differed in the extent to which families paid these costs. Among the middle class, parents customarily met all three of these expenses. Parents provided room and board, at least at home, with many providing dormitory or apartment costs so that students could live on or near the campus. Among the working class, parents typically provided room and board, but only in kind, never as a cash outlay. No working-class parents in the sample paid for a daughter to live away from home.

In a city with inadequate public transportation and colleges across town from many of its suburbs, the second major expense of college is transportation. The young women needed cars after high school graduation if they were to go across town to the main community college campus or the two universities. They also needed cars to get to work; in their residential neighborhood, only jobs in retail stores or fast-food outlets were available. Middle-class parents bought their daughters cars during high school. How luxurious these gifts were varied considerably among those in the sample, from mother's hand-me-down to a brand new sports car, but some form of transportation was provided. Some of the young women were asked to contribute toward their transportation by paying for gasoline or insurance as a token of their increasing responsibility. Few working-class daughters, however, were given cars as gifts. The majority had to buy their own cars. Daughters whose parents paid for them initially or cosigned for them got cars sooner than those who had to save up for them. The most frequently cited reason these women gave for not starting college was not having a car. Some intended to work full time to save for a car and then go to school, but none of them did return to school. The most frequently cited reason for not going to school full time but only part time was working full time to buy a car.

For the third largest expense of college, tuition, books, and supplies, the same middle class versus working class contrast could be found. Among the middle class, parents paid for these expenses, though young women sometimes paid for some part of them from their part-time or summer earnings, again as a token of their willingness to take some responsibility for their expenses. If their earnings were insufficient, however, they were not required to pay them. Among the working class, most chose community college in order to save the tuition costs for the first two years of college. Those at community colleges usually paid for their own books. The few who did begin at universities had some help from their parents. Those working-class women who went to private vocational schools usually had loans for tuition and supplies and attended full time so that they could reduce their period of dependence.

The Substitute Son

Not only the young women's class, but also their gender shaped their transition from high school to the adult world of work or college. The effects of gender were greatest for the working-class women, because their gender disadvantage was not mitigated by class privilege. The interplay of class and gender can be seen in the effects of family composition on the women's chances of going to college. For both groups of young women, there was often a special advantage in not having a brother. Daughters typically experienced increased parental ambition and investment by default due to the absence of a son in the family. This common situation made a greater difference to the working-class women, because there were fewer family resources to begin with. In middle-class families, it was not that women received encouragement to go to college only if there were no son in the family, but that they sometimes received encouragement for higher achievement when there was no son. Among the middle-class families, both daughters and sons went to college. Of those families in the middle-class group who had both a daughter and a son of college age, daughters and sons were equally likely to be enrolled at a university. The sons, however, were more likely to attend a more selective, prestigious university and to choose a more prestigious, male-dominated field of study than were the daughters. A few middle-class daughters talked about the pressure they felt because there was no son in the family, or because the son had disappointed parental expectations. One young woman, for example, was the only child of a father with a professional job. She described how she had been told she should go to medical school as far back as she could remember. Another young woman said she thought her parents pressured her to compensate for their disappointment in their drug-using son who had dropped out of college.

Only a handful of the working-class families had daughters enrolled at a university. Half of these had both sons and daughters of college age, who were equally likely to be attending college. As with the middle-class families, the sons were more likely than the daughters to be at more selective universities and to be aiming for higher-status professions. Unlike the middle-class group, however, sons often got more of the families' resources, as families concentrated their scarce resources upon them. One working-class daughter reported that she had bought her car completely on her own while attending a community college part time, eventually transferring to a university. Her brother, on the other hand, was getting help with his car payments while attending community college full time, because he was aiming for medical school and the parents felt 'they had to help him more'. Another daughter from a more affluent working-class family had gone to a local community college for an associate of arts degree, gone into the work world for a time, and eventually returned to the local state university, while her parents gave considerable economic aid to her younger brother who was enrolled as a freshman out of town at a selective state university.

In addition to these families, in which both daughters and sons were enrolled at the university level, albeit in different sorts of programs, there was an equal number of working-class families with a university attender who had only girls in the family. Thus, the working-class families producing college-going daughters in this sample were disproportionately families with no sons. Among the working-class daughters, 56 percent of the university attenders came from female-children families (against 28 percent of the non-university attenders who came from female-children families). This indicates that the working-class families sometimes invested in a daughter when there was no son. One of the few working-class women in this sample to enroll directly at a university came from a family of three daughters. Two of the three ended up getting college degrees. This daughter talked a good deal of her warm, mentor-type relationship with her father. Another working-class university attender was the last of six children. The brothers who had come before her had not gone to college. The young woman described herself as 'the last hope of the family'.

Issues of Independence

Value differences, as well as differences in material resources, affected the ability of the working-class and middle-class women in the sample to pursue their educations. Based on the interview data, there was a difference in the basic ground rules between the middle- and working-class families for granting independence to daughters in the college years. These differences may have stemmed ultimately from differences in material resources, but the rules also had a life of their own and, in some families, became a good in and of themselves.

Among the middle class, independence is granted at a certain age and status. When children reach college age and attend college, they are granted a separate residence and a separate life which parents economically support. There may be a tacit or explicit understanding that the children had to 'keep up grades'; it is usually understood, too, that they had to attend college. Variations on this idea may be that the child lives at home during the freshman year so that parents may retain supervision during a period of adjustment, or the child may remain at home for the first two years and then be free to choose any college for upper division. But it is college age that secures these resources and this freedom.

Among the working class, on the other hand, the children never receive this dependent independence. Children may move out when they can pay for it. A woman earns independence by becoming a self-supporting wage earner or a wife and mother. While most of the working-class families in the sample could not afford to support their daughters in dormitories or apartments anyway, these families did not in any event believe that it would be right to do so. The daughters often discussed moving out and paying their own way as a good in itself. In the last interviews, some saw the achievement of financial and thus personal independence in the time since high school graduation as their greatest accomplishment.

Because the biggest cost of college is room and board, and working-class families are neither able nor willing to pay for this other than in kind in the family home, a daughter's having to or choosing to move out on her own virtually guarantees she will have to drop out of school. Most of those who started out full time in school and then dropped out did so in order to work more hours to pay for living away from home. This sometimes arose because parents moved away, but it was more often due to conflicts between parents and daughters. The daughter typically found herself in conflict with parents over her right to personal independence in such matters as hours, study time, and dating. The young women chose to earn their independence rather than continue school. This conflict over independence, and dropping out of school because of it, is a working-class phenomenon. The majority of middle-class women did not experience this. Their personal independence came more quickly than their financial independence, and was acquired during the college years without a sharp break in parental financial support. Conflicts seldom arose over hours, studying, or boyfriends because women lived away from home. Even when daughters stayed at home, these matters seldom aroused conflict because their families had different ways of defining personal independence, and the parents also had less puritanical, restrictive attitudes toward daughters. Middle-class women were gradually weaned of parental financial support as they completed college and obtained full-time jobs. This was a very gradual process, not yet completed for most of the 24-year-olds in the sample.

The Burden of Family Sacrifices

During the interviews, working-class women would sometimes say that their parents had offered to help them pay for tuition or books for the university or community college, yet they had refused such proffered support and were paying their own expenses. These women said that they would worry about not doing well or dropping out if their parents paid these costs, whereas if they paid themselves, it would be their own money that they had 'wasted' and they would not have to worry as much. One young woman, Andrea, explained that she was proud of having paid for her own car and school expenses through three years part time at the local community college and one semester at the state university. Her parents had offered to help with tuition, but she had declined, both because she wanted to keep her emotional freedom to quit if she did not like college and because she was well aware that her mother would have to make major economic sacrifices. As she said, 'My mother works two jobs and it would be nice if she didn't have to work that much or could get something for herself with that money.' Another, Debbie, said that she had wanted to go to a highly regarded art school in another city and that her father would probably have covered her tuition. She decided against it, declaring that, 'If my parents were rich, it would be no big deal if I went to that school and then decided I didn't like or didn't do well or whatever, but it would be a lot of money for my father and he works hard for his money.'

Young working-class women strove for financial independence rather than take scarce resources from their families. They feared that if they accepted resources, they might not measure up, that their achievements would not be enough to offset the sacrifice their families would be making on their behalf. Such a feeling of obligation and pressure did not exist among the middle-class women, even those whose families had financial difficulties due to divorce or unemployment. Middle-class women do not view school expenditures as requiring justification, but as their birthright. They have a sense of entitlement lacking among the working-class women, which in turn supports their educational ambitions.

Experiencing College

Middle-class and working-class women had differed factors propelling them toward work or higher education, but in addition, those who chose higher education had different experiences once they arrived. This occurred because they attended different types of institutions and because only the middle-class women had college attendance as the center of their lives during their enrollment. The institutions attended by middle- and working-class women differed in such resources as faculty, library, and laboratory facilities, and in the variety of social and cultural events on campus. The middle-class women were more likely to live in dormitories or apartments near campus, to have part-time jobs on campus if they worked at all, and eventually to have internships related to their major fields. (These also provided valuable practical knowledge and contacts for after graduation.) Middle-class women learned through their college-going peers and faculty in their major departments to refine their views of prospective majors and job opportunities. Their social groups and boyfriends usually attended the same college. The friends they mentioned after graduation were the ones they met at college.

Among middle- and working-class women attending four-year colleges, there was a substantial difference in the number of hours per week they worked. Middle-class women averaged six hours per week during their first year (the only year for which information was gathered), while working-class women averaged seventeen hours per week on the job. Working-class women at the university level were much less centered at school and at a disadvantage in competition with middle-class women in hours available for academic work and other school activities.

When middle-class women attended college, they experienced an increased, more focused ambition and a general broadening of knowledge and experience. These women also increased and focused their occupational ambitions while in college. One woman changed from wanting a nursing degree to one in business administration; another changed from a major in communications to one in business management, and a third switched from the humanities to a major in public administration. Although some middle-class women remained in traditional female fields such as English, more of them ended up with majors leading to higher-status, male-dominated fields, and these majors were ones they decided upon after they began college. Furthermore, as they described their experience, college broadened and challenged them intellectually. When asked what contribution their college education had made to their lives, these women replied that they had increased their self-confidence and broadened their perspective. As their observer before and after college, I found them more self-confident in speech and manner, and more knowledgeable and articulate, once they had had their college experience.

In contrast, the working-class women were less centered in college life and attended college with fewer campus activities. They worked long hours, often full time. They selected classes around their jobs, not vice versa. They commuted to classes for one class per evening and left after class. They studied at home alone on other evenings after work. They had friends and boyfriends and a social group that was not college-going. Most made few if any friends at school, but had a host of friends at work.

The working-class women seemed largely untouched by the experience of attending college. Unlike their middle-class counterparts, they appeared no more sophisticated or self-confident, broadened or articulate than when they graduated from high school. They viewed the experience as something they at least had tried for a while. Furthermore, through the college-going years, working-class women's ambitions declined. They abandoned hopes of entering professions requiring at least a bachelor's degree and instead pursued shorter, strictly vocational programs. One left biology and considered training as a biomedical lab technician; another gave up ideas of being a nurse in favor of pursuing a two-year program in bookkeeping, and a third thought of majoring in business management but later took a program to become a dental assistant. They had trouble finding resources to support their earlier ambitions, and they also observed the highly visible vocational programs at community colleges, which had the lure of short time lines.

The Cost of Youthful Mistakes

While there are large social forces at work in the transmission of class position from one generation to the next, the process is also affected by a multitude of individual circumstances. Families can use their resources to facilitate their children's educational success, but the children themselves must have some commitment to their own schooling; the process of social class transmission is inherently risky when it comes down to individual cases, despite the broad regularities sociologists have long observed between class background and educational attainment. What is striking in the interview data, however, is that middle-class daughters can make mistakes and then recover them in a way that is much less possible for working-class daughters. For a working-class young woman to succeed, she must keep a clear path to her educational goals. Middle-class women can better afford to be diverted by personal issues or problems because they are less likely to be permanently derailed by them. Middle-class parents cannot forestall transition-to-adulthood crises, any more than working-class parents can, but they can throw down a safety net that keeps their children from a free fall into educational failure.

In the sample, there were a few middle- and working-class women who dropped out of school, and then went back, during the six-year period of the study. Some dropped out because they had no sense of academic direction, feeling they should work while they decided on long-range goals. Others had relationships with men which diverted them from their college programs. Gender plays a role in the women's situations, with the women more vulnerable than men to the consequences of early parenthood. Both working-class and middle-class women were subject to these crises, but the middle-class women had more routes to recovery. This can be seen most clearly in the contrasting cases of two women who had early become single mothers. Courtney, a middle-class woman, left her parents' house in her sophomore year and moved in with her boyfriend. She eventually married him and had a baby. Her marriage failed after eight months and she moved back to her parents' house. At the time of the last interview, Courtney had applied to be re-admitted to the university, hoped to graduate in a year and then enter law school. She did not need to work for her expenses, and child care was provided by her parents' live-in housekeeper. Her parents' resources helped her get back on the educational track. Her situation contrasted with that of Angela, whose parents had fewer resources to give. Angela enrolled full time in college after graduating from high school and thought of pursuing a nursing degree. She became pregnant by a man she had known only a short time and did not want to marry. She dropped out of college, got a full-time job as a bank teller, moved back home, and began cooking and doing housework in exchange for room and board. At the time of the last interview, her child was two years old, and Angela was back in school two evenings a week to get an associate of arts degree in accounting to improve her position at the bank.

When the middle-class women in the sample who had dropped out resumed their schooling, they picked up where they left off; they went back to the university, back to parental support, back to the degree and occupational aspirations they began with or maybe even higher ones. These women did not face easy situations and their families also went through turmoil, but the women did not face a loss of educational options. The working-class women, on the other hand, seldom had the resources to pick up where they left off. They usually ended up going to school part time while maintaining their full-time jobs, thus beginning a long and arduous path to finish school. Usually they lowered their sights. Individual temperament and choices play major roles in people's lives, but they do so within boundaries partly determined by their class positions.

Plans versus Hopes

If the middle- and working-class women are compared on the basis of their ability to predict their own educational and occupational attainments, the contrast is as great as in the attainments themselves. When first interviewed, the young women were asked what they expected to be doing in the next five years. Five years later, they talked about whether or not they had fulfilled these expectations and why. Among the middle-class women still available, 81 percent had expected to receive college degrees. Some 62 percent of those who expected to had in fact done so. Another 15 percent were within a year of graduation. Some 77 percent could thus be said to have fulfilled their own expectations for educational attainment. Among the working-class women still available for the final interview, a smaller proportion had expected to graduate from college. Only some 62 percent had said they expected to receive a college degree within the five-year period. Of this group of degree hopefuls, only 17 percent had in fact secured degrees by the time of the final interview. Another 17 percent were within a year of their goal. Only about 34 percent of the working-class group could therefore be said to have fulfilled their schooling expectations.

This difference in the rates of fulfilled expectations reflects a difference in what those expectations meant. For the middle-class women, the earlier statements represented plans. For the working-class women, on the other hand, their stated expectations were actually only statements of hopes. Annette Lareau (1989) has argued that middle- and working-class parents have similar levels of commitment to education. In a study she conducted of working- and middle-class parents and their relations with schools, she found the working-class parents were not indifferent to their children's academic progress; they fervently hoped their children would do well in school, but they lacked specific means of intervening to help bring this about. Similarly, in the present study the differences between the middle- and working-class women in their goals were much smaller than the differences in educational outcomes.

The middle-class families in this study had the skills and resources to translate the sometimes unfocused hopes and interests of their daughters into specific plans. This included making sure the daughters took college prep courses in high school, helping them prepare and apply for admission to a university, and planning transportation and living arrangements. More importantly, they had the resources to *provide* transportation and living arrangements. If focusing their daughters' interests meant a special kind of program, it included finding that program and the means for the daughter to pursue it. It often also meant having a back-up plan if the first choice did not work out. Not every daughter in the middle-class group aspired to a profession, but when the daughter wanted something else and held firmly to her goal, her parents usually helped her find a way to achieve it. One middle-class mother, for example, found an exotic animal trainer program for her unconventional daughter. The daughter is an animal trainer today. Another mother supported her daughter's efforts to become a model, accompanying her on trips to modeling locations and providing other aid, but also advising her to stay in college as a back-up plan. The modeling career did not work out, but the college major in business did.

The working-class families varied in the skills and resources they could bring to bear on the problem of turning hopes into realizable plans in the academic or other realms. A few daughters had the same pattern of high school preparation as their middle-class counterparts and at least some financial help with college. These daughters did make it to university. They foundered when they tried to take on independence while still in school, however, and dropped out. The majority of those who hoped to attend college had not given the matter much thought. They had taken few prerequisites in high school, and had not tried to get into a university at once, but believed that community college would lead to a degree eventually, that they could get half their schooling 'for free'. They had not figured out how they would get to school or how they would pay for books.

These things seemed to confront them unprepared. This may be how they coped with the fact that their hopes were not in line with their resources.

Accepting Unequal Opportunity

The United States has a high, and growing, degree of inequality between rich and poor. As in other social systems, the privileged seek to legitimate their position. In the United States, perhaps more than any other country, belief in equality of educational opportunity occupies a central place in the legitimation process. Public belief in the possibility of upward mobility through hard work and educational achievement is widespread even among the poor and the politically dispossessed. The interviews conducted for the study give insight into how this legitimation occurs.

Few of the working-class women attained their educational goals. Those who set out to earn vocational licenses had done so, while a large proportion of the rest had failed to attain their goals, college degrees. The women had different ways of accepting the disappointment of their hopes. Some did not yet accept the reality that they would be unlikely ever to get a degree. These, about one-quarter of the college dropouts, continued to define themselves as students and degree hopefuls by taking evening courses at community colleges. Another group of the dropouts in the working class, a larger proportion, had turned their attention to marriage and actual or prospective motherhood. Among the women available for the last interview, the rates of marriage and motherhood were much higher among the working class than among the middle class. For both groups, these rates were inversely related to degree expectations expressed in the first interview less than a year after high school. They were also inversely related to degree attainment reported in the last interview six years after high school. By the time of the last interview, one-half of the working-class women were married and one-third were mothers (compared with only 7 percent of the middle-class women who were mothers).

When the young working-class women became mothers, two factors eased their disappointment over their truncated educations. First, they transferred their aspirations to the next generation. The young women appeared to give up any dreams of a college education for themselves and began to dream about their children's futures instead. Second, they shifted their day-to-day energies from their jobs to their families. The women have few prospects for job advancement, given their lack of educational credentials. Many become aware of the job ceilings they face at roughly the same time as they start to have children. Their focus shifts to the home front and they avoid taking on increased responsibility at work. Some no longer want to work at all and do so only because of financial need.

Only six years after high school, most working-class women had come to accept their defeat in the educational contest. A small proportion who had no marriage prospects at that time were still taking some classes and vowing to return to school. Most, however, had turned their attention to marriage and motherhood. While working-class women recognized the inequality of the opportunity structure, they made little reference to that larger structure in the interpretation of their own failed hopes. They saw their educational disappointments in personal terms. These women had never rebelled in school as had the English working-class 'lads' described by Paul Willis (1977), and in the years after their schooling ended they remained accepting of the social order around them.

Conclusion

How it happens that class inequalities are reproduced across generations, yet are accepted as legitimate, is a central question in the study of class societies. Sociologists have emphasized the importance of education in class reproduction and its legitimation in Western democracies. Public educational systems contribute to the reproduction of class inequalities through the unequal distribution of skills, knowledge, and the credentials required for access to professional, managerial, and technical occupations. The stratified occupational system, in turn, contributes to the unequal distribution of educational credentials through the unequal distribution of family resources. Family of origin limits access to educational opportunities for the next generation, directly because of inequality in economic and cultural resources for educational attainment, and indirectly by limiting perceptions of the opportunity structure among those placed at its lowest levels.

This reproduction of class inequality from one generation to the next is legitimated in our society through the individualization and internalization of responsibility for one's class position. The ideology of equality of opportunity legitimates the obvious inequality in educational and occupational results. Many sociologists have noted that the idea of equality of opportunity through public education masks actual class biases working in the process by which knowledge, skills and educational credentials are distributed. The public educational system is presented as an objective, merit-based system of selection for occupational rewards. While it is presented in this ideology as a fair contest, selection criteria are in fact determined by dominant groups because of their dominant positions in the society's institutions.

The ideology of equality of opportunity in our society includes the belief that the educational contest need never really be over, that none of the differences in achievement in the secondary years need be permanent, that anyone can try college at any time in life. The 'free' community college system is the central structure in this ideology. It is supposed to equalize opportunity by being both 'free' and non-selective, thus providing a 'second chance' to working-class youth who have fared poorly in competition with middle-class youth in the primary and secondary educational levels, and who furthermore can ill afford the costs of higher education. Early on in the junior college movement, sociologists noted that the junior colleges provided a safety valve for the generation of ambitions beyond that which the four-year colleges and the occupational structure itself could absorb. This they did by providing the illusion of mobility without much actual mobility. Junior colleges 'cooled out' most of those who enrolled in them in the hope of attaining a college degree. 'Cooling out' was accomplished by remedial courses, low grades, aptitude testing, and counseling designed to move transfer students into terminal vocational programs considered more appropriate to students' 'abilities' (Clark 1960; Karabel 1977; Karabel and Brint 1989; Pincus 1980). This 'cooling out' function of the community colleges has continued throughout their rapid growth and has even increased through the 1980s (Karabel and Brint 1989).

While material resources are considered nearly irrelevant in the ideology of equality of opportunity, they are probably actually increasing in importance as a factor in the distribution of educational credentials because of credential inflation. In the competition for scarce occupational rewards, only those credentials which discriminate among job applicants remain valuable (Collins 1979). Thus, the amount of education required for the better occupational positions continues to increase as more people attain the lower educational reaches. The higher the credential required for entrance to professional, managerial and technical occupations, the longer the period of financial dependence required of the credential earner. The costs of such prolonged educational preparation include much more than tuition and other direct educational costs. They include living and transportation expenses for a dependent adult who must also forego more lucrative full-time employment for less profitable part-time work. The longer the period of financial support required, the more disadvantaged families of modest means become in supporting their offspring through the educational contest. The winners of the educational contest between middle- and working-class youth turn out to be those who can go the longest without working.

It is into this context of class competition for educational credentials that the middle- and working-class women in this study must be placed. Despite their often inadequate preparation and unpleasant experiences in high school (described in Finley, 1990), the ideology of equality of opportunity was still subscribed to by many of the young working-class women in this study. Many rushed to enroll in the 'free' colleges near their homes immediately after high school. They saw in these 'free' colleges their 'second chance' to succeed in their schooling; they aspired to college degrees and professional occupations. At these institutions they experienced the 'cooling out' of being placed in remedial classes, receiving poor grades, and being counseled toward vocational programs. Even more important, however, was the 'cooling out' of their ambition as its true cost began to be paid. The true cost of college for these young working-class women had to be counted in foregone income, lengthy personal and financial dependence, and strained family finances and family relationships. Many middle-class families had to bear fewer of these personal costs of educational ambition, since daughters went away to college or at least lived away from home with parental support.

In addition to the class biases at work in the educational system itself, and the limited material resources of the working-class families which handicapped the young working-class women in this study, there are the additional burdens which they bear because they are women. Working-class women suffer a greater gender disadvantage than do middle-class women. They have a lesser share of family resources because resources are especially scarce and are prioritized in favor of the male family members. They are more restricted by their families as well. They are often the recipients of ill treatment and even abuse in families with too many tensions and difficulties. Their job opportunities are limited and they cannot gain freedom from their families on their own earning power alone.

The young women in this study, high school graduates in 1982, are among the first young women to grow up in an era of widespread dissemination of beliefs in equal rights and increased independence and ambition for women. As with other groups in our society before them, women seeking increased independence and better job opportunities have turned to increasing their educational opportunities. Women of middle-class backgrounds have, in fact, made use of the new opportunities for women to gain more and better educational credentials. In so doing, the polarization between middle-class and working-class women has increased. If the new, highly educated, middle-class women are able to gain some occupational payoffs from society for their educational achievements, they may well increase class polarization generally, since they will make greater contributions to their future families than will the working-class women who were ill equipped to compete with them in the educational contest as it opened up to women.

References

ALEXANDER, K.L. and ECKLAND, B.K. (1974) 'Sex Differences in the Educational Attainment Process', *American Sociological Review* 39 (5), pp. 668–82.

BLAU, F.D. (1978) 'The Data on Women Workers, Past, Present, and Future', in STROMBERG, A.H. and HARKNESS, S. (Eds) *Women Working*, Palo Alto, Mayfield.

BLUESTONE, B. (1972) 'Economic Theory and the Fate of the Poor', *Social Policy* 2, pp. 30–54.

BOURDIEU, P. and PASSERON, J. (1977) *Reproduction in Education, Society, and Culture*, Beverly Hills, Sage.

BOWLES, S. and GINTIS, H. (1976) *Schooling in Capitalist America*, New York, Basic Books.

CARNOY, M. and LEVIN, H. (1985) *Schooling and Work in the Democratic State*, Stanford, Stanford University Press.

CLARK, B.R. (1960) 'The Cooling Out Function in Higher Education', *American Journal of Sociology* 65, pp. 569–76.

COLEMAN, J.S. et al. (1966) *Equality of Educational Opportunity*, Washington, DC, US Government Printing Office.

COLLINS, R. (1979) *The Credential Society: An Historical Sociology of Education and Stratification*, New York, Academic Press.

CURRIE, E., DUNN, R. and FOGARTY, D. (1980) 'The New Immiseration', *Socialist Review* 54, pp. 7–32.

FINLEY, M. (1990) *The Educational Contest for Middle- and Working-Class Women: The Reproduction of Inequality*. Unpublished PhD Dissertation, Los Angeles, University of California.

GIROUX, H.A. (1983) *Theory and Resistance in Education*, South Hadley, Bergin and Garvey.

HERTZ, R. (1986) *More Equal than Others: Women and Men in Dual-Career Marriages*, Berkeley, University of California.

JENCKS, C. et al. (1972) *Inequality: A Reassessment of the Effect of Family and Schooling in America*, New York, Basic Books.

KARABEL, J. (1977) 'Community Colleges and Social Stratification: Submerged Class Conflict in American Higher Education', in KARABEL, J. and HALSEY, A.H. (Eds) *Power and Ideology in Education*, New York, Oxford University Press.

KARABEL, J. and BRINT, S. (1989) *The Diverted Dream*, New York, Oxford University Press.

LAREAU, A. (1989) *Home Advantage: Social Class and Parental Intervention in Elementary Education*, London, Falmer Press.

MANN, M. (1970) 'The Social Cohesion of Liberal Democracies', *American Sociological Review* 35, pp. 423–39.

METZ, M. (1978) *Classrooms and Corridors: The Crisis of Authority in Desegregated Secondary Schools*, Berkeley, University of California.

PARKIN, F. (1971) *Class, Inequality, and Political Order*, New York, Praeger.

PINCUS, F.L. (1980) 'False Promises of Community Colleges: Class Conflict and Vocational Education', *Harvard Educational Review* 50, pp. 332–61.

ROBY, P. (1975) 'Sociology of Women in Working-class Jobs', in MILLMAN, M. and KANTER, R. (Eds) *Another Voice*, Garden City, Anchor.

RUBIN, L. (1976) *Worlds of Pain: Life in the Working-Class Family*, New York, Basic Books.

SENNET, R. and COBB, J. (1972) *The Hidden Injuries of Class*, New York, Random House.

SEWELL, W.H. and SHAH, V.P. (1967) 'Socioeconomic Status, Intelligence, and the Attainment of Higher Education', *Sociology of Education* 40, pp. 1–23.

WILLIS, P. (1981) *Learning to Labour: How Working-class Kids Get Working-class Jobs*, New York, Columbia University Press.

Notes on Contributors

David Baker is an Associate Professor of Sociology and holds an appointment at the Life Cycle Institute at The Catholic University of America in Washington, DC. In addition to studies of international comparisons of school organization and achievement, his research interests include immigration and the labor market, and immigration and institution building in nineteenth-century America.

Aaron Benavot is a lecturer in sociology at the Hebrew University of Jerusalem and an assistant professor at the University of Georgia in Athens. His areas of research interest include the sociology of education and development, and the comparative study of school curricula. He is currently examining the impact of instructional time devoted to different school subjects, especially in mathematics and science, on national economic growth.

Cynthia Dean received her BA from the University of Maine in 1988. Her fields of interest are the gay/lesbian rights movement, Latin American women's history, and women's studies. She is currently living in Minneapolis and intends to pursue graduate work in the area of social policy.

Nancy Durbin is a research scientist at Battelle Human Affairs Research Centers in Seattle, Washington. Her research focuses on how organizational structures and worker characteristics interact to affect organizational performance. Current research projects include an evaluation of how educational opportunities affect sex segregation of occupations in Sweden, and research on the relationship of job characteristics to drug and alcohol use. Previous research has included an evaluation of how the skill requirements of jobs are linked to the gender, educational level, and income level of workers. Prior to joining Battelle in 1989, she was on the faculty at Pennsylvania State University.

Merrilee Finley recently received her doctorate in Education from UCLA. Her chapter included here is based upon her dissertation research. She lives in southern California where she has worked for several years evaluating programs for urban school districts. Most recently, she has worked on a study of state-funded preschool programs sponsored by the California Department of Education.

Saundra Gardner is an associate professor in the sociology department at the University of Maine in Orono. She received her PhD from the University of New Hampshire. Her fields of interest include women's studies, feminist pedagogy, visual sociology, and the sociology of education. She is presently studying how race, class, and gender affect the educational aspirations and academic success of college students.

Linda Grant is an Associate Professor of Sociology and faculty associate of the Institute for Behavioral Research at the University of Georgia. She received her PhD in 1981 from the University of Michigan at Ann Arbor. She has published articles in the *American Sociological Review, Sociology of Education*, and *Gender and Society* (among others). She is currently researching school restructuring and student experience, and is also studying gender, mentoring and publication among university-based scientists.

Deborah Jones received a PhD in sociology from The Catholic University of America in Washington, DC, in 1989. She is a private consultant doing research on social and economic development in Dakar, Senegal.

Ingrid Jönsson received her PhD in sociology from Lund University in Sweden. Her main interest is in the sociology of education. She has worked as a researcher on a study of 4000 students in the Swedish school system. Her current research project concerns the transition to higher education and working life in relation to school success, class, and gender.

Lori Kent is Director of Research at The Leonhardt Group in Seattle, Washington. She received a BA in Sociology from the University of Colorado and PhD in Sociology from the University of Washington. Dr Kent has published articles on the causes and prevention of juvenile delinquency, and on the historical development of higher education. Currently, she conducts communications research for a variety of public agencies and corporations.

Annette Lareau is a member of the sociology faculty at Temple University. She is the author of *Home Advantage: Social Class and Parental Intervention in Elementary Education*, which is published by Falmer Press. Her current research explores class and race differences in how parents manage children's school experiences and leisure experiences outside the home.

Wendy Luttrell holds a joint appointment in the Departments of Sociology and Cultural Anthropology at Duke University. Her research and teaching is concerned with the formation and transformation of gender, race, and class identities and consciousness. These issues are explored in a book she is completing which examines black and white working-class women's schooling experiences and beliefs about knowledge, power, and femininity. She has also translated her findings into adult basic education literacy materials.

Deo McKaig received her MA from the University of Maine in 1988. Her fields of interest are women's and lesbian studies and Native American women's spirituality. She is currently working at a group home for adolescent girls in Taos, New Mexico.

Roslyn Arlin Mickelson is Associate Professor of Sociology and Adjunct Associate Professor of Women's Studies at the University of North Carolina at Charlotte. She is interested in the effects of gender, race, and class on educational processes and outcomes. Her current research is a critical examination of corporate influence on the school reform process.

Barrie Thorne is the Streisand Professor in the Program for the Study of Women and Men in Society, and Professor of Sociology at the University of Southern California. She is coeditor of *Language, Gender and Society* and *Rethinking the Family: Some Feminist Questions*. Her full ethnography of gender relations in elementary schools will be published by Rutgers University Press.

Julia Wrigley teaches in the sociology program of the Graduate Center of the City University of New York. Previously she taught at UCLA, where she served as Acting Director of the Center for the Study of Women. She edits the American journal *Sociology of Education* and is the author of *Class Politics and Public Schools*. Currently she is working on a study of social class and child care.

Index